BY
JONATHAN DARMAN

*Becoming FDR: The Personal Crisis
That Made a President*

*Landslide: LBJ and Ronald Reagan
at the Dawn of a New America*

BECOMING FDR

BECOMING
FDR

The Personal Crisis That
Made a President

JONATHAN DARMAN

RANDOM HOUSE | NEW YORK

LIBRARY OF CONGRESS CATALOGING-IN-PUBLICATION DATA

TITLE: Becoming FDR : the personal crisis that made a president /
Jonathan Darman.

DESCRIPTION: First edition. | New York : Random House, [2022] |
Includes bibliographical references and index.

IDENTIFIERS: LCCN 2021061041 (print) | LCCN 2021061042 (ebook) |
ISBN 9781400067077 (hardcover) | ISBN 9780593448502 (ebook)

SUBJECTS: LCSH: Roosevelt, Franklin D. (Franklin Delano), 1882–1945. |
Roosevelt, Franklin D. (Franklin Delano), 1882–1945—Health. | Presidents—
United States—Biography. | Poliomyelitis—Patients—United States—
Biography. | United States—History—1919–1933. | United States—
Politics and government—1919–1933.

CLASSIFICATION: LCC E807.D338 2022 (print) | LCC E807 (ebook) |
DDC 973.917092 [B]—dc23/eng/20220518

LC record available at https://lccn.loc.gov/2021061041

LC ebook record available at https://lccn.loc.gov/2021061042

Printed in Canada on acid-free paper

randomhousebooks.com

2 4 6 8 9 7 5 3 1

FIRST EDITION

Book design by Barbara M. Bachman

FRONTISPIECE:

Campaigning for the presidency in the summer of 1932,
Franklin Roosevelt looked like a political natural,
yet his real genius had been shaped by his search for
hope in his struggle with polio.

For James

"A year or two in bed should be
prescribed for all our statesmen."

—LOUIS MCHENRY HOWE,
QUOTED IN LELA STILES,
The Man Behind Roosevelt, 1954

"Every time you meet a crisis and live through it,
you make it simpler for the next time."

—ELEANOR ROOSEVELT IN
You Learn by Living, 1960

CONTENTS

PROLOGUE: Destinies
(JUNE 1920 AND JUNE 1936)   *xiii*

PART I: *The Invaders*
(AUGUST 1921)

CHAPTER 1:   On Campobello   *5*

PART II: *Ascent*
(SPRING 1919)

CHAPTER 2:   The Path   *15*
CHAPTER 3:   The Parade   *20*
CHAPTER 4:   Broken Glass   *26*

PART III: *Origins*
(1882–1919)

CHAPTER 5:   The Precious Child   *33*
CHAPTER 6:   Love Matches   *43*
CHAPTER 7:   The Orphan Girl   *48*
CHAPTER 8:   Mr. and Mrs. Roosevelt   *56*
CHAPTER 9:   Golden Boy   *60*

PART IV: *A Public Life*
(JUNE 1919–AUGUST 1921)

CHAPTER 10: Breathless and Hunted   *69*
CHAPTER 11: Persecutors   *77*
CHAPTER 12: Lonely Island   *83*
CHAPTER 13: In a Hurry   *91*
CHAPTER 14: Hurtling   *99*

PART V: *The Forgotten Man*
(SEPTEMBER 1921–NOVEMBER 1922)

CHAPTER 15:   Stranded   *109*

CHAPTER 16:   Plans   *121*

CHAPTER 17:   The Will and Determination
              of the Patient   *130*

CHAPTER 18:   Nothing to Do but Think   *138*

CHAPTER 19:   Means of Grace   *150*

PART VI: *Try Something*
(JANUARY 1924–OCTOBER 1928)

CHAPTER 20:   Time in the Sun   *167*

CHAPTER 21:   The Way It Feels   *183*

CHAPTER 22:   The Soul That Had Believed   *199*

CHAPTER 23:   The Call   *220*

PART VII: *The Return*
(OCTOBER 1928–JULY 1932)

CHAPTER 24:   On My Feet   *235*

CHAPTER 25:   The Long Fight   *248*

CHAPTER 26:   "You Must Let Me Be Myself"   *261*

CHAPTER 27:   The Prize   *277*

PART VIII: *Out of Every Crisis*
(JULY 1932–MARCH 1933)

CHAPTER 28:   "Pray for Me"   *293*

CHAPTER 29:   Spreading Fire   *305*

CHAPTER 30:   An Unfamiliar City   *317*

CHAPTER 31:   Fear Itself   *326*

EPILOGUE: The Spirit of Warm Springs
              (NOVEMBER 1933 AND NOVEMBER 1941)   *333*

ACKNOWLEDGMENTS   *349*

NOTES   *351*

SELECTED BIBLIOGRAPHY   *385*

PHOTOGRAPH CREDITS   *391*

INDEX   *395*

PROLOGUE

Destinies

JUNE 1920 AND JUNE 1936

FRANKLIN ROOSEVELT COULD SEE IT RIGHT IN FRONT OF HIM. His chance. It was a late-June afternoon in San Francisco, the opening day of the Democratic Party's 1920 convention. Only a few paces away from him, a couple of overfed party functionaries were guarding the standard of New York State. It was nothing special to look at, a wooden sign dangling above the convention floor. But to Franklin it would have been irresistible: *Here is greatness. Come and get it.*

Franklin was thirty-eight years old but looked younger. Handsome, well connected, and eager, he'd spent the better part of the last decade holding high offices—a term in New York's State Senate followed by seven years in Washington as Woodrow Wilson's assistant secretary of the Navy. He'd devoted much of his adult life to dreaming of an even higher office—the presidency and studying the things that savvy politicians did to win it. A convention, he knew, was a kind of game, often a physical one. Playing it well, and looking good while playing, an ambitious young man could prove he had the stuff of a future president—quick wits, a hint of eros, oceans of charm.

Franklin fancied himself that sort of man, and New York's hanging wooden sign offered a means of proving it. Whenever the convention-floor game got heated, states' standards became prized possessions, a signal that that state was lining up behind a cause, a platform, or a candidate. Holding the standard of New York, the most populous state in the country, was a chance to show off power. *Stealing* New York's standard in a moment of tense drama was a chance to captivate the room. That was what he now intended to do: grab the standard and everyone's attention. To get hold of it, he would use his long, lean frame and his quick, elegant stride, the same things that distinguished him on the golf course and tennis court, places where he spent much of his time. And he was also prepared to use his fists.

The trouble had started a few minutes earlier, with the unveiling of the president's portrait. Woodrow Wilson, the current inhabitant of the Oval Office, had been badly debilitated by a stroke the previous autumn and had not made the trip to San Francisco for the gathering. In his place, the convention's organizer had hung a giant likeness of the president, the only Democrat to win two consecutive terms in the White House since the Civil War. Shortly after the convention opened, they had pulled back a seven-story American flag to reveal the portrait. State after state had thrown its standard in the air and joined a bandwagon parade in Wilson's honor.

But New York had not joined the celebration. The state's delegation was controlled by Tammany Hall, the eternally powerful, endlessly corrupt New York City Democratic machine. Tammany's boss, Charles Murphy, loathed Wilson and the party's preening, moralistic "Wilsonian wing." When the Wilsonian parade had started, Murphy's delegation made sure to stay put.

Franklin had watched Murphy's intransigence from the middle of the New York delegation with a striking expression of outrage on his face. Just how real was this outrage was subject to interpretation. There were limits on Franklin's devotion to *any* politician not named Franklin Roosevelt, and during Franklin's seven years serving in the Wilson administration, the president had thwarted his ambitions for greatness as often as he'd helped them along.

But, Franklin, a privileged son of New York's Hudson Valley, was no Tammany loyalist. Indeed, as a young state legislator in Albany, he'd made a name for himself as a noisy opponent of the Hall. A flashy convention-floor display of defiance against Tammany's authority could serve him well with Democrats from outside New York

State. From his place in the middle of the New York delegation, he had loudly demanded that the state join the pro-Wilson parade. And when cries yielded no response, he had set his sights on the state's standard.

The sign was guarded by a pair of Tammany regulars. If Franklin wanted it, it would mean a fight, one that would almost certainly catch the room's attention. A fight was a chance to become a surprise star of the convention. And then, perhaps, something more.

For two decades, Franklin had been looking for chances like this. In his college years, he had idolized his distant cousin Teddy Roosevelt, then the sitting president of the United States. He had spent many hours studying Teddy's path: provocative young politician, then wartime hero, then political phenomenon, then president of the United States. All of it appeared effortless, as if it had been destined from on high.

Perhaps it had been, and perhaps destiny had a plan for Franklin too. Perhaps it was just a matter of finding the right moment to grab hold of the nation's attention and not let go.

Franklin had been looking for his opportunity ever since.

For Teddy, it had come on a summer's day in 1898 during the Spanish–American War, when he led his Rough Riders to battlefield triumph. Teddy had been thirty-nine that day, only a year older than Franklin was now.

Of course, this breezy convention hall, pleasantly lit by electric chandeliers, was not exactly San Juan Hill. In fact, if Franklin was to speak plainly of the events of his life so far, something he was not usually inclined to do, he would admit that it had supplied fewer instances of true heroism than had the career of his famed relation. At age twenty-eight, when Franklin arrived at the New York capital in Albany as a newly elected state senator, he'd quickly captured headlines, raising hell about Tammany and the urgent need for progressive reform. But there had been less fanfare when he'd left the State Senate a mere two years later; there was not a single piece of significant progressive legislation connected to his name.

Nor was there a dash for the heights with the bullets whistling by:

Franklin had spent World War I safely ensconced behind his Navy Department desk. He was a well-liked figure in Washington, where his service as assistant secretary of the Navy was widely judged able and effective. But when Washingtonians looked back on his tenure, they were more likely to remember his elegant, engaging presence at dinner dances than any brilliant policy or project he'd carried out.

It had been nearly eight years since he'd last won an election, to the New York State Senate in 1912. Many in the state's political establishment thought him an overrated dilettante. Reviewing his career, it seemed he was more than happy to play the part of hero, so long as no actual courage was required.

Nevertheless, he had a number of things going for him—a pleasing manner and knack for making other people feel good. "Roosevelt" was still the most celebrated political name of the day, even if the public principally associated it with Teddy and the Republicans.

And he had his looks. Journalists who profiled him—already there had been many of those—invariably lingered on his appearance. His angular, expressive face was the sort, a writer for the *Washington Post* observed, that "could set the matinee girls hearts throbbing." Slim and well proportioned, he stood six feet two inches tall. His was, said *New York World*, "the figure of an idealized college football player, almost the poster type." Watching him jump over a stream near his home in the Hudson Valley, one friend thought he looked "like some amazing stag."

Franklin was realistic enough to understand that, when combined, his assets as a politician were hardly enough to earn him a seat at the top of the Democratic ticket in 1920. But the bottom of the ticket was another matter altogether.

All he had to do was find a way to show the people gathered in that convention hall how much he had to offer. He ran forward, toward the NEW YORK sign.

Reaching up over the heads of the Tammany guards, he pulled the standard down and pivoted toward the center of the convention floor. Before he got more than a few paces, however, other New York delegates were scrambling toward him, grabbing for the sign. When Franklin managed to evade them, they grabbed at him too.

Soon he was in an outright struggle as more delegates tripped into the chaos, pushing and ruffling him, knocking the hat off his head. Fists flew, his and theirs. A policeman dove into the fracas, lunging at Franklin, who screamed theatrically in protest and then violently shoved the man away.

By this point, he'd caught the attention of the reporters in the press gallery. They lapped up the spectacle—an actual fight! In the dispatches they would later file, they disagreed over the details: who had thrown the first punch, whether Franklin had lost his eyeglasses, his tie, his coat. But there was no debate over the victor in the scuffle. They'd all seen Franklin easily dispatch each man who'd come at him until, after a few minutes, he escaped unmolested, the standard in his hand.

Clutching it to his chest, he bolted toward the ongoing Wilson parade, offering New York and himself. Everyone in the room was looking at him as he leapt over a row of chairs. He smiled in triumph as he turned to look up toward the galleries. By the next day, his name would be on the front pages of newspapers nationwide. By the end of the convention, his performance would help win him a spot on the ticket as the party's vice-presidential nominee.

Few would remember anything Franklin had to say at that convention. Few would even remember much he said that entire election year. But in that moment, as in so many moments in Franklin's life leading up to it, what mattered was not words but appearances. And few would forget how splendid Franklin looked as he made his fantastic run.

ON A SUMMER NIGHT almost exactly sixteen years later, Franklin Delano Roosevelt sat in the back seat of a limousine as it moved across a stadium field. It was just after sundown on June 27, 1936, the last day of another Democratic convention, this one in Philadelphia.

As his car drove slowly toward a speaker's platform in the center of the field, Franklin could see a massive crowd of one hundred thousand people who had come out to see the convention's crowning event.

Through the window of the limousine were signs of how much politics had changed in the intervening years. A portrait of Woodrow Wilson hung along one end of the stadium but only as one in a row of dead Democratic presidents, unknown and unmissed by the younger people in the crowd. The party had long ago stopped dividing itself into Wilsonian or anti-Wilsonian wings. It was a Roosevelt party now.

Franklin was fifty-four years old but looked older. The patrician angles of his face were absorbed by billowing flesh; his skin was sectioned by deep lines. Beneath his navy serge suit, his chest had filled out and his arms were thick from years of conditioning. Inside his trousers, the legs he'd used to leap like an "amazing stag" were now shrunken and contained by heavy braces of thick steel.

Franklin's performance at the 1920 convention had indeed earned him a place as his party's vice-presidential candidate, alongside the presidential candidate, Ohio governor James M. Cox. But their ticket was defeated in a landslide in the general election that November. Nine months later, in August of 1921, he had been stricken with a grave sickness while vacationing with his family on Campobello, an island off the coast of Maine. For days, he'd lain in fevered agony, unable to move below the neck. Feeling his control over his muscles and bodily functions slip away, he wondered if he would live.

The infection had passed and in time he'd regained the use of his upper body. His life, however, was transformed by the illness, eventually diagnosed as infantile paralysis, known to later generations as polio.

The disease had robbed him of the use of his legs, aged him ten years overnight, and appeared to put his old dream of winning the presidency perpetually out of reach. Political insiders mostly wrote him off for dead.

But from the earliest days of his recovery, Franklin refused to surrender his ambition of someday returning to politics and running for president. Convinced that doing so would first require regaining the ability to walk, he had spent seven long years away from the hunt for elected office—in politics, several lifetimes—devoting his days to taxing and often fruitless rehabilitative schemes. All the while, with the assistance of his wife, Eleanor, and his devoted adviser, Louis Howe, he had nurtured a strategy for an eventual return to elected office— a multiyear plan that was detailed, complex, and secret.

His moment had come in 1928 when he surprised the New York political scene with a last-minute candidacy for the state's governorship, then shocked the nation with a decisive win. He had leveraged a strong performance in that office to wage a successful campaign to be his party's 1932 presidential nominee. In November of that year, he defeated the reviled incumbent Republican president, Herbert Hoover, in a landslide.

Franklin had assumed the presidency in March of 1933, the darkest hour of the Great Depression. One in four adults was out of work, the nation's financial system was on the brink of collapse, and the republic itself seemed in mortal danger. But beginning with the extraordinary legislative activities of his first hundred days, he had reinvented the role of the federal government and remade much of American life with the sweeping programs of the New Deal.

By the summer of 1936, he was already thought to be the most significant American president since Abraham Lincoln. Most important, though millions of Americans remained hungry and out of work, Franklin's energy and magnetic charisma in office had transformed the country's spirits. The previous day, the Democrats gathered in Philadelphia had rapturously nominated him for four more years in the White House. At ten o'clock that night, he would accept the nomination in front of the crowd of a hundred thousand, in a speech broadcast over the radio nationwide.

As Franklin's car moved slowly across the field, an excited voice on the loudspeaker announced his arrival. The faces in the crowd strained for a glimpse of him, but most saw nothing. That was all right by Franklin. On that long-ago day in San Francisco in 1920, he'd had to scheme about ways to get people to look at him. Now his challenge was the opposite: making sure people did not see too much.

Despite his efforts, he had never regained his ability to walk. In private, he moved about most comfortably in a dining chair that had been refashioned as a wheelchair; at times when he'd needed to move somewhere quickly, he had been known to drop to the floor and crawl across a room. He could, with some practice, move around on crutches, placing one crutch in front of him, pivoting his weight at the hips so that his legs swung out in front of him. But without a companion's arm to steady him, his progress was ungainly and fraught with peril.

When he'd returned to active political life, Franklin's great fear had been falling in front of an audience. Over the years, he had been carried up countless sets of stairs, had been pushed through the window of a train compartment, had been dangled down onto a stage from a fire escape. Whatever it took to avoid being jostled, losing control, falling to the ground.

The car came to a stop when it reached the back of the platform. Franklin had long since perfected a method for exiting an automobile. Swiveling his torso to the side, he would extend his arms up, waiting for a pair of strong hands to pull and lift him out of the car. Outside the vehicle, he would steady himself, taking the arm of whoever was tasked with supporting him. Tonight, as on many nights, that person was James "Jimmy" Roosevelt, Franklin's twenty-eight-year-old eldest son. At the back of the convention speakers' platform, he took hold of Jimmy's arm with one hand; in his other hand he held a cane he used to help steady his weight.

On the platform, a large group of dignitaries and party leaders swarmed toward him. Among them was Edwin Markham, the eighty-four-year-old "dean of American poetry," who had just finished reciting a poem he'd composed for the occasion: "Franklin D. Roosevelt: Man of Destiny."

White-bearded, with large, expressive eyes, the aged poet approached Franklin to say hello. As he drew near, however, Markham was jostled by the crowd and lost his footing. Falling forward, he struck Jimmy Roosevelt, who in turn lost his own footing and fell into his father. Absorbing the blow, the steel brace on Franklin's right leg gave way. Franklin struggled to regain his balance, but his body crumpled. As he fell headfirst toward the floor of the platform, the pages of the speech he was about to deliver scattered in the air.

Seeing the president slip, a Secret Service agent dove forward to catch him. Just before Franklin touched the ground, the agent thrust his shoulder under Franklin's armpit, arresting his fall and scooping him up. James A. Farley, Franklin's political adviser who was now serving as chairman of the Democratic Party, quickly led a group of other officials in forming a tight circle around Franklin. They knew without being told what to do in Franklin's moment of exposed vulnerability: *Don't let people see.* Within their shelter, Franklin's heart raced—he had fallen before but never in so public a setting. He could hear the roar of the hundred thousand, waiting for him, watching for him. *Don't let them see.*

Meanwhile, Franklin's attendants held him in the air and refastened his brace. "Clean me up!" Franklin commanded. He was anxious and agitated. Seeing his pages strewn all about, he barked orders about "those damned sheets." There wasn't time to prepare a clean copy of the remarks—the radio broadcast was set to begin in mere moments.

A chaotic scene followed: people dusting him off, chasing after stray pages. "Okay," he finally announced when all the sheets had been recovered, "let's go." But as he and Jimmy resumed their progress, Franklin caught sight of Edwin Markham a few feet away, weeping over all the trouble his stumble had caused. On Jimmy's arm, Franklin went over to the old man, took him by the hand, and offered a reassuring smile. All would be well.

Soon he was at the speaker's stand, smiling broadly as the crowd cheered him. Then, with stagey exaggeration, he looked at his watch to remind his audience of the impending broadcast and signaled for them to hush. Just after ten o'clock, he began to speak.

The speech he gave that night in Philadelphia would be one of his most celebrated. In it, he sought to provide context for the work his administration had done over the previous three and a half years to save the country from ruin. Yet Franklin knew that for many listening to his words, his presidency was about something greater than just restoring the country's economic health. In his first term, he told them, he'd sought to renew the nation's spiritual purpose, to replace the pursuit of narrow self-interest with a more nourishing generosity and concern for humankind. "In the place of the palace of privilege, we seek to build a temple out of faith and hope and charity."

As he concluded his remarks that night, he spoke of destiny: "There is a mysterious cycle in human events. To some generations much is given. Of other generations much is expected. This generation of Americans has a rendezvous with destiny."

Destiny was indeed a mysterious thing; Franklin Roosevelt had learned that long ago. As a young man, cosseted in his own palace of privilege, he had believed himself destined for glory. He had thought that if he followed a straightforward path from success to success, greatness would surely come. Then one awful day, illness had surprised him, mocked his certainty, and tossed his expectations of triumph aside.

But the stroke of fate that had turned his legs lifeless had also made him the man who could inspire and lead his country that night. Polio had remade his life, created a more gifted, intuitive, compassionate politician, made him a better man. It had taught him the one thing that his country needed most: how to find hope in the darkness and how to share it with the world.

STUDENTS OF AMERICAN HISTORY have long memorized a series of moments from the life of Franklin Delano Roosevelt, moments marked by his words and deeds. March 4, 1933: the day he assumed the presidency in the midst of the Great Depression, telling a hungry nation it had nothing to fear but fear itself. December 7, 1941: the Japanese attack on Pearl Harbor, "a day which will live in infamy." June 6, 1944: the Allied invasion at Normandy, "a mighty endeavor, a struggle to preserve our Republic, our religion, and our civilization, and to set free a suffering humanity."

August 11, 1921, is not one of the dates usually cited. On that morning, the thirty-nine-year-old Franklin awoke from a night of fitful, fevered sleep to find his body under assault from the polio virus. There was no soaring oratory that day, no splendid triumph. Only a future in doubt; only pain, uncertainty, and fear. Still, it would prove to be the most important day in Franklin's life, in the life of his wife, Eleanor, and a crucial turning point in American history. For without the day when illness overtook his body, none of the subsequent Roosevelt moments of greatness would have been possible.

In popular memory, Franklin Roosevelt is the quintessential political natural, a president with greatness in his blood. He was indeed born with many advantages—wealth, charm, and intelligence; loving, attentive parents, and a famous cousin who was president of the United States. Had he never gotten polio, those things could have delivered him a life of achievement and accomplishment. Aligned with luck and timing, they might have even brought him to the White House someday.

But they were not enough to make him great. For that, he needed first to suffer and to overcome. It was only through hard years of struggle, learning, and perseverance that he became "FDR"—a man who could lead his country through crisis and preserve freedom in the world.

WHEN I BEGAN RESEARCHING the life of Franklin Roosevelt in the final year of the Obama presidency, I hoped it would shed light on a pressing question: When the country is beset by conflict, how does a president unite the nation to do big things? In the years that followed, the country grew more divided and the world became more frightening. A global pandemic killed millions and upended daily life. Political violence and sectarian hatred threatened the stability of American democracy. An escalating climate crisis imperiled life on earth. In time, the question guiding my research became more simple and more urgent: When fear and suffering are all around us, how does a true leader inspire hope?

I assumed I would find my answers in a story that began in March of 1933, a moment as fraught with fear as any this country has known. Starting with the famed Hundred Days at the outset of Franklin's presidency, I intended to follow the great drama of his twelve years in the White House. I expected to find my answers in his masterful skills as a storyteller and political performer. He was, I knew, one of history's great showmen, and I saw his presidency as an epic performance, a fantastically successful twelve-year effort to keep the country enthralled and believing in a better world to come.

The more I immersed myself in Franklin Roosevelt's America, however, the more I began to understand that his connection with the American people was about something greater than just a master performer's ability to captivate his audience. Millions of Americans believed in Franklin's promise of a better future because, on some level, they knew that *he* believed. Moreover, they understood that when he spoke to them of hardship and struggle, he was speaking from his own experience. They did not know all the details of his battle with polio and its aftermath. But when he asked them to find the courage to turn their backs on fear, they listened, because they knew he had found that courage himself.

Soon, it became clear to me that I needed to entirely rethink this man—what I thought I knew about his political successes, his wife, his marriage, and his character. I had to look from a different angle at the heroic opening days of his presidency in March of 1933. To be sure, those consequential first days as president mark the beginning of one of the great American stories, as triumphant and thrilling a story as the history of the presidency has to offer. But they were also the end of another story, at the center of which is a human drama I found deeply inspiring, important, and far less well known, about how Franklin Roosevelt became "FDR."

That story appears in the pages that follow. It takes place in the ambitious and anxious America that emerged in the aftermath of World War I, an America with striking resemblance to our own. Emerging from years of hardship and sacrifice in the Great War and the 1918 pandemic, Americans were eager to resume normal life and experience the pleasures of abundance. Yet deep, bitter divisions plagued the nation's politics. Voters in the nation's cities thrilled to the new opportunities provided by modern life and emerging technologies. Meanwhile, voters in rural areas bemoaned the change in the country's culture and moral standards and feared that an influx of new immigrants was rendering *their* America unrecognizable. A violent white-supremacist movement that had been dormant for several decades reemerged as an influential and terrifying force in the nation's politics.

The war had proved once and for all that however large the oceans surrounding America, the country's fortunes were tied up with those of an unstable global order. Many Americans, however, were exhausted by years of sacrifice and favored turning away from overseas obligation. Throwing off deprivation, the country embraced consumption, celebration, and excess; but millions of Americans were left behind, victims of a persistent systemic inequality that would threaten the nation's stability and survival.

It is in the early days of that unsettled America that we find a figure history often overlooks: the pre-polio Franklin Roosevelt, a man who was attractive, accomplished, and decidedly far from great. As the pleasant, somewhat shallow assistant secretary of the Navy, he excelled at making things look easy, because, for him, most things always had been.

But when illness upended his life and plans, he did not choose the easy path of a quiet retreat into a privileged private world. Instead, he resolved to remake himself so that, in his new condition, he could still achieve his old dream. Aware that he could no longer rely on his physical presence to dominate a room, he trained himself to become a gifted orator for the radio age, calibrating his voice, using simple language and stirring stories to distill complex ideas. Understanding that a return to politics would require intricate planning and exquisite timing, he developed powers he had never needed before—patience, discipline, and strategic thinking. In his confined state, he read and wrote and thought more deeply than he ever had before, and his conscience and consciousness grew.

He learned how to access his remarkable powers of intuition, which, in time, heightened his sense for that most important element in politics, the shifting contours of public mood. Forced to deal with his own practical difficulties each day, the problems of those less fortunate than him became real and vivid for the first time. He developed a new empathy that, when paired with his magnetism and good nature, would make him more effective at understanding and communicating with average Americans than any politician in the nation's history.

Before polio, Franklin had believed he had a duty to make the world better for those less fortunate. But, convinced that in order to do good in the world he first had to become great, he'd put most of his energy into the advancement of his own career. He was to learn the transformative power of service for its own sake.

The dramatic changes Franklin experienced in these years mirrored an equally extraordinary transformation in his wife, Eleanor, and in her life. In the winter of 1919, Eleanor Roosevelt was a beleaguered figure, her life lacking conviction, purpose, or joy. But in the 1920s, the necessities of Franklin's recovery, the emerging opportunities for women in politics, and, most important, her own powers of resilience, intellect, and will all brought her to engage more fully with the world's problems and her own ability to help solve them. In these years, Franklin and Eleanor reinvented their marriage. At the core of their unconventional but deeply rooted union were common values, the wisdom they had both gained from suffering, and their shared ability to remake themselves in the middle of life.

Franklin's return to the heights of American politics in the last years of the 1920s brought him into contact, and brutal competition, with the leading political figures of his day, among them New York governor Al Smith, newspaper publisher William Randolph Hearst, and the Republican president, Herbert Hoover. All of these men had known Franklin in his younger, pre-polio days and saw him as a shallow, vain man who lacked wisdom and true political skill. Encountering him in the years after polio, they assumed he was simply a feebler version of the same man he'd been before. Unable to see how much he'd learned, and grown, from his struggle, they paid a heavy price.

Franklin's story reveals him not as a towering deity of history but as a flawed human being who called on human virtues—work and will, fellowship and faith—to become a more able leader and a wiser human being. It offers perspective on evaluating our own leaders when they talk of "hope": When did they need hope in their own lives? How did it change them and their understanding of others and the world?

For the story of how Franklin Roosevelt became history's FDR extends beyond politics to the heart of the human experience. Many of us can point to an event, often tragic or traumatic, that feels like a river across our lives, with "before" on one side and "after" on the other. Sudden illness was the river through Franklin's life. His story is powerful because it shows that adversity, and the way we respond to it, can make us better—more alive, more aware of others, more useful, more personally successful, more awake to our own potential and to the possibilities of humankind.

To understand how Franklin made this transformation, we must look at both the "before" side of his river, when he still believed himself entitled to greatness, and at the "after" side, when he did the hard work of becoming great.

BECOMING FDR

Polio upended Franklin's life when he was 39.
Its effects on his body were immediately evident.
The change in his character, equally profound,
would take years to fully emerge.

PART I

The Invaders

===

AUGUST 1921

"I dread the time when I have to tell Franklin and it wrings my heart for it is all so much worse to a man than to a woman."

—ELEANOR ROOSEVELT
TO JAMES R. ROOSEVELT,
AUGUST 19, 1921

———

Chapter 1

On Campobello

AUGUST 25, 1921

FRANKLIN ROOSEVELT WATCHED AS THE THREE DOCTORS LEFT the room. They'd finished their examination, they said, but before they offered their diagnosis, they needed a few minutes to confer. As they disappeared into the passageway of the rambling summer cottage, Franklin was left to wait.

For two weeks he'd been here, inside his room on the tiny island of Campobello, gravely ill, unable to rise from his bed. The memory of much of that time was a dark fog. He'd suffered terrible fevers and debilitating chills. Sometimes, his flesh would grow so tender that a single blanket felt like a load of sharp glass pressing down on him. He'd lost the use of much of his body below the neck, lost the ability to control his bladder and bowels. He'd spent agonized hours in fevered delirium, not sure whether he was awake or asleep.

Whenever his mind cleared, he was too feeble to do much of anything. He could only wonder, worry, and wait.

Somehow it had been only two and a half weeks since Franklin arrived on Campobello, the remote island off the coast of Maine where he and his thirty-six-year-old wife, Eleanor, kept a summer home. He'd been a different person then—active and energetic, still expecting a happy summer vacation with his family after a disorienting, sometimes difficult year.

It had been just over a year since his performance at the San Francisco convention had earned him a spot on the 1920 Democratic ticket as the vice-presidential candidate alongside the presidential nominee, Ohio governor James M. Cox. That fall, the Cox–Roosevelt ticket had been soundly defeated in the election. Aware that his public career had reached at least a temporary end, Franklin and Eleanor made plans to leave Washington, where they'd lived for the previous seven years during Franklin's service as assistant secretary of the Navy. They settled in New York City with their five children—daughter Anna and sons James, Elliott, Franklin Jr., and John.

The spring and summer had been a hectic whirl. Franklin took on two jobs in the private sector, serving as name partner in a Wall Street law firm and as head of the New York office of the Fidelity and Deposit Company of Maryland, a bond underwriter. By early August, when he arrived on Campobello by boat, he was feeling worn down by the accumulated strain. Now thirty-nine years old, he had expected a happy interlude on the island where he'd spent summers since his childhood and where he and Eleanor owned a large rustic summer cottage. Just three miles wide and nine miles long, the island had a single telephone line, in the home of a neighbor, and was reachable only by boat. It promised a welcome respite from the busy world.

It was on his fourth night on Campobello that the pain and terrible fever had taken hold. Quickly, his world shrank to the four walls of his bedroom, and the torturous, mysterious illness took over his life. Through the fog, he saw Eleanor attending to him constantly, assisted at times by his trusted aide, the political strategist Louis Howe. After a week, his fever had broken; he'd regained his sense of reason and of time and place. But his body still felt like an occupied territory, subject to cruel and unpredictable intervals of excruciating pain. Most concerning of all was what *wasn't* happening. Though some of his muscle function had returned, he could not move his body below the waist.

Now, along with Eleanor and Louis, Franklin was waiting for the doctors to come back with an answer to the essential question: What had happened to him?

IN ANOTHER PART OF the house, Anna Roosevelt, Franklin and Eleanor's fifteen-year-old eldest child, heard the doctors coming toward her own bedroom, seeking out a quiet place to talk. More invaders in the house.

When their father had appeared on the island two and a half weeks before, Anna and her four younger brothers had been thrilled. During the Roosevelts' years in Washington, Eleanor had brought the children to Campobello for monthslong summer vacations, escaping the capital's heat. But Franklin's responsibilities in the Navy Department meant he'd been able to join them for only short stints. This August was to have been different, a long family holiday when the children could luxuriate in their father's company.

But they'd had only one day.

It was a happy coincidence, given all the unpleasantness that was to follow, that they had spent that day together. The children would long remember its sun-dappled hours—sailing on Franklin's boat, picnicking on a rocky island, swimming in the sea. A lovely, ordinary Wednesday, August 10, 1921. The last day of the Roosevelt family's old life. The last day of Before.

Anna had begun to perceive the trouble that evening when Franklin went to bed without dinner, complaining of a pain in his back. The next morning, when she looked in on her father, he said he'd be all right. But his smile had been weak.

That was when the invasions began—when the doctors started coming, when the adults' faces darkened with concern, when her father, always at the center of everything, became a passive presence on the other side of his closed bedroom door. Eleanor, serving as his nurse, was mostly behind that door as well. Louis Howe, a coarse and often imperious man whom Anna disliked, slept on a cot outside Franklin's bedroom and kept the children at bay. The adults all looked more and more downtrodden, partly from fatigue, partly from the worry that was swelling inside. The details they kept to themselves, but the general message was clear: The children's father was very, very sick.

Now, two weeks since Anna's father had first taken to his bed, there were more invaders—three doctors who had arrived that morning to examine Franklin. When they finished, they headed toward

Anna's bedroom. At the sound of their voices, Anna hurried into a closet. Crouching quietly as they entered the room, she tried to make out their words.

Anna knew all about the signals grown-ups sent when they considered their topic unfit for children's ears. Her grandmother, Sara Delano Roosevelt, would pat or squeeze her theatrically, then slow down and accentuate her words, a signal to her conversation partners that they'd best tread carefully with the children around. Her mother was more icily direct. "What do you want, dear?" she would say when she discovered Anna lingering on the fringes. These words were intended less as a question than a command: *You're not meant to be here; stop hanging about.*

But Anna had grown adept at finding out what it was the grown-ups didn't want her to hear. Perhaps it was the interest in adult topics that came with her advancing age; perhaps it was the tension, unspoken but omnipresent, that hovered between her parents in recent years. She could not make out every word the doctors spoke to one another as they summarized their inventory of Franklin's condition: "lost the use of part of his hand ... partial paralysis in the face ... nonresponsive muscles below the waist." But she did not miss the diagnosis they had unanimously agreed upon, contained in two little terrifying words: "infantile paralysis."

Soon the doctors were leaving the room again. It was time for them to tell Franklin the news.

THAT DAY WAS THURSDAY, August 25, 1921. The Great War had been over for nearly three years, but the global shifts caused by the conflict—and the terms of the subsequent peace—were, in many ways, just beginning.

That same day in Berlin, some 3,500 miles from Campobello, representatives of the American and German governments finally signed a peace treaty formally ending the state of the war that had existed between the two powers since 1917. A separate peace had become necessary after the Senate's rejection in November 1919 of the Paris Peace

Conference treaty, due to the inclusion of the proposed League of Nations.

In Germany, there was widespread disillusionment with the peace, thanks to the enfeebled economy and the high cost of reparations the defeated country was obligated to pay to the Allied powers. Right-wing political factions were propagating the idea that Germany had not lost the war on the battlefield; rather, victory had been stolen from the Fatherland by traitorous Bolsheviks and Jews who had infiltrated the government and capitulated dishonorably in the armistice of November 1918. In the last days of July 1921, as Franklin had prepared to leave New York for Campobello, a thirty-two-year-old Bavarian orator who raged against the treachery of the "November criminals" had assumed the chairmanship of an Aryan nationalist faction headquartered in Munich. His name was Adolf Hitler.

The day before Franklin's visit from the doctors, the Dow Jones Industrial Average had reached a postwar low of 63.9. The market's performance had been dismal through the first half of 1921. But on that Thursday, Wall Street traders bid prices up from the previous day's lows. As Franklin sat waiting for the doctors to return to his room, the Dow embarked on a period of growth that would, in time, turn into a multiyear boom, a boom so long and spectacular that some wondered if it would ever again come to an end.

And that same week, in the village of Broadstairs on the coast of Kent, the British politician Winston Churchill watched his beloved, not-quite-three-year-old daughter, Marigold, take her last breath. The little girl, known to her father as "the Duckadilly," had been gravely ill with septicemia. While it would be decades before history brought Franklin Roosevelt and Winston Churchill together, in late August of 1921, in two small seaside communities on opposite sides of the Atlantic, these two men found themselves confronted by grave personal tragedies at almost exactly the same time.

BEFORE LONG, THE DOCTORS had returned. Franklin, Eleanor, and Louis listened as Dr. Robert Lovett, a famed orthopedist who had come to Campobello from Boston, delivered his diagnosis: Franklin had infantile paralysis, the disease later generations would know as polio. When Lovett finished, Eleanor looked to her husband, expecting to see shock and despair. She had known for several days that infantile paralysis was most likely the cause of Franklin's illness, and she'd feared how he would take the news. But Franklin's face showed no hint of the bracing reality: His body, his plans, and his life had all been irrevocably changed.

Eager for high office, the pre-polio Franklin
wanted the public to see him as the energetic
reincarnation of his famed cousin, Teddy Roosevelt.
Voters never quite bought it.

PART II

Ascent

===

SPRING 1919

"The greatest blow the nation could sustain in the
loss of a single citizen has fallen. Theodore Roosevelt, the strongest single personality in the
world, is dead."
—Colorado Springs Gazette,
JANUARY 7, 1919

"He is put forward as another Theodore. . . .
Franklin is as much like Theodore as a clam is like
a bear cat."
—Chicago Tribune,
AUGUST 13, 1920

Chapter 2

The Path

MARCH 25, 1919

Two and a half years before the events on Campobello, the striking figure of Assistant Secretary of the Navy Franklin Delano Roosevelt strode along a breezy block of New York's Fifth Avenue between 82nd and 83rd Street, home to the Metropolitan Museum of Art. That morning, March 25, 1919, the Army's 27th Infantry Division was set to march up the avenue from Washington Square, in front of what would be the largest parade crowd in the city's history.

In front of the museum, Franklin found a crush of New York State officialdom: state senators and assemblymen, aldermen, judges and justices—"everybody," in the words of *The New York Sun*, "who was willing to be the next governor of New York." These aspirants for power were part of a crowd of five million New Yorkers gathered that morning along the grand thoroughfare that ran down the middle of Manhattan Island.

The papers called the men of the 27th Division "New York's own flesh and blood." Largely made up of National Guardsmen from the five boroughs, the division had the Army's heaviest concentration of New York City troops. Ever since these men had paraded out of the city in August of 1917, New York's newspapers had provided detailed dispatches on the division's progress through the war. In the papers' telling, it was because of the daring and bravery of these New York fighters that the Allies had been able to capture victory with the declaration of armistice on November 11, 1918.

The parade was the city's chance to welcome its victors home. But it was also a chance for the city to celebrate a definitive end to years of disruption, dislocation, rationing, and grief. Naturally, then, anyone eager to reach the heights of New York politics made it his business to be there that morning, welcoming in the new era. With Josephus Daniels, the Navy secretary, away in Europe, Franklin had come to represent the department at the parade as acting secretary. There was no better opportunity to reintroduce the city to Franklin Roosevelt, dashing young politician, returning at last to New York.

By prearrangement, much of New York's political establishment had headed that morning toward the steps of the Metropolitan Museum, where the official reviewing stand—a large, canopied platform festooned in ribbon—offered an ideal place to see the parade. On arriving, however, the politicians were distracted by the presence of a second, smaller reviewing stand on the opposite side of Fifth Avenue. They quickly discerned that this second platform, hastily erected, was the more desirable place to be, though it lacked the height and the ornament of the main platform. At the last minute, the division's commander, Major General John O'Ryan, had sent a request for the mayor of New York City and the governor of New York State to observe the parade from Fifth Avenue's eastern side. That way, when it came time for troops to salute the civilian leadership as they marched northward, they could follow military custom and turn to their right. The smaller riser was put up in accord with Ryan's wishes and, when they arrived after ten o'clock that morning, John Hylan, the mayor, and Al Smith, the governor, had placed themselves on it.

Political animals possess an innate instinct for where power does and does not reside in any situation. Soon, nearly all of the officials who were "willing to be the next governor of New York" were crossing the avenue and scrambling for a place on the small riser, the real place to be seen.

Among those vying for position was Franklin. He made his way through the crowd in the politician's way, smiling generously as he moved toward the center of the tiny stand. Before long, he was there. As the troops prepared to begin their march from Washington Square, four miles to the south, the preening politicians fell into position. At the center of the smaller platform, directly in line of sight of the passing troops, was Mayor Hylan. On his right side stood Governor Smith and, on his left, stood Acting Navy Secretary Franklin Roosevelt. Of these three officials, Franklin stood tallest. When New York's boys turned to salute the civilian leadership, it would be his face that stood out.

THIS WAS WHERE FRANKLIN knew he had to be. Just over two and a half months earlier, in January 1919, former president Theodore Roosevelt had died in his sleep at the age of sixty. For Franklin and Eleanor Roosevelt, it had been not just the loss of a revered American president but of a close family tie. Teddy was Franklin's fifth cousin and Eleanor's uncle. Teddy's younger brother, Elliott, was Eleanor's father, a troubled soul who had died in tragic circumstances in 1894, when Eleanor was nine. Her "Uncle Ted" had been an affectionate, if inconstant, presence in her life ever since. He had often welcomed her into his home, including on more than one occasion when his home had been the White House. On the day she'd married Franklin, her fifth cousin once removed, it had been Teddy who'd given her away.

For Franklin, Teddy's death held even greater significance. He too shared Teddy's blood, though less of it than did his wife. As fifth cousins, Teddy and Franklin's nearest shared ancestor had been dead for 180 years. In his boyhood, spent in the baronial splendor at Springwood, his family's home in the Hudson Valley, Franklin had known Teddy as only one in a cluster of illustrious Roosevelt cousins. The two branches of the family did not even share political allegiance: Like his father before him, Franklin was a Democrat, while Teddy had been the most prominent Republican of the age.

Nonetheless, for much of Franklin's life, few figures had loomed larger than Teddy. Franklin had been schooled along with other sons of privilege at Groton, the Episcopal boarding school in Massachusetts, and at Harvard College. In those places, he'd learned the words that men of his class used when they wanted to explain an interest in the grubby business of politics: service, obligation, duty. But in the career of his famous cousin, Franklin had seen the promise of something more alluring. Teddy, who had ascended to the presidency when Franklin was a Harvard sophomore, was more than a public servant; he was the most famous and admired man in the country, unmatched by any other figure in his ability to inspire awe. In Teddy's vocation—politics—and in Teddy's magnificent rise, Franklin saw a chance to have the most thrilling kind of existence: a life of service and duty, yes, but also of achievement and renown. It was a life of *glory,* and Franklin wanted it for himself.

By the time he reached adulthood, he'd come to believe that glory would be his if he could just make Teddy's path to power his own. He'd gotten straight to it. After Harvard and law school at Columbia, he served a brief, uninspiring stint as a clerk in a Wall Street law firm. One Saturday afternoon, Franklin and other young attorneys passed the time by speaking of their dreams for their careers. While the others spoke of partnerships and appointments to the bench, Franklin laid out a precise path of progress through politics: first a run for the New York legislature, followed by service in Washington as assistant secretary of the Navy, then election as governor of New York. Years later, one of the other young attorneys present that day would recall Franklin explaining that a man who followed this path "has a good chance to be president of the United States." This path was, the other clerks knew, roughly the path that *Teddy* Roosevelt had taken to the presidential ticket just a few years before.

As promised, Franklin won election as state senator at the age of twenty-eight and appointment as assistant secretary of the Navy at thirty-one. Along the way, he carefully molded himself in his cousin's image, a Democratic Teddy Roosevelt for the next generation who was known to exclaim "Bully!" on occasion, and dropped the well-placed reference to "Cousin Theodore" in casual conversation. When, from time to time, the papers mistakenly improved the family connection to make Teddy his *uncle,* he did not object. All the while, he watched with hungry wonder as Teddy's reputation had grown ever greater.

The newspaper editorialists had struggled to describe the scale of the loss of Teddy. It was, one wrote, "the greatest blow the nation could sustain in the loss of a single citizen. . . . The strongest single personality in the world is dead." But for Franklin, the true significance of Teddy's death was what it portended: For the first time, the path in front of him, Teddy's path, was clear. By the spring of 1919, Franklin had served six solid years in the Navy Department. It was time to move on to the next stop on Teddy's trajectory: statewide office in New York. Standing in the crowd on Fifth Avenue that morning, he surveyed the rough and noisy world of New York politics, the next Roosevelt, ready to take charge.

Chapter 3

The Parade

MARCH 25, 1919

AT TEN O'CLOCK THAT MORNING, THE CROWDS ALONG THE parade route on Fifth Avenue were so thick that it took as long as an hour to walk a single block. Fights were breaking out among bystanders vying for a view of the parade route, their sharp elbows marring the happy unity that was supposed to define the day.

A few months earlier, Americans had welcomed the new year with immense good feeling. With the Great War won, 1919 was to be a "year of endless hope," said one newspaper, "a turning point in world history as vital and meaningful as the first year of Christianity." The most prominent promoter of these grand expectations was President Wilson, who had called the European conflict "the culminating and final war for human liberty." Wilson had spent much of the first months of the year in Paris. There he and other world leaders were negotiating terms of the treaty officially ending the war. The president hoped these peace talks, and his proposed League of Nations for the adjudication of international disputes, would ensure that the days of nations settling conflicts through bloodshed had indeed come to an end.

But by late March in America, optimistic visions of the postwar future were beginning to ring hollow. Decommissioned soldiers and sailors, looking for work, were causing disturbances in the nation's cities. There was a growing panic over the threat posed by international socialism. To many, the spread of communism in Europe since

Russia's October Revolution of 1917 seemed a direct threat to America's system of government. Each day's newspapers seemed to carry more reports of discord, violence, and unrest.

In New York, even the parade itself was a source of division. Prominent New Yorkers had expressed their outrage earlier that year when Mayor Hylan announced that the committee organizing the welcoming festivities would have the newspaper publisher William Randolph Hearst as its co-chair. They remembered well that in the years preceding America's entry into the war, Hearst had heaped scorn on the Allied cause, praised the kaiser's Germany, and vehemently opposed America's joining in the conflict, promoting instead an isolationist policy based on the nation's raw self-interest.

Hearst, who'd been a fixture in American public life since he'd assumed ownership of the *San Francisco Examiner* and the *New York Journal* in the 1890s, was used to the scorn of his fellow elites. Heir to a grand family fortune, he had a knack for scandal and self-promotion. His greatest gift was a total absence of shame. In January, mere days after prominent New Yorkers led a Madison Square Garden rally attacking him, Hearst revived the prewar slogan he'd used above the banner of his newspapers. Repurposed as a rejoinder to President Wilson's high-minded ideals, the words bellowed out from atop Hearst's front pages: "America First."

ON THE SMALL PLATFORM on the eastern side of Fifth Avenue, Franklin stood beside John Hylan, the city's inelegant mayor. Hylan had won his office the year before thanks to Hearst's dogged support. Since then, Hylan's chief occupation had been serving the publisher's interest.

On Mayor Hylan's other side was the governor of New York State, Al Smith. Smith was only eight years Franklin's senior but to judge by his face they were years Smith had lived with brio. The differences in their aspects paled in comparison to the differences in their backgrounds. Franklin, the child of New York aristocrats, had launched his political career on the strength of his famed family name. Smith, the son of Irish and German immigrants on the Lower East Side, had worked his way up the Tammany ranks to become speaker of the New York State Assembly and sheriff of New York County before winning election as governor in 1918. Along the way, he had established a record as one of the most effective progressive policy makers in the country, pushing through an array of reforms that made New York a national leader in workplace protections. When the lesser figures of New York politics looked at Al Smith, they saw the kind of career they aspired to have and the kind of man they aspired to be.

And when they looked at Franklin Roosevelt? They saw a man who hadn't been elected to anything in six years. A man who had tried to get himself elected to the U.S. Senate in 1914, running a pious and preachy anti-Tammany campaign, only to be overwhelmingly rejected by voters in the Democratic primary. A man who had then discreetly explored running for governor in 1918 but hadn't quite dared to take the plunge. A man with a famous name and a friendly demeanor but, where it counted in New York political circles, few real friends.

Nor did he have a record of accomplishment that any of them would have found impressive. In 1911, Franklin had served a brief tour in the New York State Senate, where he had railed against the Tammany patronage system and preached the need for reform. But he had left for the Navy Department after a single term without any major legislative achievements. During Franklin's time in Washington, there had been many fawning profiles that portrayed him as the next Teddy Roosevelt, but there was little in the way of concrete substance and action to link the two men, beyond the shared family name.

Worst of all, he seemed to lack the human understanding that came as second nature to men like Smith. Years later, the Democratic activist Frances Perkins, a Roosevelt friend and ally of several decades, would describe getting to know Franklin in his Albany years. "He really didn't like people very much," she wrote. "He had a youthful lack of humility, a streak of self-righteousness, and a deafness to the hopes, fears, and aspirations which are the common lot."

———

IT WAS LATE IN the morning when the crowd in the reviewing stands at East 83rd Street finally caught its first sight of the parade, a black caisson covered in lilies in honor of the war dead. Next came a group of wounded men, driven in cars by female volunteers. "I got the Jerry who got me," one of these men cried, raising a German iron cross in the air.

Moments like this emphasized the indelible line between those who had risked their lives at war and those who had not. Franklin was in the latter camp. Shortly after Wilson had announced the country's entry into the war in April 1917, Franklin visited with his cousin Teddy Roosevelt. "You must resign," Teddy had told him. "You must get into uniform at once."

Franklin had tried, in his fashion. He knew well that Teddy had resigned *his* post as assistant secretary of the Navy and gotten into uniform at the outbreak of hostilities in the Spanish–American War. Franklin told Josephus Daniels, the Navy secretary, that he hoped to relinquish his civilian position and enlist. But President Wilson vetoed the idea, saying Franklin could do the most good by staying where he was: "Neither you nor I nor Franklin Roosevelt has the right to select the place of service."

Franklin had begrudgingly accepted Wilson's verdict and remained at his Navy Department desk. Throughout the war years, and after, he would complain about having been kept out of action, though some around him would wonder how hard he'd really fought the president's directive. Members of Franklin's class paid close attention to who exactly had put himself in harm's way and who had not. "For every fifty men who will express a desire to go on service . . . and will grumble if they are not selected," wrote one highborn British war-correspondent-turned-combatant in the Boer War, "there is only about one who means business . . . and will run the risk of going to the front on the chance." A real man, declared the correspondent Winston Leonard Spencer Churchill, "should get to the front at all costs."

Nevertheless, as the wounded men of the 27th division rode by that day, Franklin did have some understanding of the horrors those troops had seen. Two and a half months earlier, Franklin and Eleanor had traveled to Europe, where Franklin had been charged with making arrangements for the decommissioning of the Navy's wartime installations. After hobnobbing with Wilson's delegation in Paris, the couple had driven out to visit what had been the wartime front. As their car bumped along makeshift roads the Allied forces had cut through the mud, the landscape seemed transformed into something appalling and grotesque. The scenes from that day would remain with Eleanor for decades. "Along the road," she would later write, "there were occasional piles of stones with a stick stuck into them with the name of a vanished village."

Even Franklin, who had a deep aversion to dwelling on distressing or unpleasant information, could not conceal his discomfort with what he'd seen. In a letter to his mother and children, he described an eerie twilight drive across the site of the Battle of the Somme, where, on a single day in July 1916, more than 57,000 British troops had been killed. The landscape "was ghastly in its desertion, no longer pock-marked fields but the whole surface torn and dug and thrown apart."

These were not the sort of images a person could forget; they would quietly guide the thinking of both Roosevelts on questions of America's role in the world for years to come. Slogans like "America First" might sell newspapers. But for most who'd absorbed the war's human catastrophe, the idea of America entirely turning its back on postwar Europe would have seemed plainly impossible. The scarred European landscape revealed a barbaric unreason lurking in Europe, the cradle of the Enlightenment. If Americans wanted to be safe in the world, they had to do everything possible to see that that darkness was not unleashed again.

MIDDAY APPROACHED AND THE rest of the parading troops had still not appeared at the reviewing stand. Word came that they were delayed downtown, where the authorities had lost control of the unruly crowds. Mayor Hylan, gazing across at the larger reviewing stand in front of the Metropolitan Museum, saw something that disturbed him—a face in the crowd settling into that lesser position, someone who shouldn't have been there. Determined to rectify the matter, Hylan signaled to a nearby policeman.

Finally, at half past noon, the crowd at 83rd Street caught sight of Major General O'Ryan leading the procession, astride a chestnut mare. Behind him came row upon row of the New York troops, their tin helmets dented from bullets and shrapnel.

When they reached the official reviewing stands, they did as their general had ordered and turned to their right to salute. It was the day's climactic moment, the formal yielding of the wartime forces to civilian power. The newspaper photographers rushed to capture the scene. The dignitaries in the center of the small riser were playing a pivotal role in this ritual, and the images would capture that.

In the interval of waiting, however, one of the dignitaries had disappeared from the frame. Mayor Hylan still stood in the center of the platform. Governor Smith still stood to his right side. But Franklin had been replaced.

While awaiting the parade, Mayor Hylan had spotted his own most prominent backer, the publisher Hearst, standing on the less prestigious platform across the avenue. This was, in Hylan's eyes, an intolerable slight—no one deserved a greater place of prominence than Hearst. He had hurriedly sent the policeman to retrieve his patron. And then he had seen to it that Franklin made way.

Franklin now stood further down the riser, nearly out of sight. He had missed his moment—outmaneuvered by men with better instincts for the quick clip of a New York scramble for power. Edged to the side, he was sandwiched between representatives of the French and British militaries. These men wore the splendid uniforms of their native lands. In his plain suit beside them, Franklin barely stood out at all.

Chapter 4

Broken Glass

MAY 1919

TWO MONTHS LATER, FRANKLIN WAS BACK IN WASHINGTON, when he received an enticing invitation from the Democratic National Committee. At the last minute, a scheduled speaker at the party's annual banquet in Chicago had pulled out of the program. Might the assistant secretary of the Navy be able to speak in his stead? The banquet, Franklin knew, would gather party leaders from across the country as they contemplated the campaign for the presidency in 1920 and the party's direction moving forward. He quickly accepted the invitation and scrambled onto a Chicago-bound train.

Onboard, he saw A. Mitchell Palmer, the attorney general and Franklin's neighbor on Washington's R Street, who would also attend the party banquet, as the keynote speaker. Franklin couldn't hope to match Palmer as a celebrity guest. A few weeks earlier, the nation had been rocked by the discovery of a massive anarchist bomb plot intended for May Day, the international workers' day. Using deadly incendiary devices sent through the mail, the anarchists had targeted dozens of leaders in government, business, and finance. Though most of the bombs were discovered before reaching their intended victims, the uncovering of the May Day plot had left the country deeply unsettled.

Palmer's name had been a constant in the newspapers ever since the plot's revelation. As attorney general he had begun exploring a systematic campaign to track subversives, anarchists, and communists, particularly in the immigrant populations of the large cities.

While they did not yet know the details of this program, later known as the Red Scare, many Americans cheered Palmer's aggressive approach. Gossip pinned him as a favored choice to succeed Wilson in the White House. Newspaper stories in advance of the Chicago gathering named Palmer in the headlines and mentioned Franklin only in passing.

But in Chicago, it was the assistant secretary of the Navy who stole the show. Addressing the party committee, Franklin offered a lively analysis of where the parties stood going into the decade to come. Before the war, he said, Republicans and Democrats had each contained their own reactionary and progressive elements. In the Republican Party, Teddy Roosevelt had fought for the progressive cause. But now, Franklin said, the GOP had turned its back on Teddy's progressive tradition, embracing the politics of fear and reaction in order to advance the interests of the wealthy.

Here, Franklin argued, was the Democrats' opportunity to become the country's true progressive party, offering a bold program for reform and a hopeful vision for the future. "We are approaching the campaign of 1920 ... with the broad principles settled in advance; conservatism, special privilege, partisanship, destruction on the one hand; liberalism, common sense idealism, constructiveness, progress, on the other."

Franklin's Democratic audience was thrilled by his message: Even though the party had been in power for six years, they could run as the party of change. "Franklin D. Roosevelt burst into the limelight," wrote one newspaper afterward, "quite overshadowing ... Attorney General A. Mitchell Palmer." The author praised Franklin's "combination of gingery force with political astuteness worthy of his great cousin.... Can it be that his prophetic propensity leads him also to glimpse another Roosevelt in the White House?"

For all the admiring coverage, however, Franklin's speech failed to capture the reality of American life in 1919. He had described a nation neatly divided between the forces of prudent progress and stubborn reaction. But with each passing day, it became clearer that postwar America's politics would be powered by things that defied his easy ideological categories: by fear, resentment, and even anarchy. These sinister forces would appear on Franklin's own doorstep sooner than he could know.

After the Chicago speech, Franklin returned home to Washington. He and Eleanor had moved to the capital in 1913, when he was named assistant secretary of the Navy. They lived with their five children in a house on R Street in the city's fashionable West End. On a warm summer evening, a few nights after Franklin's return, he and Eleanor went out to dinner with friends. When they'd finished, they drove their car back to their garage near Dupont Circle and began the short walk toward home.

It was around eleven o'clock. In his own house on R Street, across the street from the Roosevelts', A. Mitchell Palmer turned off the lights in his library and retired for the evening. Outside, in the darkness, a small man in a pinstripe suit turned the corner onto the block. At number 2132, he stepped off the sidewalk and began to make his way across the lawn. In his hands, he held a suitcase and a sign with smudged words: *The powers that be must reckon that they will have to accept the fight that they have provoked.* He was about to reach the walkway leading up to the stone steps when his foot caught on an iron wicket in the grass. He faltered and crumpled to the ground as his suitcase went flying through the air.

Palmer was preparing for bed when he heard something crash against his front door. Then came an explosion so loud it sounded like the house was falling in on itself. Before he knew it, he was covered in glass.

At number 2131, eleven-year-old Jimmy Roosevelt was startled awake. Franklin and Eleanor had left their eldest son at home with the household help; his four siblings were away visiting their grandmother, Sara, at her home in Hyde Park, New York. Jimmy, who had stayed behind to prepare for his Groton school entrance exams, heard the downstairs windows shattering and the sound of a servant's screams.

A few blocks away, Franklin and Eleanor heard the explosion too.

When sirens followed, Franklin thought of his son and sprinted ahead of Eleanor.

Further down R Street, the Norwegian minister to Washington rushed into the bedroom of his own teenage son. After finding the boy unharmed, the minister looked down and recoiled in horror. Lying beside his son's bed was a sizable fragment of a human spinal column, belonging to the man in the pinstripe suit. Another section of his torso was found on S Street, more than a block away.

In time, the police would determine that this man was a disciple of Luigi Galleani, the Italian anarchist whose followers had also been responsible for the bomb plot that was exposed and foiled a few weeks earlier. At nearly the same time as the bomb ripped through R Street that night, the anarchist's followers had set off explosions in seven other American cities.

Approaching his own doorstep, Franklin saw bits of bone and human flesh. The street-facing windows were smashed. Bursting into the house, he found young Jimmy standing in his pajamas, startled but unharmed. Franklin threw his arms around the boy and held him tight.

Soon Eleanor, who had hurried along after her husband, joined them in the house. Franklin later went out to survey the scene on the street, now filled with police. The ground was littered with little pieces of pink paper, flyers the bomber had been carrying in his suitcase, with the message he'd intended to leave behind:

We will kill because it is necessary . . . We will destroy to rid the world of your tyrannical institutions.

This kind of darkness would roil American life in the months to come. To answer it, an ambitious politician would need not just a pleasing vision of the way the world ought to be but an unflinching grasp of the world as it was. Franklin did not yet have that kind of understanding in the late spring of 1919. His life up to that point had been shaped by people and places far removed from the tumult of the modern world.

Franklin sailing at Campobello in 1916. The young
Franklin was charming, yet he lacked depth.

PART III

Origins

===

1882–1919

"As a matter of fact, I do not believe I have ever seen a little boy who seemed always to be so consistently enjoying himself. . . . He seemed to me always just the average carefree small boy."

—SARA DELANO ROOSEVELT,
My Boy Franklin, 1933

"I tried continually to study him, to try to look beyond his charming and amusing and warmly affectionate surface into his heavily forested interior. But I could never really understand what was going on in there."

—ROBERT E. SHERWOOD,
Roosevelt and Hopkins, 1948

Chapter 5

The Precious Child

1882–1900

THOUGH FRANKLIN WAS NO STRANGER TO NEW YORK CITY and Washington—places where Roosevelts had long held preeminent positions—he was rooted in an altogether different place. That place, the Hudson Valley hamlet of Hyde Park, was only one hundred miles north of Manhattan but belonged to another world and a simpler time.

He was born at Springwood, the Roosevelt home in Hyde Park, on January 30, 1882. That day, the skies over the Hudson had swelled in advance of a massive snowstorm. His birth might not have happened at all. During a difficult delivery, his mother, Sara Delano Roosevelt, was administered an overdose of chloroform and slipped out of consciousness. Wrenched from her womb, the baby was blue and lifeless; the local doctor had to give him mouth-to-mouth resuscitation before he gasped his first breath.

Checking in on the Roosevelts the day after this traumatic delivery, the doctor struggled against a heavy wind and large drifts of snow. But inside, all was calm, the house already warmed by a life force that would in time prove among the most consequential in American history: the intense love that Sara Delano Roosevelt felt for her child.

She and her husband, James Roosevelt, named their child Franklin, after a favorite uncle on Sara's side. The decided tilt toward Sara's family in his full name—Franklin Delano Roosevelt—revealed the way the mother thought of her son: beautiful, glorious, *hers.*

Sara was devoted to her baby, taking charge of all aspects of his care. She carried him with her through her daily regimen about the house and grounds until he was big enough to follow timidly on his own two feet. Under her design, he was a sort of dauphin—long dresses, ringlets in his hair—with a court to provide an adoring audience at all times. Members of the household staff were permitted in his presence provided they acknowledged the supreme wonderfulness of this child. Once, Sara caught word that Franklin had acted naughty in front of his Scottish nurse. On questioning, the nurse was unwilling to confirm the young boy's misdeeds: "They tell me he has faults, but I cannot see them."

Decades later, long after she had reluctantly agreed to share her son with the broader world, Sara would author a memoir of his upbringing. In it, she dwelled on the uncommonly sunny disposition Franklin displayed almost from the moment of his birth. "I do not believe I have ever seen a little boy," she wrote, "who seemed always to be so consistently enjoying himself."

In Sara's telling, Franklin's perfect temperament was fixed by creation. She marveled at his powers of restraint; his parents hardly had to worry about rules. "In fact," she wrote, "we took a secret pride in the fact that Franklin never seemed to need that kind of handling."

But the boasts of her son's immaculate goodness obscure the strong force of Sara's own hand. Life at Springwood may have had few rules, but it was governed by one giant, inescapable expectation: that Franklin would always strive to be agreeable. This rule had roots in the Roosevelts' social class—aristocratic New Yorkers in the nineteenth century went to great lengths to avoid unpleasant topics—and in Sara's own upbringing as a member of the illustrious Delano clan. Delanos prided themselves on their ability to focus on the positive, a habit that Sara wanted to live on in Franklin. If each day was a celebration of his wonderfulness—the admiration of the household help, the indulgence of the farm staff, the parade of praise when relations came to call—Sara made sure her boy understood it all depended on his unfailing good cheer. She did not expect perfection: Her memoir recounts several instances of the young Franklin acting foolish or careless or naughty, matched with little parental response beyond a stifled laugh. But only once does the book recall the need to discipline him: when, as a boy of four or five, he lost a pony race and dissolved into an ill-tempered fit.

Always be pleasant, that was Sara's rule, and Franklin came to understand it quickly. His early letters are filled with happy tidings, wonder at his good fortune, and an unceasing wish to please. At age seven, he wrote, with the help of a governess, a letter to his mother in German: "I will show you that I can already write in German," it read, "but I shall try always to improve it, so that you will really be pleased."

It is tempting to see the adult Franklin's uncommon emotional gifts as a simple product of Sara's enveloping embrace. To be sure, her immersive love and unending praise fortified the young Franklin with a strong shell of self confidence, a deep-seated belief in his own abilities, which he would carry all through his life. But plenty of other little boys in his generation had adoring mothers who poured their considerable ambition and ability into their sons. What made Franklin unique was the subtle but implicit condition attached to Sara's affection. A child who is merely worshipped has little call to think of anything but his own wants and needs. But a child instructed to be pleasant—a child who must be delightful in order to receive delight in return—must step outside his own whims long enough to consider what it is that brings other people pleasure. Franklin learned an early vigilance for any sign that he was less than delightful. And in paying careful attention to the subtle reactions of other people—a change in tone, a twitch across the face—he developed powers of emotional intuition that went far beyond his years.

After all, the stakes undergirding his mother's system were high. Franklin's existence in Hyde Park was a lonely one. There were no other children in the house—his half brother, Rosy, was nearly thirty years his senior, an adult with children of his own. His early schooling was performed by governesses and private tutors. There were few neighboring families of sufficient social stature for their children to make suitable peers; Franklin played with those children whenever he could. There were maids and nurses and gardeners and visiting uncles and aunts; there was his dog, a sweet setter, who followed him wherever he went. But his parents were the only constant. Aside from them, life for the young Franklin felt quiet, empty, and alone.

Franklin hated that feeling, and as he grew, he worked hard to keep it at bay. For decades to come, his life would be shaped by the desire to please, to be judged uniquely wonderful in the adoring eyes of the world.

IT WAS NOT HARD to feel special if you were a Hudson Valley Roosevelt. In the early seventeenth century, the family's Dutch immigrant progenitor, Claes van Rosenvelt, had immigrated from Holland and purchased forty-eight acres of Manhattan Island when it was still New Amsterdam. (Claes's son, Nicholas, changed his surname to "Roosevelt" and dropped the prefix "van.") Like the city they lived in, the early Roosevelts were adaptable and driven by profit, trading farming for the refining of sugar as well as real estate and banking. By the time of the American Revolution, they were among New York City's first families.

In the early nineteenth century, well-to-do New Yorkers, seeking pastoral refuge, built vast baronial estates in the Mid-Hudson Valley, well upstream from the coarse metropolis at the river's mouth. The Roosevelts followed the fashion in 1819, when Franklin's great-grandfather established residence just north of Poughkeepsie in Dutchess County, not far from the village of Hyde Park. From then on, his descendants, including his great-grandson, would think of nowhere but Hyde Park and the Hudson Valley as the family's permanent home.

It was there that Franklin's father, James Roosevelt, was born in 1828. By adulthood, he understood his life's purpose: to live honorably as a gentleman in Hyde Park, where he was known as "Squire James." He married Rebecca Howland, the daughter of another esteemed Hudson Valley family, and in 1854 Rebecca gave birth to a son, James Roosevelt Roosevelt, known all his life as "Rosy," Franklin's older half brother.

In 1867, James and Rebecca purchased a substantial farm near the village of Hyde Park, handsomely positioned between the Hudson River and the Albany Post Road. The clapboard house was large and square, with two towers at either end. Inside was a large entrance hall, dining and drawing rooms, two parlors, a library, five bedrooms, and a third-floor nursery.

Its glory was in its grounds: orchards that lined either side of the post road; a long, meandering driveway; stables for horses; farm fields that supplied milk, vegetables, and cheese. James and Rebecca called this estate "Springwood." It would be Franklin Roosevelt's lifelong home.

In the 1870s, Rebecca suffered through prolonged illness and infirmity, ending at last in a heart attack and her death. James's only son, Rosy, had reached adulthood. By the customs of the region and by the pattern of his own prior life, James could anticipate more days of leisure, the arrival of grandchildren, and the approach of old age.

Instead, he turned back the clock. One evening in the spring of 1880, James attended a dinner at the 57th Street home of Mrs. Martha Bulloch Roosevelt, the prominent New York widow and mother of James's cousin Theodore Roosevelt. Among the guests was the twenty-five-year-old Sara Delano of Newburgh, a town on the west bank of the Hudson just above the Highlands. Miss Delano had a fast wit and a distinguished family name. She was tall and striking, with dark features and broad, beautiful eyes. Her conversation would have quickly revealed her to be well traveled and uncommonly well-versed in culture, even by the standards of the sophisticated society circles in which she ran. James was instantly smitten with the much younger Sara (she was, in fact, several months younger than his own son, Rosy). "He never took his eyes off her!" Martha Roosevelt marveled to her daughters after the guests had said their good nights. Things moved quickly—letters were written, promises made. James and Sara were engaged in a matter of months.

Like the man she was marrying, Sara descended from early-American adventurers—a French Huguenot ancestor, Philippe de la Noye, had arrived in Plymouth in 1621, a year after the Pilgrims. Sara's seagoing father, Warren Delano II, had amassed extraordinary wealth trading in the Far East. When the financial panic of 1857 wiped out most of his fortune, he returned to Asia to win it back again, and then some. To their bounty, Warren and his wife, the Massachusetts-born Catherine Lyman, added copious amounts of children: Catherine gave birth eleven times, with eight of her offspring surviving to adulthood. The seventh child, a girl born in 1854, they called Sara, or "Sallie" for short. The family lived overseas for much of Sara's childhood but home was always Algonac, a forty-room marvel, ideally situated on sixty river-view acres in Newburgh.

James and Sara's wedding in 1880 borrowed the customs of ancient European courts. After the ceremony at Algonac, the newlyweds departed in a Delano carriage, which transported them to a point halfway up the river toward Springwood. There, they switched to a Roosevelt carriage, which carried them the rest of the way.

Many young brides, arriving at the forbidding home that an aged husband had inhabited with his late wife, might tremble: What gothic horrors lay in wait? Sara simply laid claim. The rooms were rearranged to her specification. The servants learned her opinions on the correct way to do things—how to cook rice, preserve eggs, or finish a stocking toe. She claimed the rose garden at the property's heart for her own. And, most important, within two years of her arrival, she filled the third-floor nursery with the coos and laughter of her own precious baby boy.

JAMES ROOSEVELT WAS FIFTY-THREE years old when his son Franklin was born. Unencumbered by the worries that plague a younger man—career advancement, social position—James threw himself with zest into his second chance at parenting. Father and son toured the estate at Springwood on horseback, trekked through its fields, skated on icy ponds, and slid on toboggans in the snow. In the summers, James nurtured young Franklin's passion for sailing on visits to Campobello, the remote island off the coast of Maine where the Roosevelts purchased a cottage in 1885. In the Hudson Valley, James's naturalist passions—birds and trees—became Franklin's passions too.

The boy's happiest hours were spent with his father, walking the woods in the late spring or early fall.

James's lessons for Franklin resembled his life—simple, good-natured, plain—but they tilted toward a higher realm. A son's duty to his family, a Roosevelt's duty to his heritage, a gentleman's duty to the land. And perhaps in those occasional moments when James sensed his son's mind was particularly supple, he spoke of the most important duty of all: man's duty to God.

Despite his mild manner, James Roosevelt possessed a burning, passionate faith. From the pulpit at St. James' Episcopal Church, the parish in Hyde Park, James learned that God had demands for the here and now. Only when mankind worked to improve the wicked world that is could it begin to approach the better world to come.

James heard this call to do good works and felt it deep in his bones. In the latter years of his life, he joined the vestry at St. James'. One night, addressing the church's guild, he spoke of the terrible suffering of the age—suffering he had seen firsthand and found intolerable. Tenements and workhouses and fathers who could not find food to fill their own families' mouths. Children, "nearly nude and hideously dirty," huddled beneath "sewage and gas pipes" in makeshift homes.

"Here is work for every man, woman, child in this audience to-night," James told the guild. "Help the poor, the widow, the orphan. Help all who are suffering. Man is dear to man."

To be kind to such as needed kindness—this, Franklin's father believed, was the great privilege God granted to humankind. He and his son were no exception. They had a moral responsibility to help those who were suffering. Young Franklin was shaped by his mother's drive toward pleasantness and delight, but he was shaped too by the hours he spent with his father. In exchange for his supreme position in the Hudson Valley, Franklin had a duty to look for the goodness in others and to reach out for them as for the hand of God.

IN THE FALL OF 1890, when Franklin was eight, James suffered a heart attack, the recovery from which sent him to his bed for weeks on end. He would spend much of the next decade immobilized, plagued by heart disease, indigestion, and overwhelming fatigue.

Illness reordered the family's life. Sara became mistress not just of Springwood but of her husband's recovery, charged with keeping him comfortable and well attended at all times. Beginning in the spring of 1891, the Roosevelts decamped to Germany each year for several months at spa resorts, where James took in the restorative salt spring waters. Until he entered boarding school at age fourteen, Franklin accompanied his parents on these trips. A substantial part of his boyhood and earliest adolescence was spent in the company of the aged and infirm who strove to pass the days as quietly as they could.

When back home, with his father often confined to the sickbed, Franklin roamed the grounds of Springwood on his own. But if he felt pain, if he felt loneliness or sadness over his father's decline, he would not let the world see it. In her role as caregiver, Sara sought to banish all thoughts of illness and death. Her bargain with Franklin—*be delightful and receive delight in return*—now had a sharp and urgent edge; through his pleasant nature he could help the illusion of normalcy to flourish. "Franklin and his mother," the insightful biographer Geoffrey Ward observes, "were brought still closer together as conspirators in a loving plot to keep Mr. James alive and well." Franklin's great talent—sensitivity to minor changes in the emotions of others—was now paired with an important corollary: the ability to keep his own true feelings hidden at all times.

Even Sara marveled at his ability to play the sphinx. On one European tour, the Roosevelts retained a governess to help look after Franklin. The governess promptly fell out of Sara's favor by committing that unpardonable sin—monopolizing Franklin's time, keeping him too long away from his mother. But Sara noticed how attached Franklin seemed to be to his new companion, how much he delighted in the governess's company, so she held her tongue until it was time to return home. Then she put it in her son's hands: James and Sara would prefer to part with the governess, but if Franklin truly couldn't bear it, the woman could return with them to Hyde Park.

Franklin didn't hesitate: He most certainly did not want his attendant to come home with them; indeed, he found her "perfectly awful." Sara, shocked, wondered why he hadn't said something before. "Because," Franklin said, "I thought after Father had gone to such trouble and spent so much money to get her, it wouldn't be right for me to complain."

Keeping his feelings to himself must have made life even lonelier as he grew older. In the fall of 1896, he left Hyde Park for boarding school at Groton, the Episcopal academy north of Boston that saw itself as a training ground for the nation's Protestant elite. The school was as spartan and unforgiving as Springwood was comfortable and warm. Soon after his arrival, older boys, with their keen nose for vulnerability, pounced, poking him with hockey sticks and commanding him to "dance."

But in his letters home, he was careful to conceal any trace of unhappiness. "I am getting on finely both mentally and physically," he wrote to James and Sara during his miserable first weeks. Occasionally, he would give a glimpse of despondency and then quickly correct course and retreat to resolute good cheer before the sentence was done.

At Groton, he was steeped in a cult of "muscular Christianity" as promoted by the school's founder and headmaster, Endicott Peabody. The Christian half of this equation was cold and proper; Groton boys mostly eschewed spiritual inquiry in favor of godly attributes like punctuality, obedience, and duty. Muscle showed its worth on the playing fields, the center of scholastic life. Franklin settled for life on the fringes, managing the varsity baseball team. "He was a quiet, satisfactory boy of more than ordinary intelligence," Peabody later recalled, "but not brilliant. Athletically he was rather too slight for success."

Upon graduation, he joined all but two of his Groton classmates in the Harvard College class of 1904. There, he was confronted with more disturbing evidence of his own mediocrity. Turn-of-the-century Harvard was ruled by its own cult of manliness. Athletes were campus supermen. Franklin—scrawny, fragile, somehow smaller than his six foot two—failed to stand out. He tried out for the football team and did not make it.

He had no great record as a scholar or intellect. At the *Crimson,* the student newspaper, which eventually accepted him into its ranks after an early failed attempt, he would be remembered chiefly as a "mixer of claret punch for the semi-annual initiation of new editors."

He had long taken for granted the preeminence of his family, but upper-crust, insular Boston society did not seem overly impressed by a boy with a grand Hudson Valley name. Classmates found him friendly but cloying, bursting with noisy opinions in a place where aspiring aristocrats feigned cool disaffection. Society girls thought him a "feather duster," puny and insincere.

His early months in Cambridge were made more tormenting by grave reports from home. Writing to her son that fall of 1900, Sara described a series of attacks that left James again confined to his bed. In Franklin's letters back, anxious concern overcame his habitual optimism. "I am so glad that Papa is really better," he wrote in late November 1900, "and I only hope he will be absolutely well again in a few days and not go to New York again, for it is not necessary I am quite sure, and is bound to be bad for him, no matter how quietly he takes it."

In early December, James took a definitive turn for the worst. Alerted to the graveness of the situation, Franklin left Cambridge and rushed to his father's side. He was with James when he died. "At 2:20 he merely slept away," Sara wrote in her diary as she sank into deep grief. It was December 8, 1900. A strange new century was starting, and Franklin was as alone as he'd ever been.

——

Chapter 6

Love Matches

FRANKLIN AND ELEANOR,

1900–1905

T HE DEATH OF HIS FATHER HAD BEEN FRANKLIN'S FIRST REAL experience of hardship. The loss of a beloved parent is a challenge for any child at any age. For children who have never known real struggle, it can be particularly painful. Their faith in the fundamental goodness of the world is challenged at the same moment they lose a person who has always offered them reassurance and stability.

For Franklin, the grief and loneliness brought on by James's death might also have been an opportunity for growth. Awakened to the world's potential for cruelty, he might have tired of the quest for plea-sure and praise that had long defined him. Compelled to introspec-tion, he might have narrowed the chasm between his inner thoughts and feelings and the cheerful front he showed the world. He might have looked for deeper meaning, and found new purpose, in his fa-ther's old admonition to serve something greater than himself: *Help all who are suffering. Man is dear to man.*

Instead, having lost his most important role model, Franklin grabbed hold of a replacement: Theodore Roosevelt. In September of 1901, nine months after James's death, Teddy became president, ele-vated to the office from the vice presidency following the assassina-tion of President William McKinley. Franklin, beginning his second year at Harvard, had already caught a glimpse of the luster that came from sharing a name with this prominent politician: In the New York governor's race of 1898, his Groton classmates had cheered Teddy Roosevelt's defeat of Democrat Augustus Van Wyck. With a familial tie to a president—and a young, manly, and glamorous president at that—Franklin could not have helped noticing the improvement in his campus fortunes. When he was introduced, the name "Roosevelt" now prompted recognition and admiration, even envy. This, finally, was the thing to rescue him from his own averageness. When, in his junior year, he sought election as the *Crimson*'s managing editor, a jokey placard referred to him as *Cousin Frank, the Fairest of the Roosevelts.* (He won that contest and, the next year, an election to lead the newspaper as its president.)

Franklin's parents had little interest in the political game; service for Franklin's father was a question of duty, not personal accomplishment. Sara Roosevelt saw politics as a grubby business unfit for gentlemen. But as he basked in the ambient warmth of Teddy's sun, Franklin could see the possibilities of public life. It was a career that, not coincidentally, required the persistent pleasing of people and offered constant opportunities for praise. If his father's death had stirred up unsettling questions and uncomfortable introspection, Teddy's path offered a respite and a clear blueprint to follow. To be a successful politician, Franklin did not need to learn how to be more authentically himself. He needed, instead, to become more like his famous cousin in the White House.

By the time he left Cambridge in the spring of 1904, it was clear that was exactly what he intended to do. Politics would be his profession, he told friends, with Teddy's office, the presidency, as his goal. By then, too, he had moved considerably closer to Teddy's inner circle, thanks to a time-tested means of advancement for men in public life: love.

THEIR RELATIONSHIP, LIKE SO much else in Franklin's life, was born alongside the Hudson River. Traveling north in a New York Central railcar in the summer of 1902, the twenty-year-old Franklin was struck by the sight of a familiar face. It was his distant cousin Anna Eleanor Roosevelt, on her way to her grandmother's home at Tivoli, twenty miles up the river from Hyde Park.

The two young people had known each other longer than either of them could remember. Literally. Later, Sara Roosevelt would remind Eleanor of the visit she'd made to Springwood as a tiny child. "She remembered my standing in the door with my finger in my mouth," Eleanor would later write, "and that Franklin rode me around the nursery on his back."

As children, Franklin and Eleanor had shared a friendly acquaintance, but in their teenage years they'd fallen out of touch so that, when he spotted her on the train, Franklin knew only vague outlines of how she had spent recent years. Eleanor Roosevelt was orphaned at the age of nine. Following the death of her mother in 1892 and her father two years later, Eleanor lived with her mother's family at Tivoli. As an adolescent, she was sent to Allenswood, a school for girls, outside London. Now seventeen, she had returned to the United States and was preparing for her society debut that winter. She had transformed from the girl Franklin knew into a cultured, intelligent young woman. They talked for the entire train ride, and in the weeks that followed, Franklin found excuses to appear at the same social engagements as his cousin. Soon they were falling into a discreet but fervent romance.

To their mutual connections, Eleanor might have seemed the greater catch. In those days, acquaintances thought her attractive, even a beauty. Tall and fair, with high cheekbones and the striking Roosevelt eyes, she had, in the words of one society columnist, "more claim to good looks than any of the Roosevelt cousins." She had a set of fashionable New York friends and a name that appeared prominently in coverage of young socialites. Not least, she was the beloved niece of the president of the United States.

Eleanor was, of course, a great deal more than that, as Franklin could see from the start. Like Sara Delano, she was well traveled, well read, and opinionated, though she lacked Sara's confidence and tart tongue. By her late teens, Eleanor had already developed a passionate concern for the underprivileged and felt solemnly obliged to lessen their affliction where she could, tendencies in which Franklin would have seen traces of the father he still missed. In her spare time, Eleanor taught young girls at Rivington Street Settlement House, an aid organization amid tenements on the Lower East Side of Manhattan. She brought Franklin for a visit, and what Eleanor showed him was a revelation. He "simply could not believe human beings lived that way," he told her afterward.

When, in November 1903, Eleanor came to visit Franklin at Harvard, he surprised her with a marriage proposal, and she thrilled him by accepting. "I am so happy," she wrote to him afterward. "So *very* happy in your love dearest, that all the world has changed for me."

Their elation was premature, however, for they had not accounted for an essential force in Franklin's affairs: his mother. Sara's attachment to her only son had grown even tighter in the years since her husband's death. "Now, dear Franklin," she told him, "you are *everything* to your dear mother." Sara liked Eleanor enough but thought it altogether too early for Franklin to think of marrying (and, more important, to think of leaving *her*).

Advising the young couple to wait a year before announcing their engagement, Sara spirited Franklin away on a long visit to the Caribbean, in the hopes that distance and tropical breezes would cool his ardor. But Franklin and Eleanor's resolve did not falter. Finally, after extracting a vow of devotion from her son, Sara said she would not stand in their way. In mid-December 1904, the New York papers announced that the two cousins intended to wed.

"We are greatly rejoiced over the good news," Teddy Roosevelt wrote to Franklin after the engagement announcement. "I am as fond of Eleanor as if she were my own daughter and I like you, and trust you, and believe in you." Marriage to Eleanor would bring Franklin closer to his idol, a fact that doubtless enhanced his enthusiasm for the match. The happy couple chose March 17, 1905, St. Patrick's Day, for their New York City wedding, in part because Teddy would be in town to attend the parade.

The wedding was held in the home of Eleanor's cousin, Susie Parish, on East 76th Street. Teddy gave the bride away. After standing through the ceremony—and joking about how happy he was that his niece was keeping the name "Roosevelt" in the family—Teddy moved to Mrs. Parish's library in search of refreshments. Franklin and Eleanor watched as their guests briskly took off after him. Eventually they decided to join the crowd, hovering at the periphery of their own wedding reception, watching the great man preside. "I cannot remember," Eleanor later wrote, "that even Franklin seemed to mind."

Chapter 7

The Orphan Girl

ANNA ELEANOR ROOSEVELT,

1884–1905

E LEANOR AND FRANKLIN ROOSEVELT WERE FIFTH COUS-
ins in a family that smiled on intermarriage: How to find a gentleman
sufficiently distinguished to marry a Roosevelt bride? Easy. Select a
Roosevelt groom.

Viewed from a distance, their upbringings appear interchangeable.
Their parents were blessed with the same exalted social position, their
actions governed by the same exacting social code. But the inner lives
of Roosevelt offspring were influenced by the same things as those of
other children: stability or chaos, sorrow or joy. And in this respect,
the difference between Franklin and Eleanor's upbringings could not
have been greater.

A pair of vignettes tell the tale. In 1885, at the age of three, Franklin
joined his parents on a trip to England. Returning home by steam-
ship, they encountered stormy weather. They were gathered in their
private cabin when they felt the ship take a precipitous plunge. James
Roosevelt went above deck to see what was wrong. He returned to
report that an enormous wave had overtaken the vessel and the ship
was starting to flood. A strong current of water entered the Roosevelts' cabin. As the sea rose around them, Sara fretted over her beloved child, shivering inside his berth. Reaching for a nearby hook,
she pulled down her fur coat and used it to envelop her child. "Poor
little boy," she said. "If he must go down, he's going down warm."

They did not drown that day; the captain managed to right the
ship before the water overtook the little family. Still, the experience

would have been terrifying enough to traumatize any child. But for Franklin, the dominant memory of the occasion was of his mother wrapping him up in her warmth. The episode left no lasting mark. Indeed, he would go on to have a lifelong passion for the sea.

Eleanor's parents had also planned to bring their daughter to Europe as a small child. But in a thick fog one day out from New York, their own ship was rammed by a passing steamer. On deck, Eleanor and her family encountered screams, bloodied passengers, fires burning. This ship certainly was going down. Eleanor's parents raced to join the crowds near the lifeboats.

Handing his small daughter to a nearby crewman, Elliott Roosevelt first helped his wife into a lifeboat along with the baby nurse. Then he got on board the small boat himself. Only then did he call to the crewman to throw his daughter down. Young Eleanor, only two years old, dug herself into the crewman and screamed and cried. Finally, the man forcibly unlatched her grip. The little girl was sent hurtling toward her father below.

All her life, she would remember the terror of that fall. She landed safely in her father's arms and, with her parents, was eventually transported to safety. But no sooner were they back on dry land than her parents began looking for substitute passage to England. Two-year-old Eleanor, still understandably terrified from the ordeal, didn't want to return to sea. Her parents' solution? Leave the frightened child behind and sail for the continent on their own. Little Eleanor Roosevelt, having just endured the greatest trauma of her young life, would not see her mother and father again for months. Fear of heights and fear of water would haunt her well into adulthood.

No parents wish to be judged by their actions in a single moment of crisis. Anna and Elliott were hardly the only wealthy nineteenth-century parents who inflicted long absences on their children. But the two episodes capture, in miniature, the difference between Franklin's and Eleanor's upbringings. If the key force in young Franklin's life was an enveloping love, provided by parents obsessively attending to his comfort and needs, the essential fact in Eleanor's childhood was the absence of those things.

Anyone who ever met Eleanor's mother, Anna Livingston Ludlow Hall, remembered her beauty. As a descendant of the Livingstons, an ancient and powerful New York clan, Anna had lineage to match the Roosevelts' and a snobbery about social position that surpassed theirs. She was raised in a forbidding New York townhouse and a sprawling mansion near Tivoli on the Hudson, known as Oak Terrace. By the time Anna reached maturity, her pristine birth and beauty combined with a congenital coldness to give her an archaic, otherworldly air.

She met Eleanor's father, Elliott Roosevelt, in the early 1880s, when she was a star debutante of the New York season. Desperate to marry her, Elliott nonetheless worried about his own worthiness for such a partner: "She seems to me so pure and so high an ideal that in my roughness and unworthiness I do not see how I can make her happy."

Elliott was beautiful too, and also gentle and kind. He was Theodore Roosevelt's younger brother, separated by a mere fifteen months, a great man's changeling twin. In their early childhood, Elliott was the family favorite—sweet-natured, attractive, and adaptive, while his sickly brother, Theodore, could be difficult and prone to hysterics. Life was a struggle for the young Theodore; for the young Elliott, a lark.

Then, with adolescence, came the reversal in fortune. The emotional makeup of the two boys was near but not identical. Both were possessed by a manic intensity, which in Teddy made the world seem a place of wonder, ripe for exploration and conquest; in Elliott, the same stimulations came at too swift a clip. By early adulthood, they were set on their divergent paths. Teddy was a Harvard graduate, established in his community, a rising, respected public man. Elliott was a dropout who drank too much and chased wild fancies that took him on expeditions to far corners of the earth.

He was strikingly handsome, however, and blessed with a sincerity and an earnest attentiveness that enthralled the young women of New York society. He even managed, in the early 1880s, to capture the affections of the elusive Anna Hall. Putting aside worries about his unstable nature, Anna assented to Elliott's marriage proposal after only a brief courtship. "Believe me," she assured him, "I am quite strong enough to face with you the storms of this life."

Life would put that statement to the test. Their first child, Eleanor, was born in October 1884, ten months after her parents' marriage. Her mother was only twenty-one, her father twenty-four. Elliott quickly cratered under the world's expectations for a respectable family man and gave his life over to leisure—hunting and yachting and carousing, all of it soaked in drink. He raged and wept and occasionally lost control altogether, his body convulsed with violent fits. To his peers, he appeared an unfortunate dilettante who would not put aside childish things. In a later age, he might better have been described as a man tormented by alcoholism, epilepsy, and manic–depressive illness, bearing down upon a psychotic break.

As the demons set in on her husband, Anna sank into her own misery. She was left alone with a fussy infant daughter and felt like a marooned matron of only twenty-one years old. She implored her husband to change his ways, writing, "I shall never feel you are really your dear old self until you can give up all medicine and wine." But his struggles, she could see, eluded his own willpower. Even his wounds to her dignity—there was talk of love affairs—were beyond his control. She summoned a sympathy for her husband that his own family, particularly his brother, Theodore, would not abide.

Unwilling to blame Elliott for her painful day-to-day existence, Anna sought other outlets for her rage. She found one in her firstborn daughter, who, annoyingly, did not seem to fit the part of a beautiful dreamer's child. By the time she could speak, the child could tell her mother judged her harshly. "Come in, Granny," Anna would sigh when little Eleanor hovered uncertainly in the doorway. Once, when the tiny girl was acting up, her mother snapped in irritation and revealed her true thoughts: "You have no looks," she told the child. "See to it you have manners."

The young Roosevelts put their faith in unsatisfactory treatments for Elliott's illnesses—harsh doctors prescribing rest cures. They tried flimsy remedies for a troubled marriage—journeys abroad, a second and third child. None of it worked. By 1891, Elliott was adrift on the European continent, uninterested in the bonds of matrimony. Scandal beckoned when a former servant approached the family, asking for money, saying she would soon bear Elliott's child. Teddy feared a permanent black mark on the Roosevelt name. He insisted his brother be institutionalized against his will. Anna, by now exhausted and devastated, assented. Eleanor's father, always unreliable, now disappeared entirely from her life.

Plagued by terrible headaches, Anna would pass hours of the day sobbing under her covers. Stroking Anna's hair as her mother drifted in and out of consciousness, Eleanor found rare moments of tenderness, connection, and love at her mother's bedside.

In the fall of 1892, at the age of twenty-nine, Anna contracted diphtheria. Her diagnosis was grave, her spirit broken. Her family, left in Elliott's absence to look after her and her children, could see the end was near. Elliott, exiled in a sanitarium, begged to be allowed to visit his wife's bedside. But the family declined: Only after Anna's death, in early December, was Elliott allowed to return.

As Eleanor's only surviving parent, Elliott promised her that they could make a family at last. Since her two younger brothers, Ellie and Hall, were still small, he explained, it would fall to Eleanor to be not just daughter but mother too. In her memoir, Eleanor recalled the world her father promised: "Someday I would make a home for him again, we would travel together and do many things which he painted as interesting and pleasant, to be looked forward to in the future."

Whatever the rest of the world thought of her father, Eleanor knew him as that most rare and cherished of creatures: someone who looked at her with affection and love. Hearing his voice in a downstairs hallway, she would cast aside her habitual fear and caution, sliding down the banisters and barreling into his embrace.

That Elliott soon disappeared once more, to a sanitarium in Virginia, mattered little. More and more, Eleanor lived in a "dream world" where father and daughter lived the thrilling existence Elliott described for her in his vivid letters. She was too young to admit to herself, or even to know, that this would never be reality.

Only the grave would make that plain. In August 1894, while Eleanor was vacationing with family members in Maine, Elliott returned to New York City. In the grips of a manic episode, he went on a multiday bender, at the end of which he threw himself out of a parlor-level window. He survived the fall but soon slipped into a convulsive fit and died. The next day, his brother arrived from Washington. Teddy, his sister Corinne would write, "cried like a little child for a long time."

Following Elliott's death, Anna's mother, Mary Livingston Ludlow Hall, took custody of her granddaughter Eleanor and Eleanor's younger brother, Gracie Hall Roosevelt, known as Hall. (Another younger brother, Elliott Jr., called Ellie, had died of scarlet fever the previous year.) Eleanor was given only vague details of her father's passing. Only years later would she learn that in his final frenzied hours, Elliott had knocked on a neighbor's door to ask "if Miss Eleanor Roosevelt were at home." When the confused neighbor explained that Eleanor was not there, Elliott grew resigned. "Tell her her father is so very sorry not to see her."

SALVATION FOR ELEANOR CAME in adolescence, across the sea. At fifteen, she was sent to England to attend Allenswood, a school for girls near Wimbledon. There, daughters of well-to-do families from Europe and the United States pursued a rigorous curriculum in history, literature, languages, ethics, and politics and exerted themselves on the playing fields. All of it was under the confident leadership of Mademoiselle Marie Souvestre, a formidable French intellect and educator.

Mademoiselle Souvestre could quickly see that Eleanor had a sharp, untapped intellect. The headmistress showered Eleanor with things the girl had previously known only from her father: interest, attention, and affection. And in Mademoiselle Souvestre's warm library, stuffed with books and flowers, looking out on a placid garden, the orphan girl found safety and comfort, things she had never known before.

Soon, Eleanor discovered a haven, not in her old realm of dreams and fantasies but in the world of ideas. Allenswood made clear that it cared more about how its girls thought than how they acted or looked. Reports to Grandmother Hall raved about Eleanor's intelligence, work habits, and character. She had, Mademoiselle Souvestre wrote, "the warmest heart that I have ever encountered."

The more time she spent at Allenswood, the more Eleanor saw it was her duty to share that heart with the world. Underlying Mademoiselle's lofty discourses on history, literature, and politics was a pragmatic, progressive vision for the world as it ought to be. Allenswood girls learned of the moral outrage that was poverty in the midst of rich, enlightened societies and of the special obligation that children of privilege had to ease the suffering of those less fortunate. Though its headmistress professed atheism, the school was more influential in shaping Eleanor's concept of Christian ethics than was Episcopal Groton to Franklin's. Allenswood turned Eleanor's attention from her own misfortune to that of others.

By Eleanor's eighteenth year, Grandmother Hall insisted Eleanor return to New York permanently to prepare for her society debut. Still, the spirit of Allenswood was fresh in her when she encountered her cousin Franklin that day on the train in 1902. In the months that followed, the manner of thinking and speaking and the principles that Mademoiselle Souvestre had instilled in Eleanor drew Franklin irresistibly in.

She returned Franklin's affection. In this handsome, doting Roosevelt cousin, there were traces of her father: the lust for life's adventure, the good looks, the effortless charm. And yet life had taught her that she could not count on love's permanence.

Indeed, when Sara Roosevelt ordered the yearlong moratorium on announcing the engagement, Eleanor sensed the return of the old, dreaded pattern: a beloved man proclaiming his intention to start a life together, only to disappear. "I feel lost without you somewhere near," she wrote to her fiancé during his vacation in the Caribbean with Sara. "Well, honey, when this is over you won't leave me again will you dear?"

———

ON THE DAY OF her wedding to Franklin, Eleanor received a telegram from Madame Souvestre consisting of a single word: "Bonheur!" Happiness—the thing that had so often eluded Eleanor. Their honeymoon—a three-month tour of Europe—was a collage of blissful summer visions: brisk walks through the Scottish Highlands, sun-dappled drinks at Italian cafés. "It is deliciously cool," Franklin wrote to his mother from Venice in late June, "almost too cool for going out in the evening." Uncertain and inexperienced, they explored the possibilities available to a newly married couple intent on staying in.

Yet there were brief glimpses of pain to come. While visiting the Alpine village of Cortina in northern Italy, Franklin developed a hankering to summit a nearby peak. Eleanor, terrified of high places since childhood, said she'd prefer to stay at the hotel. She would also have preferred that Franklin stay with her, but she said nothing and watched with disappointment as her husband ignored her signals and made preparations for the trek. Her disappointment turned to dread when she discovered that, in her stead, an attractive, confident, and single American woman who was also staying in the hotel would accompany Franklin on the hike.

In the hours they were gone, Eleanor's old loneliness returned. She was cold to Franklin when at last he came back to the hotel. Ignoring unpleasantness, as he always did, he said nothing and simply waited for her mood to improve. The whole episode left him bewildered.

It might have been a trivial quarrel if it hadn't hinted at a sad reality of their union: The equation linking Franklin, Eleanor, and love would always be unbalanced. Franklin's life had taught him that love was a force determined to multiply—the more of it you gave to the world, the more it would grow and come back to you. From her own experiences, Eleanor had learned the opposite lesson. Love, she knew, was a finite quantity, fleeting and rare. It must never be wasted, for it might never appear again.

Chapter 8

Mr. and Mrs. Roosevelt

1905–1913

WHILE FRANKLIN AND ELEANOR WERE AWAY IN EUROPE, Sara secured a house for them in New York City, where Franklin was attending law school at Columbia. She also took the liberty of helping with the furnishing and staff. She was determined to keep a close eye on the young married couple. Three years later she designed and built a pair of conjoined townhouses on East 65th Street—one for herself and one for Franklin and Eleanor. Outside, the households appeared separated; inside, they were interlaced. Every floor contained a retractable door or a passageway connecting Eleanor and Franklin's space with Sara's, making it all, effectively, Sara's realm.

Franklin didn't mind. Growing up a lonely, only child, he'd learned to love a full house. Servants, visiting family members—all were an audience for his exploits. It was natural that his mother would perform the same role in his adult home that she'd played in his childhood: observer and admirer in chief.

The Roosevelts' domestic arrangement reflected Sara's broader influence in their lives. Eleanor had no mother of her own and knew so little of the world; it seemed only natural that Sara, never one to hesitate with an opinion, would offer suggestions on how her daughter-in-law went about her life. Eleanor was grateful for the attention in those early days of marriage and felt intense pressure to measure up. Before long, she'd settled into an adulthood where her primary concern was how others—Sara, Franklin, the world—thought she should do things. She could barely remember her own preferences and desires at all.

Among the greatest expectations was that she give Franklin children. Franklin, the only child of Sara and James, wanted lots of them. A year after their marriage, Eleanor gave birth to their first child, a daughter, Anna, named for Eleanor and Eleanor's mother. A son, James, named for his grandfather, followed the year after that. A second son, named for Franklin, appeared healthy when he was born in the spring of 1909 but suffered from a heart condition and died after just seven months. They buried him in Hyde Park, in November 1909. "So many years later," she wrote in her memoir, "I can stand by his little stone in the churchyard and see the little group of people gathered around his tiny coffin and remember how cruel it seemed to leave him out there alone in the cold."

However great her grief, Eleanor set out to conceive again. Another son, born the following September, was given a name freighted with unique sentiment: Elliott.

That fall, 1910, marked Franklin's first run for office, a campaign for the New York State Senate. After his victory that November, the Roosevelts moved to a grand house on Albany's State Street. Franklin quickly drew attention to himself by joining a group of Democratic "insurgents" in opposition to William Sheehan, the corrupt former boss of Buffalo, who was Tammany's choice to fill New York's U.S. Senate seat. (New York's legislature was still responsible for selecting the state's senators. The seventeenth amendment, establishing the direct election of senators by voters, was ratified in 1913.) The Tammany Democrats held a majority in New York's legislature and thus controlled selection of the Senate seat, but they needed the votes of Franklin and his fellow insurgents to form their majority.

For weeks on end, Franklin and his co-conspirators met in the library of the Roosevelts' State Street house. Franklin, with his famous last name and his aura of freshness, was the star. A profile in *The New York Times* depicted him as a dashing, principled fighter, buttoning his coat to weigh his heavy responsibilities on a "long, lone walk" through the winter cold. This was stagecraft—during his own fights with Tammany as a young legislator, Teddy Roosevelt had been famous for brisk rambles around Albany and the surrounding countryside, strategy and oratory swirling in his head.

After three months and sixty-two ballots, Tammany withdrew its support of Sheehan and offered up a compromise candidate, State Supreme Court justice James Aloysius O'Gorman. The episode brought Franklin attention that most first-term state senators could only dream of, but it also earned him the lasting enmity of his party's power brokers in Albany. Performing a satirical song at a dinner shortly after, newspaper reporters taunted him with a lyric: "Franklin D., like Uncle 'The.'/Can't compete with Tammany."

Her husband's entry into politics might have been an opportunity for Eleanor to reconnect with the ideas and principles that had animated her years at Allenswood. As the twentieth century entered its second decade, other progressive activists and politicians were organizing to expose the ugly underbelly of industrialization—immigrants jammed into unsanitary tenements, women and children working long hours for slave wages in dangerous, poorly ventilated factories. Franklin's principles called for him to support these causes, but he had no passion for them. His old instinct—don't look too closely at uncomfortable things—prevented deep engagement with the scourge in the nation's cities.

Eleanor had no such aversion. In another circumstance, she might have urged him to see addressing the suffering in the cities as an opportunity to do good. But she was overwhelmed in Albany by the expectations of how political wives should pass their time—paying calls on other ladies, listening silently in the Senate galleries, attending to their husband's needs and promoting their interests whenever the opportunities arose. Here was yet another intricate code of adult responsibilities that left her feeling exposed and insecure. It did not occur to her that she had found a venue for putting to action the ideas that had excited her in her youth. "I took an interest in politics but I don't know whether I enjoyed it," she wrote. "It was a wife's duty to be interested in whatever interested her husband, whether it was politics, books, or a particular dish for dinner."

It was soon clear, anyway, that Franklin did not intend to stay a mere state legislator for long. By 1912, Teddy Roosevelt had grown bitterly enraged toward William Howard Taft, the man he had chosen to succeed him in the White House. Teddy sought to win back the presidency for himself. First, he challenged Taft for the Republican nomination. When that failed, he launched a third-party candidacy from the Bull Moose Progressive Party. Franklin made it clear that, despite family affections, he would back the Democratic nominee, Woodrow Wilson, over Teddy.

After Wilson defeated both Teddy and Taft in November 1912, the incoming president's lieutenants remembered Franklin's support. Wilson had run on a program of progressive reform—an energetic young Democratic Roosevelt with a colorful record of opposing the bosses of Tammany Hall might serve him well. In March of 1913, Franklin traveled to Washington for Wilson's inauguration. In the lobby of the Willard Hotel, he encountered Josephus Daniels, the North Carolina newspaperman who would serve as Wilson's secretary of the Navy. "How would you like to come to Washington as assistant secretary of the Navy?" Daniels asked. Franklin was thrilled at the prospect—Daniels was offering him Teddy's old job. "How would I like it?" Franklin replied. "I'd like it bully well."

Soon Eleanor was making plans for the family's move to the capital. This next phase of life might have been another opportunity to connect with her old longing for purpose. Away from the omnipresent eye of her mother-in-law, surrounded by the missionary zeal of Wilson's reformers, she might have found a calling at last. Had things gone differently, Washington might have been another Allenswood, a scene for rebirth. Instead, it would prove the setting for the lowest days of her life, filled with embarrassment, alienation, and despair.

Chapter 9

Golden Boy

1913–1919

FRANKLIN COULD NOT HAVE BEEN MORE THRILLED TO ASSUME the post of assistant secretary of the Navy in the spring of 1913. He swiftly came to treasure life in the nation's peculiar little capital with its particular customs. Washington reporters, he perceived, were friendly to subjects who presented them with ready-made stories. Franklin knew he could offer them an enticing angle—the reincarnation of Teddy Roosevelt in the Navy Department. In popular memory, Teddy had helped to start the Spanish–American War while filling in as head of the Navy Department when the Navy secretary was out of town. When Franklin served as acting secretary for the first time, he hammed it up for reporters. "There's another Roosevelt on the job today. . . . You remember the last time a Roosevelt held a similar position?" Reporters loved it. Before long, the assistant secretary of the Navy was among the most recognizable faces in Wilson's Washington.

For their first Washington residence, he and Eleanor took a house on N Street belonging to Eleanor's aunt, Anna "Bamie" Roosevelt Cowles. The location pleased him: It had been the Washington home of *Teddy* Roosevelt several decades before. (Despite the house's lineage, it struggled to contain the five Roosevelt children, and Franklin and Eleanor moved their family to a larger house on R Street after a few years.)

Franklin and Eleanor quickly settled into the highest echelons of Washington society, thanks to a number of Harvard and New York friends who had become prominent in the city's affairs. The most regal was Eleanor's cousin Alice Roosevelt Longworth, Teddy's eldest daughter and the wife of Nicholas Longworth, a Republican congressman from Ohio. By then, Alice had established herself as an imperious leader of the Washington social scene, her power springing not just from her family name and her husband's position but from her self-possession and mordant wit. In later years, she would keep a pillow in her drawing room with an embroidered message: *If you haven't got anything nice to say, come sit here by me.*

Franklin and Eleanor's fast move up the city's social ladder was also aided by the fraught, frenzied moment at which they'd arrived in town. When Wilson came to Washington in the spring of 1913, he was the first Democratic president in sixteen years. His party had held the White House for only eight years of the last fifty. Republicans had long dominated the city's social life. Wilson, with his bizarre hybrid of progressive idealism and parochial prudery, was an unwelcome outsider.

Still, the city and its citizenry lived by one simple dictum: When presented with newcomers wielding influence—however off-putting their preferences, whoever they might be—the first order of business was to find a way in. And in a genial, handsome young Wilson appointee called Roosevelt, Washington's shrewd hosts and hostesses saw an avenue of approach. After all, this new Roosevelt in the Navy Department not only was willing to accept invitations to dinner but proved an enchanting guest. With his high position in the administration, he was, indisputably, a coming man. His table talk dripped with valuable observations—and delicious gossip—about the strange Wilsonian occupiers in their midst. But with his clubbable manner, his fancy friends, and his famed family name, he was, even more indisputably, one of their own.

In Washington, Franklin found success by adopting the guiding principle of his youth: Good things come to the man who strives to please. Before backing Franklin's appointment to the Navy Department, Josephus Daniels had sought input from Elihu Root, the Republican grandee who'd served as Teddy's secretary of war. Root had offered a warning: "Whenever a Roosevelt rides, he wishes to ride in front." Daniels, however, quickly found himself overcome by Franklin's charms. At their first meeting, the Navy secretary, who was twenty years Franklin's senior, thought him "as handsome a figure of an attractive young man as I had ever seen."

Franklin was thirty-one when he assumed his Navy Department post but hardly looked his age. One afternoon in the spring of 1916, a Wisconsin congressman, arriving for an Appropriations subcommittee meeting, was annoyed to find a fresh-faced boy smoking in the committee room. "Young man," the congressman chided, "I wish you would throw that cigarette away; it is offensive to me." The young man, not intending to cause offense, pleasantly obliged. In a few minutes the meeting of the committee was called to order. "We'll hear you first, Mr. Roosevelt," the chairman said. As the assistant secretary of the Navy rose to his call, the Wisconsin congressman shrank in horror: The witness was none other than the boy smoker.

So, the happy balance reigned: Franklin was willing to be charming; Washington was willing to be charmed. His was not just the workaday Washington of Pennsylvania Avenue between the White House and the Capitol but the more rarefied Washington of Connecticut Avenue, the long thoroughfare that passed through the countryside toward Maryland, along which the capital became a small village of big personalities. Leaving his office in the State, War, and Navy Building on a given day, Franklin might head to the Metropolitan Club, where he frequently lunched with gentlemen of both parties. From there, he might follow Connecticut Avenue toward his home. Along the way, he'd pass the British embassy, the center of the city's social life in those years, where he was a frequent guest. The British ambassador, Cecil Spring-Rice, lived in a townhouse farther up the avenue, across the street from the home of Germany's envoy, Count Johann von Bernstorff. In the years before the Great War, the two men would pause their morning ablutions to exchange an amicable wave through their bathroom windows.

He might then catch a passing trolley car heading north out of the city to the exclusive Chevy Chase Club. There he could pass a happy afternoon playing tennis or golf, a game to which he'd become addicted. In the evenings, he and Eleanor might return for a dinner dance.

A certain kind of privileged young man takes a life of comfort, leisure, and adulation too much for granted. His wit slackens; his charm fades away. But Franklin was that rare man who bloomed under adoration. Catching a glimpse of attraction in the eyes of others, he saw, at last, the confirmation of the exquisite splendor he had always known he possessed.

And if there were parts of him that were less than perfect, Washington was willing to overlook them or make them into a charming joke. One day, Josephus Daniels showed him a picture of the two of them standing on the eastern portico of the State, War, and Navy Building, across from the White House. Daniels asked a rhetorical question of the ambitious young man: "Franklin, why are you grinning from ear to ear, looking as pleased as if the world were yours?" Daniels then answered himself: "I will tell you . . . We are both looking down at the White House and you are saying to yourself . . . 'Some day I will be living in that house.'"

FRANKLIN HAD BEEN IN his Navy Department post for over a year when the Great War began in August 1914. Many in the eastern establishment, like Theodore Roosevelt, favored entering the war on the side of the Allied powers—Britain, France, and Russia. Franklin had been a consistent voice for engagement within the dovish administration and had been frustrated with his superior, Daniels, for not taking more steps to get the Navy onto a war footing.

When at last, in April 1917, Wilson decided America should join the Allied cause, Franklin began his unsuccessful (and perhaps half-hearted) campaign to leave his Navy Department office for the front. He did eventually get to the front, though not in uniform. In the summer of 1918, he spent six weeks in Europe, inspecting naval forces and the broader war effort. This trip seemed to galvanize him, in some fashion. "Somehow I don't believe I shall be long in Washington," he wrote home to Eleanor near the end of his trip. "The more I think of it the more I feel that being only 36 my place is not at a Washington desk, even a Navy desk." When he got back, he put out word to the papers that he intended to soon join the fight. Even if he was speaking truthfully, it was too late. When the war ended a few weeks later, on November 11, 1918, he remained deskbound.

Franklin's civilian wartime service was not without value. It provided him with a wealth of practical knowledge he would carry into his later career: how to get results from a cumbersome bureaucracy; how to negotiate contracts and leases for gargantuan government enterprises; how to manage relations with Congress, other government agencies, and allies. But at his Navy Department desk, he was never forced, in the horrific manner that so many soldiers in the Great War were, to confront the gap between life as imagined and life as it really was. He had emerged from the war a man still dependent on his lifelong habit: avoid unpleasantness, however pressing or real.

That was the Franklin who was pushed aside at the Fifth Avenue parade in March of 1919. That was the Franklin who in late May 1919 pleasingly predicted a new progressive order, only to be surprised a few nights later by a scene of horrific anarchist carnage right outside his own front door. As spring turned to summer that year, it was apparent that if Franklin's country had been irrevocably changed by the war years, he himself had not. He still had the same fixation with surface appearances, still gave the world artifice at the expense of substance and feeling. For much of his career in Washington, these deepseated tendencies had served him well. In the months ahead, however, they would pose a threat to his promise of becoming something more.

Eleanor Roosevelt at the time of
her marriage to Franklin in 1905.

PART IV

A Public Life

───

JUNE 1919–AUGUST 1921

"Nothing ever happens to us except what happens in our minds. Unhappiness is an inward, not an outward, thing. It is as independent of circumstances as is happiness."

— ELEANOR ROOSEVELT,
You Learn by Living, 1960

"This past year has rather got the better of me. It has been so full of all kinds of things that I still have a breathless, hunted feeling."

— ELEANOR ROOSEVELT TO
ISABELLA GREENWAY,
JULY 11, 1919

Chapter 10

Breathless and Hunted

JUNE–DECEMBER 1919

I N THE INFERNAL HEAT OF HIGH SUMMER, ANYONE WHO COULD get out of Washington did. That summer of 1919, not long after the explosion outside the Roosevelts' home on R Street, Eleanor had taken the five children to the Delano family's seaside compound in Fairhaven, Massachusetts. Franklin made brief visits but mostly stayed in Washington at his Navy Department desk.

In previous summers, Eleanor had taken their children to Campobello. But that year she did not dare venture quite so far. By the summer of 1919, great distance was no longer a thing that the Roosevelts' marriage could bear.

It had been fourteen years since Franklin and Eleanor said their vows under Teddy's approving gaze. Thirteen years since she'd given birth to Anna, the eldest of their five children, and three years since she'd delivered their youngest, John. Six years since they'd moved to Washington, less than one year since the end of the war.

And it had also been less than a year—nine endless, unbearable months—since the Roosevelts' marriage nearly came to an end.

The blow had come in September 1918, when Eleanor discovered that Franklin had been, for several years, carrying out a passionate, semi-public affair. Worse, his lover was no stranger but Lucy Page Mercer, a young Washington beauty who had, for a time, served as Eleanor's own social secretary. Worst of all, it was no passing fancy. For Franklin, it was genuine, passionate love.

History does not record when Franklin Roosevelt fell in love with

Lucy Mercer. Perhaps it was the moment she entered the Roosevelts' lives during their first year in Washington. Eleanor was struggling to manage the varied demands on the time of an assistant secretary's wife and decided to hire a social secretary. Lucy Mercer was a pleasant young lady from a nice Washington family. Tall and slender with refined features, she was striking to behold.

Her life story had vague touches of tragedy and romance. She was descended from the Carrolls of Maryland, one of that state's grand old families. Her father, Carroll Mercer, had the pleasing aspect of his antecedents, but his life was mostly given over to drinking and losing money. By mid-1913, the twenty-two-year-old Lucy was living with her mother, Minna, in Washington in a series of leased apartments. In the society columns, Lucy was "daughter of Mrs. Carroll Mercer, who was a social leader here before her family met with financial reverses."

Life on the frayed edge of Washington society could not have been easy for Lucy. Well-born women without fortune in that era lived a precarious, hard life—think of Lily Bart, the heroine of Edith Wharton's *The House of Mirth.* In the company of more-affluent acquaintances, such a woman was never to miss an opportunity for advancement but also never to forget her place. She was to appear always carefree and accommodating while never taking her mind off the clock, counting the seconds until her youth and her chance at marriage were gone. This tangle of pressures had driven Miss Lily Bart to calamity. But if Miss Lucy Mercer felt similar danger, she kept it contained. To the outside world, she appeared placid and prodigiously talented. Encountering a hopeless pile of invitations scattered around the Roosevelts' sitting room, Eleanor's fashionable young secretary needed only a few moments before emerging with everything in perfect order.

Lucy "had the same brand of charm as Father," Franklin's son Elliott would later write, and "there was a hint of fire" in her eyes. At some point, lingering pleasantness had become flirtation, and then flirtation had become romance.

By then, even the ever-optimistic Franklin would have known that not all was perfect in his and Eleanor's union. After the birth of John in 1916, Eleanor had made it known that she wanted their sexual relationship to end.

Lucy was an escape, a portal back to youth. In the hot summer of 1917, America's first summer in the Great War, Eleanor had decamped with the children to the family's cottage on remote Campobello. With the war on and Eleanor away, Lucy joined Franklin's office as an assistant. The pleasures left to Franklin as a "summer bachelor" in Washington were all too apparent. Life in the swampy city, drained of its inhabitants, created a heightened awareness of his physicality. He could not cross the street without feeling sweat gather beneath his suit jacket, could not make it through the night without dunking himself in an ice-water bath at 3:00 A.M. And with Lucy always near, he could not escape desire.

Their romance became consuming passion. On weekends, they fled to the Potomac for pleasure cruises on the *Sylph*, a Navy yacht. Coming ashore one afternoon at an old Virginia plantation, they wandered through a lush garden and a sudden thunderstorm swelled around them, leaving them drenched.

The enamored lovers were not discreet, and Washington soon took notice. After one of their jaunts, the society doyenne Alice Roosevelt Longworth, Eleanor's mean-spirited cousin, approached Franklin with devilish confidence. "I saw you out driving with someone very attractive indeed, Franklin," she said slyly. "Your hands were on the wheel but your eyes were on her." Franklin didn't bother to feign ignorance. "Yes, she is lovely, isn't she?" he replied.

As the summer wore on, the muffled hurt and worry in Eleanor's letters grew and grew. In late July, Franklin wrote to her of their chauffeur, who had taken the family car out for an illicit adventure and got into an accident. "Isn't it horrid to be disappointed in someone," Eleanor wrote in response. "It makes one so suspicious!" By late summer, Franklin sensed enough resentment to finally make his way north.

But even when summer ended and both he and Eleanor were back in Washington, he remained in Lucy's thrall. The war raged on and their affair did too. Perhaps he could love Lucy while married to Eleanor. Perhaps things could continue as they were.

They couldn't, of course. During Franklin's return from a wartime trip to Europe in September 1918, his Navy ship was beset by the influenza epidemic ravaging the globe. Franklin took ill, developing pneumonia in both lungs. Eleanor and Sara greeted his boat in New York, transporting him to Sara's Manhattan townhouse, where he would recover. Unpacking his things, Eleanor found a parcel, which on inspection revealed love letters from Lucy.

That was when Eleanor, clearly devastated, had presented him with his opportunity: If he wished to end their marriage, she would not stand in his way.

Franklin had seriously considered the offer. Divorce, if not yet common in the Roosevelts' circle, was not the unspeakable act it had been a generation earlier. Still, there were complicating factors. Lucy was a Catholic, and her church would not recognize a marriage to a divorcé. Sara's opposition to his leaving Eleanor was strong, and she accentuated it with a threat: If he chose to end his marriage, he could no longer count on receiving money from her.

Most of all, one plain fact would have made this path unthinkable: Voters would not tolerate a divorced president, certainly not one whose first marriage had unwound in scandal under Washington's watchful eye. Leaving Eleanor for Lucy would mean the end of his political career.

However much he cared for Lucy, the choice was no choice at all. In the last months of 1918, he told Eleanor the affair with Lucy was over.

Through the spring of 1919, Eleanor had continued to go through the motions as "Mrs. Franklin Roosevelt," putting on fancy dress, walking through vestibules on Franklin's arm. But as the seasons turned, her life grew smaller and smaller, walled in by hurt, paranoia, and gloom. She was the wife of a high government official, living in an emerging global capital in an age of earth-moving events. Yet her letters from the summer of 1919 suggest that those events—the passage of the nineteenth amendment by Congress that summer, race riots in segregated Washington—were at the far periphery of her thinking, if she thought of them at all.

She struggled to see much of anything beyond her own despair. "This past year has rather got the better of me," she wrote to an old friend that summer. "It has been so full of all kinds of things that I still have a breathless, hunted feeling about it." She did not explain what those "kinds of things" were. Perhaps she did not know. If the precipitating cause for her pain was lingering worry over Franklin and Lucy, its source was something deeper. The sorrow and yearning inside Elliott and Anna Roosevelt's daughter sprang from something older than the betrayal, older than her marriage, older even, perhaps, than Eleanor herself.

THE TAR OUTSIDE THE house on R Street seemed to sizzle. The day after her return from Fairhaven, Eleanor went to the White House for a ladies' tea. Because of the heat, the event was moved inside; guests crammed into the green parlor off the Oval Room on the building's shady side. It was a sought-after invitation, the only social event First Lady Edith Wilson had hosted in some time and perhaps the last one she would host for months to come.

In late June 1919, President and Mrs. Wilson's months in Europe had reached a crescendo at Versailles, where the Allied powers and Germany signed a treaty formally ending the Great War. Under its terms, Germany would assume responsibility for the conflict and agree to pay massive reparations to its adversaries. Punitive and flawed though the treaty might have been, it contained a covenant for a League of Nations, the body for arbitrating international disputes of which Wilson had long dreamed. The president had presented the treaty to the Senate for ratification in mid-July.

Wilson had known he was in for a fight. Public tolerance for a president preoccupied by international affairs was waning, a fact the Republicans were eager to exploit. The GOP controlled both the House and the Senate, where Henry Cabot Lodge, the Republican leader, strongly opposed the League of Nations. Wilson knew that the league's international credibility depended on American participation, but a conflict over ratification of the treaty might well last into the next year's presidential election.

One thing distinguished the coming battle over the league from previous debates over international affairs: American women were expected to play a part in deciding the league's fate. With the passage of the Nineteenth Amendment by Congress that summer, it was possible that the amendment would be ratified by the states in 1920 and the 1920 election would be the first in which women were granted the right to vote nationwide. For the first time, the two political parties had reason to care what women thought on major issues of the day. That summer, the suffrage leader Carrie Chapman Catt was inviting journalists into her airy apartment on Manhattan's Upper West Side. Millions of new female voters, Catt told one reporter, would be paying careful attention to where the two parties came out on the question of the treaty. The League of Nations, she ventured, was favored by women "passionately longing, as they do, for the success of some as yet untried project whereby the horrors of war may be rendered obsolete."

Yet even as other women in her generation organized to determine the league's fate, Eleanor, sweltering in her formal wear at the White House, remained far apart from it. In the days that followed the tea, her name would appear in society columns nationwide. As was the case with nearly every event Eleanor attended in these years, the women's names were printed followed by descriptions of what they had worn, as if they were no more than walking dresses, their thoughts and words on the vital issues of the day left out.

Eleanor was still in Washington two weeks later when she received word that her maternal grandmother, Mary Livingston Ludlow Hall, had died. It was Grandmother Hall who had taken in Eleanor and her siblings at Tivoli after their parents' deaths. As she and Franklin headed home to the Hudson Valley for the funeral, Eleanor reflected on Mrs. Hall's life: rigid, proper, and small. She wondered what it might have been like if her grandmother had chosen a different path, guided by her own needs, talents, and mind. She and her family might have been better off, Eleanor later wrote, "had she insisted on bringing more discipline into their lives simply by having a life of her own."

ELEANOR TURNED THIRTY-FIVE THAT fall. She spent the season making social rounds in Wilson's Washington, an increasingly grim task. In September, while on his speaking tour promoting the League of Nations, the president had suffered a small stroke. Under advice of his doctor, Wilson's aides had canceled the remainder of the tour. Back in Washington, on October 2, Wilson suffered a far more serious stroke, which left him entirely paralyzed and barely able to speak.

Wilson's hopes for an American-led League of Nations died in the Senate that fall. Lodge had proposed a number of revisions as requirements for Senate passage. Rather than engage in a negotiation, the Wilson administration asked the Senate to vote up or down on the treaty as it was. The Senate voted it down altogether on November 19.

By then, rumors about the true state of the president's health were running rampant in the city. Following her husband's stroke, First Lady Edith Wilson, with the help of her husband's doctor, had designed an elaborate subterfuge for members of Congress, to give the false impression that the president was still fully in command. In fact, for the remainder of Wilson's presidency, much of the decision-making in the executive branch would be carried out not by him but by his wife. Her husband's illness had taken Edith Wilson out of the realm of society pages, parties, and dresses and into the realm of action. She would not be the last woman of the era to see her life transformed in such a fashion.

As 1919 reached its closing months, however, Eleanor remained in the old realm—attending holiday gatherings and debutante parties. One night at the Chevy Chase Club, she watched Franklin, aglow on the dance floor with an array of society beauties. Eleanor could bear no more. It was only ten o'clock and they had brought guests from out of town with them, but she told her husband she had to go home. Franklin did not accompany her.

It was nearly dawn when he did arrive home, punch drunk, guests in tow. On the front doorstep they saw a pitiful figure cowering against the cold. It was Eleanor. She had forgotten her key, she explained, and hadn't wanted to go back to the party to get someone to let her in. "I knew you were all having such a glorious time," she said. "I didn't want to spoil the fun."

Chapter 11

Persecutors

JANUARY 1920

A GRAY MIRE SETTLED OVER THE ROOSEVELTS' WASHINGTON life that winter. The skies were often overcast, and the streets were coated in the residue of dingy rain. For several weeks, the house on R Street became a sick ward, as the children suffered from chicken pox and other ailments. Franklin himself was frequently ill and, with the children's nurse away on vacation, much of the care for the family fell to Eleanor, who seemed ever more weighted down. One night while she and Franklin were receiving guests for a dinner party at home, she disappeared from the room. When Franklin went off in search of her, he found her weeping. "I just can't stand to greet all those people," she explained. "I know they all think I am dull and unattractive."

The strain on Franklin and Eleanor's nerves was compounded by worries about money. In addition to his Navy Department salary, they both received income from sizable family trusts that made them more than comfortable, if not fabulously rich. Still, faced with a sprawling family and large house to keep up, multiple servants to pay, and an active social life to support, the Roosevelts often found it hard to make ends meet.

Franklin's greatest troubles that winter were professional. Seeking ammunition for the upcoming 1920 elections, Republicans in Congress had launched a series of investigations into the Wilson administration's management of the war, including at Franklin's Navy Department. None of these inquiries had yet inflicted lasting damage on Franklin's reputation, but the Republicans were about to get a new, lurid source of scandal. For months, the Navy Department had been dogged by shocking allegations about its handling of a morals investigation at the Naval training center in Newport, Rhode Island. As 1920 dawned, the burgeoning Newport scandal had not yet publicly touched the Navy's senior leadership. But Franklin knew that it soon would.

THE TROUBLE BEGAN, as political scandals often do, with the peculiar obsessions of an obscure underling deep inside the government. In early 1919, Ervin Arnold, a fourteen-year Navy veteran serving as a chief machinist's mate, arrived at the hospital of the Newport naval station to receive treatment for a rheumatic condition. There he found himself horrified, and captivated, by idle talk about sexual activity between men in and around the naval base. Though he was quick to avow his bitter hatred and disgust for gay men, Arnold nonetheless sought out as much of this talk as he could; most of his convalescent hours in the Newport hospital appear to have been spent gathering lavishly detailed descriptions of young sailors engaging in gay sex. After a few weeks, he was loudly opining on the nature of the "fairy" menace in Newport and sharing his own thoughts on the proper method for rooting it out.

Arnold's newfound obsession with the Navy's gay subculture came at an opportune moment. During the war years, Newport had gained a reputation as a place where off-duty sailors could easily find prostitution, drugs, and a gay underworld of the sort that had thrived in many American cities since the last years of the nineteenth century. The notion of a Sodom on Narragansett Bay was particularly upsetting to Josephus Daniels, whose southern religious sensibilities were offended by the notion of the pure American sailor ensnared by sin. In early 1919, he tasked a special court of inquiry with investigating homosexuality in Newport. Franklin, too, expressed his revulsion at the rumored behavior. "This department," he said, "desires to have the horrible practices stopped."

The man the department charged with stopping those practices, a Navy doctor named Erastus Hudson, quickly found his way to Ervin Arnold. With Hudson's blessing, Arnold launched an elaborate scheme to identify as many gay men in Newport as possible and document their conduct in graphic detail, with the goal of prosecuting them in Navy tribunals.

Arnold's innovative method for fulfilling this task was to recruit a special unit of young sailors—"good-looking" men "from the average of 19 to 24." In mid-March 1919, these agents set out into Newport's bars, hostels, parks, and beaches, looking for men to entrap. Their inspection was thorough. An average vice detective in that era might have suggested sexual activity to a stranger, only to arrest him at the first sign of receptiveness. Following instructions, Arnold's recruits went further—not just suggesting an interest in sexual contact but following through. Some even made appointments for repeat engagements.

In mid-April 1919, Arnold led a massive raid on the men he'd been surveilling, arresting more than twenty sailors in a single night. These men were taken to a ship, the USS *Boxer*, where they were confined in unsanitary conditions and subjected to inhumane interrogation. They were still there two weeks later when Arnold and his supervisor, Dr. Hudson, traveled to Washington to report on their investigation to their ultimate superior in the Navy Department, Assistant Secretary Franklin Roosevelt.

What exactly Franklin knew about the manner in which his department was rooting out gay men in Newport would be a matter of dispute. Arnold and Hudson later claimed that when they met with Franklin in Washington in early May, they provided him with a thorough overview of their investigation, including the methods they had used to identify their quarry. Franklin disputed this, claiming the meeting had been perfunctory, that it had lasted only five minutes, and that he had never been briefed on the methods used to entrap suspects. Who to believe? Both sides would give their version of events later, when the tactics of the Newport investigators came under public scrutiny. It was in Arnold and Hudson's interest to say they'd acted with Franklin's full knowledge and sanction and in Franklin's interest to say that they hadn't.

But Franklin's account seems less plausible. It would have required Arnold, in his meeting with Franklin, to become suddenly endowed with tact and restraint, which were otherwise absent in his dealings with the Newport affair. Franklin's actions also suggest that he knew more about Arnold's questionable investigative techniques than he let on. In a confidential memo to the director of naval intelligence four days after his meeting with Arnold, Franklin acknowledged that the nature of the investigation was sensitive. "It is requested that this be the only written communication in regard to this affair," he wrote, "as it is thought wise to keep this matter wholly secret."

To later generations, with more-enlightened attitudes on sexuality, Arnold's tactics were quite obviously persecutory and cruel to the men he sought to ensnare. But even to Americans of 1919, Arnold's approach would have been shocking: The Navy was ordering young sailors to perform the very activity that their investigation sought to eradicate. How could Franklin, encountering such a risky plan, not instantly see danger?

Viewing Franklin's actions through the prism of his ambition and the limitations of his character provides a clue. Public outcry over loose morals in and around the Newport base began immediately after the war. This was the same period when Franklin was beginning to think about life in politics after the Navy Department. His reputation might be damaged were it to come out that he had impeded an investigation aimed at expelling gay men from the Navy.

Moreover, voicing skepticism would have required Franklin to do something he did not like to do: look closely at things that were un-comfortable or unpleasant. Hudson and Arnold, with their zeal about the "fairy" menace, were presenting Franklin with both a displeasing problem and its solution in nearly the same breath.

However much or little he really knew about Arnold's methods, what is most striking about Franklin's handling of the Newport matter is his lack of empathy. The men arrested and imprisoned under Franklin's authority were kept in horrific conditions and held without having formal charges levied against them. When these men did ultimately face Navy tribunals, Franklin was presented with documents to sign that described, in detail, the evidence against the individuals on trial. Putting his signature on these charges would blacken the names of those men, almost all of whom were less privileged and well known than he, some of whom were quite young. Yet sign he did. If, as he later claimed, he was truly in the dark about the methods Arnold used, that merely suggests he made these men pariahs without bothering to consider if the evidence against them was accurate or justly obtained.

IN AUGUST 1919, SAMUEL KENT, an Episcopalian minister caught up in Arnold's raids, was put on trial in federal court for "lewd acts." Under defense questioning, Arnold's undercover agents admitted they had been ordered to become sexually involved with the men they were trying to ensnare. The shocking testimony about the Navy investigators' actions left much of Rhode Island's respectable citizenry appalled.

With the public outcry, Franklin, at last, began to see the mess that Arnold and Hudson's team had created. But by then, the focus was no longer just on the minor officials who had given the Newport orders; it was on the department leadership that had given them free rein. In the last months of 1919, John Rathom, a Rhode Island newspaper editor, used the pages of *The Providence Journal* to excoriate the department's conduct of the investigation. Rathom and others were looking to lay ultimate blame for the scandal far beyond Rhode Island. In late 1919, Eleanor received a letter from Anne Sims, the wife of William Sims, a revered Navy admiral who had commanded forces in Europe during the war before falling out with his civilian bosses in the Wilson administration. "I heard something recently, which I feel it is only fair to pass on to you and Mr. Roosevelt," the letter read. "A high-ranking officer in Washington told a lady there that the order to use enlisted men as decoys in the sad business which has stirred Newport so deeply came from the Assistant Secretary of the Navy."

SO IT WAS THAT in late January 1920, Franklin woke to find a displeasing headline in *The New York Times:* "VILE PRACTICES" IN NAVY PROSECUTIONS OF SEAMEN. The piece, drawn from Rathom's charges in *The Providence Journal*, was the beginning of a small flood of press coverage that winter examining the Newport affair. In these stories, Josephus Daniels and Franklin Roosevelt were the saga's named villains. Daniels, who had not overseen Hudson and Arnold's investigation and did not like what he'd learned about it, was no longer inclined to serve the needs of Franklin's ambition. Daniels made a point of telling reporters that Assistant Secretary Roosevelt was more familiar with this matter than he.

On January 30, 1920, Franklin turned thirty-eight years old—still young by the standards of politics but no longer unvarnished or fresh. He faced a dreary winter slog through scandal. He had no broader network to support him. Washington was a tribal place, and its laws were catching up to him. When things had been going well for him, he had belonged to everyone. Now that things looked bad, he belonged only to himself.

Chapter 12

Lonely Island

JUNE–JULY 1920

FIVE MONTHS LATER, IN THE LAST WEEK IN JUNE, FRANKLIN arrived in San Francisco for the Democratic Party's 1920 convention. That afternoon, the Navy's entire Pacific fleet passed through the Golden Gate into San Francisco Bay, where it would remain at anchor for the duration of the convention. Franklin set up a headquarters for himself aboard the super-dreadnought *New York,* a not-so-subtle reminder to the party's delegates that a handsome young New Yorker had helped lead America's Navy for the past seven years.

Franklin's political prospects had improved since the dark winter months. Though a Senate subcommittee had launched a confidential inquiry into the Newport scandal, it had not yet publicly revealed damaging information about Franklin, and, for the time being, public interest in the topic had waned.

It was widely expected that the required three-fourths of U.S. states would ratify the Nineteenth Amendment by summer's end, meaning that women would have the right to vote in the 1920 election. Yet while political insiders—almost all of them male—had begrudgingly agreed to give women the franchise, they did not place much faith in female voters' deliberative powers. Would women, some male political columnists wondered, prove superficial voters, drawn to candidates by the quality of their clothes and the comeliness of their looks? No one rated Franklin among the party's best orators, thinkers, or vote-getters, but he was better-looking than most politicians of the day.

In private, Franklin did not rate the Democrats' chances highly in the coming election. Overseas, it was already becoming clear that the reality of President Wilson's utopian vision for the postwar world might not come to pass. The previous winter, a young Cambridge economist named John Maynard Keynes had published *The Economic Consequences of the Peace,* an indictment of the Treaty of Versailles. In the book, Keynes, who had attended the peace talks at Paris, argued that the reparations the Allied powers had imposed on Germany would leave the European economy destabilized and in danger of falling back into conflict. By summer, the book was a bestseller not just in Europe but in the United States and already seemed prescient: In elections that summer, Germans had expressed broad dissatisfaction with the centrist government in Weimar, the city that was the center of the new postwar republic.

At home, meanwhile, Americans had tired of Wilson's pious preaching about America's enlightened mission in the world; they were eager for something simpler and more boring. At their convention a few weeks before, the Republicans had nominated Ohio senator Warren G. Harding, an avuncular, attractive, apparently harmless politician. Franklin knew and liked Harding, a sometime golf partner at the Chevy Chase Club, as well as the man selected as his running mate, Massachusetts governor Calvin Coolidge. No one would ever mistake either man for Lincoln, but that was the point. The Republicans were offering the country a return to normal, ordinary politics. Already, Franklin was telling friends he'd be back in New York by year's end and, in preparation for private life, had launched plans for a new law firm bearing his name.

Still, his hopes for good fortune in San Francisco carried more urgency than he let on. Once the Democrats lost power in Washington, who knew how many years it would take for them to regain it again. During those years, his youth would fade and the name Roosevelt would diminish in the public's mind. His shimmering political future might even disappear into oblivion.

He believed his chance of glory could still be at hand. It had to be. A splendid early triumph in national politics was the idea in whose name he had turned his back on love and brought his relationship with Lucy Mercer to an end.

ELEANOR HAD NOT JOINED Franklin on the journey to California for the convention. Instead, she'd stayed a continent's length away, on Campobello Island with the children. The little island was not even part of the United States: Though Lubec, the tiny port from which it was accessed, belonged to Maine, the island itself was the sovereign territory of Canada. James and Sara Roosevelt had first purchased a home on the island in the 1880s, and it had changed little in the intervening years. Eleanor's main connection to the outside world was the daily mail, delivered by boat.

For Eleanor, the island was that rarest of gifts: a place where she belonged. In her married life she'd had many houses—65th Street in New York, State Street in Albany, N Street and R Street in Washington—but no real home. Only Campobello felt like hers. Shortly after Franklin and Eleanor's marriage, Sara had given them a large cottage on the island to call their own. It was separated from Sara's own house by a mere hedgerow, but it was that rare boundary that Sara actually honored. She took little interest in what Franklin and Eleanor did with their cottage, a rambling red old-world structure lit by candles and gas lamps. Little, remote Campobello provided Eleanor with the thing she'd needed too often in recent years: escape.

ELEANOR HAD NEVER QUITE taken to life in the nation's capital. From the start of their time there, it was clear that she and Franklin would see the place differently. He reveled in the smallness of the town, the ease with which it could be maneuvered and mastered. She felt the same smallness and it made Washington a fishbowl.

She struggled with the odd profession of "Washington wife." Eleanor would later recall of these years: "I was always part of the public aspect of our lives. Still, I felt detached and objective, as though I were looking at someone else's life." That person often seemed to come up short. On Sundays, the cook's night off, she typically served scrambled eggs, the one meal she knew how to prepare. Her son James later recalled one Sunday evening when the family's normal domestic peace was interrupted by an unexpected ring of the doorbell. Eleanor, already in her nightgown, listened from another room as guests expecting a dinner party made their way into the house. Horrified, she realized she'd written the wrong date on an invitation for a dinner she'd intended for the following night. She was hardly the first hostess to make such an error. Another Washington wife might have made a show of laughing at herself, improvised quickly, and tucked the memory of the occasion into her supply of charming, self-depreciating anecdotes. Eleanor simply froze. Franklin mixed drinks, she scrambled more eggs, and the unsatisfied guests went home early.

She struggled too as a parent. Eleanor wished fervently to be a good mother, but her troubled upbringing had left her with no notion of how a mother was meant to act. She fell back on a system of sharp discipline and rules. This came off as cold to her children; there was something forced about her rigidity, her timing was off, her tone unsure and not quite believable. She was so different from Franklin, a lovable, huggable father who would jauntily throw himself on the floor to roughhouse with them (before just as jauntily disappearing to pursue his child-free career outside the house).

Sara still hovered over Eleanor's parenting—an adviser, a specter, a judge. Sara adored her grandchildren, an extension of her perfect little boy, and the children adored "Granny" too. "I am more your mother than your mother is," she told them. "Your mother only bore you."

And then along came Lucy Mercer. Youth, beauty, social comfort—everything that Eleanor thought wanting in herself, the world found in abundance in Lucy. The very position in which Lucy had entered Eleanor's life—social secretary—was a tacit admission of Eleanor's shortcoming, her hopelessness at managing the knotty intersection of Franklin's public and private life.

Eleanor had known about Franklin and Lucy's affair long before she ever found the proof of it in his love letters in the fall of 1918. In the summer of 1917, the year America entered the war, she'd delayed her departure for Campobello as long as she could, perhaps realizing what Franklin would get up to as soon as she left. That was the summer of Franklin and Lucy's golden weeks romping through the Virginia countryside. His letters to Eleanor had been deeply unsatisfying, dripping with guilt and protesting too much. "You were a goosy girl to think or even pretend that I don't want you here all the summer, because you know I do!" he wrote to her in July. "But honestly you ought to have six straight weeks at Campo, just as I ought to, only you can and I can't!"

Eleanor may have tried to convince herself that there was nothing there, but when she returned to Washington that fall, the reality was worse than she'd feared. The rest of the city seemed to be in on the Franklin and Lucy affair. Worst was Alice Roosevelt Longworth, her cousin and inconstant "friend." Alice and Eleanor might have been close—both were the daughters of the Roosevelt brothers, both had lost their mothers at a young age—but both, too, had been raised with sparse helpings of familial affection, and Alice had long resented Eleanor's incursions into the meager portion she received. Alice kissed Eleanor's cheek but mocked her when her back was turned. Her impersonation of Eleanor's laugh—teeth stuck out, neighing like a horse—was lethal.

Eleanor did not know how Franklin had invited Alice into his confidence about Lucy—"Isn't she perfectly lovely?"—but it was clear that Eleanor's oldest rival, and Washington's most ruthless gossip, had information on the matter that she intended to use. Encountering Eleanor in the fall of 1917, Alice made a vague allusion to how Franklin had been spending his time. "She inquired if you had told me," Eleanor wrote to Franklin afterward. "I said no and that I did not believe in knowing things which your husband did not wish you to know so I think I will be spared any further mysterious secrets!"

The old fog settled over Eleanor's life: feeling jealous blurred with feeling unloved blurred with feeling alone. That fog was still there on that fateful day in the fall of 1918 when Franklin returned by ship from Europe, gravely ill with pneumonia. That black day when she'd unpacked his bag and seen the letters from Lucy—she would never speak of it in public and only rarely and obliquely made mention of it with her closest friends. But she would carry the pain of it with her for the rest of her life.

Nor did the pain and sorrow depart when Franklin agreed to end the affair. It remained with her, the "breathless, hunted feeling," through the long year of 1919, as America adjusted with difficulty to the new postwar landscape. Eleanor would have been aware that, when her husband ended the affair, he had been choosing many things over Lucy: his inheritance, his reputation, his political career. But he hadn't been choosing her.

Gradually, though, her perspective had shifted. More and more, as the months passed in Washington, she sought solace in Rock Creek Cemetery, staring at a statue honoring a woman whose life had been stamped out by betrayal. In 1885, Henry Adams's wife, Clover, a formidable Washington hostess, had killed herself by swallowing potassium cyanide. Stories passed through the decades told the tale: Clover had been so distraught over Henry's infatuation with another woman that she concluded life was no longer worth living. After his wife's death, Henry Adams had commissioned the sculptor Augustus Saint-Gaudens to build a memorial to her. Hour after quiet hour, Eleanor stared at the bronze-and-granite monument. In Washington, the statue was popularly known as *Grief.* Its sculptor, however, called it *The Mystery of the Hereafter and the Peace of God that Passeth Understanding.* It was a peace, he said, "beyond pain and beyond joy."

Eleanor and Clover had much in common. But Eleanor had not died. She was still walking the earth, within reach of pain but also within reach of joy. Franklin had made his choice, but she had choices to make too. When Grandmother Hall had died, Eleanor wondered what if her grandmother had had an existence of her own. She now asked herself the same question.

Discovering the affair would always be one of the greatest sources of pain in Eleanor's life. It would also be the thing that transformed her. In time, she made it clear to her husband that, from then on, their marriage would not be the same. They would live publicly together but privately apart. It was 1920 and she was thirty-five years old. Too old to believe in a fairy-tale future. Still, she was too young—and had survived too much—to believe the world had nothing to offer her in the years ahead. The question was how to find it. And where.

THE PAPERS CAME SLOWLY to Campobello in the summer of 1920. Had she been reading them in real time, Eleanor would have learned about a remarkable series of events at the San Francisco convention, about Franklin catching the eye of the world once more. How, when the convention broke out in a bandwagon parade for President Wilson, the Tammany-controlled New York delegation had refused to join in. How Franklin, outraged at the disrespect, had risen to challenge them, actually wrestling the New York standard away from two Tammany retainers and then wielding it proudly as he joined the Wilson procession. How his performance had made quite the impression in the room; how, indeed, his entire performance at the convention had earned praise for his attractiveness, his energy, his bearing. How, in the eyes of more than one seasoned professional, he was exactly the sort of man that the Democratic ticket needed that year.

On July 7, Eleanor received a telegram from Josephus Daniels, who had also traveled to San Francisco for the convention. He relayed extraordinary news: IT WOULD HAVE DONE YOUR HEART GOOD TO HAVE SEEN THE SPONTANEOUS AND ENTHUSIASTIC TRIBUTE PAID WHEN FRANKLIN WAS NOMINATED UNANIMOUSLY FOR VICE PRESIDENT.

THE NEXT DAY A reporter from *The Boston Post* arrived on Campobello in search of an original angle, the Democratic vice-presidential candidate's wife in the intimate confines of the family's idyllic summer retreat. Eleanor was pleasant with the reporter but reserved, even timid. She spoke of Franklin like he was a man she knew only from the papers: "I am very much pleased and happy to know of Mr. Roosevelt's nomination. While he may not have looked for the honor, I am very proud of his nomination and hope that he will be elected."

When the reporter asked for her thoughts on women's suffrage, she demurred. "I don't think I have any ideas about it at all," she said. "I haven't thought a great deal about it either way and yet I don't think it would be truthful to say that I advocate it. Personally I am happy and contented with my husband and my children."

When, a few days later, the story ran in the Boston paper, the headings in the piece showed how little the reporter believed there was to say about Eleanor Roosevelt:

TELLS OF HUSBAND'S CAREER

ALWAYS WITH HER CHILDREN

HER LIFE BOUND UP WITH HIS

On July 17, Franklin wrote to her, offering a brief account of the momentous events of recent days. "I still hope to leave Saturday p.m. And be with you all on Sunday evening. I can hardly wait. I miss you so so much. It is very strange not to have you with me in all these doings."

It was his same-old tone: affectionate, sunny, reassuring. Franklin's wager, it appeared, had paid off. The political career for which he had worked and sacrificed still promised greatness ahead.

Chapter 13

In a Hurry

JULY 1920–AUGUST 1921

AYOUNG MEN'S CANDIDATE: THAT WAS WHAT ONE NEWSPAper called the Democrats' newly selected vice-presidential nominee, Franklin D. Roosevelt, in a headline. Franklin leaned into the role. One week after the convention in San Francisco, he joined his party's presidential candidate, Ohio governor James M. Cox, to call on Woodrow Wilson at the White House. It was a bittersweet, passing-of-the-torch moment, made more so by Wilson's shattered health and wrecked dreams for his presidency. But Franklin, strutting for the White House press corps in crisp white pants, a double-breasted blue blazer, and straw hat, looked like a carefree undergraduate heading off to a lawn party.

Franklin's improbable task in the 1920 campaign was to convince the country that, despite their eight years in power, the Democrats were the party of the future, not the past. As the campaign ramped up, Franklin was careful to create the image of constant motion wherever he went, scheduling twice the number of events as a normal candidate on a given day. He was always hurrying to his next engagement, always late from his last. In August, he left the East for a cross-country tour—the first of two—in which he would visit fifteen states in seventeen days. In Illinois, his car was pulled over for violating the speed limit. Between stops in rural Indiana, a tire blew out on his vehicle, sending the car flying off the road. When, in Missouri, a stranger offered Franklin an airplane ride to his next campaign stop, a half day's drive away, Franklin quickly accepted. After touching down at his destination an hour later, Franklin emerged from the cockpit, looking, in the words of a local journalist, "like an enthusiastic schoolboy after a speedy coast down a steep hill."

It was Franklin's familiar move: channel his cousin Teddy, the indefatigable political athlete who had, in 1903, famously stampeded the West with a fourteen-thousand-mile tour of twenty-five states. Yet Franklin found the act harder to pull off than ever before. With the presidency on the line, the Republican press was quick to savage him as a pale imitation of his cousin. Among Franklin's fiercest critics was the conservative *Chicago Tribune*. "Franklin," the paper declared, "is as much like Theodore as a clam is like a bear cat."

In their efforts to de-Roosevelt Franklin D. Roosevelt, the Republicans now had the enthusiastic support of Teddy's family. Edith Roosevelt, Teddy's widow, called Franklin "nine-tenths mush and one-tenth Eleanor." Harding's campaign managers sent Theodore Roosevelt Jr., Teddy's thirty-three-year-old combat-veteran son, to chase Franklin through the West. Even Anna "Bamie" Roosevelt Cowles, Eleanor's beloved aunt, said she'd be voting for Harding and Coolidge.

The attacks from the Roosevelt family amplified a growing sense that Franklin was not turning out to be as impressive a candidate as promised. His speeches were pleasant to listen to, but when he was done speaking, it was hard to remember anything he'd had to say. The best part of his public appearances, for both the candidate and his audiences, came before and after his address, when he'd shake hands and rub elbows with the crowd. But when his car disappeared over the horizon, hurrying on to the next event, he left little impression in voters' minds. A vote for this man's ticket was a vote for energy. But energy toward what end?

Presidential campaigns are festivals of fakery, but, in their length and their brutality, they reveal candidates for who they are. On the campaign trail, Franklin showed off all the gifts of his upbringing—his ability to please, perform, and seduce. But the campaign also revealed his lack of substance; his lines about "progress" never fully landed, because he had not given sustained thought to what "progress" actually meant. Even his biography came up lacking. Reform-minded legislator, able Navy Department administrator—these were résumé lines that sounded good. But his life story lacked memorable courage, struggle, or perseverance—the moments that left voters not just impressed but inspired.

The farther from the East he traveled, the more Franklin encountered voters who seemed genuinely to despise Wilson's league. Isolationism had long had greater purchase in the West—the problems of Europe and the Atlantic seemed considerably less pressing when viewed from the Rockies or the Pacific coast. Franklin, ever the pleaser, had an easy solution: the farther west he went, the more he adapted and softened the Democratic ticket's support for the entire League of Nations idea.

In Butte, Montana, he went too far. A chief attack line from Hearst and the other isolationist publishers had been that the league would render America a vassal state of Great Britain. After all, thanks to the reliable support of its colonial holdings, Britain would have six votes in the league, while the United States would have only one. That day in Butte, encountering a question along these lines, Franklin summoned a creative answer: There would be no such deficit. America, he argued, would for all intents and purposes have multiple votes as well, since it would control the actions of smaller nations in the Caribbean and Central America. "I have something to do with the running of a couple of little republics," he bragged. Until he'd resigned from the Navy Department to campaign, "I had two of these votes in my pocket. Now Secretary Daniels has them. One of them was Haiti. I know, for I wrote Haiti's constitution myself, and if I do say it, I think it was a pretty good little constitution."

Before the day was out, his comments were everywhere, denounced not just by the Republican ticket but also by the governments of Haiti, Cuba, and Nicaragua. "We would very much like to know where Mr. Roosevelt got his authority to run two other countries," read the Hearst editorial page that week. "And we would also be pleased to know whether that is the present Administration's idea of democracy and self-determination for small nations."

Franklin had no good facts with which to defend himself—he had no authority over Haiti or any other republic; he had simply gotten lazy and bent the truth. To save himself, he bent it again, claiming the press had misquoted his words.

No one believed him, and before long no one much cared. Republicans were left to conclude that this Democratic Roosevelt would prove less of a problem than they had once feared. When Republican senators complained about unpleasant things Franklin had said about them that fall, a newspaper cautioned them not to worry: "You who have been bludgeoned over the head by THEODORE ought not wince when tapped on the wrist by FRANKLIN."

WHATEVER IDEAS SHE HAD about a new, independent life, Eleanor knew that, as long as she was married to a politician, she would be expected to appear on campaign stages at her husband's side. In the fall, after leaving her eldest son, James, at Groton, she joined Franklin on his second cross-country trip.

Unaccustomed to presidential politics, she struggled to understand the bizarre and, to her, unbecoming subculture in which Franklin was now enmeshed. Franklin adored the company of campaign reporters, with their high-quality gossip and their willingness, when given the proper attention, to write flattering things. On board the train, a willow basket on a secretary's desk was labeled *Drop clippings and suggestions for speeches here*—as though the people writing the news clippings and the people writing the speeches were one and the same. At day's end, when reporters and staffers tempted the candidate to join in long nights of drinking, card playing, and bawdy storytelling, Franklin always said yes.

Eleanor put up a good front, but she was miserable. All her life, she hated being around alcohol, the demonic force that wrecked her father's life as well as the lives of two of her mother's brothers, and the campaign featured an endless stream of booze. She could not have helped but notice, too, the pretty women who seemed to crowd around her husband whenever the campaign train made one of its stops. Franklin flirted energetically and indulgently with them, bowing as they threw garlands at his feet. At a stop in Wheeling, West Virginia, a reporter noted that when Franklin appeared "clean shaven and fairly spark[ling] with virility," the city's "sister citizens" were enthralled. "In truth, it was momentarily forgotten that Mrs. Roosevelt was accompanying her illustrious husband."

Eleanor got used to saying good night early and heading to her sleeping compartment on the train alone. Then one night she was surprised by a knock on the door from Louis Howe, her husband's long-serving political adviser, asking if she might like company. Louis had been part of the Roosevelts' lives for nearly a decade. A reporter turned New York political guru, Louis had attached himself to Franklin during his State Senate days, seeing a gifted performer whose talents he could shape. Franklin had taken Louis with him to the Navy Department, where he'd served as a dogged defender and promoter of the assistant secretary's interests. Franklin delighted in Louis's attention and valued his strategic mind. Whenever his career had hit a snag, he found comfort in Louis's confidence that all would be well.

But Eleanor had always been repelled by Louis. He was a decrepit-looking wretch of a man, whose intense brown eyes jumped out above hollow, pockmarked cheeks. Weighing less than a hundred pounds, he wore cheap, ill-fitting suits that he rarely changed. His chief source of sustenance appeared to be cigarettes and newspaper columns, the detritus of which—ash and newsprint—congealed to form permanent black stains on his fingers and hands. In Washington, he had frequently appeared uninvited at Eleanor's breakfast table, demanding coffee and barking commands.

On the campaign trail, however, she began to see that Louis was a different kind of man than she'd thought. He was generous and thoughtful; he listened to her problems and sympathized with her plight. She sympathized with him too. Though he was along for the ride, he had no control over Franklin's vice-presidential campaign. One veteran of later Roosevelt campaigns would observe that when it came to Franklin, Louis had the "jealousy . . . of a one-man dog who felt that anybody who came close to the master came with the idea of hurting the master or hurting the dog." But on the 1920 campaign, Louis watched Franklin invite new aides into his confidence, whether Louis approved or not. He was learning what it felt like to be outside Franklin's sun, a feeling that Eleanor knew well.

Soon they were inseparable. Eleanor began to share her opinions with Louis, offering thoughts on what Franklin ought to be saying in his speeches, what the campaign ought to do. Louis, too, began to see Eleanor in a different light. Reviewing the complex mosaic of a presidential election, Eleanor could see problems and possibilities that even a seasoned professional might miss. Louis recognized something in Eleanor that she could not yet see in herself: a brilliant political mind.

AS THE WEEKS WORE on and they traveled to far-flung corners of the country, Franklin seemed to be fighting a futile cause. The Harding campaign's simple promise of a "return to normalcy" had perfectly captured the postwar American mood. In public, Franklin displayed his usual optimism, talking up a "silent vote" swinging swiftly toward the Democrats that fall. Privately, he was more realistic. A letter to a servant reveals how he viewed his chances: "Please take the enclosed note and go to the Chevy Chase Club and get Mr. Roosevelt's golf sticks and other things out of his locker. Then fix them in a nice strong box and express them to Hyde Park." He would have little use for golf sticks during the cold Hudson Valley winter; Franklin knew that his years in Washington were coming to an end.

Franklin woke up on November 3, the morning after the election, to headlines proclaiming the GREATEST REPUBLICAN SWEEP IN HISTORY. In the end, 60.3 percent of Americans would vote for the Harding–Coolidge ticket over Cox and Roosevelt, the largest proportion of the popular vote won in a presidential election in a hundred years. The result in New York State was even more embarrassing for Franklin and damaging to his political future. He had failed miserably at keeping the Democrats competitive in his home state—the

Republicans carried New York by more than a million votes. The Democratic ticket hadn't even managed to carry Hyde Park.

For years, his enemies had rated Franklin a mediocre politician, and now they'd been proved right. The *New-York Tribune* described the scene on election night at city hall, where a crowd of ten thousand had watched results come in on a giant screen. When the image of Al Smith, the Democratic governor, appeared, the crowd burst into wild exuberance. When Franklin's face appeared, it was met with silence. "Who is that fellow?" one man in the crowd asked. "Oh," said another, "I think he was Daniels's secretary or something."

Perhaps the only development in the 1920 election that would prove advantageous to Franklin's long-term political prospects was one that neither he nor many others noticed at the time. On election night, those few residents of Pittsburgh who thought to fiddle with their wireless radio devices while waiting for the returns to come in encountered a ghostly voice: "This is KDKA of the Westinghouse Electric and Manufacturing Company.... We shall now broadcast the election returns.... We'd appreciate it if anyone hearing this broadcast would communicate with us, as we are very anxious to know how far the broadcast ... is being received." These words, the first live radio news broadcast in history, reached only a few miles that night. But soon the radio would remake the world.

FRANKLIN TRIED TO PUT his disastrous election showing in the best possible light. The Democrats' landslide loss had been inevitable, he told friends; the country was entering a cycle of consumer glut, and Republicans, running as the party of business and normalcy, had benefited. "Every war brings after it a period of materialism," he wrote to one friend. "People tire quickly of ideals." The Democrats, he ventured with startling prescience, might not win the White House again until a major financial crisis upset the political order once more.

His own political future looked worse than ever before. Up to that time, no failed vice-presidential candidate had gone on to win election to the presidency. Any future run for office in New York State would have to account for his embarrassing 1920 showing as a statewide vote-getter. And while he might joke about his "comparative" youth, the eventual Democratic revival in national politics he imagined might take as long as twelve years to come to pass. By then he would be nearly fifty-one, older than Teddy Roosevelt had been when he'd *left* the White House.

For the first time in more than a decade, Franklin had to contemplate a life out of government service. He joined the law practice of two old friends, Grenville Emmet and Langdon Marvin, who renamed their law firm Emmet, Marvin & Roosevelt. In addition, a Baltimore tycoon, Van Lear Black, chairman of the Fidelity and Deposit Company of Maryland, offered him a position as head of the firm's New York office, at a salary of $25,000 a year. Franklin accepted the offer, eager to get some of the benefits of the "period of materialism" for himself.

"We move to N.Y.—47 E. 65th Street on January 3, and will be there from Monday to Friday every week," he wrote to Steve Early, his campaign press secretary, from Hyde Park at year's end. "If you come up at any time we really count on your letting us know, or if you can get off for a Sunday, come up here and spend it with us—very quiet but plenty to eat and wash it down."

Chapter 14

Hurtling

JANUARY–AUGUST 1921

THE BEGINNING OF 1921 FOUND ELEANOR BACK TO A WEEKLY shuffle between Sara's homes at East 65th Street and Hyde Park. Eleanor was determined to at last proclaim the independent life she had imagined for herself, but she still wasn't sure what that life should include. She signed up for cooking and business classes, and to placate Sara, who seemed disturbed by her daughter-in-law's new independent streak, she joined a sewing circle for society ladies. These activities would pass the time, but it was unclear how they might provide the higher purpose for which she longed.

Then, a few weeks after her return to the city, purpose found her. In January 1921, she was asked by Narcissa Vanderlip, a social acquaintance who had worked as a suffrage advocate, to join the board of New York's chapter of the League of Women Voters. Carrie Chapman Catt and other activists had founded the league a year earlier as a successor organization to the groups that successfully passed the Nineteenth Amendment. Vanderlip assumed that, after her years in Washington, Eleanor would have much to contribute to the league and asked her to be in charge of reviewing national legislation for the New York chapter. This would be quite a change for Eleanor, who only six months earlier was telling the reporter from *The Boston Post* that she had no real opinions on suffrage. When Eleanor protested that she really did not know much about the goings on in Congress, Vanderlip proposed she work with Elizabeth Read, an adept and knowledgeable league member who could assist Eleanor in her work.

This introduction proved a boon. Read, a University of Pennsylvania–trained lawyer, was indeed knowledgeable. Once a week, she and Eleanor would review the text of bills currently before the Congress, which Eleanor would then dissect in monthly reports to the league. Read helped Eleanor to see that women's participation in politics was not just an end in itself; it could be used to help make America, and the world, a better place. By bringing women into the political process and organizing them within the parties, female political leaders could create a powerful constituency for progressive aims like the League of Nations and the promotion of international peace. By April, Eleanor was attending the league's national conference in Cleveland, where she watched women leaders in action. She was perceptive about how these leaders did their work, noting the difference in their styles—Catt's "clear cold reason" versus the "emotional and idealistic" style of a Texas activist who "nearly made everyone cry." A month later, Eleanor's efforts outside the home had gained sufficient notice for the *New York Daily News* to call her "an indefatigable worker."

Even more important was the world to which Read introduced Eleanor. Read shared her life, and a home on East 11th Street in Greenwich Village, with Esther Lape. Lape, like her partner, was an activist and intellectual whose mind and manner enticed Eleanor. More and more in the spring of 1921, Eleanor slipped away from the house on 65th Street to spend evenings downtown with Read and Lape and their circle of friends, many of whom were also lesbians. There she found good food and refined conversation. It was, in one sense, a foreign landscape for a society matron from Hyde Park and the Upper East Side. But it was also deeply familiar. In Read and Lape's home, Eleanor found books and ideas and female companionship, the very things that, at Mademoiselle Souvestre's Allenswood, had saved her life.

She was beginning to see the small hints all around her that the world was not quite as she'd been conditioned to believe. Perhaps suffering and happiness were not locked in a perpetual struggle. Perhaps suffering could, in fact, lead to a deeper, fuller knowledge of oneself.

As the summer of 1921 approached, she began making plans to take the family to Campobello once more. But she did so with the knowledge that, this time, there would be a life waiting for her when she came back.

WHILE ELEANOR STROVE FOR deeper meaning, Franklin's chief concern upon his return to New York seemed to be never having to sit still. In the first half of 1921, in addition to his two jobs, he took on a host of philanthropic and social commitments. He did not mind the amount of time Eleanor was spending away from East 65th Street, if he even noticed, because he was rarely at home himself.

He was hurtling through a strange new orbit, unsure how to live outside the thrilling game of politics. The work of a gentleman lawyer bored him as much now as it had in his youth. He had no special acumen for business (which was fine because Van Lear Black, his boss at the Fidelity and Deposit Company, had made clear that if he contributed his good cheer, his good name, and his good connections to the wooing of clients for the firm, he would more than earn his keep). Cast away from high purpose, he indulged in pleasure, to excess. Returning home to East 65th Street one afternoon that spring, Eleanor learned from a servant that Franklin was in bed, having taken ill. Upstairs she found him recovering from a rough bout of drinking the night before. The next month, he and Eleanor attended a family wedding with the Oyster Bay Roosevelts, their tormentors from the 1920 campaign. Franklin sought comfort in alcohol and was soon visibly drunk. The Republican Roosevelts snickered.

In mid-July, Franklin was on Campobello when he received a telegram from Josephus Daniels: COMMITTEE READY TO REPORT MONDAY ON NEWPORT. LIBELLOUS REPORT OF MAJORITY. CAN YOU GO TO WASHINGTON AT ONCE ANSWER.

For months, a Senate subcommittee, led by Republicans, had been quietly but diligently gathering testimony on the Wilson Navy Department's handling of the Newport vice allegations. Alarmed and enraged to learn that the committee planned to report its findings without giving him and Daniels a chance to respond, Franklin hurried to the capital, where he demanded to review the document before it was made public.

Franklin tried to take in the report—an avalanche of calumny coming his way. "That Franklin D. Roosevelt," it read, "ever permitted or directed as he did . . . the use of enlisted personnel for the purpose of investigating perversion, is thoroughly condemned as immoral and an abuse of the authority of his high office." He tried to catalog his objections, but it was too late. Before he'd even arrived in Washington, the newspapers had the report—fully six thousand pages of testimony.

The headlines the next morning were as bad as could be: LAY NAVY SCANDAL TO F. D. ROOSEVELT and USED ENLISTED MEN IMPROPERLY TO CATCH MORAL PERVERTS. The text of the articles was even worse: "Former Secretary Daniels and Former Assistant Secretary Roosevelt of the Navy are denounced for the methods used in investigating the war time scandal among enlisted men at the Newport training station. . . . Most of the details of the Newport scandal, as disclosed in the investigation, are of an unprintable nature." Those who got to the bottom of these stories found a robust response from Franklin to the congressional report: "Through their report I accuse them of deliberate falsification of evidence, of perversion of facts, of misstatements of the record, and of deliberate attempt to deceive." But the damage was done. Public recognition of his name had dimmed in the months since the campaign. Now it was revived, but only as that of a man who dealt in perversion and crimes too unspeakable to name.

Twelve months had passed since that day when Franklin, resplendent in his white pants and navy blazer, gazed down at the defeated-looking Woodrow Wilson. Now, as he headed back to New York, it was Franklin himself who felt worn out, exhausted by a frenetic, disappointing year. He planned to rejoin the family on Campobello in August, but he had a number of obligations before then.

One afternoon in late July, Franklin joined a group of prominent New York men at the Hudson River landing of the Columbia Yacht Club at the end of W. 86th Street. After boarding a yacht, the group of men headed upriver to Palisades Interstate Park for an inspection tour of the eighteen Boy Scout camps at Bear Mountain. On arrival, Franklin and the other men observed the Scouts canoeing on a lake and inspected their campsites. Over a dinner of fried chicken, Franklin served as toastmaster, leading a series of speeches about what men of accomplishment owed to the younger generation. Posing for pictures with the Scouts, Franklin looked happy and at ease, though the wear and exhaustion from recent weeks was evident in the dark circles under his eyes. The whole trip lasted only a few hours, during which, almost certainly, Franklin came into contact with standing water carrying the polio virus—an unremarkable moment that would change his life.

He finished his obligations in the city, fighting off what felt like a summer cold. In the first week in August, he at last headed back to Campobello, in the comfortable quarters of Van Lear Black's yacht. On board, he mixed congenially with a group of well-heeled guests who planned to spend several days fishing on Campobello.

At the voyage's end, the ship dropped anchor at the edge of the island. Franklin set to work, baiting hooks and ferrying supplies to the shore. Sliding along the side of the yacht's launch, he lost his balance and fell into the water. He emerged laughing, and his guests laughed too. But Franklin was struck by the moment. He'd been swimming in the bracing tides off Campobello for much of his life. That day felt different, the water "so cold it seemed paralyzing."

After a few days, the guests departed, and Franklin was left in comparative solitude with his family. They were joined by Louis Howe, his wife, Grace, and their young son, Hartley; Eleanor had maintained her friendship with Louis after the campaign and had invited the Howes to join them for the summer holiday. Franklin could now feel in his bones the fatigue that had been chasing him for weeks.

On the morning of August 10, he took Eleanor and the children for a long sail in his twenty-four-foot single-masted sailboat, the *Vireo*. Passing through the rocky shoals of the Bay of Fundy, they came upon a forest fire burning its way through one of the small isles.

They scrambled ashore and spent hours trying to subdue the flames with evergreen branches. When they'd extinguished the last of the embers, they headed home.

Arriving on their own island, Franklin felt the wave of exhaustion once more—but, as always, he was determined not to stop moving. With the children, he ran two miles to a favorite swimming hole, where they all splashed happily about. Again, the water felt strange, not cold and regenerative, just *cold*.

Returning home, he found that the mail had arrived, bringing news of the world. Without bothering to change out of his bathing suit, he sat down on the porch to go through it. Before long he was overcome, his body roiled by chills. There was now no denying it: He needed a rest. Getting up, he told Eleanor he would skip dinner that evening and went upstairs, where he collapsed into bed.

There he passed a long, torturous night, the chill inescapable even under his blanket. The following morning, August 11, he resolved to get up, to get going. He found, though, that he could barely get off the mattress. When he tried to stand, the legs beneath him felt like they would give way. Defeated, desperate, he returned to bed.

With his body transformed by the effects of polio,
Franklin had to find new ways to distinguish himself
as a public figure and political performer.

PART V

The

Forgotten Man

———

SEPTEMBER 1921–NOVEMBER 1922

"You people must have faith; you must not be stampeded by rumors or guesses. Let us unite in banishing fear."

—FRANKLIN DELANO ROOSEVELT,
FIRST FIRESIDE CHAT,
MARCH 12, 1933

"Mr. Roosevelt, don't worry, whatever you do. It won't help any."

—LAWRENCE ERVING BROWN TO
FRANKLIN DELANO ROOSEVELT,
SEPTEMBER 20, 1921

Chapter 15

Stranded

AUGUST 11–25, 1921

THAT MORNING, ELEANOR WAS SO ALARMED BY FRANKLIN'S condition that she summoned Dr. E. H. Bennet, the local physician in nearby Lubec, Maine. The doctor, who tended to the routine medical problems of the community on Campobello, was a Roosevelt family acquaintance of long standing. He was not concerned by what he saw when he examined Franklin. The patient was merely suffering from a bad cold, Bennet declared, one from which he would soon recover.

But Franklin's condition worsened considerably, leaving him to pass another night of fevered horrors. The next morning he found himself unable to control any muscles below the waist; he couldn't even urinate without Eleanor's help. It was clear to anyone that this was no mere cold.

Franklin's world shrank quickly in the days ahead; his horizon became his bedroom, then his bed. Minutes were indistinguishable from hours and days. In his lower body, it felt like someone was hammering nails into the bone. He screamed in agony. He lay in suspended agony, no longer able to move his legs.

Faces came and went. He drifted back and forth between sleep and waking. Spotting Louis Howe, Franklin was able to muster only a few pitiful words: "I don't know what's the matter with me, Louis. I just don't know."

By then, Eleanor and Louis could see the full gravity of the situation. Franklin had taken seriously ill in a house without electricity on a remote island. As Franklin lay in his ongoing misery, his caregivers realized just how far from good fortune they had fallen.

THE GROUP ON CAMPOBELLO was still weeks away from understanding what exactly was happening to Franklin: the ravaging of his body at the hands of polio. The virus poliomyelitis is contracted when traces of polio-infected fecal matter enter the digestive tract, either through direct contact with the mouth or through a viral way station like warm standing water. (Less commonly, it can be transmitted by breathing in droplets from an infected person's cough or sneeze.) The virus takes control of cells within the gastrointestinal tract, where it multiplies. Sensing the presence of an infectious agent, the body will often mount an inflammatory response, which might cause fever, chills, and fatigue. Usually, this response is effective at halting the virus's progression. For most people, the virus ends with this gastrointestinal phase, causing stomach upset, or mild flu-like symptoms, or no symptoms at all.

In some cases, however, the virus continues to replicate and expand to other systems. Evading the body's defenses, the virus can reach the central nervous system, where it becomes a truly dangerous, even deadly disease. As they replicate in the central nervous system, polio-virus cells conquer and render useless motor cells in the brain and spinal column. Depending on the severity of the infection, this motor destruction can leave the body disabled or partially or fully paralyzed. If the infection progresses far enough, it destroys neurons required for the movement of the lungs, leading to death.

For an American family in the summer of 1921, there were few diagnoses more terrifying than polio. In the first years of the twentieth century, Americans became aware of a strange new syndrome affecting previously healthy members of their communities. An afflicted person would go to bed with what seemed like an upset stomach or fever and wake up unable to move their legs. The disease, which appeared highly contagious, was so frightening in part because of its mystery and novelty and in part because the overwhelming majority of its victims were children. Panicked mothers would arrive at hospitals with babies rendered suddenly motionless, earning the disease its widely known description: infantile paralysis.

In 1916, New York City was badly shaken by an epidemic of infantile paralysis centered in Brooklyn that ultimately caused more than six thousand cases. *The New York Times* warned its readers of a disease that appeared "to pick the strong and well children in preference to the weak" and that could turn "a healthy baby . . . into a cripple overnight." Under the false impression that insects transmitted the virus, public-health officials urged urban citizens to rid their homes and neighborhoods of flies. Runny noses became objects of dread as officials cautioned parents that by simply wiping the face of an afflicted child, they could infect their entire family.

Health officials found themselves besieged by a virus whose transmission they did not understand and whose symptoms they were usually unable to treat. When New Yorkers fled the besieged cities, neighboring localities banned their passage. In cities as far away as San Francisco, children from the East were greeted by medical teams searching for signs of infection. Babies and toddlers with detectable fevers were whisked away into quarantine.

The ghastly accounts of the 1916 epidemic had left even the normally cool-headed Franklin gripped by fear. His children had spent that summer with Eleanor on Campobello, far from the heart of the epidemic. But Franklin, writing to his wife from Washington, had conjured scenarios for how it might find its way to the remote island. "The infantile paralysis in N.Y. and vicinity is appalling," he wrote to Eleanor that summer. "Please kill all the flies . . . I think it is really important."

In the summer of 1921, five years after the New York epidemic, fear of the virus was still universal in the Northeast. Unfortunately for Franklin, the emerging understanding that the virus was spread through contact with warm standing water was not. Considering the typical life cycle of polio, it is almost certain that Franklin came into contact with the virus during his visit to the Boy Scout camp on July 27, 1921.

Later, Franklin's assistant, Marguerite "Missy" LeHand, would recall that he'd been somewhat under the weather in the days after the trip to the camp. Had he sought medical attention for the first symptoms of infantile paralysis, it is possible that he could have been given convalescent plasma, the one effective means of stopping the polio virus before it has its worst effects.

But polio would not have been high on Franklin's list of worries. Though it was known that adults could contract the virus, infantile paralysis was largely thought to be a children's disease. It was also widely, and wrongly, believed to be a disease of the urban poor, particularly immigrants—many noted that the explosion of polio cases in the United States coincided with the waves of mass immigration from southern and eastern Europe. The Franklin Roosevelt of 1921, a vigorous adult, a patrician scion of the pristine Hudson Valley, was the last person anyone imagined getting infantile paralysis.

He was, in fact, *more* likely than many other adults to suffer from the worst of its effects. A study would later determine that adults from rural areas of upstate New York had a greater chance of experiencing severe polio infections than did adults from New York City, who were more likely to have been exposed to a mild form of the virus in childhood. Franklin's upstate childhood, spent in relative isolation from other children and their germs, would have left him especially vulnerable.

What's more, despite his healthy appearance, Franklin's immune system was not in perfect condition in the late summer of 1921. Over the previous three years, he'd been ill a great deal of the time—the double pneumonia that had left him bedridden for weeks in the fall of 1918; the bouts of sickness that had required him to get a tonsillectomy in the winter of 1919–20. The stresses and strains of the past year—the decline in his political prospects, the Navy scandal, the continued unhappiness of his marriage—had all left Franklin worn down at precisely the moment the virus entered his system.

PERHAPS THE ONLY PIECE of good luck the Roosevelts had in those vexing early days of Franklin's illness was Louis Howe's presence on

Campobello. It was not ordinary in those days for out-of-office politicians to bring political advisers—much less their families—along
with them on vacation. But Franklin and Louis's relationship was not
ordinary.

In the winter of 1911, when Franklin was a newly elected New York
State senator, Louis, working at the time as a journalist, had gone to
interview Franklin at a large house the Roosevelts had rented in Albany. A servant had ushered Louis through the grand entranceway
and shown him into the library. Louis was still taking in his
surroundings—the coat of arms above the fireplace, the elegant
furniture—when Franklin burst into the room. Over the course of the
next hour, Louis had watched the young state legislator pace the
room, his words overflowing with enthusiasm, energy, excitement. All
of it, just for him! Louis was just another member of the capital press
corps then, but Franklin made it clear that for those moments he was
the most important person in the world. And yet Louis was canny
enough to recognize that this wasn't entirely genuine; Franklin was
putting on a performance, and an effective one, for Louis's benefit.
Louis was struck by the young politician's talent. Soon he was working as Franklin's chief strategist.

They had made an odd-looking pair, Franklin the matinee idol
beside Louis, known in Albany as "the gnome." Their differences
transcended the physical. Where Franklin greeted newcomers with
instinctive pleasantness and accommodation, Louis was brusque,
skeptical, and mistrustful. But Louis's coarse exterior shielded a heart
that was moved by romantic, heroic drama. When he was young, he'd
been drawn to the theater, not as an actor but as a writer and director
of scenes. In Franklin, he saw his star.

Franklin too was drawn to Louis—to his talent for publicity and
strategy. As a matter of survival, a feeble man pushed to the fringes
develops a sophisticated understanding of how power works and
where it resides. Franklin could see that understanding in Louis and
perceived how it could prove crucial for his own rise.

He'd given Louis charge of his political organization in Albany
and then brought him to Washington when Franklin was named as-

sistant secretary of the Navy. There, Louis had launched complicated schemes for using the Navy's big footprint in the various states to make friends for Franklin nationwide, all the while making sure Franklin's name stayed in the papers back home in New York.

Louis called himself Franklin's "toe weights"—the force that pulled him back to earth when the admiring hordes and Franklin's own ambition lifted him heavenward. But there was no one who adored Franklin as much as Louis did. "His whole object in life was to make himself helpful" to Franklin, Secretary of the Navy Josephus Daniels would later say. At one point in the Washington years, Franklin took ill while Louis was off touring the Caribbean on a Navy Department vessel, and Eleanor wondered if perhaps Louis ought to be notified of Franklin's condition. Louis's wife, Grace, had said no, not "unless you want him to jump right off that ship and swim ashore and rush right back here to him."

In truth, Franklin, with his brilliance, beauty, and promise, was the bright spot in Louis's often troubled life. His marriage to Grace was unhappy. Their children knew Louis as an itinerant presence, eternally rushing off to answer Franklin's call. In a 1919 letter to Grace, complaining that he hadn't heard enough from their son, Hartley, Louis revealed the desperate loneliness and insecurity he always struggled to keep at bay. The boy was "the only person in the world that cares for me," Louis wrote, "and I'm afraid it wouldn't take him very long to forget. Everybody else is indifferent or hates me or is afraid of me or sees me to get what they want."

The Howes' visit to Campobello in the summer of 1921 was bittersweet. Louis planned to take a job that fall as an executive with the company New England Oil. The position was well paid, the responsibilities reasonable. With no political office beckoning Franklin, it made sense for Louis to find occupation elsewhere. Still, the change was painful to contemplate. This new job would take him out of the Roosevelts' orbit, perhaps forever.

Now, however, with Franklin ailing, Louis sprang instinctively to action. His skills as a journalist and political professional made him

invaluable in this particular hour of need. A reporter's work is guided
by the faith that at the center of the most mysterious story, there is a
man or woman who knows everything. And the political pro knows
that at the heart of every intractable problem, there is a person who
has the power to get things unstuck. The well-placed call, the un-
swerving faith that the right person can be found—this was life for
men like Louis Howe.

From Dr. Bennet's office in Lubec, Louis worked the phone lines.
He soon discovered that Dr. William Williams Keen, a famed Philadelphia surgeon known as "the grand old man of American medicine," was spending his holiday at Bar Harbor, the summer colony on
Maine's Mount Desert Island. Louis got ahold of Keen there and
filled him in on Franklin's condition. The doctor agreed to leave for
Campobello at once

Louis met Keen that evening at the boat launch in Lubec. He may
well have sensed instantly that this doctor would not be the savior for
whom they'd hoped. Keen was eighty-four years old that summer and
had been working as a surgeon since the Civil War. His most famous
case was in 1893, when he had helped to remove a cancer from the jaw
of the sitting president, Grover Cleveland, aboard a presidential yacht
floating in Long Island Sound. By the time Louis summoned him to
Campobello, Keen had been retired from the practice of medicine for
more than a decade.

Keen did not, however, seem deterred by this interlude, exuding
confidence as he examined Franklin. What he saw was plain: a patient who was exhausted, suffering extremes of hot and cold, unable
to urinate and express his bowels on his own, and apparently unable
to move the lower portion of his legs, save for a few tiny wiggles in his
toes.

Upon completing his examination, Keen delivered his diagnosis:
Franklin was suffering from a blood clot that had gotten loose and
congested his spinal cord. This congestion had caused him to lose
ability in his legs. The damage was not permanent—the twitching
toes were the vital proof of that—and Keen was certain Franklin

would regain full mobility in time. He advised Eleanor to send to New York for a trained masseur, who could stimulate the leg muscles. In the meantime, it was essential for Eleanor and Howe to perform the massage themselves.

This opinion would turn out to be yet another stroke of bad luck. The years out of practice had not served Dr. Keen well. As the historian James Tobin notes, a competent doctor ought to have known that Franklin's debilitating temperature shifts could not be attributed to a blood clot; vacillating heat and cold were a sign of fever, and fever was a telltale sign of infection. The misdiagnosis came at a high cost: For a person in the grips of a serious polio infection, there are few things so likely to increase the risk of permanent damage as vigorous massage.

BUT ELEANOR ROOSEVELT DID not know that. After Keen left the island, Eleanor was careful to follow the doctor's instructions. "Louis and I are rubbing him as well as we can," Eleanor wrote to James "Rosy" Roosevelt, Franklin's older half brother. "The doctor thinks absorption has already begun as he can move his toes on one foot a little more which is very encouraging."

Eleanor had been nursing her husband round the clock, catching rare moments of sleep on an upholstered chair at his bedside. Tending to a man who had lost control over much of his body, including his bladder and bowels, was arduous, anxiety-producing work. Just as exhausting was the emotional toll, a burden she bore nearly alone. Keen's diagnosis and his precise instructions had allowed Eleanor to put her trust in an external authority.

Still, for all Keen's assurances, Franklin seemed to be getting worse. For a period of time, he lost the use of his hands; at one point, he complained of difficulty seeing. A few days after Keen's departure from Campobello, a letter from the physician reached the island. In addition to a bill for his services—a summer house call from the "grand old man" of medicine came with an accordingly grand price of six hundred dollars—the letter contained an amendment to his earlier diagnosis. On further consideration, he said, he wondered if perhaps the problem wasn't a blood clot at all but "inflammation" in the spinal cord that had caused residual damage in the nerves. If so, complete recovery was still possible but might well prove "a longer business."

Eleanor knew her husband would be crushed by the prospect of prolonged infirmity. "I dread the time when I have to tell Franklin," she wrote to Rosy, "and it wrings my heart for it is all so much worse to a man than to a woman."

BY THEN, LOUIS WAS nurturing his own doubts about Keen and looking for another source of help. This time he turned to Franklin's uncle, Frederic Adrian Delano, a gregarious and well-connected railroad executive and former member of the Federal Reserve Board. Writing to Delano at his home in Washington, Louis described the state of Franklin's condition, his concerns about Keen, and his fears about the true nature of Franklin's illness.

Delano was the only surviving brother of Sara Delano Roosevelt—Franklin's beloved "Uncle Fred." In recent years, when both were living in Washington, Delano had enjoyed spending time with his nephew. In the early mornings, they'd suffered together in a training regimen led by the acclaimed fitness guru Walter Camp. Delano was troubled to think of his graceful, athletic young nephew confined to his bed, unable to walk.

Putting down Louis's letter, Delano immediately sought the opinion of a Washington doctor. On hearing of Franklin's symptoms, this physician offered a disturbing diagnosis: It sounded, he said, like Franklin had infantile paralysis. The doctor went on to say that the foremost expert in that illness was Robert Williamson Lovett, a famed orthopedic surgeon who ran an infantile-paralysis clinic in Boston. Rather than wait for further word from Campobello, Delano rushed to catch a train for Boston.

When he arrived there, he found that the esteemed Dr. Lovett was not available to see him. In the middle of the August holiday, only Samuel Levine, a thirty-year-old infantile paralysis specialist at the Peter Bent Brigham Hospital, was in town. After reviewing the symptoms described in Louis's letter, Levine told Delano there was no way Franklin was suffering from a blood clot in the spinal cord. He had infantile paralysis. The doctor was sure.

ON CAMPOBELLO, ELEANOR RECEIVED word that Delano was on the phone from Boston. When she came on the line, he began to tell her about his meeting with Levine and the doctor's conviction that Franklin had infantile paralysis. Delano tried to explain the rest of what the doctor had said—that it was imperative to act quickly—but the connection was bad and it was hard for Eleanor to grasp what he was saying.

In a letter to Eleanor following the call, Delano laid out the case more clearly. They had to dispense with Keen and his diagnosis, he told her. What they needed was for an expert in infantile paralysis to examine Franklin at once. Delano urged Eleanor to summon Dr. Levine to Campobello: "A telegram to his office will get him."

Yet Eleanor hesitated, not sure what to think. The implications of a polio diagnosis were terrible to contemplate—and not just for Franklin. She feared for her children, sleeping under the same roof as their father. Stray sniffles now seemed a portent of doom.

When she shared Dr. Levine's view with Dr. Keen, Keen strongly rejected the possibility of infantile paralysis. Eleanor was left with a difficult choice: Should she discard Keen, the one voice of authority in whom she'd placed her trust?

She worried what a polio diagnosis would do to the precarious state of Franklin's mood. For a week, Keen's hope-inspiring prognosis had been their watchword, the light at the end of the tunnel. What would happen to Franklin's already faltering spirits if the light was stamped out?

"On Uncle Fred's urgent advice," she wrote to Rosy, "I have asked

Dr. Keen to try to get Dr. Lovett here to determine if it is I.P. or not."
Soon, it was arranged: Lovett would come to Campobello, and he and
Keen would examine Franklin together.

In the meantime, Eleanor tried to lighten Franklin's countenance
however she could. Eleanor, Louis, and Grace took turns reading the
newspapers aloud, hoping to rekindle his interest in the world beyond
Campobello's shores.

Most of the time, Franklin listened in silence. One day, however,
when Grace was reading to him in his bedroom, he surprised her by
raising his voice. "Grace," he said, "read ... that story again." She
obliged and repeated the article she had just finished. It was about a
curious subject: a recent outbreak of infantile paralysis in parts of
upstate New York

Eleanor and Louis were talking in hushed tones, believing they
were sparing Franklin from their polio worries. But Grace Howe
would come to know better. That was the moment, she would later
say, when Franklin came fully to understand exactly what had happened to him.

THE OFFICIAL CONFIRMATION CAME on August 25, when Dr.
Keen and Dr. Lovett came to Campobello, along with Dr. Bennet.
After examining Franklin, they repaired to Anna Roosevelt's bedroom for their conference, with Anna listening through the closet
door. Keen gave up his resistance; he agreed that Franklin had infantile paralysis.

Finally, the doctors returned and Lovett delivered the diagnosis to
Franklin, Eleanor, and Louis. As the doctor continued to speak,
Franklin and Eleanor were relieved to find the news was not all bad.
Later, Lovett would recall saying that while "no one could tell where
they stood," he'd also explained to them that Franklin's "case was evidently not of the severest type, that complete or partial recovery to
any point was possible, that disability was not to be feared, and that
the only cut about it was the long continued character of the treatment." Writing Eleanor a few days later, Keen would remark that "the

prospect is so bright for Mr. Roosevelt's restoration I think to complete (or at worst almost complete) health and activity."

THESE ASSESSMENTS FILLED THE beleaguered group on Campobello with hope: Disability was not to be feared! The diagnosis sounded dire, the Roosevelts told intimates afterward, but all would be well again. And soon.

Chapter 16

Plans

SEPTEMBER 1921

L OUIS HOWE WATCHED AS A GROUP OF LOCAL MEN CAME to carry Franklin out of the house on Campobello for the first time in more than a month. Six pairs of hands surrounded Franklin from head to toe, pulled him off his bedsheets, suspended him in the air, and then laid him gently on an improvised transport device. To call it a "stretcher" was too generous. A canvas sail draped over several pieces of pine—that was what Campobello could provide.

It would have to be good enough that morning. Good enough to get Franklin out of the house, down the lawn, and off the island, all in accordance with Louis's plan.

It was September 14, 1921, three weeks since Dr. Lovett had delivered the news that Franklin had infantile paralysis. Listening to the doctor that day, Franklin had gotten the distinct impression a complete recovery was assured. But Louis, the former newspaper reporter, knew how to spot the escape hatches experts leave for themselves, the caveats and qualifiers they can use for shelter later on. In a private aside afterward, Louis asked plainly if Franklin would walk again. "Few people possess the courage and determination to make the fight," Lovett replied. "But if Mr. Roosevelt's interest in resuming active life is great enough, his will to recover strong enough, there is undoubtedly a chance."

That was one reason Louis had pushed to leave the island—to get back to the arena of active life, to help Franklin recover and find his chance. How they would find it was not yet clear. But Louis was determined to come up with a plan.

Louis always had plans, intricate and exacting plots that strove to anticipate every thinkable scenario. Eleanor teased him about it, reminding him that sometimes one must deal with life as it comes. She knew how much he loathed that idea. Preparation was essential to Louis, she would later say, the way he "dominated circumstances."

Franklin had never been like Louis; his experiences had never made strategizing necessary. With his charm and his social instincts and his good looks, he could walk into most any situation and let the room tilt toward him. Louis, on the other hand, was the kind of man rooms swallowed up. Life had taught him to think things out in advance.

That was why Franklin had always needed Louis, whether he knew it or not. Grand visions were well and good, but in politics you needed someone thinking through your next step and the step after that.

On this day, Louis's plan called for getting Franklin out of the house and into a small boat that would cross the harbor to Eastport, Maine, where a train would carry him south to New York. All of it was intended to keep Franklin safe and comfortable. And, no less important, Louis's plan was carefully designed to keep the eyes of the world at bay.

THE WEEKS AFTER FRANKLIN learned he had polio were a trying time for the beleaguered group charged with his care. Following his visit to Campobello with Dr. Lovett, Dr. Keen, the famed surgeon who had initially misdiagnosed Franklin, wrote Eleanor and implored her to take care of herself. "You have been a rare wife and have borne your heavy burden most bravely," the doctor assured her. "You will surely break down if you do not have immediate relief."

Fall was coming; the children needed to start school. If Franklin was to have a real shot at recovery, he needed to do it in a proper hospital with proper care. It was time to get off the island.

So they had turned to the challenging question of how to get

Franklin—who was supposed to move as little as possible—all the way back to New York. In any condition, the journey home from Campobello wasn't easy; it required taking a boat to a slow train, with connections along the way. No one liked imagining Franklin forced onto a stuffy, crowded train. "What a pity he is not still in the Navy," his brother, Rosy, had written to Eleanor, "and a destroyer handy to take [him] right through to Hyde Park." Finally, Frederic Delano had arranged a private car on a train that could transport Franklin directly from the station at Eastport, Maine, to New York. The day of departure had been the family's watchword for Franklin, proof that help was on the way.

Now that day had come. Louis watched as the men moved cautiously down the staircase, then out the door of the Roosevelt cottage and across the lawn toward the sea. Franklin was calm as his procession made its way, a chalky raft in the air. Louis had always marveled at Franklin's gift for rising to the occasion, for sensing an audience's needs and suppressing his own. His audience this time was small but significant: the five children he had barely seen in a month.

The Roosevelt children looked on as the men carried their father out. Franklin could see that the faces of the two littlest ones, Franklin Jr. and John, were marked with heavy concern. He gave them his broad smile and then, somehow, a reassuring wave. "Don't worry, chicks," he shouted from his makeshift stretcher, "I will be all right."

THESE WERE THE EARLY DAYS of a new way of living, a life guarded by careful acts of omission, thoughtful concealing, half-truths. For a month, Franklin and his caregivers on Campobello had worried over how to keep rumors of his illness from spreading. For all its disadvantages, Campobello's remote location at least provided an expansive interlude of anonymity. In New York or even Hyde Park, with Franklin's busy professional and social schedule, mere fever would attract notice after a day or two.

Dr. Lovett's diagnosis had accentuated the importance of remaining quiet about the illness. If infantile paralysis had spared Franklin's life, it now posed a dire threat to his career. Americans associated polio with all sorts of politically unpalatable things—poverty, poor hygiene, squalor. The deadly words "infantile paralysis" made people think of pitiable, permanent incapacity, the opposite of the image Franklin had cultivated over the past decade as a premium specimen of the virile American man.

His caregivers were mindful of whom they wrote to and sparing in the news they shared. Their confidants knew to be cautious too. "Your Aunt Annie knows nothing of Franklin except that he has been very ill," Frederic Delano wrote to Eleanor at the end of August. "The secret has been pretty well kept considering all the telegraphing."

Without explicitly saying so, they became conspirators. The Roosevelts and their intimates invented new rules for the discussion of Franklin's health: speak elliptically, accentuate the positive, use vague language to conceal and distract. They worked on Franklin's behalf to maintain appearances. New York State Democrats had been pleased to receive a letter from the island bearing Franklin's signature, agreeing to join their executive committee. They were unaware that the signature had been forged by Louis. Franklin was not even able to hold a pen.

Rumors spread all the same. At Franklin's office in New York, his secretary, Missy LeHand, received a call from a family acquaintance, asking to speak to Mr. Roosevelt. Mr. Roosevelt was unavailable, LeHand told the caller, a woman, who then tried to draw LeHand out in conversation. She had "heard from Eleanor" that Franklin was ill and wondered what news LeHand could supply. LeHand, like any good gatekeeper, mistrusted outsiders claiming intimacy. If this caller had really been in touch with Eleanor, why had she asked if Franklin was there? "I have made an attempt at not telling people that Mr. Roosevelt was ill," LeHand wrote to Eleanor on Campobello. "But apparently it is known."

After receiving the infantile paralysis diagnosis, the Campobello group knew they had to put out some word of Franklin's condition, heading off the full truth. On August 26, the day after Dr. Lovett's visit, Louis released word to the press, confirming that Franklin D.

Roosevelt had taken ill. The statement made no mention of infantile paralysis. It allowed that Franklin had been quite unwell but promised that a return to health was assured. "Franklin D. Roosevelt, former Assistant Secretary of the Navy, has been seriously ill at his summer home at Campobello, N.B.," *The New York Times* told its readers. Under the headline F. D. ROOSEVELT RECOVERING, *The New York Herald* explained that Franklin had "caught a heavy cold and was threatened with pneumonia."

Franklin's original teacher in the art of concealment arrived on Campobello at summer's end. Sara Roosevelt had been touring Europe when Franklin took ill. Concerned over her reaction, the family had kept the infantile paralysis diagnosis secret from her while she was away. The first hint her son had suffered any trouble came on the sea ship journey home, in a breezy letter from Eleanor. "Dearest Mama," the letter read. "Franklin has been quite ill and so can't go down to meet you on Tuesday to his great regret, but Uncle Fred and Aunt Kassie both write they will be there so it will not be a lonely homecoming." Eleanor tried to make Franklin's illness sound like a mere blip in an otherwise unremarkable month: "We are having such lovely weather, the island is really at its loveliest."

Upon disembarking in New York, Sara insisted on traveling to Campobello at once. By then, the Roosevelts had had several days to digest the doctors' opinion that Franklin had polio. Yet he was determined his mother would see no sign of distress. Led up to the house by Eleanor, Sara found her "brave . . . & beautiful" son freshly shaved and beaming brightly at her. "Well, I'm glad you're back, Mummy," he said. "I got this party up for you."

Sara appreciated the show he put on. "He & Eleanor decided at once to be cheerful & the atmosphere of the house is all happiness," she wrote approvingly to Frederic afterward. "So I have fallen in and followed their glorious example." Yet she stayed on the island only briefly, departing soon after her arrival for a Delano niece's wedding in Massachusetts. This was an unusual decision—Sara was generally disinclined to leave other people in charge of anything, least of all the care of her darling boy. But the visible change would have been wrenching to Sara. Perhaps she knew that she was incapable of re-flecting her son's sunniness back onto him. "My thoughts are with you & our dear invalid all the time," she wrote to Eleanor after departing, "& I even wake at night with a longing to know how Franklin is."

As the first weeks of September had passed, the press noticed that news of Franklin's further improvement did not come. It was clear that he had more than just a bad cold. Reporters sensed a story. They had headed toward Campobello, and they were waiting at the train depot in Eastport to catch a glimpse of him before he headed home. Thus Louis's intricate plan for getting Franklin to the train, the urgent need for a grand deception. A need that would not go away.

LOUIS HAD SENT WORD to the reporters in town, notifying them that the next day Franklin would arrive by boat in Eastport to take the train south. He knew the demands facing newspaper reporters—how they would jostle and crowd up to the edge of the dock where the Campobello boat typically came in, eager to capture the pathos of this stricken man. He knew as well that the first reported descriptions of the incapacitated Franklin Roosevelt could shape perceptions of the man for years to come. So he'd encouraged the reporters to gather at the main Eastport dock at the appointed time.

On the day of Franklin's departure, while the reporters waited at the dock, Franklin and his attendants rode across the bay in a little motorboat. It was not a large craft—there was no space to put Frank-lin but on top of the floorboards, laid out flat on his back, away from the wind and waves. Louis ordered the boat's captain to find another landing on the opposite side of the harbor. The reporters at the dock-side did not notice the little motorboat passing them by. Nor did they see the famous passenger, lying on the floor.

When they reached land, Franklin's escape team loaded him onto a baggage cart, which they then encircled, forming a protective shroud. Upon arrival at the station, though, they discovered that the train doors were too small for the canvas stretcher to fit inside. The men from the boat lifted Franklin up through the window of the sleeper car instead.

It was an elaborate subterfuge, riddled with vulnerable moments, yet through some stroke of luck the reporters failed to catch on before Franklin's minders had situated him comfortably on the train. Only then did Louis send word to the gang waiting at the dock that the passenger had already arrived. The reporters raced over to the departing train, where they found a relaxed Franklin lying on his berth, smiling and chatting through the window. He had a cigarette in his mouth, his hat covering one hand, and the Roosevelts' small Scottish terrier, Duffy, settled comfortably on his chest. They didn't know that the hat was placed strategically, concealing a thumb and forefinger that had been disfigured by the disease. They also didn't know that, since Franklin could not yet control his hands, the cigarette had been placed and lit by someone else.

All in all, it was a masterfully orchestrated ruse. F. D. ROOSEVELT IS BETTER, read the headline in *The New York Times* the next day. "Mr. Roosevelt," said the *New York World*, "was enjoying his cigarette and said he had a good appetite." There was little doubt, readers of *The Boston Globe* were assured, that Franklin was "on the road to recovery."

But as Louis well knew, this was not the sort of story he could control perfectly, no matter how clever his plan. Sure enough, one line, written in a wire-service dispatch and reprinted in newspapers across the country, mocked his attempts at control. The words it contained would have been startling to any reader with even a cursory knowledge of Franklin Roosevelt's career to date: "He was unable to walk or to sit up."

THE TRAIN MOVED SLOWLY southward toward New York City. At Louis's direction, a crowd of Franklin's intimates had gathered at Grand Central to greet him. Even in the midst of his grueling journey, at the end of a terrifying month, Franklin couldn't help but anticipate other people's emotions. As the train approached the city, he worried about his friends' reaction to his condition: What could be done to keep them from feeling down? He greeted them buoyantly, calling each one by name. Catching the eye of Tom Lynch, an old Democratic ally from the Hudson Valley, Franklin was solicitous, eager for news from the home territory. The next day, Lynch was quoted in the *Poughkeepsie Eagle*. Franklin "looked like his old self and didn't seem a bit down-hearted," he reported. He was "in the best of spirits and had every confidence of his complete recovery."

That was the version Lynch gave the paper. The reality of the scene at the station had been far harder to take. Lynch was overcome by Franklin's condition, a thin shadow of the man he had once known. He begged off Franklin's invitation to join him for the ambulance ride to Presbyterian Hospital, muttering that he would "be along later." Then he turned to keep Franklin from seeing the tears that had filled his eyes.

At the hospital, the Roosevelts met with Franklin's personal physician, Dr. George Draper, who, after a cursory examination, confirmed Dr. Lovett's diagnosis. The New York papers knew their way around the city's hospitals—there was no keeping this story quiet any longer. The time had come to tell the world. Louis put out a statement that accentuated the positive as much as possible.

In his efforts to shade the truth, he had a surprising collaborator: Dr. Draper. While the patient had temporarily lost the use of his legs, the doctor said in his statement, his case was not a serious one. Indeed, he was on the way to complete recovery. The headlines reflected this positive slant: F. D. ROOSEVELT HAS PARALYSIS IN MILD FORM, said the *New-York Tribune*. *The New York Times* quoted Draper's reassuring diagnosis: "He definitely will not be crippled. No one need have any fear of any permanent injury from this attack."

Draper would have known his statement wasn't true. Beyond his own examination, he had received a thorough debriefing from Dr. Lovett on Franklin's case. Even if he still believed Franklin *might* fully recover the use of his legs, there was nothing about his condition to merit a categorical declaration that Franklin had nothing to fear.

Why didn't Draper, a man of science, tell the truth? Perhaps he simply folded under Louis's pressure. Perhaps, as a social peer of the Roosevelts, he felt a greater obligation to his friends than to the grubby reporters prowling the hospital's halls. Or perhaps he too got caught up in Franklin's cheery performance and momentarily came to believe that, despite the available evidence, a complete recovery was under way.

Yet the doctor's statement to the reporters may well reveal a broader strategy guiding Franklin's early medical care. In his second volume on the life of Franklin Roosevelt, biographer Geoffrey Ward posits that Draper may have intended to use the papers to send an encouraging message to Franklin himself. Politicians, after all, pay attention to their own news coverage. It is plausible that Draper was using the news reporters to infuse his patient with some much-needed optimism. Sure enough, on reading the *Times* report that he "definitely will not be crippled," Franklin dictated a happy letter to the paper's publisher, Adolph Ochs. Reading these words in the paper of record, he said, "I feel immensely relieved because I know of course it must be so."

—

Chapter 17

The Will and Determination
of the Patient

SEPTEMBER–OCTOBER 1921

IN LATE SEPTEMBER, A WEEK AND HALF AFTER FRANKLIN ENTERED the hospital, Dr. Draper wrote to Dr. Lovett in Boston to update him on the patient's progress. There was some good news: Franklin had recovered enough power in his hands to write his own name. His arms appeared to be returning to normal function: His biceps were mainly operative and, clutching a leather strap from above, he could hold himself up off the bed. The medical staff could detect some faint twitching in the toes and occasionally in the hamstrings.

But mostly the news was dreadful. A month had passed since Lovett examined the patient on Campobello. Not only had Franklin not recovered leg function, but much of the muscle mass in his arms and legs had disappeared, and his back muscles were so depleted that Draper did not dare even try to sit him up. "I am very much concerned at the very slow recovery," he wrote to Lovett, "both as regards the disappearance of pain, which is very generally present, and as to the recovery of even slight power to twitch the muscles."

These words had an ominous implication. It was well over a month since the onset of infection. An inability to twitch his muscles suggested that the motor neurons in Franklin's legs had been destroyed. Once destroyed, neural function was gone for good; no feat of medical science could bring it back. It was appearing more and more likely that Franklin would never walk again.

"I feel so strongly after watching him now for over a week that the psychological factor in his management is paramount," Draper's letter continued. "He has ... such an extraordinarily sensitive emotional mechanism, that it will take all the skill which we can muster to lead him successfully to a recognition of what he really faces without utterly crushing him."

What the doctors could not see was that Franklin, all on his own, was using his "extraordinarily sensitive emotional mechanism"—his powers of feeling, perception, and intuition—to create a foundation of hope.

The mind of a patient facing a long road back from serious illness or injury is like a house that has been badly damaged by a catastrophe—a flood or an earthquake or a fire. The extent of the damage or what exactly will be required to rebuild is not evident in the early aftermath. What is clear is that the house is dangerously unsteady and, without some immediate intervention, it is in danger of collapse. So the homeowner puts up a scaffolding to keep the walls and roof from collapsing and to serve as a base of operations in the long effort to rebuild.

Similarly, in the early days of a serious illness or injury, the mind is destabilized. It is inundated with questions: What is causing pain; how can it be alleviated; when will it end? What has happened to my body; what normal tasks and functions are impaired; what can I do to adapt and get by? Will I survive; how will I recover; will I ever feel normal again?

Hope is the scaffolding that protects the traumatized mind. Modern study of the psychology of illness suggests that hope provides clear emotional and physical benefits to the seriously ill. Pain becomes more bearable when it has a horizon. Suffering is more survivable when it has the promise or even the *possibility* of an end. And recovery seems more possible when it is spelled out in a detailed plan.

When a patient is seriously ill, hope is among his earliest medicines. Provided with a truthful and reality-based vision of his path out of suffering, he regains his powers of reason. He can see his symptoms of distress for what they are and rationally evaluate potential treatments to manage and diminish his struggle. For some people, hope can even spur physical processes of recovery and remission.

Lying in his hospital room, as September gave way to October, Franklin needed hope to help him heal.

In a sense, it was harder to find and even more essential to his well-being than it had been in the worst days on Campobello. The frantic fight for survival on the island was terrible, but its worries were short-term and practical: Was he going to get worse? Was he getting the proper care? Would he make it off the island alive? His return to the city and admission to the hospital had relieved him of short-term worries—it was now someone else's responsibility to ensure that he stayed alive. This meant his mind could turn to the big unsettling questions: What would this mean for his life? Did he have a future in politics? Would he walk again?

Franklin needed a vision of the future that was both positive and realistic. If he was going to walk again, his rehabilitation would require hard work and concentration, rehabilitation sustained over months and years. But even before he resumed walking, he could begin the important work of adapting to return to a full and productive life. His doctors needed to offer him the truth from which he could build his hope.

On Campobello, Dr. Lovett had delayed this process, with his slippery words about the possibility of complete recovery. In New York, Dr. Draper was concerned about what the plain truth would do to Franklin's psyche. Somehow, Draper wrote to Lovett, Franklin had convinced himself that within two or three weeks he would be able to walk out of the hospital on crutches—an unthinkable possibility. While Franklin was "very cheerful and hopeful" at present, Draper feared that his optimism was grounded in delusion. He suspected that the inevitable intrusion of reality would prove "frightfully depressing." Worried about what that depression would look like—perhaps worried that Franklin simply couldn't bear the bad news—the New York doctors had backed down further. If they didn't explicitly lie about his prognosis, they continued to downplay and diminish the severity of his situation, holding their tongues as his own forecasts for recovery became ever more self-assured.

Their reluctance to temper him was understandable. All his life,

Franklin had led with a resolute pleasantness. Few had not responded pleasantly in return. Why should his doctors now prove the exception? They may have reasoned that his psyche was still vulnerable, his prognosis still uncertain. Why not spare him what emotional discomfort they could?

After a few weeks' time, Missy LeHand began coming to the hospital in the mornings to take dictation and help him catch up on his correspondence. Friends visited and found Franklin in shockingly good spirits. Arriving at the hospital, Josephus Daniels was crushed to see Franklin, his beloved exemplar of gilded youth, in such a beleaguered state. But when he approached the patient's bedside, Daniels was greeted with a smack to the stomach. "You thought you were coming to see an invalid," Franklin cheerily declared. "But I can knock you out in any bout." Even the further deterioration of Franklin's body that Draper had worried about did not come to pass. In mid-October, the hospital staff sat him up in bed. Franklin's ragged back muscles were still alive and strong enough to hold him up.

The doctors were wrong to assume it was too early to provide Franklin with the full picture of his recovery. It may well have been too late. This was Franklin, who in earliest boyhood had trained himself to pay attention to the slight variations in other people's speech—the emphasis that wasn't there, the word that wasn't said. He often anticipated changes in other people's moods before they felt them themselves. Franklin, with his subtle powers of human understanding, would not have missed the careful hesitation in the doctors' voices, the qualified hedging in their speech. He would have understood it for exactly what it was.

How early had he seen it, his altered destiny, the shape of his new life? Perhaps as early as that day on Campobello when, listening to Grace Howe read about the polio outbreak in upstate New York, his mind began to turn.

Franklin's behavior during his first weeks in the hospital suggests he had chosen to believe in the possibility of full recovery. He had decided to announce to the world that it would be so. His was a life of many layers—concealing and deceiving and denying so splendidly he could almost fool himself. But even as he dissembled, he could see reality. He could also see hope.

IN THIS WORK, he had a few trusted voices. Shortly after Franklin first received his polio diagnosis, his uncle, Frederic Delano, spent a long waking night worrying about his nephew's fate. He could see how hard the path ahead for Franklin would be. Rising the next morning, he sat down to write Franklin a letter. "I came to the conclusion," he said, "that I might give you fatherly advice."

What Franklin needed, Delano went on, was a framework for approaching his recovery, a "philosophy" for life that would get him through the hard days ahead. "To my mind, Philosophy means in substance, 'making the best of the situation,' or in other words taking things as they are, analyzing the facts, above all not fooling yourself and by intelligent reasoning determining the right course to pursue."

Take things as they are; never fool yourself. On the face of it, this was hard counsel for Franklin, whose lifelong habit had been to focus on the positive and banish unpleasant thoughts. But Delano believed that looking squarely at painful truth was not the enemy of positive thinking but rather its source. It was his very "philosophy" that made him able to experience optimism. Armed with a thorough knowledge of the world as it is, Delano told Franklin, "I never worry, I accept things as they are, I look forward and not back.

"Now as to your recovery," Delano continued, "the doctors and nurses can do much. Experience can warn you what to avoid, but, after all, the constructive work of getting well depends largely on your own character. . . . Marvelous cures have been effected by men I know, in consumption, paralysis, etc. by the will and determination of the patient."

In the hard days ahead, Delano wrote, Franklin ought to follow his doctor's instruction and offer his prayers to a loving, almighty God. But if he wanted to be well, he must, above all, look within. "You are up against a hard problem, and hard cruel facts, and yet I feel the utmost confidence that you will emerge a better and stronger man."

——

LOUIS TOO WAS GIVING hard thought to the state of Franklin's mind. He kept close to his chief during his weeks in the hospital, managing press coverage of the illness. He successfully spread the idea throughout the city that Franklin's health was moving in the right direction, and reporters stopped haunting the hospital. Not long after Draper wrote to Lovett of his frustration over Franklin's stalled recovery, an item appeared in *The New York Herald* with the happy headline ROOSEVELT IS IMPROVING.

But Louis himself was under no illusions. When, that fall, Herbert Pell, the chairman of the New York Democratic Executive Committee wrote to Franklin, inviting him to attend the group's next meeting, Louis appended a note: "Mr. Pell had better wake up & hear the birdies!"

It was October, long after Louis was supposed to have left the Roosevelts' employ for his new job at the oil company. By then, however, he'd informed the company that he would be unable to take the position after all. From what he could gather from the doctors, Franklin's chances of a full recovery depended on his remaining as active as possible. Louis believed he could help.

When Franklin lost the ability to walk, Louis lost something too: the old strategy that had carried them thus far. If Franklin's public image had emphasized his graceful athleticism and youthful vigor, it had been Louis who did the emphasizing. He believed in that image, believed that the alchemic combination of Franklin's age and personality and physical aspect would hurtle him to the highest heights. It had been clear to him since the earliest moments of their acquaintance, watching Franklin perform in front of the fireplace at Franklin and Eleanor's Albany home: "Nothing but an accident could keep him from becoming president of the United States."

Now the accident had come, but Louis sensed that Franklin still needed a future to believe in. If he did not have something to work toward, a vision of himself returning to meaningful work, Franklin not only would never walk again, he would lose his will to go on. So

Louis, who needed a future to believe in too, set to work doing what he did best. He began to create a concept of Franklin's life, still devoted to politics but dependent on a new and radically different plan.

In late October, Franklin was finally ready to leave the hospital. His recovery would be ongoing, under the care of a nurse at home. He did not walk out on crutches, as he'd hoped; he was carried up the stairs of his townhouse on 65th Street and placed in yet another bed. Eleanor reorganized the house to accommodate Franklin's recovery.

With her beloved child released from the hospital, Sara Roosevelt was ready to resume control. She believed that there was only one way to restore her boy's health: to bring him home to Hyde Park. That was where she had cared for her husband in his years of infirmity; she could care for her disabled son in much the same way. He could pass the time as Roosevelt men were supposed to: looking after the farm accounts; tending to the needs of their tenant farmers, the village school, and the church; taking care of their immortal souls.

Yet Sara was irritated to discover that Franklin did not want to move permanently back to Hyde Park; he seemed intent on remaining in the city, resuming an active life. He even had the absurd idea that he might resume his political career.

To Sara, this was madness. She'd never liked the squalid business of campaigning and self-promoting; now she was convinced it would kill her beloved boy. She cast about for allies. Grubby Louis Howe had never been her favorite accomplice, but she knew him to be someone who spoke honestly about what he thought. "You have good common sense," she said to him. "Can't you see that a political future is now out of the question for my son?"

Staring back at her that fall of 1921, mere weeks after Franklin was struck by illness, Louis offered his reply: "I expect him to be president of the United States."

At some point in those early weeks of recovery, Louis shared this expectation with Franklin too. He laid out his plan—years of hard work for Franklin to recover his health, enduring setbacks and pain but keeping his eye on the ultimate goal, the greatest prize a politician could want. Years later, Louis would describe to his associate (and later biographer) Lela Stiles the pitch he'd made to Franklin. "You are a man of destiny ... and I will go along with you every inch of the hard way." Franklin's disability, Louis told him, only half joking, would be the thing that *made* him president. "You'll get the sympathy of the public and you will be spared ... all the political nonsense that ruins so many men."

Louis would recall Franklin listening in silence, taking in the enormity of what Louis was proposing. When Louis finished speaking, he looked at his chief, waiting for Franklin's reply.

"Well," said Franklin, "when do we begin?"

Chapter 18

Nothing to Do but Think

OCTOBER 1921–MARCH 1922

IT WAS A MISERABLE FALL FOR FRANKLIN AND ELEANOR'S fifteen-year-old daughter, Anna. On the family's return to New York from Campobello, she'd enrolled at Miss Chapin's School, where she felt painfully out of place—a country rambler amid society girls. James, her closest sibling in age, had started Groton the previous year, leaving her a teenage island in a house of young boys—eleven-year-old Elliott, seven-year-old Franklin Jr., and five-year-old John. Her Victorian grandmother had little interest in offering guidance on approaching womanhood. Her mother had little idea how. At one point, Eleanor awkwardly informed Anna and James that she wished to speak to them about "the birds and the bees." She proceeded to give them a strange lecture, James would later recall, that was literally about the biological habits of birds and bees. Both children left the lesson vexed.

But worst of all was her father's illness hanging over the family, not as a cloud but as the sky itself. His return to East 65th Street from the hospital at the end of October had filled Anna with anxiety. Upon arrival home, he promptly had rings placed above his bed as a means to hoist himself up. On his first full day out of the hospital, he began practicing swinging his lifeless legs out of bed. Predictably, he pushed himself too hard, too fast. Soon a fever raged through his body once more, crowding the house with renewed fear. He complained of a new pain in his eyes. Sara passed nervously back and forth through the doors connecting her townhouse to Franklin and Eleanor's. She worried her son was going blind.

The older children—Anna, Jimmy, and Elliott—were capable of understanding more information about what their father was facing, but Eleanor and Franklin decided not to give it to them, a choice Eleanor would later regret. Elliott, who had turned eleven a week after Franklin entered Presbyterian Hospital, would walk by the hospital building on Madison Avenue at 70th Street on his way to the Buckley School each day, left to wonder about the fate of his father inside.

Franklin was sensitive to his children's worries and did what he could to adapt. After returning home from the hospital, he had his bed moved closer to the window so he could wave cheerily at Elliott in the mornings as the child went to school. When the fever had passed and the pain in his eyes subsided, he resumed his physical-improvement routines. He quickly became comfortable crawling on the floor. Before long, he was challenging the younger boys to wrestling matches, pinning them to the ground.

At Groton, James was farthest from their father's plight. When he wrote to his parents that fall, filling them in on his efforts in academics and football, he paused only briefly on Franklin's condition: "It was great to hear how well Father was getting on, I hope he will continue." And yet he understood everything. Standing with his siblings while the men carried Franklin out of the house on Campobello, he'd remembered his father taking him to see a heavyweight boxing championship earlier that summer. At that moment he'd wondered: *Will he ever take me anywhere again?*

At Christmas, James came home from Groton to a house transformed. Nervously climbing the stairs to his father's room, he imagined Franklin's "withering legs" and told himself not to cry. His father, the performer, was ready for him. "Come here, old man!" Franklin exclaimed, all smiles and sunshine. James hurried into his father's embrace. He noticed that the arms that gripped him were surprisingly strong. But the boy's eyes still filled with tears.

It was Anna, the eldest, who had the hardest time. Her discomfort gradually morphed into hot rage. She focused her anger on a single target: Louis Howe.

Louis had taken up permanent residence in the Roosevelt townhouse after Franklin's return from the hospital. His wife, Grace, stayed at a rented house up the river in Poughkeepsie, with promises from Louis to visit on weekends. To find a path back to politics, Franklin needed to maintain his network and his profile in the wider world. But he also needed to regain the ability to walk, a project that, at least for the foreseeable future, would require all his effort and concentration. Only with Louis inches away, acting as a kind of surrogate for the otherwise-occupied Franklin, could the important work of maintaining the political lifeline get done.

Louis moved into a large third-floor bedroom with its own bathroom. The room was just across the hall from Franklin's. He made himself at home, taking long breakfasts with cigarettes and the papers, ordering the servants around, critiquing the children on their comportment.

The rest of the household was squeezed to discomfort. To accommodate Franklin's nurse, Edna Rockey, and Louis, the littlest boys moved to a spare bedroom in Sara's house. Anna, to whom Louis's third-floor room had previously belonged, was displaced to a tiny room in the rear of the house. It was a cruel affront to a sensitive teenage girl; Eleanor bore the brunt of her daughter's understandable outrage over the move. Anna critiqued and teased and attacked Louis. Once, when he objected to her behavior and went off to alert her mother, she chased after him up the staircase, pulling at his legs until he was sent toppling down below.

Anna was mystified that her parents would tolerate this arrangement. In her younger days, her mother had loathed Louis too. But now Eleanor seemed to delight in having Louis around. On occasion, the children would find her sitting at the foot of Louis's bed, talking away as he lovingly stroked her hair. "Mother had changed completely," Anna would later say. "When I wanted to see her, she and

Louis would be in very deep conversations, talking about things. Obviously I wasn't wanted."

There was more to her anger, of course, than just irritation with Louis Howe. In loudly pointing to Louis's faults, she was voicing a deeper wish to return to the way things had once been. Children of fractured marriages learn to live along the dividing line between their parents. The Roosevelt children had grown conscious of the icy expanses that separated the adults in their family—the gulf between Franklin and Eleanor, between Eleanor and Sara—and they had also grown expert at navigating them. But now the alliances had shifted: Franklin and Eleanor and Louis all seemed to be working in lockstep. Beyond just adapting to the new limitations facing their father, their family had to invent new ways to coexist.

Meanwhile, there was Sara, pacing the floorboards next door. She was still convinced that a return to political life was madness. She had never liked Louis and had counted on Eleanor as an outlet for her dismay. But now Eleanor and Louis were inseparable. And, amazingly, Franklin and Eleanor seemed to have acquired a new resolve against Sara's entreaties. At one point, Eleanor even moved a large piece of furniture in front of one of the connecting doors, an act of rebellion that would have been unthinkable before.

It would take more, though, than some old bureau to thwart Sara's will. Ever resourceful, she cast about for a new ally and found one in her eldest grandchild. She whispered in Anna's ear: Wasn't Mr. Howe awfully vulgar? Wasn't it inexcusable that Anna should be inconvenienced for the sake of Mr. Howe? Egged on, Anna's protests grew louder and louder. "You don't care about me anymore," Anna cried to Eleanor. "You never consider my feelings."

Anna's attacks on Eleanor were not entirely fair. Eleanor could point out that the sleeping arrangements were partly Anna's choice. She had been given the option of remaining in the third-floor room if she was willing to share it with Franklin's nurse, but Anna had opted for her attic room instead. Mostly, though, Eleanor endured her daughter's abuse.

When Anna's rebuke did arrive, it came from the one person she had always relied on for warmth and support. One night during dinner, when she launched into her objections to Louis, her father interrupted: "Anna, I will hear no more from you. You may leave the table whenever you choose." She fled the room in tears.

Franklin hated conflict, hated to be the disciplinarian, hated to make anyone cry. But Louis was going to stay. What he offered to Franklin was too important to be risked.

LOUIS'S PLAN WAS FAST developing, informed by the emerging reality of Franklin's condition. In November 1921, a month after Franklin returned from the hospital, Dr. Lovett paid a call on him at East 65th Street. The specialist examined his patient, considered Franklin's progress, and then briefed the Roosevelts on where things stood. Despite the alarming symptoms Franklin had experienced on first returning from the hospital, he told them, the critical phase of the disease had passed. Franklin's body would experience no further damage directly caused by the polio infection.

Then he described the path ahead. In the next two years, the muscle tissue that had been damaged by the infection could be healed and brought back to fuller function. Franklin could regain some use of his legs and perhaps experience dramatic improvement in his mobility. But to accomplish that, he would need to follow, with discipline, a specific regimen. He would have to work closely with a physical therapist, perform daily exercises prescribed by Lovett, and get used to moving around easily on crutches. Most important, he had to be vigilant never to take on too much too fast, lest he re-injure his already damaged form.

Louis absorbed the doctor's time frame and its implications. As he saw it, the long horizon of recovery would be fine. He had always cautioned Franklin not to move too quickly in politics. He ought not to jump into a race just because someone suggested it; rather, he should wait for the moment when he—or, more precisely, Louis—believed it to be the right move. But Franklin always had been taken with his own mythology as the young man in a hurry. Too often, he'd shirked Louis's restraints. The results were usually disastrous, as they had been in 1914 when, ignoring Louis's counsel, Franklin made a run to be his party's Senate nominee from New York and got trounced.

Now, though, Franklin would have to bide his time. Louis began to lay out an exceptionally long arc for their return to political glory. The years ahead, he told Franklin, should be devoted first and foremost to regaining the ability to walk, the essential requirement for Franklin's eventual comeback. Meanwhile, they would work on elevating his national profile. There would be calls for his candidacy—Louis would use his publicity skills to see to that—but Franklin would have to resist them. He would learn a more sophisticated set of rules for political courtship, come to see the advantages in being the man who demurs when others prevail. He would lend his name and stature strategically, collecting favors and biding his time. At some point in the future, perhaps in 1932, he could make a ferocious reappearance with a run for the New York governorship. Then, four years after that, he could capture their shared objective, the presidency of the United States.

Better than most men, Louis knew the hidden gifts presented by a period of convalescence. He himself had spent much of his life battling one illness or another and had seen the interesting places the mind goes when the body is confined. With Eleanor's assistance, Louis worked to transform the Roosevelts' home into a kind of retreat of its own, a place designed to facilitate Franklin's recovery while keeping in mind his need for contact with the outside world. They made sure he had a steady flow of visitors—friends at first and then, later, experts on topics of substance. They made sure he always had a book at hand. Louis saw the opportunity inside this adversity, the rare midlife chance to deepen Franklin's knowledge and refine his powers of analysis. "A year or two in bed," Louis would later say, "should be prescribed for all our statesmen."

Frederic Delano also saw the hidden advantages of a long convalescence. A mandated period of recovery, Delano told Franklin, "will give you a time for reflection and that alone is worth a good deal! In your rushing and busy life you have not had that."

In truth, Franklin's peripatetic habits—racing off to play a round of golf or sail up some coast—had prevented him from deep thinking. Convalescence meant he could no longer search for distraction at the first hint of a difficult or uncomfortable idea—the way he had, for instance, distracted himself with frantic activity and too much drinking after losing the 1920 election. Too often in his career, he had paid the price for acting before thinking. Had he given more reflection to, say, the means by which the Navy was surveilling gay men, he might have spared himself involvement in that scandal. Or had he thought more deeply, and less cleverly, about selling the public on the League of Nations, he might not have embarrassed himself as badly on the 1920 campaign trail. Now he was on his back, as Louis later put it, with "nothing to do but think." In convalescence, Louis would later tell Lela Stiles, Franklin "began to see the other fellow's point of view. He thought of others who were ill and affected and in want. He dwelt on things which had not bothered him much before. Lying there, he grew bigger by the day."

FRANKLIN HAPPILY ASSENTED TO Dr. Lovett's recovery program, promising to do just as told. But the muscles in his legs did not return. In January 1922, the tendons behind his knees faltered and his legs began to contort backward. (Dr. Lovett, Franklin would later recall, "found that the muscles behind the knees had contracted and that there was a tendency to foot-drop in the right foot.") To keep them from deforming permanently, his legs were placed in plaster casts. Once a day, an attendant would attempt to stretch the tendons by driving a wedge further into the back of the cast. The brutality startled the family. "Mother," young Franklin Jr. asked, "how does he stand the pain?"

But the smile did not fade from the elder Franklin's face. It was only for a moment, at the deepest point of that winter, that his good cheer faltered. After the plaster casts came off, it was clear that Franklin's leg muscles were too weak for him to stand on his own. If he was going to follow Dr. Lovett's program and learn to navigate the world on crutches, he would need some additional support. Accordingly, he was fitted with braces—each leg entrapped by seven pounds of steel running from his waist to his feet. Franklin didn't mind the awkward, elaborate dance of trying to move himself across a room, his arms poking ahead on crutches, his torso bent precariously forward, his heavy legs dragging behind. What bothered him was what the braces represented: the fixed immovability of steel, the gnawing permanence of deadweight. He hated his braces because they suggested his disability was there to stay.

In truth, even as he'd listened to the doctors' prognosis, Franklin had never quite given up the notion that he would be up and walking again soon. At least, not that he showed the world. In his letters to friends over the months that followed, he kept emphasizing that the hard part was always behind him, the victory near at hand. An early letter to Josephus Daniels was typical: "The doctors are most encouraging and express great pleasure at the speed I am making towards complete recovery." He was quick to assure people that he would soon be up on crutches, a process that in fact took nearly seven months. When at last he did get up on crutches, he was a teetering colossus, lurching about the floor drenched in sweat, trying not to fall. But he told his correspondents that his muscles were making great strides and soon he wouldn't need crutches at all. "By next Autumn," he wrote to Admiral Richard E. Byrd, the famed explorer, "I will be able to chase the nimble moose with you."

He began receiving his visitors in the downstairs drawing room at 65th Street, where they generally entered to find him seated in a chair. Few saw him being carried up and down by some combination of his nurse, Eleanor, the butler, or the chauffeur. Even fewer saw him crawling, his preferred method for getting around the house, including up and down the stairs to his bedroom on the third floor.

In person, he was all bravado and theatrics, but visitors were startled by just how badly his body had been transformed. That spring, James Cox, Franklin's 1920 running mate, paid a call while on a visit to New York. Cox, who had received typically breezy and reassuring reports, was shaken by the extent of Franklin's disability. Franklin could see the tears filling Cox's eye. Later that year, Cox wrote to him with frank, fatherly affection. "You have been in my thoughts for a long time," he wrote. "Tell me how you are. What progress is being made since I saw you last and what are you feeling about further improvement? I felt you were pretty badly bunged up, but your spirit was hopeful and courageous and I said to the gentlemen who were with me that day that you would pull through."

Franklin's reply was prompt, friendly, and impenetrable: "Except for my legs I am in far better physical shape than I have ever been in my life."

His closest intimates knew better than to address his condition directly. Livingston Davis, an affable Harvard classmate who was among Franklin's best friends, wrote and visited frequently. An expert at keeping things light, "Livy" would share jokes, seek Franklin's advice on his own messy personal life, and make suggestive comments about Edna Rockey, Franklin's attractive young nurse. Only occasionally, and obliquely, did he let the anguish he clearly felt over Franklin's plight slip through. Near the end of one gossipy letter, he turned suddenly serious: "You are constantly in my thoughts and I wish to gosh there was something I could do." That was about as close to Franklin's pain as the people who loved him could get.

YET, WHILE HE KEPT this pain away from many of his intimates, he also knew there were other people—strangers—who shared in his pain. Beyond his political and social circles, there was a group of people, across America and indeed around the world, who read the articles about the former vice-presidential candidate's illness with intense interest. They were those, near and far, whose lives had also been touched by polio. People who had made a full recovery from the effects of the disease and people who had seen their abilities permanently curtailed by it. People who had watched a loved one struggle with polio's aftermath and people who were in recovery themselves.

Some were drawn in by Louis's clever publicity. From the papers, it sounded like Franklin had made a miraculous recovery. Naturally, others dealing with the disease wondered if he had advice to impart. A particularly urgent request came from a G. S. Barrows of Lancashire, England. "I read in our English press that you were suffering from Infantile Paralysis and were likely to be cured," he wrote. "Now my son who is only 10 years of age is suffering from this complaint which has partially taken the use of his right arm & leg, and I was wondering if you would kindly let me know what form the cure takes, whether it is electrical treatment or what, as I am most anxious to do everything that lays in my power to get my boy alright again."

Barrows was a stranger on the other side of the ocean, but Franklin sent him a prompt and thoughtful response. "I hope you will pardon me for not answering ... before this, but I have only just returned home from the hospital. I hope you will allow me to extend to you my great sympathy in that your son is also suffering from infantile paralysis," he wrote. He then proceeded to give a far more detailed account of his treatment than had appeared in the press or even with his close friends. "What is considered the best treatment over here is to allow absolute rest and quiet until such period when all soreness has disappeared from the muscles." He went on to warn against the mistake that had been made in his own care: "Absolutely no massage is given until this takes place. ... The doctors here feel that the old method of using massage from the beginning is not nearly as likely to produce permanently good results."

Three weeks later, he received another letter from England, bearing good news from G. S. Barrows. "I am delighted to be able to tell you that my boy has been doing wonderfully well since I last wrote you, and he is now able to walk and go about almost as well as ever he did." While the boy did still have traces of a limp, it was "not noticeable to anyone unless they looked very closely." Barrows thanked Franklin for his concern. "You will no doubt be pleased to hear that his treatment has been exactly as described in your letter, our doctor would not hear of any kind of massage until all soreness had gone."

Franklin, still mostly bedridden at that point, would have seen the sad irony in Barrows's letter—in just a few short weeks, the boy had progressed far past the "cured" man his father had sought out. Replying to his new English acquaintance, he shared his enthusiasm at the good news. But the vulnerability on display in his earlier letter was gone, replaced by his usual optimism. "I too am getting along well," he wrote. "The doctors say there is no question but that by Spring I will be walking without any limp."

Other people who'd had polio wrote to Franklin merely to offer fellowship and support. Though some of them came from backgrounds vastly different from his own, they felt compelled to share with him what they had learned. Lawrence Erving Brown, a former railroad worker from Massachusetts, shared the story of his own struggle. At the age of twenty-six, he had contracted polio and spent seven years in the hospital. For a time he had been paralyzed and unable to hear, speak, or see. Now thirty-seven, he used a wheelchair; his vision, hearing, and speech had returned, but he remained unable to walk. His two daughters had grown from toddlers to teenagers all while their father battled the disease.

"I really think I would be walking today," he told Franklin, "only I was poor and proud and when it came so I could not care for my family it made me most crazy." He warned Franklin not to give in to similar despair. "Mr. Roosevelt, don't worry, whatever you do. It won't help any." Brown was two years younger than Franklin, had experienced a more devastating case of the disease, and lacked all of the other man's advantages of wealth and social position. Still, this impoverished man offered his help. "Drs. Here [have] taken blood from a person that has had infantile paralysis to help another person that has got it. Now Mr. Roosevelt I stand ready to give blood to you or anyone else. . . . I am not much good to my own . . . family, so if I could be of any use to you I will be glad to." He enclosed a picture of himself, sitting upright in his wheelchair, smiling in the sun.

Franklin was touched. "That was a most generous offer and I very greatly appreciate it. . . . I am going to be as cheerful in my case as your picture . . . indicates you have been."

From these strangers speaking frankly and vividly about the trials of their affliction, Franklin received a model of how to think about his own illness and his own path toward hope. It was, in a sense, the same message he had received from Frederic Delano: Never fool yourself, never worry, accept things as they are, look forward and not back. These strangers were living examples of how a person might start to embody that message.

Franklin began to share more of the truth with his children. When they came to visit him in his bedroom, he could feel their trepidation, could see the way they looked with anxiety at his legs concealed by the blanket on his bed. And so he gathered the children at his bedside and pulled the blanket back. He showed them his legs as they were: battered, shriveled and small. But he also showed them what he believed his legs could still become. He taught them the Latin name of every muscle in his lower body and gave them precise reports on his progress.

Writing many years later, James recalled the sight of his father working hard to wiggle a single toe, the children his captive audience, looking on. "'By golly, I can really feel those muscles coming back,' he would say. And we believed him because he believed it."

———

Chapter 19

Means of Grace

MARCH–NOVEMBER 1922

ONE AFTERNOON, IN EARLY SPRING OF 1922, ELEANOR WAS reading a book to her two youngest children, Franklin Jr. and John, in the downstairs sitting room at East 65th Street. She felt tears running down her face. Before she knew it, she was dissolving, eyes flooded, composure gone. Peeking into the room on his arrival home from school, eleven-year-old Elliott found his mother so overcome with sadness that he quickly scuttled away. The two little boys soon departed too. Eleanor's wailing aroused Louis, who came in offering consolation, but he found she could not be calmed.

Eleanor wasn't sure why she was crying. Nothing in the story she had been reading set her off. Conscious of the scene she was making, she searched for privacy in the cramped townhouse. She crossed the passageway into Sara's house—hardly the place to go seeking solace but, happily, her mother-in-law was away in Hyde Park. There at last she found an empty room.

It had been, she would later say, "the most trying winter of my entire life." At Campobello, the labor of caretaking had been back-breaking, borne by Eleanor and Louis alone. That had been relieved by the arrival of Nurse Rockey, though there were hours in the day when the nurse was off. In New York, though Franklin now liked to be independent, he still needed constant help getting started in most activities—people to help lift him in and out of a chair, people to hold up his body while attempting to place his legs inside the braces.

It had been months since Eleanor had a comfortable bed to call her own. The packed quarters in the house meant she spent most nights sleeping on a spare bed in one of the younger children's rooms. And there was the constant climbing and descending of the narrow house's four stories, with someone on every floor who needed her.

Where was it all headed? She'd heard the doctors' forecasts and was clear-eyed about what it meant: Franklin's incapacity could last for years, perhaps forever. A person in her position would inevitably wonder if this constant labor was ever going to end.

And Franklin was fretting noisily about expenses. The costs of his illness and recuperation had been great. It was getting hard to make ends meet. He wondered if he needed such an elaborate retinue; perhaps it would be best to dismiss both Nurse Rockey and the physical therapist, Kathleen Lake. They could manage on their own. What would that mean for Eleanor? Most likely, more hours of her day spent lifting and tending. More years of her life spent climbing up and down those stairs. Dr. Draper shuddered when he heard of Franklin's plan of economy. "Mrs. R is pretty much at the end of her tether with the long hard strain she has been through," he wrote to Dr. Lovett.

Everyone—the doctors, her friends, even Sara—marveled at the selfless devotion she'd given to Franklin's care. But constancy did not signal contentment. Franklin was grateful to her, but he was not close; if he felt grief or melancholy, he never confided it in his wife. Certainly his charm was not reserved for her; the house on 65th Street was filled with the appreciative laughter of Missy LeHand, and of the enthusiastic and attractive Nurse Rockey.

It had been little more than a year since they'd moved back to New York from Washington, dreams of a new life running through Eleanor's head. In their first months back, that first half of 1921, she'd made inroads toward that life—the promising work in politics, her smart, sophisticated new female friends with their enticing Greenwich Village world. Tentatively, she'd begun to try on new identities. When she'd left for Campobello in the summer of 1921, the summer of Franklin's illness, she had confidence that she would eventually return to a full life in New York. But, in fact, polio and her old obligations had swallowed all her energy and time. Her explorations of the previ-ous year began to look like little more than a brief costume play.

She carried on—threw water on her face, calmed her breathing, went back across the passage to her own house. Eleanor had *always* carried on. This time, though, salvation was closer than she knew.

If Franklin's physical recovery was really going to be a long busi-ness, a multiyear affair, he needed to find ways to maintain his profile in the wider world. Eleanor and Louis tried to bring the wider world to him at East 65th Street with important thinkers, writers, and Democratic Party bigwigs. And Louis could serve, as he liked to put it, as Franklin's "legs." Each day, he headed downtown to Franklin's office at the Fidelity and Deposit Company, the bond insurer where Franklin had retained his position as vice president, to keep a close eye on his boss's affairs. But that wasn't enough to keep Franklin's name in the papers, to preserve the value of the Hyde Park Roosevelts in the fast-moving political marketplace. For that, Franklin needed an ambassador, someone who would be noted by people who mattered.

Louis knew the interest that people took in Eleanor—she was tall and well spoken, Teddy Roosevelt's niece, Franklin Roosevelt's wife. Louis had spent those long hours talking to her on the campaign train in 1920; he knew how quickly she absorbed political realities, how expansive were her visions for potential public action, how hard she was willing to work. And he had spent long hours in the last two years serving as Eleanor's confidant. An adept student of human na-ture, he would have come to see that Eleanor Roosevelt needed, and wanted, to devote her life to something big.

Despite the new demands on Eleanor's time, Louis encouraged her to maintain and strengthen the ties to the emerging world of fe-male political activists she had begun to form a year before. So when, one day that spring, Eleanor received a call from Nancy Cook, the secretary of the Women's Division of the Democratic State Commit-tee, asking her to host and speak at a fundraising luncheon, Eleanor surprised herself by saying yes.

She had never given a speech in front of a large audience and had no idea what she was going to say. And she had never met Nancy

Cook in person, though she knew, simply from their telephone calls, that she liked her a great deal. And so, on a mild afternoon in early May, she walked to the National Democratic Club on Madison Avenue, a bouquet of violets in her hand. The violets were for Nancy Cook. The two women greeted each other happily, warmed by the intuition of a bond about to form, a bond that would prove to be electric.

She was only a couple of dozen blocks from the prison of East 65th Street, a few weeks from the most trying season she had ever known. But now there was warm air, sunshine, and bright-purple flowers, a fast and stirring world.

AT THE END OF May 1922, Franklin traveled by train to Boston, to spend ten days under Dr. Lovett's care. It was the farthest he had traveled from home since the escape from Campobello. The public remained unaware of his true condition. As he readied for his journey to Boston, a *Chicago Tribune* correspondent reported on the New York political scene: "Franklin Roosevelt for Governor, Al Smith for United States Senator. That's the ticket that appears to find most favor among the big chieftains of Tammany Hall." Franklin had no illusions about an imminent return to the campaign trail, but he knew the value of keeping his name among those mentioned. His travel plans, he wrote to Livingston Davis, were "to be kept strictly confidential as it is of the highest importance that the papers do not get hold of it."

In Boston, Franklin settled into Phillips House, a private hospital, and submitted himself to Dr. Lovett's inspection. Lovett had kept track of Franklin's condition in the intervening months. "Below the knee I must say it begins to look rather hopeless," Dr. Draper had written to Lovett in March, "but I know that even at this stage one cannot tell." Examining Franklin, Lovett judged that his progress in recovery had been adequate if not entirely encouraging. Franklin's upper body was considerably stronger than at the outset of the illness, but progress below the waist was minimal. (This evaluation did not stop Franklin from telling Davis that his recovery was moving "away ahead of schedule.") Lovett was most concerned with how little Franklin was adapting to his incapacity. He had not yet gotten comfortable on crutches, the instruments that would truly liberate him from his sickbed.

Lovett introduced Franklin to Wilhelmine Wright, an orthopedic nurse who worked at his clinic. Wright was an expert in improving mobility in disabled people. During his stay in Boston, Franklin listened attentively as she instructed him on how he could use the superior strength he was building in his upper body to compensate for the lack of ability below. Franklin left the clinic with some new braces and instructions to devote the months ahead to making progress on crutches.

That summer, Franklin went home to Hyde Park. A long summer under his mother's disapproving eye might have been an unbearable strain, but Sara set off for Europe halfway through the season, taking with her Anna and Jimmy, her two eldest grandchildren. With the distance of an ocean, the sharp tone of Sara's disappointment dulled, even if it did not quite disappear. "I am glad you and Franklin have had plenty going on," Sara wrote to Eleanor at one point that summer, "and am not surprised at Franklin's not having written at all, he really has not had time."

Anna's absence made things more peaceful too. Her frustrations had not slackened with time. In June, Eleanor had found her in the library at Springwood, writing a letter to a cousin. Anna was startled by her mother's entrance and looked guilty. When Eleanor asked her daughter to hand over the letter, Anna burst into tears. Reading it, Eleanor discovered Anna had been describing afresh the horrors of Louis Howe. Eleanor was icy when she finished reading: "I shall have to make sure that you have no further contact with Mr. Howe when you return to school in the fall."

With both of Louis's antagonists, Anna and Sara, far away from Hyde Park that summer, he was always near at hand, supplying Franklin with a steady stream of political visitors and political gossip. But his main project was Franklin's mood. Louis made Franklin's passions his own. Together, they spent hours inspecting Franklin's stamp collection or designing miniature boats.

Eleanor was there too, close but not too close. Her mood was lightening by the day, thanks to her burgeoning political world. Nancy Cook, the Democratic activist, became a regular at Hyde Park. So did her partner, a tall, kind schoolteacher named Marion Dickerman. At the sight of their car coming down the long driveway, Eleanor would race out onto the porch to greet these two women. Quickly, the three of them formed an intimate bond, Cook and Dickerman dazzled by Eleanor's mind and worldly connections, Eleanor equally dazzled by the ease and joy with which they sauntered out into the world.

Eleanor's new friends were also in Franklin's thrall. Meeting him for the first time at Springwood, Dickerman found him to be the center of everything in the house, emanating strength and quick wit. He was bursting with "immense joie de vivre" even as he remained seated, Dickerman later told the biographer Kenneth Davis. It was only afterward that it occurred to her: Franklin had remained seated the entire time because he was unable to stand. She was flabbergasted: He didn't *act* like he had a disability at all.

As the first anniversary of his illness approached, Franklin was once more at the center of things, surrounded by appreciative supplicants, a radiant sun. And yet he was still alone.

That first summer back at Springwood, familiar delights were near but out of reach. There were the trees he had loved, but he could no longer stand under them. There were only a few trails in those woods, and they were too rough to pass in a wheelchair or car. He thought of riding out on a horse but knew the risks were too great: What if the animal threw him off? In the past, he'd led his children on long chases over miles of woods and fields. Now he sent the little boys out on their own with detailed routes to pursue, making sure they knew exactly which tree, deep in the forest, would mark the spot at which they must turn.

After visiting Dr. Lovett's clinic, Franklin had resolved to work hard at walking on crutches so he could reach the end of the driveway, the long driveway, by summer's end. Yet he was discouraged to find that it did not come easily, that progress did not appear with each passing day. That had always been his pattern for learning things—how he'd learned to sail a boat or climb a tree. In Boston, Lovett had advised him to keep his new braces on as much as possible. But he dreaded them. Difficult to put on and painful to maneuver, they were a weight on his spirit, a constant reminder of his disability. He wondered if he really had to wear them—wasn't the whole point of his exercises to get his muscles and tendons to a point where he didn't need the braces at all? He began leaving them off for longer and longer stretches of the day. Perhaps, like the child thrown into deep water who learns in an instant to swim, his unaided legs would be forced by necessity to stand.

But it didn't work. He would set out for the driveway and not come close to finishing, giving up in sweaty, exhausted defeat. The next day he would try it again, only to find the struggle had not diminished but grown. When Eleanor told Lovett that Franklin hadn't been wearing the braces, the doctor was horrified and sent word that they really *had* to stay on.

Yet even as he failed to transform his body that summer, his mind and spirit began to shift. The Hudson landscape would have provided countless reminders of how temporary, and how eternal, life can be. In the farm fields were massive oak trees that had lived through the time of the oldest American Roosevelts and of his father and grandfather. His father, who in the midst of his own prolonged illness had seen and spoken of the life of meaning: "Here is work for every man," James had said. "Help the poor, the widow, the orphan. Help all who are suffering."

Occasionally, Franklin attended services at St. James', the Episcopal church where, like his father, he served on the vestry. He spoke the prayer of thanksgiving: *We bless thee for our creation, preservation, and all the blessings of this life; but above all for thine inestimable love in the redemption of the world by our Lord Jesus Christ; for the means of grace, and for the hope of glory.*

This was the summer he discovered swimming. Eleanor was learning to drive, a signal of her independence, her new confidence, her wanderlust. She would drive him up to Vincent Astor's house in Rhinebeck, where the tycoon kept a heated pool. In the water, Franklin was weightless, fast-moving, transformed. Without the strain of his body, his legs could move. The logic was divinely elegant. "The water put me where I am," he cried out from the pool one day. "The water has to bring me back!"

Those late-summer afternoons had a powerful duality that would guide him through the years ahead. He could work toward great things in the future at the same time as he opened his eyes to the potential available to him in the present. Both would now sustain him in his struggle—the hope of glory and the means of grace.

THAT SUMMER OF 1922, not only Franklin but much of America was turning inward, away from the wider world. To mark the eighth anniversary of the beginning of the Great War, peace activists, most of them women, planned a large protest on the streets of New York City on July 29. It was intended as part of a coordinated demonstration in cities around the world, demanding an end to war. But only five hundred people showed up for the New York rally, and the speakers were heckled by others in the streets. Just three years had passed since the March 1919 parade when five million New Yorkers crowded Fifth Avenue to celebrate the returning troops, but the specter of world war and its horrible toll had already faded into distant memory.

In Europe, with its fresh graves, the war was nearer. The reparations from the Paris Peace Conference had left Germany's economy in tatters; on the day of the peace rally, the German mark reached an all time low of 600 to 1 on the dollar. German nationalists were plotting a campaign of terror and sabotage to bring back a kaiser-led monarchy that could avenge the country's humiliation. In late July, French prime minister Raymond Poincaré left Paris for his country home under heavy guard after his government unveiled a German monarchist plot to assassinate him. In a speech timed to the anniversary of the outbreak of the Great War, David Lloyd George, the British prime minister, despaired that "there is a growing assumption that a conflict is coming again sooner or later," one with "more terrible machines than even the late war ever saw."

OCCASIONALLY THAT SUMMER, New York politics pierced Franklin's seclusion. In June, William Randolph Hearst had launched an aggressive effort to be the Democrats' 1922 nominee for governor. This was surprising given that Hearst had spent much of the past three years in California, where he was building an actual castle for himself, high above the Pacific. But for three decades, Hearst had been trying to transition from being a man who influenced the course of American affairs to a man who actually *ran* the nation as the president of the United States. The New York governorship, a perennial launchpad for the presidency, seemed a gettable prize.

Many leaders of Tammany Hall, former Hearst enemies, resigned themselves to his candidacy, figuring that the publisher's money and unmatchable media presence made him a hard candidate to beat. One notable exception, though, was Tammany's favorite son, the now ex-governor Al Smith. Smith had been enjoying life in the private sector since his narrow loss in the 1920 gubernatorial election, earning real money for the first time in his life. He had made it known he was not interested in seeking the office again in 1922. (In the first decades of the twentieth century, New York governors' terms were only two years long.) But the idea of Hearst, whose papers had menaced Smith during his years as governor, as his party's standard bearer was more than Smith could tolerate. As summer progressed, it was clear he was willing to return to public life if that was what was required to keep Hearst out.

Smith liked to brag of his unbreakable hold on the hundreds of thousand Democratic votes "below the Bronx County line." But to succeed, he needed support upstate. Though Franklin's reputation was banged up after the 1920 election and he was rumored to be in worse condition than the papers let on, he was nonetheless an attractive option. Upstate party leaders knew of Franklin's long history as a Tammany foe; his endorsement would make it easier for other Tammany skeptics to back Smith over Hearst.

Franklin was thrilled by Smith's call for help. From Springwood, he and Louis wrote to Democratic leaders upstate, urging them to join Smith's effort. In mid-August, he wrote Smith a letter—not accidentally shared with all the newspapers—urging him to put aside his personal interests and save New York State from Hearst. "Dear Al," he wrote, "I have been in touch with men and women voters from almost every up-State county and there is no question that the rank and file of Democrats want you to run. . . . Something must be done and done now." Smith promptly offered a "Dear Frank" response, equally preplanned and well publicized, in which he announced that he would indeed answer the call. The tidy exchange made Franklin appear a man who could hold sway in the party without having to leave Hyde Park.

Louis saw the Hearst-Smith fight as an early opportunity for Eleanor to be Franklin's surrogate in the wider world. Eleanor was game: In late June 1922, she hosted a meeting of Democratic women leaders, urging "the nomination of such candidates as supported the Democratic National and state tickets in 1920, and who are honorable and honored members of the communities in which they live." This was, quite obviously, a shot at Hearst, who had lived in any number of communities during his years in public life, but never with a surplus of honor.

For rising female power brokers like Eleanor, Hearst was an easy man to loathe. He demanded a return to the party's turn-of-the-century populist past, an era when neither the women leaders' prized issues—international cooperation and peace efforts—nor women themselves had driven the party's fate. Kicking off his candidacy, Hearst declared himself uninterested in "the attitude of the women."

Yet while Franklin's needs and Hearst's flaws may have drawn her to the 1922 campaign, Eleanor soon came to believe in the cause of Al Smith. Smith, a traditional Catholic and a backslapping son of Tammany, seemed an unlikely champion for women's causes or women in politics. But Smith understood that women could think as effectively and work as hard as men. His devoted group of advisers included several formidable women, among them the labor activists Frances Perkins and Mary Dreier.

Frances Perkins had first gotten to know Governor Smith after the tragic Triangle Shirtwaist Factory Fire of 1911, when she was charged with investigating factory conditions for a statewide commission. She made a point, she later wrote, of taking Smith "to see the women, thousands of them, coming off a ten-hour shift on the rope line." This was a revelation to Smith, who proceeded to become one of the party's leading reformers on the cause of workers' rights.

No one was closer to Smith than Belle Moskowitz, the social-worker-turned-elite-Albany-operator. "Mrs. Moskowitz," as she was universally known, was a ruthlessly unsentimental infighter who possessed a multidimensional understanding of the levers of power in government. Nonetheless, in the back rooms of politics, she'd learned to downplay her influence so as not to offend the sensibilities of insecure men. She would often sit in a corner, silently knitting, while men talked over one another, until Smith turned to her to ask, "What do you think, Mrs. M.?"

In the women circulating in Smith's orbit, Eleanor would have seen an alluring new model for her life in politics. These were women who didn't just talk about political principles but who actually possessed, and used, political power. Moreover, in the broader Smith organization, Eleanor found deeply passionate and knowledgeable progressive activists with big plans for Smith's future in Albany and beyond. It was something she had never really encountered in her husband's circle: people with bold ideas for social reform and practical plans for achieving it.

Eleanor became a true believer, appearing and speaking in public on Smith's behalf. With Louis she practiced her oratory, repeating his simple rule: "Have something you want to say, say it, and sit down." He policed her nervous habit of abbreviating sentences with girlish laughter, firmly pointing out that what she was saying wasn't funny.

She was a skilled student. Faster than anyone had imagined, she emerged as a sought-after political performer.

When the Democrats held their 1922 nominating convention in Syracuse that fall, Eleanor, not Franklin, appeared in support of Smith. By then she'd begun to see that the way for women to effect change in the Democratic Party was to organize and stick together. At the convention, she and a group of other upstate women pressured women delegates from New York City to break with their local party bosses and declare that they would under no circumstances support Hearst or any candidate other than Smith.

Two years earlier, Franklin had chased after the New York standard in San Francisco. Now it was Eleanor who joyously ran to join a bandwagon tribute to her chosen candidate at a convention. Smith won the nomination, trouncing the dreaded Hearst so forcefully that the publisher would swear off New York politics once and for all. By November, when Smith easily won a return trip to the governor's mansion, Mrs. Franklin Roosevelt was on her way to establishing herself as an independent political force.

THAT FALL OF 1922, when he returned to the city, Franklin wrote to his old 1920 running mate, James Cox, the man who had embarrassed him with pity earlier in the year. "The combination of warm weather, fresh air and swimming has done me a world of good. . . . I am still on crutches but get about quite spryly and, in fact, have resumed going to my office downtown two or three times a week."

One October morning, Franklin's chauffeur pulled up to the curb outside the company's office at 120 Broadway. As an impatient motorist behind them beeped his horn, the chauffeur struggled to pull Franklin out of the car—an awkward act that sent Franklin twisting around inside the car while his braced leg was pulled straight out, suspended in the open air. When Franklin was at last upright on the pavement, he flailed for his crutches and slipped back against the car, losing his hat. After a passerby chased it down and placed it, crum-

pled, on Franklin's head, Franklin using his crutches, began to move
gingerly across the sidewalk.

Basil O'Connor, an attorney who knew Franklin by sight, watched
him as he approached the entrance. His head was down, focused on
his legs and crutches, but O'Connor, who kept an office in the same
building, could see the sweat forming on his back. The building's interior was a nightmare—the elevator far from the entrance, separated
by an ocean of marble floor. Every time Franklin moved a crutch, it
slipped across the slick surface. The chauffeur hovered near Franklin,
using his own foot to stop the crutches' slide. Eventually, the slick
floor defeated them: the crutch slipped too swiftly and Franklin toppled to the ground.

He was facedown on the marble, his hat flown off once more.
When he looked up, he saw a crowd of onlookers, their faces filled
with pitying concern. This was the scene that he had been trying to
avoid for more than a year. His chauffeur tried, fruitlessly, to pull him
up again, but Franklin was too heavy, and they continued to slip and
flail. Franklin signaled gamely to some men in the crowd, O'Connor
among them, who stepped forward to help. After a moment they had
him upright again. "Let's go," Franklin declared confidently, hat back
on his head. O'Connor would always remember how quickly Franklin regained his pleasant composure, smiling as if nothing had happened.

But the lesson was learned. Though he would retain his position at
the F&D, Franklin would not be a regular presence at the office that
winter, or any winter thereafter. He looked toward the recovery ahead,
which, deep down, he knew would take years. If he was going to make
it through, succeed in the trial that had been given him, he would
have to take himself far away. If he was really going to be president,
he needed first to take himself to the hardest place for any politician—
out of sight.

Franklin at Warm Springs, Georgia, a place he initially hoped would give him back the full use of his legs. What Warm Springs actually gave him was an understanding of hope and his own ability to inspire it in others.

PART VI

Try Something

===

JANUARY 1924–OCTOBER 1928

"It is common sense to take a method and try it: If it fails, admit it frankly and try another. But above all, try something."

— FRANKLIN DELANO ROOSEVELT, ADDRESS AT OGLETHORPE UNIVERSITY, MAY 22, 1932

"I shall be here next week and go then to Warm Springs, Georgia. . . . I have a hunch that this swimming pool filled with hot water is going to do a lot of good."

FRANKLIN DELANO ROOSEVELT TO VAN LEAR BLACK, SEPTEMBER 24, 1924

"Human relationships, like life itself, can never remain static. They grow or they diminish. But, in either case, they change. Our emotional interests, our intellectual pursuits, our personal preoccupations, all change. So do those of our friends. So the relationship that binds us together must change too; it must be flexible enough to meet the alterations of person and circumstance."

—ELEANOR ROOSEVELT, *You Learn by Living,* 1960

Chapter 20

Time in the Sun

JANUARY–JUNE 1924

IN JANUARY 1924, THE DEMOCRATIC PARTY SELECTED NEW York City as the site of its presidential nominating convention. Democrats from other parts of the country, particularly the South and West, shuddered at the news. To them, New York was a Gomorrah on the Hudson, whose institutions—Tammany, Broadway, Wall Street—were synonymous with vice, corruption, and greed. Its selection, they feared, would bring rancor to the party, followed by electoral doom.

Many Democrats believed the party had a real shot at recapturing the presidency in 1924. The year before, the sitting president, Warren Harding, had died in office, replaced in the White House by Calvin Coolidge, his sturdy but uninspiring vice president. The Republican Party was mired in scandal. In 1922, it had been revealed that in order to secure exclusive access to the Teapot Dome oil fields on federal land in Wyoming (the name referred to a prominent nearby rock outcropping), the oil barons Edward Doheny and Harry Sinclair had provided large bribes to senior members of the Harding administration. Two years later, the circle of prominent Republicans caught up in the scandal continued to expand and included the interior secretary and the attorney general.

A New York setting, however, would most likely mean a convention spent focused on the things that were tearing the party apart. First among these was prohibition. Although the Eighteenth Amendment was losing popularity nationally, the abolition of alcohol remained the preeminent moral cause of conservative Christian "Drys," who dominated the Democratic Party in the South and parts of the Midwest and West. To them, New York City, with its notoriously lax adherence to the Volstead Act, the prohibition-enforcement law, and its "Wet" anti-Volstead politicians, was a singular threat to the moral purity of the United States.

Even more divisive was the Democratic Party's stance on the Ku Klux Klan. The racial terrorist organization had seen a remarkable nationwide resurgence since the end of the Great War, capitalizing on white Protestant Americans' resentment for blacks, Catholics, and recent immigrants from southern and eastern Europe. Its power extended far beyond the Deep South to states such as Indiana, New Jersey, and Maine. The Klan had infiltrated the mainstream of both parties. In the mid 1920s, writes the historian Robert K. Murray, it had helped its favored candidates secure as many as seventy-five seats in the U.S. Congress.

Traditionally, a convention was the place for a party to work through its divisions, to find consensus where it could and agree to disagree on the rest. But it was hard to imagine a New York convention pulling that off, because the New Yorkers didn't want consensus—they wanted the presidency for their governor, Al Smith.

Smith, fifty years old and halfway through his new term as governor, was more popular than ever before. If he could effectively govern the nation's largest state, why shouldn't he lead the country as a whole? Smith's closest aides saw the challenge of selling a Catholic New Yorker with a long, Wet record to the party at large. His best chance would be to fight things out on the floor as a dark horse. With the right combination of stagecraft, noise, and brute force, they might be able to convince wavering delegates that there was a broad base of Smith support.

Looking forward to the convention in late June, they began to plot a spectacular Smith show. To pull it off, they needed a front man. They had a good idea who that person should be.

THAT WINTER OF 1924, as his party prepared for battle, Franklin was far away, floating through mangrove trees in a pleasing salty haze.

He had left behind New York and Washington, left behind politics and his professional responsibilities, left behind his children and Sara and Louis and Eleanor. He had turned his back on all of it and headed south in the name of his consuming project: getting well.

It would be his second consecutive winter spent outside New York. After he'd fallen in the lobby of his downtown office, he had indeed taken himself away from the eyes of the world for the winter of 1923. Having discovered the restorative promise of swimming during the summer in Hyde Park, he hated the idea of waiting through a long winter before the water could do more magical work. He had set forth for Florida, in search of the sun.

For a man in Franklin's position, Florida's shimmering new resort hotels came with challenges—navigating stone patio steps, maneuvering on crutches through sand, avoiding strangers with their prying eyes. Rather than bothering with it all, Franklin had elected to spend the season on a rented houseboat, the *Weona II*. There, surrounded only by the ship's crew and a circle of trusted intimates, he crawled around on deck in the sun and slipped into the palliative salt water, lowered down on a canvas sling.

The experience had been a revelation. "The result has been most satisfactory and I am convinced that there is a vast improvement in the leg muscles," he wrote to Dr. Lovett on his return. "I am tremendously keen about life on a boat, especially in Florida waters."

He'd immediately begun to search for a boat of his own. "What I am looking for," he said, "is a boat that is fairly low in the water so that I can easily drop overboard and crawl back on deck. Also, if possible a boat whose cabin is not down a ladder." Joining forces with John Lawrence, a social acquaintance who was also disabled, Franklin found a dilapidated seventy-one-foot barge powered by unreliable engines. With peeling paint and shaky construction, it was not luxurious—a "floating tenement," co-owner Lawrence called it. Still, after some haggling, they purchased the boat for $3,750. At Franklin's suggestion, they christened it *LaRooco*—a mash-up of the owners' names ("*La*wrence" and "*Roo*sevelt") and the word "company."

The cost of *LaRooco* and its crew and upkeep would put a sizable dent in Franklin's finances, which were already strained. He continued, despite his long absences, to draw his salary from the F&D. Van Lear Black had no illusion that Franklin would earn his keep toiling behind his desk. His chief value to the F&D was in his ties to the New York political world.

He drew income as well from the law firm Emmet, Marvin & Roosevelt, though he found the firm's work to be dry tedium. Adding to his distaste was the firm's location: 52 Wall Street, a building with large stone steps at its entrance. To visit the office, Franklin had to be carried up the steps, with all of Wall Street looking on. Soon enough, he would decide to end his association with the firm.

The costs of his illness and the support of a family of seven attended by multiple servants seemed to suck up every penny he brought in. Great wealth was always nearby—as the Roaring Twenties heated up, people in Franklin and Eleanor's social circle seemed to be doubling their fortunes daily with a simple wave of the hand—but never quite near enough. Sara continued to share her largesse with Franklin and Eleanor when asked, but only when asked. That winter, the rector of St. James' Church in Hyde Park wrote with a helpful reminder that Franklin was in arrears of three hundred dollars on a pledge to the church's endowment fund. "I will send you $100 this spring," Franklin replied. "I could no more send you $300 than $3,000,000." His son James would later recall that "at one point, cash was so low that Father had to sell off some of his beloved marine and naval prints to raise a thousand dollars."

Still, when Eleanor wondered aloud if *LaRooco* was really worth the expense, Franklin's reply was swift and adamant. Yes, he said, he needed the boat because he needed to recover. "I want to be as little of a burden to you all as possible," he explained. She was struck by his plain honesty, so much that she remembered it for decades to come. It was, she said, a rare glimpse of the things he "felt deeply" but never said.

And so he headed to Jacksonville, Florida, where, in the first week of February 1924, the maiden journey of the *LaRooco* was launched. Heading first down the St. Johns River, Franklin's party would spend the next two months traveling as far south as the Florida Keys. Franklin would pass the time with a rotating cast of friends, swimming, fishing, practicing on his crutches, and leading a nonstop revel in the sun.

ELEANOR KEPT AS FAR from the *LaRooco* as she could. She had joined Franklin for part of his 1923 trip to Florida and lived to regret it. The atmosphere on board *Weona II* was not to her liking: days lacking in apparent purpose, boozy and flirty nights. The tropical landscape was strange and uninviting. "When we anchored at night," she later wrote, "it all felt eerie and menacing to me."

She preferred to stay in New York, where she was taking on increasingly important work. In February, she accepted an invitation to head up a special committee of female members of the Democratic National Committee. Their task was to advise on issues of special interest to women to be considered in the party's platform at the convention in July. Floating down the coast that month, Franklin received a letter from his wife: "I'm up to my eyes in work for the convention preparations and trying to raise our budget which is going to be an endless job."

In the papers she was still "Mrs. Franklin Roosevelt," but in the sentences that came after, her public comments became more passionately ideological, even radical. That spring she was invited to address the YMCA on the safely conventional topic of "motherhood." But her speech struck a fiery note. "I do not believe," she said, "the older generation has made such a wonderful success in the world as to be in a position to lecture the younger generation." Better, she told her audience, to "keep your minds open to new thoughts, ideas and ideals. . . . If you have no desire for new things the nation will never make any progress."

She was finding her own voice, and the sharp side of her elbows too. Four years after women had gained the right to vote, male political bosses were happy to invite them to their meetings but were surprised when those women wanted to be heard. In April, when Tammany

Hall tried to seize control of the selection of female delegates from upstate New York to the state party's convention, Eleanor was outraged. How exactly, she wondered, could a party claim to represent women if it denied them the right to choose their own representatives? She staged a public revolt, making her displeasure known in the press and appealing privately to Al Smith. When Smith acquiesced, the headline in the *Times* was definitive: DEMOCRATIC WOMEN WIN.

People took note of Eleanor's new prominence, particularly as her husband seemed to have dropped from sight. "Like you I have fought for years to keep my name on the front page," Franklin wrote to Josephus Daniels that spring, "and relegate the wife's to the advertising section. My new plan, however, seems admirable—Hereafter for three years my name will not appear at all, but each fourth year, (Presidential ones) I am to have all the limelight. Why don't you adopt this too?"

Eleanor clearly worried that her husband might envy her turn in the limelight. In her letters to *LaRooco,* she took pains to downplay her work, complain about the strain of it, and insist that she was doing it all on her husband's behalf. "You need not be proud of me, dear," she told him in an early-February letter. "I'm only being active till you can be again." She now had her own life, her own serious interests, her own conviction that she could make a difference in the world. Yet, ministering to Franklin's ego, she would deny even these. "It isn't such a great desire on my part to serve the world and I'll fall back into habits of sloth quite easily! Hurry up for as you know my ever present sense of the uselessness of all things will overwhelm sooner or later!"

Only the final line of her letter alluded to a broader, more permanent change in how they conducted their lives: "My love to Missy, and to you."

Missy LeHand was at Franklin's side for most of the Florida trip. She had joined his retinue in the 1920 presidential campaign. During Franklin's illness and early recovery, her discretion and devotion cemented her place in his innermost circle. Raised in a working-class family in Somerville, Massachusetts, she had suffered rheumatic fever as a teenager, which left her frail into adulthood; she understood what it was like to have one's health imperiled and was fluent in the convalescent rhythms that now ruled Franklin's days. But she was also strong-willed and sharp-tongued and could sometimes needle Franklin, a contrast to Eleanor's studied correctness. Most of all, though, she adored everything about Franklin. Day and night, she provided Sara Delano's son with his oldest, most familiar comfort: a gaze that told him he was the most wonderful person in the world.

By 1924, Missy had taken charge of every aspect of Franklin's life: his correspondence, his travel arrangements, his comfort, and his care. This necessitated an intimacy between them; she helped him in and out of his braces, saw him in various states of undress, took care of his sleeping arrangements. Given this closeness, many have wondered about the nature of their relationship. In a 1973 memoir of his parents, Elliott Roosevelt would claim that Franklin "shared a familiar life in all its aspects" with Missy, implying that their intimacy extended to the bedroom. The other Roosevelt children disputed this idea, and in a subsequent memoir of his own, Elliott's brother James speculated that Franklin's sexual function had ceased with his disability. Still, even James allowed that "after his forced break with Lucy ... she filled a need and made him feel a man again, which Mother did not do ... I suppose you could say they came to love one another but it was not a physical love."

If Eleanor resented this love, she mostly kept her feelings to herself. She fully accepted Franklin's secretary as a member of the family and household. She was not above irritation with Missy's constant presence, but her objections usually concerned the younger woman's ceaseless indulgence of Franklin's ego. She knew better than to feel threatened. Lucy Mercer had been her social and intellectual peer; Missy LeHand was not. What's more, the things that Missy longed to do for Franklin—tend to his needs, laugh at his jokes, bolster his ego—were the very things that had left Eleanor feeling imprisoned in the first winter after his illness. The other woman became an essential part of the Roosevelts' marriage: Franklin may have blessed Eleanor's independence, but it was Missy who made it possible.

———

THROUGH FEBRUARY AND MARCH 1924, the *LaRooco* slowly floated south. Every few days it would find mooring in a Florida port, where the other passengers would collect mail and news from the outside world. Louis, who had stayed behind in New York, peppered Franklin with gossip about the fight between William Gibbs McAdoo and Al Smith for the Democratic presidential nomination. McAdoo, who was both Woodrow Wilson's son-in-law and former Treasury secretary, was the leading choice of prohibition-supporting Drys and other cultural conservatives in the party, but his chances were considered tarnished by peripheral involvement in the Republicans' Teapot Dome scandal. Al Smith's backers liked their chances at the convention more and more, though everyone anticipated a big blowup over prohibition. "I took lunch with some of the Albany boys," Louis wrote, "and they told me in one way at least Smith is much drier than he used to be. How long he has sworn off for this time, God knows. Let us trust until after the national convention."

Though nominally a supporter of his fellow New Yorker, Franklin took a dim view of Smith's chances. He was dismayed by how little Smith concerned himself with "national questions" and how much he underrated the dangers of the party's rural–urban divide.

But even with the convention looming, Franklin had a surprisingly easy time tuning out the chatter from New York and Washington. Swimming was what gave purpose to his days. He continued to have a near mystical devotion to its curative powers. The previous summer, he'd written to Reginald Bulkley, a fellow polio sufferer he'd met at Dr. Lovett's clinic in Boston. "I much hope that you will be able to in some way try swimming, even if you have to lie on your back with some bamboo poles as a support under you to help [you] float. I feel certain that you would find you could do a good deal more in the water with your arms and legs than you have any idea of."

He had developed, too, a strong belief in the curative powers of warm air and sunlight. He seemed to do so much better when his skin was warmed by the sun. Perhaps, he conjectured, prolonged exposure to the sun's rays triggered an electric response in his spine, jolting dormant nerve centers awake. This theory performed a convenient function: explaining why, a year and a half after he'd first started swimming, he had not yet regained the ability to walk on his own. Too much time in the cold and dark! "I know that it is doing the legs good," he wrote to Sara from Florida, "and though I have worn the braces hardly at all, I get lots of exercise crawling around, and I know the muscles are better than ever before."

In reality, the chief benefits of the time in Florida were psychological. He was intoxicated by whole days spent feeling good and a course of rehabilitation that was entirely of his own design. In New York, concentrating on the doctors' prescribed recovery meant endless drudgery—exercises that never brought improvement quickly enough, crutches that taunted him with how far he still had to go. On his boat, he had agency again. He could do as he liked. An afternoon of poor fishing conditions was a chance to do his exercises. A frustrating hour with the crutches could be swiftly set aside in favor of a rejuvenating swim.

Above all, Florida offered Franklin a break from all the things polio had put out of his reach. On the water, he was the sole emperor of his circumstances. Sometimes in the afternoons, he and Missy would row out into the warm Florida waters on the boat's dinghy, with Franklin at the oar. As he steered the tiny vessel, her eyes would rest on him lovingly. In that small universe, he was still splendid, still in control.

In mid-April, *LaRooco* docked in Miami. Franklin and Missy gathered their things and made arrangements to travel home by train. Back in the city, he quickly resumed his routine—journeying down town in a chauffeur-driven car to visit the F&D office, taking meetings at East 65th Street. At the end of the month, he received a delegation of New York Democratic operatives, who had come with a request.

TWO MONTHS LATER, IN late June, the Democratic convention began under Madison Square Garden's gleaming glass roof. In the months leading up to the convention, backers of McAdoo, the Dry candidate, had worried that the Wet forces in New York would drown his delegates in liquor, rendering them prostrate when it came time for a convention-floor fight. (What role the individual delegates would play in their own liquor-drowning was left ambiguous.)

Meanwhile, New Yorkers' worst suspicions about *their* enemies within the party were confirmed when Ku Klux Klan members appeared in New York. While McAdoo claimed no allegiance to the Klan, his managers staunchly opposed any action by the convention denouncing Klan activity. This was a tacit acknowledgment of the substantial Klan presence within McAdoo's ranks. "There may not be enough Kluxers in the convention to nominate McAdoo," wrote the columnist H. L. Mencken, "but there are probably enough to beat any candidate so far."

The convention quickly devolved into venomous rancor. On the day when California's delegation was to put McAdoo's name into contention, Smith's forces stampeded the convention floor and mocked the California delegates with cheers of "Ku Ku, McAdoo." The experience left the McAdoo forces looking for revenge. On the day designated for Smith's nomination, anticipation was electric in the Smith galleries above the Garden, and there was palpable hatred in the McAdoo delegations below. The convention's chairman struggled in vain to bring the room to order.

But then something unexpected did what the chairman's pounding could not. It unified the room in silence and rapt attention. The angry, rivalrous factions of the Democratic Party were captivated by what they saw at the speaker's platform. It was moving and a little pitiful and it was impossible to ignore. Rising up in front of them was Franklin Roosevelt. Seated in a wheelchair, he was being lifted onto the podium, carried in the arms of other men.

HIS JOURNEY TO THE convention floor had begun shortly after his return from Florida, when Smith's backers had visited him at East 65th Street. In late April, Charles Murphy, the Tammany boss and the chair of Smith's effort, had suffered a heart attack and died. Smith's advisers saw the opening as a chance to find a non-Tammany chief for their campaign, someone who could prove more palatable to the national party. Would Franklin, they wondered, consider taking the job?

After consulting with Louis, Franklin had accepted. He warned Smith's advisers, Belle Moskowitz and Joseph Proskauer, that his mobility was limited and that he would need to do much of his work from the East 65th Street house. That would not be a problem, Moskowitz and Proskauer assured him. In fact, the arrangement was ideal for their purposes: Franklin would be the figurehead, languishing uptown, while they did the real work of winning the nomination for Smith.

Franklin and Louis, hardly innocents, could see what Proskauer and Moskowitz were up to. They didn't much care. Smith's cronies could do all the wheeling and dealing they liked; the campaign chairmanship was a chance to revivify Franklin's national profile. But when the Smith campaign had returned with another request—that Franklin place Smith's name in nomination on the convention floor—Franklin hesitated. By tradition, a distinguished member of a candidate's home-state delegation made nominating speeches during the calling of the roll. Done right, a nominating speech would be Franklin's best chance in years to prove to his party that he was still in the game.

The risks, though, were impossible to ignore. Conventions were still about spectacle, the clamor for attention, the whole room turning at once to look. The game you played there was physical, mostly brash and brutal, sometimes elegant and inspired. Franklin knew this better than anyone. Leaping over the chairs in San Francisco four years before, he had stopped the convention, pulling the broad room toward him like a kite on a tight string.

For the last three years, Franklin had carefully curated the public image of his illness. He and Louis had salted the news pages with encouraging reports of his swift progress and produced orchestrated photos to hide the extent of his disability. The highly public setting of the convention floor had the potential to wipe all that away. There, Franklin could not hide the simple, unspoken fact at the center of his life: He remained unable to walk without assistance.

Still, the chance to step back into the light was too good to waste. Franklin again accepted the Smith campaign's offer. He drafted a speech with Louis, which the Smith cronies swiftly rejected, preferring to supply a version of their own. Franklin acceded to their demands; his real concerns were more practical. Now, with the help of his son James, he spent long hours practicing the choreography he'd need just to appear onstage. Standing beside a chair and shifting his weight, he slowly passed his crutch to the boy and fell gently into his seat. Walking a few feet on crutches was still a precarious proposition, but he was determined that, when the moment came, he would walk to the speaker's rostrum on his own.

Each day, Franklin would arrive at the convention floor early, before most of the other party notables had shown their faces, before the proceedings officially commenced. That way, as few people as possible would take notice of his slow entrance, clutching James's arm. In the New York delegation, he sat in a special upholstered chair he'd brought in, with cushions to provide comfort for the long stationary hours. It looked like a throne. Seated on it, he became a kind of way station for arriving delegates, stopping by to trade gossip. At the end of the day, he and James would make their way out.

Louis's usual handiwork was evident in the convention coverage. "The work of restoring his limbs . . . has progressed so satisfactorily," the *New York Herald Tribune* told its readers a few days into the convention, "that within a year he will need no more than a cane to get about with and eventually not even that." But the particular challenges of the convention setting made the reality plain. First among them was the platform from which Franklin was to deliver his nominating speech, rising high off the ground. It was so tall that people passed underneath like it was a bridge. All of those eyes—thousands of them—now watching Franklin being carried up onto the platform in the arms of two men, could see just how far from walking Franklin really was.

———

FRANKLIN WAS NOT SUPPOSED to have to wait on the platform for long. The roll call of states was still in the early part of the alphabet. By prearrangement, Connecticut had agreed that, when its turn came, it would yield to the delegation from New York. At that point, Franklin would deliver his speech nominating Smith. But after the convention attendees got over their hushed shock at seeing Franklin carried onto the stage, the bickering between the Smith and McAdoo forces in the room had recommenced, leaving the roll call stuck at Colorado.

Through the endless screaming and catcalling, Franklin sat in his wheelchair, under the harsh convention lights. Many in the room fixed their eyes on him. The giant stage loomed, with all the delegations crowded close around it in the center. The galleries were hard to make out from the stage, obscured by giant orange and purple shades on the lights and a sea of American flags floating from the ceiling. For Franklin, exposed onstage, the effect was devastatingly intimate. The press, the party's leaders and financial backers—all the people he needed to convince he was still among the quick—were staring right at him.

They judged his condition harshly. "Franklin Roosevelt sits in his wheelchair," wrote one reporter describing the scene. He was "gray faced and tired," said another. Hearst's *San Francisco Examiner* recalled the Franklin of 1920, "a vigorous young man in the flower of his youth." Now he was "still rich in the vigor of his mind but fighting gamely against the creeping inroads of infantile paralysis." Few could look at him without making the same comparison. "It was Roosevelt but not the same Roosevelt," another reporter wrote.

Waiting beside his father on the platform, James Roosevelt felt Franklin's fingers dig into his arm. When the screams finally abated and Connecticut's delegation started to speak, Franklin signaled to a committee member standing nearby, saying, "Shake the rostrum!" The man looked puzzled, James later recalled, until Franklin explained that he wanted to make sure the stand would not fall over when he used it to support his weight.

When Connecticut yielded to New York, James helped his father to his feet. The younger Roosevelt could feel *himself* shaking. Then he watched as Franklin, holding his own weight up on a crutch, let go of James's arm, took hold of a second crutch, and slowly began to make his way forward. Franklin moved from the back of the platform awkwardly, the crutches in his hands sliding forward, his hips swiveling his legs along. Slowly, he neared center stage. He could not throw his arms up in hearty salutation—the typical politician's move—for he did not have a hand to spare and his progress required deep concentration. Instead, as he approached the rostrum, he offered a beaming smile.

For the first time since the start of the convention—for the first time, really, all year—the Democratic Party was united. Genuinely moved, the cynical convention-goers joined in a common ovation for Franklin.

Franklin leaned forward, using the podium to support his weight. The audience could not quite make out his inability to stand on his own, thanks to a novel innovation in the speaker stand's design. In the four years since the parties had last held their conventions, radio had injected itself into the bloodstream of American politics. Convention organizers, worried that orators would be tempted to pace out of range of the radio microphones installed on the stand, had put up railings to constrict the podium and force speakers to stand where their voices would be captured for the audience listening at home.

Those listeners, millions of them, had not seen Franklin hobbling to the podium. Their ears provided a simpler story. As the radio announcer spoke the name of Franklin Roosevelt, that dashing young Democratic Roosevelt who'd run on the ticket the last time around, the room was overtaken with an ovation that went on and on. The cheers had a hearty, good-natured quality, an *energy* that had been absent in the convention up to that point.

From their crackling devices, radio listeners gathered that something about this particular speaker, Franklin Roosevelt, had illuminated the convention hall. And when at last the cheers ended and he began to speak, they understood what.

The years had not just transfigured Franklin's body; they had also changed his voice. The accent was the same, a honking aristocratic lockjaw charmingly discordant with the plain words it pronounced. But his voice was deeper, more grounded, more sure. Gone was the breathy, flighty urgency of the earlier Franklin, a young man overcome each moment with a new idea of how to please his audience. This Franklin spoke in a more earthy, inviting register. He took his time, judiciously allocating his breath. Most orators, speaking to a room, let their words trail up and away as they reached the end of a sentence, trusting the audience's enthusiasm to fill in the gaps. Franklin stayed alluring and interesting to the end, ensuring that the listeners at home got the message.

His speech crescendoed with a line that would live for many years. Describing Al Smith, he said: "He has a personality that carries to every hearer not only the sincerity but the righteousness of what he says. He is the 'Happy Warrior' of the political battlefield."

By the time Franklin was done talking, the Smith forces had filled every aisle of the convention hall. With bands playing and noisemakers blowing, they paraded Smith's likeness around the Garden. As they joyously rioted, the party activist Frances Perkins turned her gaze back to Franklin, still gripping the speaker's stands. His hands, she noted, were white. It had been an eternity since he had left his wheelchair. Someone needed to help him escape. "I saw around him all those fat slob politicians—men," she later recalled, "and I knew they wouldn't think of it." With the help of another woman, she formed a shroud around Franklin; he at last departed the stage, shuttled away in his wheelchair by James.

The Smith demonstration went on for seventy-three minutes, an eternity. But in the eyes of many in the room, the day was Franklin's. There would even be talk of drafting him as a compromise candidate (talk that Franklin and Louis were quick to dispel). But to many, his triumph somehow transcended the grubby convention setting, transcended politics itself. "This fellow Roosevelt," wrote one Hearst columnist, "there is a man and I use the word as a term of great respect and sincere admiration . . . I never was present at so fine a display of

high mental courage than this morning when Roosevelt carried himself to the front of the speakers' tribune "

After the convention closed for the day, Franklin returned home to
East 65th Street. That night, Eleanor hosted a reception at the house
for the New York delegation, but Franklin was too tired to attend.
Arriving at the Roosevelts' that evening, Marion Dickerman received
word that Mr. Roosevelt wished to see her upstairs in his room.
Franklin had developed a special affection for Eleanor's sensitive
friend. She found him in his bed, arms stretched out and beaming.
"Marion," he said, "I *did* it!"

Chapter 21

The Way It Feels

OCTOBER 1924–MAY 1926

THREE MONTHS AFTER THE 1924 CONVENTION, FRANKLIN and Eleanor boarded a train for the South. They were drawn by miraculous tales of healing waters at a place called Warm Springs, near the town of Bullochville, Georgia. There, Franklin explained in a letter to an acquaintance, sat "a remarkable swimming pool of natural highly mineralized water which comes out of the hillside at a temperature of 90 degrees." He had come to believe that this warm, buoyant bathwater might be the thing to finally get him walking again.

Warm Springs had gripped his imagination for months. He'd first heard of it from the banker George Foster Peabody, a social acquaintance, who was a part owner of the spa resort there. Peabody had written to Franklin that summer to share the enticing account of Louis Joseph, a man left paralyzed by polio who after three years of therapy in the springs had regained the ability to walk. Franklin had responded with eager interest.

Peabody's partner in the venture, Tom Loyless, had hurried to New York to talk up the resort. Meeting with Franklin, he described a mystical opening in the central Georgia hills. The piping-hot water of the springs had inexplicable powers—you could swim in them for hours without tiring. For centuries, people had flocked to these waters seeking cures for physical ailments.

Franklin was so intrigued that he made plans to travel to Georgia in October, skipping the final weeks of the presidential campaign. He wouldn't be missing much. His speech had been the last moment of grace at the Madison Square Garden convention. Though McAdoo had managed to win a majority of delegates on the early ballots, Al Smith prevented him from securing the necessary two-thirds required to be the party's nominee. Custom dictated that McAdoo and Smith should withdraw and allow party leaders to select a compromise candidate. But the ill feeling between Smith and McAdoo had turned to downright hatred, and neither man would agree to release his delegates until the other had bowed out.

The deadlocked convention had gone on for sixteen days, far longer than any other convention in history. Finally, after more than a hundred calls of the convention roll, both Smith and McAdoo stood down in favor of the compromise Democratic candidate, John W. Davis, a former ambassador and congressman from West Virginia. When someone congratulated him on winning the nomination, Davis was fatalistic: "Thanks, but you know what it's worth." The endless infighting had been catastrophic for the Democrats. No one expected Davis to defeat Coolidge.

So Franklin boarded a train for Bullochville, with Eleanor, Missy LeHand, and his personal valet, Irvin McDuffie. Loyless's seductive pitch had confirmed many of Franklin's own notions: the importance of light and warm water and the hidden powers of trees. (Warm Springs's magic waters had some relation, it was believed, to the thick pine forests that covered the hills.) Franklin had an old faith in spa water, born in his childhood when his family had visited German resorts, seeking to ease his father's pains.

If Warm Springs had a vague aura of mystery and miracle, that would have appealed to him too. Increasingly, Franklin needed to believe in miraculous cures. Earlier that year, Dr. Draper had written to Lovett in Boston with a dire assessment of Franklin's improvement. "I am very much disheartened about his ultimate recovery," he had confided. "I cannot help feeling that he has almost reached the limits of his possibilities." Franklin, expert in detecting subtle changes in people's affect, would have noticed that his doctor seemed to emphasize adapting to his disability more and recovery less. He was keenly aware of the conventional wisdom about polio patients—after the first two years, damaged but functional muscles could gain strength, but muscles that had not recovered their function were most likely not going to come back. It had now been three years since he'd taken ill.

Yet he needed to believe he would walk again. He clung fast to the notion that running for office again *required* walking again—that had been his plan. Thus the appeal of a place that science could not fully explain, of waters whose healing properties predated modern medicine, of a cure that had taken another man with polio and put him back on his feet. "I have a hunch," he wrote to Van Lear Black that fall, "that this swimming pool filled with warm water is going to do a lot of good."

But when he arrived at the Meriwether Inn, the centerpiece of the Warm Springs resort, Franklin saw that his promised oasis was a derelict, cobweb-filled mess. In the late nineteenth century, the resort had briefly been a favored summer getaway for Atlanta society, but it had suffered long decades of obscurity and neglect. The remote setting meant few provisions were available, and as mealtimes approached, Eleanor watched uncomfortably while the cook chased a chicken around the yard, slaughtered it, and then cooked it for that night's dinner. At the inn, knives and forks were hard to come by, and most of the plates and dishes were broken.

Peabody and Loyless had assumed ownership of this place earlier in the decade. They had imagined reviving it as a hybrid spa resort that could offer respite, for the wealthy and well-to-do, and remedy, for the sick and aged. In Franklin Roosevelt, they saw an intriguing opportunity to appeal to both audiences. Imagine, they'd thought, having so distinguished a statesman as poster child for Warm Springs.

The resort did not appear, in other words, a place that offered salvation so much as a place that needed saving.

Still, the next morning, lounging outside the small cottage that had been prepared for his use, Franklin felt warmth on his face and breathed in air that was heavy with the scent of pine. And then he saw Louis Joseph walking toward him on the path.

This was the young man Peabody had described in the first letter. Joseph had been an engineer on assignment in South America when his body was stricken with a polio infection. Left unable to walk, he'd returned to his native Georgia, where he went with his family to a summer vacation cottage near Warm Springs. Joining them in the pool one day, he was shocked to discover he could move his limbs. He'd spent three years in the water, trying to walk. Now here he was, on dry land, moving his legs awkwardly but certainly, helped by nothing more than a cane. Franklin watched him, transfixed.

In his 1953 book *Roosevelt and the Warm Springs Story*, Turnley Walker recounted Franklin's delighted reaction on seeing Joseph maneuver the steps: "How grand to be able to do that." It was the result, Joseph said, of the waters at Warm Springs. Franklin then turned to Loyless. "Let's go down to the pool right now."

The pool was unadorned but massive, one hundred feet wide and one hundred fifty feet long. The water inside it began as raindrops on Pine Mountain, seeping down through rich soil into the old earth. It hurtled through miles of ancient rock sentiment before pouring up out of the ground at 89 degrees Fahrenheit. With the help of McDuffie and Joseph, Franklin eased into this water. As soon as it touched his skin, he felt the difference. It was delightfully warm but not so hot as to drain sweat and energy from his form. It was invigorating, an ancient life force pulsing into his depleted form.

For some time he just floated, awed and content. "Try moving your legs," Louis Joseph said. Franklin wasn't sure: He had been trying swimming therapy for some time but had never been able to do that. "This water is different," Joseph assured him. "You float so easily." Franklin clutched the side of the pool and focused on moving his right leg, the less damaged of the two. Looking down, he couldn't quite believe it. His limbs were moving in a way they hadn't for three years.

His joy burst upward: "The way it feels!" And then, close behind, Franklin offered another thought: "It does seem a pity that Louis and I have this all to ourselves."

———

AFTER HELPING FRANKLIN SETTLE in at Warm Springs, Eleanor returned north, eager to lend her hand to the Democratic Party effort for the fall elections.

She was particularly drawn to the governor's race, where Al Smith was seeking another term. She was inspired by Smith's program—and the chance to settle some old scores. The Republican nominee for governor was Eleanor's first cousin, Theodore Roosevelt Jr. Eleanor well remembered the 1920 campaign, when her Oyster Bay relations had mocked Franklin. Ted Jr. had gone on to serve as assistant secretary of the Navy in the Harding and Coolidge administrations, where his reputation was damaged by his peripheral involvement in the Teapot Dome scandal. Traveling around New York State that fall, the Republican candidate found himself stalked by a group of Democratic women in a seven-passenger car made to look like a boiling teapot. The design for the vehicle was Eleanor's, and among the passengers was her eighteen-year-old daughter, Anna.

In the November election, Smith defeated Theodore Roosevelt Jr. handily. Nationally, as predicted, President Coolidge trounced his Democratic challenger, John W. Davis, in a landslide.

Eleanor's experience at the 1924 convention had been both dispiriting and instructive. For months leading up to the event, she had worked in her appointed capacity for the party's platform committee, gathering recommendations from female members of the Democratic committee. But when the platform committee met at the convention, the men who ran it rejected her group's recommendations without even considering them. When Eleanor and other women leaders objected to egregiously weak platform language on child labor, male party leaders told them that "if they were not satisfied with the plank as approved by the committee, they might vote for another party."

It was an eye-opening humiliation for Eleanor. Going forward, she knew, women wouldn't gain influence in the party by accepting nice-sounding titles from men. If they wanted to shape the party's destiny, they had to organize and take power on their own.

POLITICS TOOK UP LESS space in Franklin's head that fall than ever before. Warm Springs, and its promise, blotted out everything else. "The legs are really improving a great deal," he wrote to Eleanor, "the walking & the general exercise, & the water is fine. This is really a discovery of a place & there is no doubt that I've got to do it some more."

He could feel it, the thing he'd been waiting for: his limbs coming back to life. In the water, his bare skin glowing under the sun, he could methodically trace the proof A year earlier, he had not been able to stand up in fresh water unless it came up to his chin. Six months ago, he'd been able to stand erect in water that just covered his shoulders. Now he could stand in water that came up only as high as his armpits. Imagine where he would be in another six months. And then six months after that.

Later that month, Franklin was enjoying his morning routine by the pool when Tom Loyless approached, accompanied by a man named Gregory from Atlanta, who was eager to hear about Franklin's progress at Warm Springs.

After hauling himself out of the pool, his body still dripping, Franklin proceeded to give this stranger a closer look at his condition than he had given most people, including many of his friends, in the past three years. "I've been greatly helped, and I've only been here two weeks," he explained. His depleted lower limbs were stretched out on the ground, tiny and naked in the warm air. "This leg," he said, pointing to the right side, "I hadn't been able to move for three years. I can use it a little now. The other is much better too."

It was remarkable for Franklin to speak so plainly about his recovery with anyone, but it was truly remarkable in this instance. Mr. Gregory, it turned out, was Cleburne Gregory, a correspondent for *The Atlanta Journal* who'd come to write a piece about the famous politician seeking a cure in the Georgia hills.

Later, Franklin would claim he was unaware he'd been talking to a reporter, but that is hard to believe. Gregory ended up spending three days at Warm Springs, during which time he kept a careful record of Franklin's words and even got him to pose, grinning, for a photograph in his swimming suit. More likely, caught up in the joyous strangeness of autumn days floating in an enchanted pool, Franklin had concluded he was too far from the real world for anything he said to have any impact on his normal life.

But by the time he traveled home in late October, a lengthy, intimate portrait of his time in the South had been published as a Sunday supplement to *The Atlanta Journal*. To Franklin's displeasure, Gregory's story was then sold in syndication to newspapers across the country. Editors jumped at the chance to run the sensational picture of Franklin at poolside. The image shows him in his swimming costume, a broad smile bursting across his face. He seems to be relaxed as can be, his right arm draped across his right leg, bent at the knee as if getting ready to stand up. Only the careful eye can see the staging—his arm is twice the size of the leg it is resting on. The left arm, also massive, is planted firmly on the ground, bearing the brunt of Franklin's weight.

The *St. Louis Post-Dispatch*, the influential newspaper owned by the Pulitzer family, ran a particularly grim full-page version of the story. With crisp efficiency, this account obliterated many of the half-truths and omissions Louis Howe and Franklin had for so long used to cloak the reality of Franklin's illness. His was not, the article made clear, simply a "mild case" of infantile paralysis, characterized by limping and occasional walking with a cane. At the onset of illness, "his home in New York became a place of tiny hopes," the piece went on. "He got a little better under treatment by specialists, enough better to leave his bed and walk around on crutches."

Franklin would later suggest the stories based on Gregory's reporting had been filled with exaggerations and inaccuracies. In fact, they were among the most accurate accounts of Franklin's illness and recovery to appear during Franklin's lifetime. They were also among the most revealing. Gregory even managed to get Franklin to reflect, briefly, on the emotional toll of his disease. "I knew when the first attack came, that I'd pull out of it some day," he said. "I told them all I would, from the start. Of course, I was pretty blue for a time, but I'm coming out of it."

And as much as Franklin may have disliked the picture painted by that article, the revelations proved an important source of connection and hope for polio sufferers across America.

Later that year, a recovering polio patient named Fred Botts was sitting by a fire at his parents' home in Pennsylvania when his father put down the paper he was reading. "Have you ever heard of Warm Springs, Georgia?" the elder man asked.

Fred Botts had contracted polio in the 1916 epidemic. The disease had left him paralyzed below the waist. Now in his mid-twenties, he remained in a wheelchair, frustrated by the meager advice on recovery the medical establishment had to offer, advice that never worked. For "eight long years," he would say, that had been "the narrow and vicious circle of my life."

His father began to read aloud a story about springs flowing from a Georgia mountainside, which had helped a polio patient named Louis Joseph regain the ability to walk. That fall, no less a figure than Franklin D. Roosevelt had gone to the springs, in the hopes they might have a similar effect on him. After just a few weeks at Warm Springs, the article said, Roosevelt "is now convinced that the water holds true merit and that very soon science will heartily endorse hydrotherapy as invaluable in the treatment and cure of infantile paralysis."

Botts's mind raced. *Swim your way back to health and strength!,* he thought. *That's the thing!*

BACK IN NEW YORK, Franklin spent the remainder of 1924 reengaging with the things he'd neglected. There was his work at the Fidelity and Deposit Company and at the new law firm he was starting with Basil O'Connor, the affable downtown attorney who had helped him up from his fall in the lobby of the F&D building in the autumn of 1922.

But Franklin couldn't get Warm Springs out of his head—the progress he'd made standing in the pool, the way his spirit had revived. He imagined what more it could offer him, and others too.

"How are you getting on?" he wrote in early January 1925 to Paul Hasbrouck, a polio survivor from Poughkeepsie. "I hope your legs are improving as fast as mine are. I should much like to tell you about Warm Springs, Georgia, and how much it helped me this autumn."

Hasbrouck, a twenty-eight-year-old veteran of the Great War, had written to Franklin the year before, one of the many polio survivors who had reached out to the nation's most famous polio patient, seeking advice. Franklin had been characteristically accommodating and open, sharing an accurate account of his own struggle and his theories about the curative powers of warmth and light. In the winter of 1925, Hasbrouck was studying political science at Columbia University. Replying to Franklin that January, he expressed his frustration at how little support he had found in his efforts to accelerate his recovery. "Consultation with the University physician did not offer any constructive suggestion of anything that I might do down here to secure special benefit." He was intrigued by the place Franklin described in Georgia. "So much of the information is negative," he wrote, "that it seems good to receive some from you which is positive. Please tell me more about it."

Franklin answered him the very next day. "I really believe that Warm Springs would do you a lot of good. . . . My month down there did more good than anything I had done before. . . . The water may or may not have peculiar building up qualities, but at least you feel wonderfully after staying in for several hours and can do a great deal of exercising.

"Up to now," he continued, "it has been impossible to stay there in the winter as the indoor pool had no heating arrangements even though the water is warm. Hereafter, however, the hotel is to be kept open the year around and the bath houses will be heated so that it will be an all year-round place."

He was beginning to sound less like a guest at Warm Springs and more like a promoter and proprietor. He knew that Loyless had high hopes for what his involvement in the resort would mean, that he would partner in the venture, help to shape and publicize the vision of a vacation resort that doubled as a colony for the ill and infirm. Franklin was drawn to the concept and began looking for money to buy out Peabody's position and assume control of the resort.

Franklin's advisers and associates thought it a crazy scheme. The amount of money required—$200,000 to assume Peabody's interest— was staggering for a man who was struggling to meet his monthly expenses. Eleanor too was wary. Franklin assured her that with time and proper management, Warm Springs might become a profitable enterprise, but she never really had faith in his business acumen. "Georgia is somewhat distant for you to keep in touch with what seems a rather big undertaking," she reminded Franklin tentatively.

Still, as the winter months went by, Franklin became more and more convinced that his new destiny was somehow tied up in that place. He returned to Georgia in April, a month before the resort was scheduled to open for the season. He was startled to find it already filled with people. Fred Botts was not the only reader who'd taken an interest in the article about Franklin's success at Warm Springs. Just as the early press coverage of his supposedly miraculous recovery had captured the attention of people who'd had polio, the Warm Springs piece had sparked broad interest in the resort and enticed other paralysis patients to make the trip to Georgia.

The staff at the resort was threadbare—no one seemed to know what to do with the new arrivals or where to put them, let alone how to direct their rehabilitation. Seamlessly, Franklin took charge, offering the new arrivals a structured approach to their days at the resort and a plan for their broader recovery.

All his life, Franklin had been drawn more to practical challenges than to philosophical debates. Warm Springs put any number of solvable problems in front of him that spring. Proving difficult to get patients in and out of the pool? Hire some strong young men from the nearby town to take on the task. Hard for patients to hold up the bar on which they did their exercises in the water? Install a long rod fixed to the ground at the poolside, extending out over the water. The cottages for guests lacked running water, toilets, and heat? He would redesign them himself.

In April, Fred Botts had boarded a southbound train, where, in his wheelchair, he was placed in an undignified position in the baggage car, surrounded by luggage, mail sacks, chicken crates, and a casket. Arriving at Warm Springs, he'd been alarmed by torn screens and peeling paint. But when he was lowered into the pool, it was just as the article had promised. The water was warm and his body felt light in it. For the first time in as long as he could remember, his legs were moving.

It was in the pool that he first encountered Franklin, his sturdy voice calling out, "Hello there." Joining Botts and the other patients in the water, he swiftly took command, instructing them on how to do their exercises on the bar that had been installed over the pool. "Catch hold of the bar this way," Botts recalled him saying, "now—swing—in and out—hard! *Harder!*" As the group worked, Franklin provided an explanatory monologue on the springs: why the body felt weightless in the water, how warm air and sunlight helped muscles, how to move damaged limbs in as close to a normal manner as possible.

Every couple of weeks, a doctor from a nearby town would visit to inspect the patients' progress. At Franklin's instruction, the staff diagrammed the musculature of each Warm Springs patient, to track the recovery of affected limbs. Patients lay on their backs beside the pool while the doctor and Franklin examined them, looking for hints of improved movement.

"Old Doctor Roosevelt," it turned out, had developed a number of very specific ideas on the proper treatment of infantile paralysis. He had been eager for some time to share this knowledge with the wider world. A year earlier, a physician had written to him for suggestions on how to help a polio patient. Franklin had provided a self-crafted list of dos and don'ts. "The following treatment is so far the best," he wrote, "judging from my own experience and that of hundreds of other cases which I have studied:

1. Gentle exercises especially for the muscles which seem to be worst affected.
2. Gentle skin rubbing—no muscle kneading—bearing in mind that good circulation is a prime requisite.
3. Swimming in warm water—lots of it.
4. Sunlight—all the patient can get especially direct sunlight on the affected parts. It would be ideal to lie in the sun all day with nothing on. This is difficult to accomplish but the nearest approach to it is a bathing suit.
5. Belief on the patient's part that the muscles are coming back and will eventually regain recovery of the affected parts. There are cases known in Norway where adults have taken the disease and not been able to walk until after a lapse of 10 or even 12 years."

This last item was particularly crucial to him: belief that he would get better and a plan for how he would do it. From the past four years, he'd learned that a patient's psychological well-being and physical condition were closely linked—it was impossible to adequately attend to one if you did not consider the other.

Perhaps not accidentally, he spoke happily and frequently that spring about the future. Gathering the patients around a table, Franklin described an array of practical improvements they could expect at the resort: dedicated doctors and nurses, an enclosed winter pool with skylights to let in the sun's healing rays. His own experience had taught him how moments of transition—getting dressed, being placed in or out of a wheelchair—made paralytics feel vulnerable, exposed to strangers' eyes. Soon Warm Springs would have special steam-heated changing rooms for patients too. The resort would soon get better, he told them, and so would they.

And they did. Fred Botts would later describe a remarkable pattern of improvement among the Warm Springs patients that first year—a man who had come on crutches and braces and left using only a cane; people who had arrived using wheelchairs who'd barely needed them by the time they left. Botts himself was among the most encouraging success stories. Later that year, his case was included in a summary of patients' progress at the resort:

> Mr. Botts from Pennsylvania—a case of 8 years' standing . . . Five or six important muscles of which there was no trace can now be felt, glutei greatly improved, quadriceps in one knee returning, abductors strengthened and adductors have reappeared. He uses braces. When he came here he could walk only a few steps, yesterday he walked half a mile in them. It is, of course, doubtful if he gets rid of the braces but his improvement has really been extraordinary.

The author of these observations signed his name at the end of his report: Franklin D. Roosevelt.

"IT LOOKS AS IF I had bought Warm Springs," Franklin wrote to Sara in the spring of 1926, "If so, I want you to take a great interest in it, for I feel you can help me with many suggestions."

Events had forced him to act. In March of 1926, Tom Loyless, the visionary promoter who had helped to bring Franklin to Georgia, died of cancer. With him gone, there was no one else who could steer Warm Springs toward a better future.

So Franklin had taken the plunge. In the end, he paid nearly $200,000 to assume ownership—a substantial portion of his net worth and no small gesture from a man who strove for frugality. Taking on the place would mean not only a major commitment of resources but an astonishing commitment of time for someone who had five children, two jobs, and an ambition to become president of the United States. It is even more remarkable considering that, up to that point, much of Franklin's life had been organized around his own needs and interests. This purchase, by far the largest risk he ever took with his own capital, was one whose benefits were chiefly to be derived by others.

"You needn't worry about my losing a fortune," he told Sara, "for every step is being planned either to pay for itself or make a profit." At first, he was drawn to the old idea of Warm Springs as a hybrid place of healing and a resort for the affluent. In a statement to the press after taking control, he announced plans to build a "cottage colony" country club for wealthy vacationers, complete with a world-class golf course. Yet pursuing these dual missions for the place proved predictably disastrous. Wealthy vacationers who found their way to Warm Springs were terrified of sharing space, let alone a pool, with polio patients. For a brief period, patients at the resort were banished from the main outdoor pool and forced to take their therapy in makeshift huts with dirt-hole tubs filled with water from the springs.

Whatever his moneymaking dreams, Franklin did not want his patients to be second-class citizens. He began to think of the leisure facilities at the place as a way for patients' families to pass the time while their loved ones sought treatment. To further ease his financial burden, he ultimately transferred ownership to a charitable entity, the Georgia Warm Springs Foundation, and began seeking gifts to cover the cost of hiring new staff and making improvements in the physical plant.

Franklin had spent his entire life around the "best" people and had paid dues at numerous exclusive clubs. Warm Springs provided him with an altogether different sense of belonging. The more time he spent there, the more he was awakened to what other people who had polio—most of whom were less fortunate and connected than he—had gone through. Getting to know these people, hearing their stories, and seeing what the disease had done to their bodies, he saw that they were linked by their shared struggle.

He was indignant over how little help most patients had received before coming to Warm Springs. "We have so many cases here that come from the so-called leading doctors where the treatment has been *criminal*," he wrote to Sara, "and left permanently bad results that could with knowledge have been avoided. We don't of course take any cases till all soreness is gone, but we know from the history of dozens of cases."

This he now believed was his duty, to provide the treatments that the "so-called leading doctors" would not. To help enhance his legitimacy, he hired Dr. Leroy Hubbard, a retired head of the New York State Department of Health, as medical director of the facility. There was also talk of testing the water at Warm Springs in the hopes of identifying what exactly explained its remarkable effects. In truth, beyond its buoyancy and its warm temperature, it had little to distinguish it from the water of other springs. If there was any special mixture helping patients at Warm Springs to recover, it was the unique combination of elements Franklin brought to the place.

First among these was his accumulated wisdom on the treatment of infantile paralysis. Franklin's famous name and expansive network had gained him access to polio and paralysis specialists all over the world. His doctors were at the cutting edge of the field. But rather than simply trusting in his primary caregivers and doing as they said, Franklin actively sought out other opinions, near and far. When he encountered new information or an idea he thought might prove useful, he quickly synthesized it into his broader understanding of the disease. All his life he'd excelled at absorbing relevant facts from a single conversation—Eleanor referred to it as his habit of "rubbing his mind up against someone else's." He was not a doctor, but he had a more encyclopedic knowledge than most doctors of what did and didn't work to treat a body damaged by polio.

Patients who came to Warm Springs also found a refreshing emphasis on practical action. Swimming was at the center of every patient's day, weather permitting. A person recovering from polio in the 1920s might well have heard of the benefits of swimming therapy, but finding a way to do it was a challenge. Getting to a pool was difficult for people who couldn't walk, and at public pools they risked shame and stigma. For most who came to Warm Springs, floating in any water—magic or not—for days on end was a new and transformative phenomenon. By organizing the place around the pools, Franklin helped patients to reshape not just their bodies but their minds as well. Together with physical therapy in and out of the pool, swimming gave Warm Springs patients a sense of agency and control over their recovery that, in some cases, had been utterly absent in everyday life.

Another key innovation Franklin brought to the resort was a focus on community. From his own experience, he knew how paralysis could isolate victims of polio. In its old configuration, the colony was somewhat dispersed, with guests often remaining in their cottages or rooms. Franklin ordered the cottages connected by wheelchair-accessible walkways. These were populated by "push boys"—young local men who were hired to move wheelchair-using patients from building to building. Meals were communal, as was instruction in the pool.

Most important of all, Franklin's Warm Springs nurtured hope. Everything in a patient's experience was geared toward a brighter future. Change in musculature, strength, and body weight were all carefully measured by medical professionals. If possible, a patient using a wheelchair worked to walk with braces; a patient on crutches worked to transition to canes; patients with canes worked to walk on their own. The place itself was marked by ceaseless renovation and construction. Pain becomes more tolerable, Franklin had learned, when a path out of it seems clear.

Gather the best available wisdom. Focus on practical action. Strengthen community. Nurture hope. These had been the cornerstones of his own attempts at recovery, and Franklin replicated them at Warm Springs. Later, when faced with the challenge of lifting his country out of an economic crisis that had spread dire terror and hopelessness throughout the land, these same principles would form the backbone of his response.

Chapter 22

———

The Soul That
Had Believed

1925–1927

DRIVING IN TO WARM SPRINGS THAT FIRST OCTOBER IN 1924, Eleanor had been shocked by the squalor of the Georgia countryside. Unlike her husband, she was instantly appalled by southern segregation and the way their Georgian hosts seemed to accept it as an immutable fact of life. Taking Franklin and Eleanor out in the car one day, Tom Loyless had shown them the local schools—schools, Eleanor noted, for white students only. "What about the schools for Negro children?" she asked pointedly. Loyless's muttered answer was noncommittal. Who lived in such a place, she'd wondered—was anything being done to help *them?*

At night, she'd slept poorly, kept awake by squirrels rampaging on the flimsy roof above her head. During the day, she could see sunlight through the cracks in the wall. She'd known early on that the place was not for her.

But it was for Franklin. That had been clear from his first morning floating in the pool. And so she had not objected as the place moved closer to the center of her husband's thoughts. Despite her worries and reservations, she had not prevented him from devoting such a substantial portion of their assets to assume ownership. Nor had she objected to the days and weeks he spent away. She hadn't even objected when it became clear that Warm Springs would be a true home for Franklin. And for Missy too.

It was Missy, after all, not Eleanor, who made each trip to Warm Springs with Franklin and stayed there by his side. Eleanor knew full well how closely her husband shared his life with his young female secretary in Georgia, and she also knew how it looked. At one point early in the Warm Springs endeavor, she alerted Franklin that his mother was hurt at never being asked to stay at the colony. "I think you ought to ask her down and stay for a week," she wrote. "I'll bring her if you want and Missy could move out while she stayed." Her message was hardly subtle: Not *everyone* was as broad-minded and accepting of Franklin's tie to Missy as was his wife.

For the most part, Missy remained a blessing for Eleanor, who knew that Franklin needed someone to nurse him, to serve as a hostess alongside him, to give him his required daily servings of admiration and affection and love. With Missy devoted to the cause, Eleanor could offer her life to other things.

As a result, Mr. and Mrs. Franklin Roosevelt were rarely in the same place in those middle years of the 1920s. The separate life Eleanor had imagined in the aftermath of the Lucy Mercer affair had finally come to pass. Franklin's year was spent chasing wellness and warmth, with long trips to Warm Springs in the spring and fall, winter trips to Florida on *LaRooco,* parts of the winter and early summers in Hyde Park.

Eleanor too was always on the move. Having devoted herself to political work, she found she was regularly asked to speak somewhere—there were women all over New York State who wanted to get involved in politics. She became a fleeting presence at both East 65th Street and Hyde Park, putting her bags down on return in one moment, picking them up to depart again the next.

Writing to Franklin, Sara Roosevelt remarked on Eleanor's frequent absences from her home and family with passive–aggressive disapproval. "Eleanor left again at 7:30," she wrote in one letter. "It was lovely to have her here for a few hours. . . . I fear [the children] were not very good when poor Eleanor was here. They do stand a little in awe of me."

Eleanor was acutely aware of Sara's disapproval of her new ways. "I wish you could read Mama's last letter to me," she wrote to Franklin during one of his absences. "She is afraid of everything! Afraid of your going over bad & unfrequented roads, afraid I'll let the children dive in the shallow water & break their necks, afraid they'll get more cuts!" But where once the strong undercurrent of criticism in her mother-in-law's queries had tormented Eleanor, now she could see how anxiety imprisoned Sara. "She must suffer more than we dream is possible," she wrote.

Eleanor's compassion for Sara, a compassion born of Eleanor's own struggles, came easier in these days. Besides, Eleanor's life was mostly out of the older woman's reach. Franklin's frequent absences meant fewer days with the whole family stuck in the townhouse, a serving of Sara's judgment waiting around every corner. And starting in the middle years of the decade, Eleanor finally had a home of her own in Hyde Park.

It had been Franklin's idea. Marion Dickerman would recall an achingly beautiful late-autumn day when she and Nancy Cook had joined Franklin, Eleanor, and two of their children for a picnic at Hyde Park, on the banks of the Val-Kill Creek. Eleanor mournfully remarked that this would be their last weekend in the country—Sara would be closing up the place for the winter. "But aren't you girls silly," Marion recalled Franklin saying. "This isn't Mother's land. I bought this acreage myself. And why shouldn't you three have a cottage here of your own, so you could come and go as you please?"

Soon plans were in the works. Franklin fancied himself an expert in the design of houses and took a proprietary interest in the construction of the cottage, which would be about two miles from the Springwood house. "I have been awfully busy . . , getting price on lumber, stone work, plumbing, etc.," he wrote to Anna in the summer of 1925, "and yesterday telegraphed a bid to Mother and Nan and Marion . . . which, if they take [it], will save them over $4,000! Your pa is some little contractor!"

However proud of his contributions to the cottage he may have been, he made no claim to the place. Warm Springs was Franklin's haven; Val-Kill was Eleanor's. And Marion and Nancy's too. Franklin provided Eleanor's friends a life interest in the land on which the cottage sat, and Eleanor's two friends joined in the construction costs.

The three women shared their first meal in the still-uncompleted cottage on New Year's Day 1926, eating off a crate.

Franklin jokingly called the cottage "the love nest on Val-Kill." Just how much truth lay inside this jest is cloaked in mystery—most of the correspondence between the three women has not survived. From what remains, there is no doubt that a deep love of some kind flourished between Val-Kill's walls. Nancy and Marion, who had been in a committed relationship for a decade, embraced Eleanor as a kind of honored guest and auxiliary to their union. Both women were passionately attached to Eleanor, adoring her when she was in their presence and pining for her when she went away. With her charisma and her prominent connections, her powerful will, and her extraordinary mind, she held her two friends in a kind of thrall. She knew it too. When she was absent from them, she was quick to swear her undying affection. "Much love to Nan & to you," she'd written to Marion at the end of a letter from *LaRooco* in the winter of 1926. "Life is quite empty without your dear presence."

This was a novel sensation for Mrs. Franklin Roosevelt—to be the one promising faithful feeling rather than the one in need of reassurance. Writing to Marion in May of 1926, she noted a trace of hurt feelings in her friend's last letter. It made her feel guilty. "I hate to think you have been unhappy dear," she wrote. "It is new for me to have anyone know when I have 'moods' much less have it make any real difference & if you'll try not to take them too seriously I'll try not to let myself have them." The previous summer, writing from Campobello, where she had taken her children for vacation, she told Marion how much she'd rather be alone with her two friends, forsaking the rest of the world. "Marion dearest," she wrote at the letter's end, "I love you and miss you and no amount of excitement could make me miss you less."

Did this love ever take physical form? Possibly. Eleanor's closest friends now included a number of women in long-term partnerships. Before Marion and Nancy, she had developed a close tie to the activist attorney Elizabeth Read and her partner, Esther Lape. Prominent women in their circles were adept at letting the world think one thing about the nature of their relationships while living another reality behind closed doors.

While it is possible that Eleanor and her friends played this game too, it is worth noting that Eleanor never displayed any self-consciousness about the nature of her connection to her female friends. At Val-Kill, where the embroidered linens read E M N (Eleanor, Marion, Nancy), she frequently brought her younger children to stay and even hosted her mother-in-law. "Eleanor is so happy over there that she looks well and plump," Sara wrote to Franklin after one visit in the summer of 1926. "Don't tell her so, it is very becoming, and I hope she will not grow thin."

Perhaps Eleanor's relations with the two women existed in a kind of middle place, a romance of passionate, if not erotic, intensity. Eleanor might well have appreciated the gray area. Up to then in her life, clearly defined relationships as Anna and Elliott's daughter, as Franklin's wife—had left her wanting. A more ambiguous, undefined connection allowed her to experience what she'd never had in her old ties: freedom. That, after all, was the great gift of her new life—freedom to live, most of the time, as she pleased.

Being Eleanor Roosevelt was now a sprawling enterprise, with commitments that seemed to increase by the hour. By the latter half of the decade, her impressive arsenal of titles included director of the Bureau of Women's Activities for the Democratic National Committee, finance chair of women's activities for the New York State Democrats, vice chair of the Women's City Club of New York, chair of the Non-Partisan Legislative Committee, board member of the Foreign Policy Association and of the City Housing Corporation. Presenting this list, her biographer Blanche Wiesen Cook concludes that, by 1928, Eleanor "held the most powerful positions ever held by a woman in party politics."

Amazingly, Eleanor found these obligations not enough to fill her time. Shortly after the completion of the cottage, she and Nancy and Marion launched Val-Kill Industries—a business that manufactured replicas of Early American furniture. It was a for-profit enterprise with broader, altruistic aims: The women envisioned factories in rural areas for young men in need of jobs. "Here was the answer to the problem of keeping the young men of the community from going to the city for work," Eleanor later said. "Teach them to build fine furniture, to be craftsmen." The business was part of a larger plan to reengineer the economy of the countryside. "There is a great acreage in the Hyde Park estate and I'd like to turn some of the back farms into experimental stations for girl farmers. They can do it. It's healthful, happy, fascinating work."

She had plans for young women in the city as well. In 1927, she and Marion and Nancy assumed control of Todhunter, a progressive Manhattan school for girls. For the remainder of the decade, she would balance her political commitments with several days a week of teaching English, history, and civics. There was a fitting symmetry in this role. In the midst of her unhappy childhood, Mademoiselle Souvestre's Allenswood had awakened her to the possibilities of the wider world. Now awakened once more, she shared those possibilities with the next generation.

Visiting Eleanor in these years, the writer S. J. Woolf marveled at her: "Seated at a small desk . . . she posed for a drawing, spoke about women in politics, answered innumerable phone calls, arranged for her son's departure from the city and directed household affairs; and all this before 10 o'clock in the morning, for at that time she had to leave to give a talk at the girls' school at which she teaches." Even her rare moments of relaxation were filled with work. At the end of one weekend, she wrote to Franklin of the joys of a "quiet evening" with Cook at Val-Kill: "I've written two editorials and three letters and we have had supper and the peace of it is divine."

Her energy was freed up by letting go of old anxieties. As a young woman, the proper management of a large household had vexed her. Now she gave it barely a thought. "It takes me exactly five minutes every morning to do my 'keeping' in this house," she told a reporter who visited her in Manhattan. "I've had my servants a great many years. They know exactly what is expected."

By the latter part of the 1920s, Eleanor had grown savvy in the management of her public profile. She was one of the first women to regularly speak about politics on the radio, participating in debates with Republican women leaders and delivering addresses on topics like "Increasing Power of Women in the World's Work." Women in politics, she knew, were usually covered by female reporters from the women's or society pages, whose editors expected copy filled with dresses, children, and chores. Eleanor understood that if she simply gave the reporters what they needed, they'd be happy to also include multiple paragraphs of her thoughts on serious topics.

So she developed a gift for the artful change of subject. One society reporter who visited Eleanor at East 65th Street in 1926 found herself treated to tea with the family, where conversation touched on vacation plans, French lessons, and the loneliness of "Chief," Anna's aging Belgian police dog. But when the children scurried off for a moment, Eleanor launched into a gripping explanation of the difficulties rural women faced in accessing healthcare and education—all of which the reporter included in her column. As a result, Eleanor delivered her political program to a whole audience of women who might have skipped over it had it appeared on the paper's front page.

This was a cornerstone of the politics she practiced: to go to women where they lived. In 1928, a reporter visited Eleanor's office in New York, where she was organizing campaigners for Al Smith. One volunteer was writing personal notes to the department-store buyers, mostly female, who'd come to New York from out of town to purchase their fall collections. The notes invited them to come in and hear about Smith. It was an efficient way to reach women nationwide. After all, the volunteer explained, "a buyer in a department store talks to more women than any other woman in town."

She caused a national stir in a 1928 article for *Redbook* in which she bluntly declared that women's suffrage had so far proved a failure. Women in both parties, she wrote, "have no actual influence or say at all." Indeed, "beneath the veneer of courtesy," women in politics encountered "a widespread male hostility—age-old, perhaps—against sharing with them any actual control."

The only solution was "to organize as women . . . and to pick efficient leaders—say two or three in each State—whom we will support and by whose decisions we will abide." With masses of votes to offer, "women bosses would be in a position to talk in terms of 'business' with the men leaders."

She still hated to see her picture in the papers. According to Joseph Lash, Eleanor's friend and biographer, she and Louis Howe would teasingly compete for who could take a worse picture. In the old days, the papers had always run the same gloomy portrait of her, with dark circles swallowing her eyes and her mouth half open as if in feeble protest. But the more she did in public life, the more frequently her picture was taken. Now people reading about Eleanor Roosevelt saw a woman whose piercing eyes looked like her famed Uncle Theodore's—touched by fire and hungry for life.

AS TIME WENT ON, Franklin's reports from Warm Springs emphasized the improvement of the colony more and more and improvements in his own physical condition less and less. While other patients who came to Warm Springs were having miraculous breakthroughs, abandoning wheelchairs, crutches, or braces once and for all, Franklin was not among them.

By the late summer of 1925, four years had passed since Franklin's initial infection with polio. Patients in recovery from polio have two kinds of affected muscles: those that have been damaged or weakened, and those that have been functionally destroyed. A sustained period of physical therapy could help people whose paralysis was caused chiefly by weakness. What it could not do was bring back destroyed tissue.

Thus, even as he promoted the resort in the press and exaggerated his progress to his friends, he began to look for other methods. He knew that Warm Springs wouldn't be enough. This had become his practice, in accordance with the "philosophy" Uncle Fred Delano had shared with him in the first days of his illness. Outward: pure confidence and optimism. Inside: unsparing truth.

In the summer of 1925, after his second long visit to Georgia, he traveled to the town of Marion on the south coast of Massachusetts, where William McDonald, a charismatic and strong-willed neurologist, ran a rehabilitative clinic. Franklin quickly fell under his spell, in part because the doctor's method confirmed Franklin's own prior prejudices. "Braces are of course laid aside," he wrote to Sara in late August from Marion. "He is hot against them and confirms what I have told you for two years and you would not believe." With the blessing of Van Lear Black, his understanding employer at the F&D, he stayed at the clinic through the fall of 1925.

Like the other experts Franklin had worked with, McDonald emphasized finding ways to exercise afflicted muscles without crushing them under body weight. While the weather stayed warm, Franklin spent his mornings splashing around in Buzzards Bay. But McDonald broke with standard thinking about the prospects of nonresponsive tissue. Nerves, he believed, were more likely to revive when the regions of the brain that fired them expected them to function. To that end, he viewed leg braces as counterproductive—the brain didn't task muscles with work that it knew the braces could handle.

At McDonald's urging, Franklin tried daring, precarious positions, being placed erect on both feet with only a single cane to support him. Yet in his heart, where he would not fool himself, Franklin must have been skeptical. The "walking" he was doing was nothing like what he'd seen Louis Joseph and other recovered paralytics perform. When he returned home to Hyde Park that winter, his everyday mobility had not demonstrably improved from where it had been before he left. His second trip to the clinic the following summer yielded even less exciting results. In time, the doctor's spell wore off entirely.

In fact, if there was any one person responsible for helping Franklin make progress in this period, it was neither an orthopedist nor a neurologist but a physical therapist named Alice Lou Plastridge, who had achieved national renown for her work with paralysis patients.

Plastridge came to stay with the Roosevelts at Hyde Park for a brief period in late 1925 and early 1926. On her arrival at Springwood, she was greeted enthusiastically by Eleanor, Anna, and Sara. Franklin was on the other side of the house when she entered, but powerful men have a knack for noticing when a fuss is being made over someone other than themselves. Plastridge found him waiting in the library, feigning exasperation. "Aren't you *ever* going to come and speak to me?"

Plastridge's method focused on helping patients make the best use of the functioning muscles they already had. She was an expert at studying a patient's gait to determine what muscles they had the use of and whether they were putting too much or too little strain on them. The goal was not normal walking but walking that appeared normal and felt easy.

After a few days at Hyde Park, Plastridge was surprised at how little of this compensating work Franklin had learned in the past four years. With his crutches, "he would pound on the floor," she later observed. "His arms were enormously strong," but "his hands always shook and he used everything with great force."

Plastridge knew that for Franklin to make progress, she had to push him out of the comfortable habits he had developed over the previous four years. Arriving for therapy one morning, she found him in bed with a bad back.

"What are you here for? Have you forgotten about my back?" Franklin snapped.

"Will it hurt your back to move your toes?" Plastridge asked him.

"Yes," said an indignant Franklin, "it will."

"Then you're not doing it right," Plastridge replied.

This was the heart of Plastridge's teaching—to help patients focus their minds on individual muscles needed for motion rather than taxing all muscles at once. Under her instruction, Franklin learned to shift his weight from the hips as he moved forward on crutches, rather than swaying his body wildly as his legs moved behind. Using these techniques, his crutch-walking was transformed from the heavy struggle that it had been at the 1924 convention into something more sedate in appearance and far easier to endure.

Still, Franklin was not ready to devote himself entirely to the Plastridge method. At its heart, Plastridge's plan was based on the belief that Franklin's damaged muscles were not going to come back. He would not, she believed, ever really "walk" on his own again.

———

IN APRIL OF 1927, Paul Hasbrouck, the recovering polio patient from Poughkeepsie with whom Franklin had corresponded, at last arrived in Warm Springs for several weeks of treatment. "Our rate is $42 a week," Franklin had written to him earlier in the spring, "this including board, lodging, medical and therapeutic treatment, pool charges, etc.—in fact, everything except your traveling expenses and cigarette money! I hope you can come soon."

Arriving at the colony, Hasbrouck found a place coming into its own. Earlier that year, an American Orthopedic Association study had concluded that the Warm Springs method had in fact demonstrably improved the conditions of its patients. The official sanction, along with Franklin's ardent publicizing, had flooded the place with new patients. Everything was new: The strong sulfur smell from the waters now mingled with the scent of newly seeded grass and fresh paint.

Franklin, who had already been in Georgia for a month, was summoned north a few days after Hasbrouck's arrival. On his way to the station, Franklin spotted the young man and shouted from the car, "I'll be back in ten days!" But whether he was physically in Warm Springs or not, Franklin's presence was everywhere. Warm Springs patients' days followed the pattern Franklin had established for himself in the first years of his illness. At ten each morning, following a leisurely breakfast, patients were driven down to the pool. After entering the pool via a gradual slope, guests spent the morning engaged in physical therapy. Early afternoons were for rest and sunbaths. From three to four o'clock, patients practiced their walking under the supervision of Warm Springs staff, who critiqued and corrected technique. There were rails, Hasbrouck explained, "for those, like Mr. Roosevelt, who need something to take hold of on both sides; but the aim is to become independent of the rails." In the evenings, patients gathered for meals and card games. On days of poor weather, they were taken out in motor cars to explore the surrounding countryside.

Decades before, Franklin's father had urged the guild at St. James'

Church to "help all who are suffering." Service had ostensibly been Franklin's reason for pursuing public life. But it had always seemed self-evident that to do good, he must *first* become great. The true guiding force of his public career had not been service but the public career itself.

His work at Warm Springs was something different. This was service when no one was watching, service for its own sake. There was no grand scheme guiding the hours he spent absorbed in the particular problems of individual patients at the colony; the path to his own glory was not evident when any one of them made progress. As the years went by, the waters of Warm Springs did not bring Franklin's legs back to life. Instead, they awakened something else in him: awareness of other people's pain, and awareness of his own ability to ease it.

IN NOVEMBER 1927, ELEANOR traveled to Warm Springs. There, she and Franklin hosted the staff and patients, eighty of them, for a large Thanksgiving celebration. She was deeply moved by what she saw. "The complete gallantry of all the patients always brought a choke to my throat," she later wrote. "Some of them were on stretchers, some in wheelchairs, some on crutches. Some hoped to get well, many faced permanent handicaps, but all were cheerful that one evening at least."

For all the changes in her life, Mrs. Franklin Roosevelt's identity was still chiefly defined by the man to whom she was married. She continued to believe in Franklin's political career and the importance of her supporting it, if only because it would structure his days and guide his recovery. Part of her believed—or at least claimed in public to believe—that the wife of a politician had an obligation to subordinate her own views in service of her husband's career. In a 1928 pamphlet, she wrote approvingly of how, when several friends of Al Smith's had disparaged one of his policies, his wife, Catherine, had "turned quite pink" and chided them: "You must not say that, the governor is always right." Eleanor went on to bemoan how many public men "suffer because their wives cannot hide their own personal likes and dislikes."

Yet she was not afraid to at times break publicly with her husband. As the 1928 campaign approached, Franklin remained opposed to prohibition (even as he tried to downplay his opposition, to mollify Democratic Drys). Eleanor, the child of an addict father, remained in favor of banning alcohol. "We don't always agree politically, my husband and I," she told a reporter. "I'm a Dry . . . in practice as well as in theory."

Every so often she showed hints of irritation at being consigned to her husband's shadow. In January of 1925, while she was working at the New York Democratic headquarters, a reporter poking around the office wanted to interview her for a feature on "Wives of Great Men." Eleanor was brusque: "I can only give you two minutes." The reporter tried to make her questions quick.

"What are Mr. Roosevelt's hobbies?" she asked.

"He has no hobbies," Eleanor replied.

This was a startling statement to make about Franklin—how to explain all the hours he had spent stamp-collecting, designing and building toy boats, researching naval and Hudson Valley history, if not in pursuit of a hobby?

The reporter kept prospecting: "Does he like the theater?"

"No," said Eleanor.

"Reading?"

"No."

"Games?"

"No."

"Clothes?"

"No."

The reporter was growing desperate: "Has he any outstanding idiosyncrasies of any kind whatsoever?"

"No."

The reporter began to worry there was nothing remotely interesting to say about Franklin. But then Eleanor went on.

"He did like golf," she said, "before he was sick. He can't play now."

The reporter finished the interview, perhaps unaware of how close she had come to the splendid feast of rage that Mrs. Franklin Roosevelt usually kept to herself. It *was* rage, born righteous in the Lucy Mercer days, never fully to depart. Her smoldering antipathy toward Franklin had, in its way, provided yet another passage to her liberation. His betrayal had freed her from the illusion of the perfect Franklin. After Lucy, she could assess him more clinically, more clearly see the defects behind his virtues. If he was energetic, he was also flighty. If his mind was supple, it was also undisciplined. If he was charming, he was also shallow and vain.

Yet her heart was not so hardened that she could not see the truth—that if the years had changed her, they had also changed Franklin. He was more serious now and more focused. He was aware of, and interested in, a wider world than he had been before. He read more books, took an interest in a wider range of people, and had gotten better at learning from them. She marveled at his ability to glean information; topics that others would have to carefully study, he could master through a single conversation.

She noted too how he'd gained remarkable powers of self-control. Before, things had come easily to him; he saw what he wanted and took it, with little waiting involved. But that would not work in the years after polio. It had been clear in the early days that to make improvements he would have to learn patience—and he had. She admired his capacity to banish worry, his unique ability to "pull a curtain down and go to sleep."

In truth, the things that had once made marriage to Franklin so frustrating—his emotional distance, his refusal to talk about unpleasant things—now made it easier for her to live the life of her choosing. If he kept things to himself, he also did not ask too many questions or bother her with complaints. Certainly Franklin was aware that Marion and Nancy were not everyone's cup of tea. "Parlor pinks," his half brother, Rosy, called them; "she-men," said Louis. But rarely, if ever, did Franklin object to them.

To the contrary, he embraced Eleanor's dear ones as if they were

Raised under the vigilant, adoring gaze of his parents, James and Sara Roosevelt, Franklin Roosevelt developed a talent for pleasing others—and for concealing his true feelings. Pictured here: Franklin as a toddler; at age 16 months, held by James; and at age 11, with Sara.

A young Eleanor Roosevelt with her father, Elliott Roosevelt. Elliott was Teddy Roosevelt's younger brother, charming and troubled.

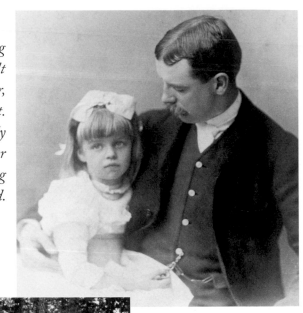

A traumatic, love-starved childhood left Eleanor shy, frightened, and unsure of herself.

Marie Souvestre, the formidable head of the Allenswood school in England, Eleanor's safe haven and salvation following the death of her parents. Souvestre introduced Eleanor to the life of the mind and the possibilities of the world.

A young Eleanor with her soon-to-be mother-in-law, Sara Roosevelt. James Roosevelt, Eleanor's son, later observed that his mother lacked "confidence in her ability" as a parent. Sara, on the other hand, "had confidence in her own ability to do anything."

A Campobello summer, 1910: Franklin (age 28) lounging with Eleanor (25), and in the waves with daughter, Anna (4).

*"The Next Roosevelt":
As the young and
energetic assistant
secretary of the Navy,
Franklin styled him-
self in the image of his
famed cousin, Teddy
Roosevelt. Pictured
climbing a Navy ship's
rigging in 1913, and
with Teddy in 1915.*

Lucy Mercer, the Washington socialite whose romance with Franklin nearly brought the Roosevelts' marriage to an end.

A Roosevelt family portrait in the unhappy period after Franklin's affair. Clockwise from top left, Franklin, Sara, Eleanor, and children James, Anna, John, Franklin Jr., and Elliott. Only Sara and Chief, the family's Belgian police dog, appear content.

Franklin campaigning as the 1920 Democratic candidate for vice president, with the presidential candidate, Ohio governor James M. Cox.

Franklin touring a Boy Scout camp at Bear Mountain, New York, July 1921. Most likely, he came into contact with the polio virus during this expedition.

The Roosevelt cottage on Campobello Island, scene of the terrifying first weeks of Franklin's illness with polio in August 1921.

Franklin with sons Franklin Jr. and John in one of the first photographs after his illness.

The heavy steel braces that Franklin used to support his legs. Wearing leg braces was a source of torment for Franklin in the early years of his recovery, a constant reminder of his upended life.

Franklin in 1924 with his closest adviser, Louis Howe. In the difficult early days of Franklin's recovery, Howe offered an alluring plan for Franklin's return to politics and his eventual rise to the presidency.

At the 1924 Democratic convention, Franklin used crutches to slowly cross the stage at Madison Square Garden. Then he delivered a moving and rousing speech. "I never was present at so fine a display of high mental courage," wrote one journalist who witnessed the scene.

Franklin poolside during his first stay at Warm Springs, Georgia, in October 1924. A visit to Warm Springs from a journalist that month resulted in all-too-revealing national coverage of Franklin's disability and his plans for recuperation.

at 120 Broadway, N.Y.C.,
January 5, 1925.

Dear Mr. Hasbrouck:

How are you getting on? I hope your legs are improving as fast as mine are. I should much like to tell you about Warm Springs, Georgia and how much it helped me this autumn. I am going back there next April. I shall be at Hyde Park over New Years.

I am returning Dr. Bidou's letter which I forgot to send you last spring.

Very sincerely yours,

Mr. Paul D. Hasbrouck,
Poughkeepsie, New York.

A letter to Paul Hasbrouck, one of many fellow polio victims with whom Franklin corresponded during his years of convalescence. Polio opened his eyes to other people's suffering and his own ability to ease it.

Eleanor Roosevelt in 1925, already a public figure with her own political base. Her husband's illness helped propel Eleanor into a new life as a political organizer and progressive activist.

Eleanor with close friends Nancy Cook (left) and Marion Dickerman (center). The three women shared the stone cottage at Val-Kill, Eleanor's private haven on the Roosevelt Hyde Park estate, a symbol of her hard-won independent life.

Franklin seaside in 1924 with friends including Marguerite "Missy" LeHand (left), his assistant and closest companion LeHand's intimate devotion to Franklin helped Franklin and Eleanor reinvent their partnership and lead often-separate lives.

The patients' pool at Warm Springs in the late 1920s, Franklin's attachment to his work at Warm Springs contributed to his reluctance to re-enter the political fray in 1928.

Franklin at the wedding of his daughter, Anna, and son-in-law, Curtis Dall, in 1926.

*Franklin with his predecessor as New York governor, Al Smith.
A one-time ally, Smith came to resent Franklin's success and
fought bitterly to prevent his ascent to the presidency.*

*Frances Perkins, the
Democratic activist and
later Franklin's labor
secretary. "I would like to
think that he would have
done the things he did
without his paralysis,"
she observed of Franklin,
"but . . . I don't think
he would have unless
somebody had dealt him a
blow between the eyes."*

Across the early decades of the twentieth century, publisher William Randolph Hearst leveraged his vast fortune and media empire to bend the political system to his will. In the summer of 1932, an eleventh-hour deal with Hearst saved Franklin's presidential candidacy from ruin.

Franklin's traveling campaign party in the fall of 1932. In the front row, with glasses, is Joseph P. Kennedy, an emerging Democratic power broker and the key emissary between Hearst and Roosevelt.

Forgoing custom, Franklin flew to Chicago to receive in person his party's nomination for the presidency. "Let it be the task of our party to break foolish traditions," he told his audience. "We will break these traditions and leave it to the Republican Party to break promises."

Eleanor with Lorena Hickok, the campaign reporter with whom Eleanor formed an intimate bond.

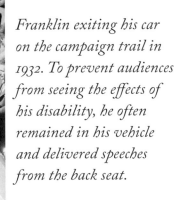

Franklin exiting his car on the campaign trail in 1932. To prevent audiences from seeing the effects of his disability, he often remained in his vehicle and delivered speeches from the back seat.

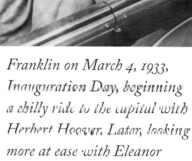

Franklin on March 4, 1933, Inauguration Day, beginning a chilly ride to the capital with Herbert Hoover. Later, looking more at ease with Eleanor and son James.

Franklin delivering his "Fear Itself" inaugural address. The reading copy of his speech shows the first sentence—"This is a day of consecration"—added at the last minute in Franklin's own hand.

INAUGURAL ADDRESS OF
PRESIDENT FRANKLIN D. ROOSEVELT
MARCH 4, 1933.

This is a day of consecration.

    I am certain that my fellow Americans expect that on my induction
into the Presidency I will address them with a candor and a decision which
the present situation of our nation impels. This is preeminently the
time to speak the truth, the whole truth, frankly and boldly. Nor need
we shrink from honestly facing conditions in our country today. This
great nation will endure as it has endured, will revive and will prosper.
So first of all let me assert my firm belief that the only thing we have
to fear is fear itself, — nameless, unreasoning, unjustified terror which
paralyzes needed efforts to convert retreat into advance. In every dark
hour of our national life a leadership of frankness and vigor has met with
that understanding and support of the people themselves which is essential
to victory. I am convinced that you will again give that support to
leadership in these critical days.

    In such a spirit on my part and on yours we face our common difficulties.
They concern, thank God, only material things. Values have shrunken to
fantastic levels; taxes have risen; our ability to pay has fallen;
government of all kinds is faced by serious curtailment of income; the

*Eleanor visiting a Bonus Army camp outside Washington in 1933.
The transformation in her life following Franklin's illness helped make
Eleanor perhaps the most influential First Lady in American history.*

*Franklin outside the "Little White House" at Warm Springs, in 1935.
From his battle back from polio, he gleaned a set of principles for
sustaining hope that would form the backbone of the New Deal.*

equally dear to him. Before one of Eleanor's visits to Warm Springs, Franklin wrote to the two other residents of Val-Kill Cottage. "A great deal of love to you both," he concluded. "I wish you could be here too. Perhaps next year we can make it a real family party." Missy wrote her own note on the letter: "Dear Nan & Marion: I just want to send my love to you both, also. I wish you were both coming. It will be nice to have Mrs. Roosevelt."

Franklin and Eleanor had found their way to what they needed—separate, distinct lives joined by pathways of shared service and shared ambition. And by shared affection too. They spent less time together than ever before, but the years of illness and recovery had brought them "much closer into a very real partnership," their daughter, Anna, would later say. "Their overall goals were very much the same. They had a great deal in common, a great deal to talk about."

Hardship had opened their eyes to their own potential. Years later, Eleanor would write that Franklin's illness had been "a blessing in disguise, for it gave him strength and courage he had not had before. He had had to think out the fundamentals of living and learn the greatest of all lessons—infinite patience and never-ending persistence." She'd had to do all those things as well.

Her old pain never really went away. In 1926, the poet Virginia Moore published a volume, *Not Poppy,* to strong reviews. Eleanor clipped the final lines of one poem to save:

> . . . *The soul that had believed*
> *And was deceived*
> *Ends by believing more*
> *Than ever before.*

On her clipping, Eleanor wrote "1918," the year when she'd discovered Franklin's betrayal with Lucy.

Franklin and Eleanor's relationship had been born of genuine love. But the things that were supposed to make them a good match—their shared family and social standing—had not delivered a durable happiness. Indeed, they had obscured the vast differences in their emotional makeup, differences that made the early years of their marriage so unhappy. Now, in midlife, they at last discovered what they truly had in common. Franklin and Eleanor Roosevelt were both brave enough to remake their lives anew.

THEIR CHILDREN, MEANWHILE, STRUGGLED to find their way in these years. Both Franklin and Eleanor were away from home often. Neither parent appears to have felt much guilt over that fact. The more years Eleanor spent as a mother, the more she came to feel it was bad for parents to spend their lives hovering over their offspring, that children did better when they did not feel they were at the center of their parents' world. She admired and agreed with an article by Angelo Patri, the educator and expert in child psychology. "You are entitled to one life," Patri told parents, "your own. Live it, start the children on their way and then plunge back into your own again."

Still, an unmistakable pain runs through the children's letters in the early- and mid-1920s. "The night that John came here he cried for you," eight-year-old Franklin Jr. wrote to his parents in 1922, referring to his six-year-old younger brother, the baby of the family. "I hope that you are coming soon." Three years later, he wrote to his sister, Anna, about her dog. "Chief is very well but seems to grow more and more lonesome, like me and Johnny. The house seems just like an empty wastebasket. Now that Father has left, Mother seems always to be on the go."

It was more than just time apart that upset the family order. Indeed, it was the teenage children—Anna, James, and Elliott—who seemed most to mind the new regime. They were old enough to remember the old days, when the family had their own private life. Now nearly everything was public; intruders and interlopers everywhere. With the world forced to come to him, Franklin's attendants and retainers were a permanent presence around the houses in Manhattan and Hyde Park. Eleanor's political friends were ubiquitous too. Anna would later reflect that her parents, with their many responsibilities, did not have "time available to think . . . about their teenage children as they were growing up and their problems.... That just didn't happen in our family." Franklin and Eleanor "were driven by their destinies," James Roosevelt would write, "and we raced along behind them."

In her public appearances, Eleanor spoke enthusiastically of the changes in the lives of women. Yet she seems to have had little interest in helping her own daughter find her way. After Anna graduated from Miss Chapin's School, Sara insisted that she spend the summer season in Newport, where she would have a society debut. Anna, who loathed the idea of gowns and gloves, protested to her mother, who, surprisingly, backed up her mother-in-law in advocating a debut.

Eleanor "didn't help me a bit," Anna would later say. The result was "a very difficult atmosphere to think through. Because on the one hand, here were my parents with their political and social views, and the people and the conversations I was listening to at meals; and, on the other hand, here I was being *forced*. I couldn't go out with a young man without a chaperone."

Ultimately, it was the memory of pain that helped mother and daughter to form a more meaningful connection. When Anna was twenty years old, she came home from a night out and found her mother waiting up for her. It was late, but Eleanor was in a cozy, confiding mood. As the early-morning hours slipped away, mother told daughter of Lucy Mercer, of the affair that had nearly ended her marriage, of the pain she had felt and how she'd found her resolve to go on.

Anna had already gathered pieces of the story from a gossipy relative. But hearing it from her mother's lips was like turning on the lights in a room. So often in those years she'd found her mother inscrutable, while her father remained the romantic hero of her childhood. Now she began to see things through Eleanor's eyes and began to take Eleanor's part. "I was *mad*," she later told the writer Bernard Asbell, "mad at Father for having at one time hurt Mother."

Anna enrolled in college courses at Cornell but stayed for less than a year; by the spring of 1926, she was engaged to marry Curtis Dall, a Princeton-educated Lehman Brothers stockbroker. Ten years her senior, Dall was conventional and unlikely to be a portal to a new world.

She was married in St. James' Church, Hyde Park, in June of that year. Her veil, wreathed in orange blossoms, was rose point lace, the same lace that her mother and her mother's mother had worn on their wedding days. In photos from the day, she stared soberly, straight into the camera. Like the two women who'd worn the veil before her, she was twenty years old, without a college education, and soon to be with child.

IN THE YEARS 1926 through 1928, Franklin devoted more energy to Warm Springs than he had to any endeavor outside politics in his adult life. He spent 150 days there in the year 1927 alone. Ironically, in this same period his political fortunes prospered as never before. The affection he prompted with his speech at the 1924 convention had generated a warm afterglow, whose heat seemed only to strengthen with time.

Franklin became a figure of consensus, the thing everyone seemed to think the Democratic Party now needed most. "Unity" was the new party watchword after the catastrophic 1924 convention, and in his strategically timed public appearances, Franklin made sure it was always on his lips. "Democratic success," he told an audience of Georgia Democrats in early 1927, depends on the "hope the party will present a militant and united front."

Nothing helped enhance his image more than his frequent trips below the Mason–Dixon line. If southerners in the party saw Smith and his supporters as foreign devils, they came to view Franklin as an altogether different sort of New Yorker. In *The Atlanta Constitution*, he was not a visiting New Yorker but "the New York–Georgia-farmer-politician" whom Georgians loved "as one of our very own."

He was happy to encourage the perception. In a column he wrote for *The Macon Telegraph*, he aped southern sensibilities, fondly recalling a visit to "Jefferson Davis's splendid home." In one column, he told readers of a trip he'd made to the top of Georgia's Pine Mountain. "There, stretching out for many miles to the horizon, was a large portion of Meriwether County. It was good looking country—and good to live in."

It bears noting that when Franklin gazed out approvingly from Pine Mountain, he was looking at a landscape of racial segregation, where white supremacy was enforced by brutal violence. He could not have been oblivious to the fact—black people lived in and around Warm Springs, maintaining its grounds and cleaning its facilities. In his 1953 account of Franklin's years at Warm Springs, Turnley Walker pointed out that the poolside area and dressing rooms were tended by a black woman known as "Aunt Sarah." "She loved the pool," Walker wrote, "even though, since it was for white folks only, she had never felt the water on her body."

Franklin's letters from the period leave little trace of a man bothered by the way Georgia treated its black citizens. This was not unusual—wealthy white northerners in the 1920s, progressive or otherwise, were mostly indifferent to the cause of racial justice. Still, the irony is striking. Warm Springs did so much to open his eyes to the suffering of others; it replenished his sense of obligation to those who had less than he. And yet the suffering of Georgia's black population does not appear to have fired his conscience in these years.

The uncomfortable reality is that advocating for racial justice would have complicated Franklin's planned return to politics. Public criticism of Jim Crow would have alienated him from influential southern Democrats. When he made his call for "unity" in the party, he was implicitly saying the party ought to put aside divisive fights over not just prohibition but matters of race and religion as well. Making it clear he was not interested in challenging their customs, Franklin gave white southerners permission to accept him as a northerner with whom they could do business.

His physical condition was now a central part of his public image. Press accounts of his recovery continued to be overly optimistic: He would walk with a single cane, the papers claimed, when in fact he was still struggling to make his way on two crutches. One newspaper account promised to describe "How Hot Sun and Water—Nothing

Else!—Cured Franklin Roosevelt's Paralysis," even as his paralysis remained essentially unchanged.

Democratic leaders spoke of him as a potential nominee for the presidency, perhaps in 1928. He had pledged himself to Smith, who was mounting an organized effort to be the nominee that year. But if the South and West once again deemed Smith an unacceptable choice, Franklin was thought to be a logical compromise candidate. Franklin protested he had no interest in running for anything in 1928, even after Coolidge, the popular incumbent, announced that he would not seek reelection that year. Franklin explained that his work at Warm Springs helping others was too consuming and too important for him to resume his political efforts.

Naturally, his reluctance enhanced his political profile even more. "Helping humanity more satisfying than helping himself," one newspaper editorial remarked. "Giving scientific discovery to the future more vital than rolling up headlines on page one—that's IDEALISM."

THE REAL EXPLANATION FOR Franklin's reluctance to reenter politics was the same as it had been since 1921. He still believed he needed to recover more. With the help of Helena Mahoney, the chief physical therapist at Warm Springs, he had improved his technique on crutches and canes. But he was not ready to give up the idea of the greater breakthrough. He still believed he could walk again, with time.

Louis, tending to his political profile, told him there was no rush. His plan for Franklin called for a run for the New York governorship in 1930 or 1932 and a run for the presidency in 1936. In the meantime, it was best to remain unavailable. When Franklin went to appear before a group of New York pols, Louis advised him to "assure them that you are still nigh death's door for the next two years. Please try and look pallid, and worn, and weary . . ."

As 1928 dawned, Al Smith's presidential campaign began in earnest. But Franklin's thoughts remained in Georgia. Edsel Ford, the president of his family's motor company, had visited the colony and agreed to pay for the construction of a heated enclosure for the swimming pool, making it possible to swim in the waters on even the coldest days of winter. The water, Franklin still believed, would deliver him from his disability. If he could only have more time.

Time, his old enemy. In the past, he had made every effort to keep up with its swift progress and still found himself left behind. The dilemma he was about to face would be altogether new: what to do when the march of events and the busy world slowed down for him and commanded him to get on board.

Chapter 23

The Call

I N THE SUMMER OF 1928, THE DEMOCRATIC PARTY GATHERED in Houston, where it tapped Al Smith to be its nominee for president, running against the Republican secretary of commerce, Herbert Hoover. The women's committee was fully engaged in the fall campaign, organizing volunteers for Smith nationwide. All of those volunteers were female. "Women, women, women," a reporter wrote, "hundreds of women, thousands of women, laughing, chatting, drawing off their gloves, tucking jocks of hair up under their hats." At the center of the effort, seated behind a desk "equipped with [one of] those one-hand French telephones you see in the movies," was the leader of the committee: Eleanor Roosevelt.

The person describing this scene was Lorena Hickok. In August, Hickok, a veteran reporter for the Associated Press, had gone to visit the headquarters of the National Women's Committee of the Democratic Party in Manhattan's General Motors building. The office was spartanly decorated and smelled of fresh plaster, but it pulsed with activity. Hickok was impressed—Eleanor, she wrote, was "tall, quiet, dignified, soft voiced and deliberate in speech and manner." She was, along with her counterpart in the Republican Party, Pauline Sabin, one of "the two most powerful women leaders in America."

Franklin too was working for Smith, though with less ardor than was his wife. In Houston, he had reprised his 1924 performance as Smith's nominator from New York State. Once more, he had pulled off a brilliant, unexpected performance. Reporters and party stalwarts had remarked on the noticeable improvement in his appearance. With his skin baked by the Georgia sun, he looked far less sickly than he had four years before. He looked considerably more formidable too—his upper body filled out and muscular, his face broadened, his neck thick. Most dramatic of all, he had disposed of his crutches. Gripping the arm of one of his sons—this time seventeen-year-old Elliott—he'd approached the podium using only a single cane, with a gait that appeared smooth and unbothered.

Though it lacked the drama of his Madison Square Garden appearance, Franklin's speech was a rousing hit. Knowing what people wanted to hear, he concluded with a phrase from his earlier address: "Victory is his habit—the happy warrior: Alfred E. Smith!" The "happy warrior" line had become not only a shorthand for Smith but the most famous phrase Franklin had ever uttered.

In fact, Franklin was devoting far less of his life to Smith's effort in 1928 than he had in the previous election. In 1924 he had tolerated serving as a figurehead leader of the Smith effort, because it helped him prove he was still in the game. By 1928 he no longer needed the publicity, and he wanted no credit for the Smith presidential strategy. Privately, he did not have high hopes for his fellow New Yorker. His time in the South had impressed on him just how deep was the antipathy for a Tammany-backed New York Catholic opposed to prohibition. He continued to marvel at how little effort Smith made to broaden his appeal beyond his New York demographic. When Smith chose the businessman John Jakob Raskob—an exemplar of the dreaded New York values so detested in the South and West—to be the party's campaign chairman, Franklin wrote to Van Lear Black: "I do not know yet what the effect will be except that a number of southern states are in almost open revolt. . . . Smith is burning his bridges behind him."

As summer turned to fall, the campaign turned vicious, with Klan-backed attacks on Smith's Catholicism. Fantastical rumors spread through the South and West: Should Smith be elected, the pope would have dominion over American policy; Protestant marriages might be declared null and void. It was, Franklin knew, the dark underside of the Republican campaign, paired with the GOP's chief message: that a vote for Hoover would be a vote for continued prosperity. As the stock market continued its climb upward, Franklin believed that message would be hard to beat. Voters liked Hoover and, in Franklin's view, he was well prepared for the presidency. Too close an association with Smith's nearly-certain-to-lose effort offered Franklin little gain.

There was talk of New York Democrats drafting Franklin to run as their candidate for governor to replace Smith that year. It was the old strategy—let Franklin find the upstate Democratic votes to pad Smith's margin below the Bronx County line and thus deliver New York State's electoral votes. (Franklin's Protestantism, too, was seen as a necessary counterweight to Smith.) The chatter was loud enough to concern Louis Howe. Ever the careful planner, he did not like the idea of Franklin returning to the stump ahead of schedule. Besides, he told Franklin, 1928 was a bad year to run as a Democrat. Franklin heeded his advice and decided to head to Warm Springs, as far from Smith as he could get.

Arriving in mid-September, he felt the embrace of his surroundings and was immediately certain he'd made the right choice. "The weather is heavenly," he wrote to Sara. "The new winter pool comes along well and will be ready in a month." A whole winter's worth of practice walking in the pool—his mind raced with the possibilities. He had made better progress with his cane techniques in the past year than at any point since he'd first come to Warm Springs. Another year of concerted work, he believed, and he would truly, finally, be able to walk on his own.

And so, that fall, Eleanor was once more the principal representative of the Roosevelt family at the heart of a political campaign, arriving at Democratic headquarters in the midday after teaching her classes at Todhunter and then working late into the night. Still, to most of the men on the campaign, her chief value was in being Mrs. Franklin Roosevelt. And by the last week of September, they had concluded that having Mrs. Franklin Roosevelt in their corner was a very valuable thing indeed.

Interest in Franklin as a gubernatorial candidate grew with Smith's troubles. Smith's problems in the South and West were so severe that it would not be possible for him to win the presidency without New York's forty-five electoral votes. His advisers all believed he *needed* a strong gubernatorial candidate from upstate on his ticket to help get him over the top. Franklin, they agreed, was the only logical choice.

Smith was not nearly so enthusiastic about the idea. THE REAL PRESSURE COMES FROM LEADERS AND JOB HOLDERS, Louis Howe told Franklin in a telegram to Warm Springs. GOVERNOR DOES NOT REALLY CONSIDER YOUR NOMINATION VITAL TO HIS PERSONAL SUCCESS. Smith's reticence was rooted in a number of factors. He couldn't quite accept that he needed anyone's help winning the Empire State. Furthermore, he had been elected governor of New York four times and had strong ideas of how the job ought to be done. He wanted a successor who owed him things, a man he could influence, if not control. Franklin was not that.

But his primary objection to the idea was more basic and more base: *How weak would he appear if he had to seek help from a cripple?* Franklin's frequent protestations that he needed more time to focus on his recovery proved his point. Franklin simply wasn't up to the job of governor—he had said it himself.

All the same, to appease his managers, Smith called Eleanor from the campaign trail to see if Franklin couldn't be convinced. She demurred, saying *he*, not she, must speak to Franklin. Yes, but couldn't she prevail on her husband, Smith wondered. No, she told him, she would not. She knew what Franklin's wishes were. However much she wanted to help Smith's candidacy, she would not abuse her role as Franklin's wife.

They left it there, but Eleanor was a shrewd-enough politician to see that the issue wasn't settled. And she was a shrewd-enough student of her husband's nature to wonder if, deep down, his true wishes were probably more complicated than he'd let on.

The last weekend in September, she boarded a train for Rochester in western New York. There, New York State Democrats would hold their own convention and choose their gubernatorial nominee for the

November ballot. As the state's most prominent female Democrat, Eleanor knew she was duty-bound to go, but she would have preferred to skip it. "Everyone makes me so uncomfortable," she wrote to Franklin. "They feel so strongly about your running and even good explanations can be made to sound foolish."

By long practice, the most important words that passed between Franklin and Eleanor were the ones left unspoken. Receiving her letter in Georgia, Franklin would have noticed what she *wasn't* saying: what exactly *Eleanor* thought he should do.

ON THE LAST MORNING in September, a Sunday, New York Democrats arrived in Rochester and gathered in the lobby of the Hotel Seneca, all of them eager to discuss the one big piece of drama surrounding the convention: who should be the party's gubernatorial nominee. Smith was said to like State Supreme Court justice Townsend Scudder. Others thought Herbert Lehman, a Smith backer and scion of the famed New York banking family, would be the choice. But the consensus was that Franklin Roosevelt would be the ideal man for the job. As happens in such settings, half-true rumors and speculative fancies, when combined with idle hours and alcohol, began to make a new reality.

By the early hours of Monday morning, when the morning edition of the Rochester *Democrat and Chronicle* reached the lobbies, it had fully formed. GROWTH OF ROOSEVELT'S BOOM MAIN DEMOCRATIC DEVELOPMENT, the four-column headline blared.

Louis, still in Manhattan but, as always, at the nexus of press and politician gossip, was getting anxious. He remained convinced that a run that year would prove calamitous. Still, he knew that Franklin Roosevelt's real intentions were never plain, not even to those closest to him. He noted, uneasily, that though he had implored Franklin to release an unqualified statement declaring himself unavailable for the governorship, Franklin had yet to do so. Louis blitzed Warm Springs with anxious telegrams, reporting on newspaper rumors that Franklin was secretly planning to run. PLEASE LET ME KNOW IF YOUR DECISION

NOT TO RUN IS STILL FINAL. He was right to be concerned: The Roosevelt boom had even found its way into Franklin's own family. GO AHEAD AND TAKE IT, Anna enthusiastically wired her father. (YOU OUGHT TO BE SPANKED, was his reply.)

The Democratic presidential candidate arrived in Rochester on Monday morning. At the Hotel Seneca, in his fifth-floor suite, Al Smith found a message from Franklin waiting for him: "Confirming my telephone message, I wish much that I might even consider the possibility of running for Governor this year, especially if by doing so I could further help you. . . . My doctors are very definite in stating that the continued improvement in my condition is dependent on my avoidance of cold climate and on taking exercise here at Warm Springs during the cold winter months. It probably means getting rid of leg braces during next two Winters and that would be impossible [if] I had to remain in Albany. As I am only 46 years of age, I feel that I owe it to my family and myself to give the present constant improvement a chance to continue."

But Smith's political advisers, along with top party bosses from around the state, were now convinced that a Roosevelt candidacy was essential. The ticket needed a Protestant anti-Tammany candidate from upstate. Word from the delegates was that only Franklin would do. Franklin would "make a good candidate," said Smith's lieutenant Robert Moses, "but a poor governor." (The thirty-nine-year-old Moses was already known for the ambition and brutal instinct for power that would make him a legendary figure of twentieth-century New York.) Oddly, this had the effect of bringing Smith around to the idea of a Roosevelt candidacy. If Franklin would merely be a name on the ballot, an ineffective figurehead, perhaps that was a good thing. They could find a trusted Smith ally, if not Smith himself, to take care of the proper governing of the state.

For much of the remainder of the day, Smith and his circle tried to reach Franklin on the phone at Warm Springs. But when they were put through to Georgia, they were told repeatedly that Franklin was not reachable by phone. UNDERSTAND GOVERNOR TRYING TO REACH YOU ON TELEPHONE, Louis wired in warning. BEWARE OF GREEKS

BEARING GIFTS. Taking the advice, Franklin used the primitive technology at Warm Springs as a shield—the only phone was inside the Meriwether Inn, a half mile from Franklin's cottage.

Of course, as the leader of Warm Springs, if he'd wanted to make himself available for incoming phone calls, he certainly could have found a way to be notified. But, like Ulysses strapping himself to the mast to avoid the Sirens' call, he had made sure he would be unreachable. Fully aware that his fellow New York Democrats were desperately hoping to make him their gubernatorial candidate, he spent the day on a picnic in the countryside with Missy.

Smith and his advisers could see what Franklin was doing. They found an operator at the AT&T office in Atlanta and implored her to leave a long-distance line open from Rochester until Franklin was located, all through the night if necessary. In the meantime, Smith saw another avenue of approach. He sent word that he wished to see *Mrs.* Franklin Roosevelt.

Eleanor had been trying to keep a low profile in Rochester. When a reporter followed her into a quiet corner of the Hotel Seneca lobby to ask about the chances of the Roosevelt boom, she'd kept mum. "I never presume to speak for my husband, and I do not see how it would be possible for him to accept the nomination, because of his health." But there was talk that she secretly favored Franklin's running, and when she got to the suite on the fifth floor, Smith immediately pressed the case. Had Franklin's doctors truly prohibited a run for the governorship? What did he mean that he owed it to his family to stay out of the race? Most important: Did she think he should run?

Eleanor reached for her script from a few days prior: Smith should talk to Franklin. But he had *tried* to talk to Franklin, Smith protested; Franklin wasn't taking anyone's calls! Now Eleanor was caught. Smith seized the advantage: Perhaps, he suggested, Franklin would be willing to take a call from his wife.

Eleanor knew that if she refused to help, they might never reach Franklin. He might never be governor; Smith might never be president—all of it might slip away. By declining to get involved, she

had left it up to Franklin. But if she placed the call, she would at last
be taking a side.

DOWN IN WARM SPRINGS, Franklin had returned from his picnic,
ignored the pile of messages waiting for him, and hurried off to the
nearby town of Manchester, where he was scheduled to make an evening speech on Smith's behalf. Georgia was still the heart of the
Democrats' "Solid South" and an essential piece of Smith's strategy
for victory. A few nights earlier, addressing a packed audience in Atlanta, Franklin had adapted his standard Smith booster speech to appeal to white Georgian sensibilities. The crowd had given him a
rousing ovation. Tonight would be more of the same.

At the school in Manchester, Franklin had to be carried up several
flights of stairs to reach the setting for his speech, a packed audito-
rium. Sweaty and depleted from the climb, he was just regaining his
composure when someone approached him with an urgent message.
The operator from the AT&T office, it turned out, was quite resourceful. Somehow she'd managed to learn that Franklin was speaking in
Manchester. She found a phone in a drugstore, but the person who
answered said that almost everyone in town had gone to see Franklin's
speech at the school. Well, the operator asked, could someone go get
him and tell him he was urgently needed on the phone?

Franklin was prepared to turn the caller away, just as he'd been
doing all day long. But the caller this time wasn't Al Smith or one of
his cronies. This time, the call was from his wife.

Franklin was startled. He was about to speak; there wasn't time to
make his way back down the three flights and across town to the
drugstore. But he sent word to Eleanor that he would call her at the
Seneca as soon as his speech was done.

He began his performance, a variation on his standard pitch for
Smith that fall. Always adept at processing information while appearing fully engaged in another task, his mind may well have raced
as he delivered his stump speech:

"The gentleman who heads the Republican ticket is an old friend of mine. He is internationally minded. He is so internationally minded that he never even voted in a presidential election in this country before the one before last."

Which should he choose? A chance to be governor or a chance to walk again?

"They say that the women believe that Hoover invented the vacuum cleaner and that Hoover provided food for the people during the world war. Well, I am rapidly reaching the conclusion in this race that there is more intelligence among the women than among the men and that the women are not being misled."

What did it mean that Eleanor was calling? Did she want him to run?

He kept talking, longer than he'd planned, as if resisting the reality that was waiting for him at the speech's end. When he finally concluded, he was carried back down the stairs and over to the drugstore. There, he was connected to Rochester and Eleanor. Hearing her voice, he admitted to his wife that he wouldn't have returned the call if it had been anyone but her, that he'd been dodging Smith's calls all day. Eleanor cut him off—that was why she was calling. Smith had asked her to get ahold of him and was standing right there. Then Smith took the phone from her: "Hello, Frank."

Franklin knew he was caught. The connection was bad and the phone booth was cramped. It had gotten quite late in the evening, but he agreed he would call Smith in a little while from the phone at the Meriwether Inn. On the car ride back to Warm Springs, Missy sat beside him, repeating the same phrase over and over: "Don't you dare take it, don't you dare."

For years, Missy would recall that fall at Warm Springs as a time of golden triumphs. To certain sympathetic listeners, she would emotionally confide the story of a day, just before the convention at Rochester, when Franklin had walked across the living room of their cottage on his own, without even the support of a cane. That was how close he'd been to walking again, she'd assure her listeners, before he'd taken the call from New York.

Did it really happen? It is hard to believe that Franklin did in fact walk unaided. First and foremost, it was beyond his capacity—his legs were simply not capable of holding up his weight as he shifted to move forward. Further, while Missy claimed that Leroy Hubbard and Helena Mahoney had witnessed it as well, no contemporaneous account of the miraculous act has survived. Franklin was meticulous about recording progress made at Warm Springs, his own included. It's hard to imagine that he would have failed to note such a monumental breakthrough. Most likely, if Franklin walked across the living room in the fall of 1928, it was with the assistance of canes, and Missy's memory improved the scene over time.

This would be an understandable thing to do. As Franklin's closest confidant and greatest admirer, Missy believed in his rosy assessment of his own prospects. Like Franklin, she had convinced herself that walking was a realistic goal for him; he just needed a little more time. Accordingly, she believed that a run for the governorship would come at far too high a cost. Grace Tully, who would begin a long career of service as an assistant to Franklin that year, would later recall how Missy's "eyes filled up" when she told the story of Franklin's triumphant performance in the living room. "She was firmly convinced that he would rather have walked than be elected to any office, including the Presidency."

Missy was still at Franklin's side when he called Smith from the Meriwether Inn, still whispering . . .

Don't you dare!

The two men talked for some time. Franklin put up a weak defense, but Smith soon realized the conversation was moving his way. Sometime after midnight, he reemerged in the Seneca's lobby. There was a smile on Smith's face.

IT WAS EARLY THE next morning when Eleanor pulled into Penn Station. She had fled Smith's fifth-floor suite in Rochester as soon as she handed the phone to him, heading for an overnight train to New York. She was greeted by Franklin's name and face on the front page of morning papers like the *New York Daily News.*

BULLETIN.

ROCHESTER, N.Y. OCT. I—

Franklin D. Roosevelt will head the Democratic State ticket. Over the telephone tonight from Warm Springs, Ga., he consented to Gov. Smith's pleas and put aside his own personal desires, based on his wishes to remain south for his health.

It was a gigantic story—a man profoundly disabled by disease, reluctantly convinced to sacrifice himself for his party. Editors had raced to find a photo to run with the late-edition front-page headline ROOSEVELT TO RUN FOR GOVERNOR. Soon they had one to sub in. It was a recent file photo, but, in the tabloid fashion, it somehow managed to tell the whole story. His face was heavy and half-cloaked in shadow. His eyes, surrounded by tiny lines, looked somber, almost haunted. His expression was resigned. But he was staring straight ahead.

Franklin, beaming in the aftermath of his 1930
re-election as governor of New York. The story of
his experience with polio was no secret; it was central
to his re-emergence as a political phenomenon.

PART VII

The Return

====

OCTOBER 1928–JULY 1932

"A real economic cure must go to the killing of the bacteria in the system rather than to the treatment of external symptoms."

—FRANKLIN DELANO ROOSEVELT,
"THE FORGOTTEN MAN" RADIO ADDRESS,
APRIL 7, 1932

Chapter 24

On My Feet

EIGHT YEARS HAD PASSED SINCE THE NAME "FRANKLIN D. Roosevelt" appeared on an electoral ballot, as the Democratic vice-presidential candidate in 1920. It had been fourteen years since he last attempted to win office in New York State. And it had been sixteen years—more than a third of his life—since Franklin was reelected to the State Senate in 1912, his last successful electoral campaign. That campaign had belonged to another age, before the Great War in Europe, when buggy traffic still clogged Fifth Avenue and living rooms still rested undisturbed by the crackle of radios.

When he agreed to head the Democratic ticket in New York in October 1928, there was only a month until Election Day. His victory was far from assured: The Republicans, hoping to rout Smith at home, had built a formidable organization in New York State. Franklin's opponent, Albert Ottinger, was a well-respected attorney general, who had proved adept at securing votes both in New York City and upstate.

Yet when Franklin awoke in Warm Springs the morning after his fateful phone conversation with Smith, he displayed no extra urgency. He rose late and breakfasted, went to the pool for his exercises, bathed in the sun. He was hesitant to return to New York, preferring to keep to his planned schedule of appearances for Smith in Georgia, Ohio, and New England. In a statement to the press, he suggested the campaign would be but a temporary distraction from the work he was doing in Georgia. "I'll be back in Warm Springs—win, lose or draw—two days after the election," he said.

There was no trace of the old Franklin, the hyperactive campaigner who gave elections all he had. Some of it was the effect of Warm Springs, with its tranquil setting and limited technology. Most likely, though, his languorous attitude reflected a lingering ambivalence: Was he really going to alter the course he'd planned for his recovery and his life?

Among his intimates back home in New York, the enthusiasm was no greater. Louis Howe was distraught and fatalistic. "By way of congratulations," he wrote Franklin after news of the nomination broke, "dig up telegram I sent you when you ran in senatorial primaries." He was referring to 1914, when Franklin had likewise ignored Louis's counsel and run abortive and unsuccessful Senate campaigns.

In the next day's *Daily News,* the lead story was about the governor's race, and its terse first line was brutal: "They nominated today a man on crutches for Governor of New York." The tight focus on Franklin's physical condition was no accident. Republicans worried he would prove a formidable candidate. Quickly, they launched a sly attack on Franklin's health. Making use of Franklin's statements in the days leading up to his nomination—his avowals that his doctors had said a run for the governorship was out of the question on grounds of his health—they cast his candidacy as the product of Smith's selfish cruelty. "Who can defend the risking of another's health and whole future career in the cause of one's own vanity and ambition?" asked the *New York Herald Tribune.*

And then came the unhelpful intervention of Al Smith. Smith, who had more than enough to worry about in the presidential campaign, was affronted by the suggestion that he had done anything to harm Franklin's well-being. With his own doubts about Franklin's abilities stuffed just beneath the surface, he summoned reporters. He wanted, he said, to "set right" a story that had been going around, that Franklin had agreed to run for governor with the understanding that most of the actual responsibilities of the job would be handled by others. "Of course," Smith protested, "that is, on its face, an absurdity."

In fact, while such a story might have been getting around, it had not made its way into the papers. That is, not until Smith gave voice to it. Smith also denied a second rumor—another with which the reading public was unfamiliar—that, in order to preserve his strength, Franklin would have to forgo the usual rigors of campaigning. Anyway, Smith added, if he did, it wouldn't matter if he was unable to travel. What with the radio, there was really no need nowadays for a candidate for governor to haul himself all over the state.

The result of Smith's comments was that Franklin appeared a sickly wastrel and his health became the central focus of his fledgling campaign. Whatever Franklin's "fine qualities of mind and heart," one upstate newspaper fretted, "the people of this state ought to recognize and keep in mind the fact that it is not wisdom to elect to the office of governor a man who may not be able to perform the duties of that office."

It was the central question Franklin had spent the past seven years preparing to answer. Hearing it seemed to rouse him from his dreamy interlude. He knew he had to respond to the charges himself. At week's end, he traveled to Columbus, Georgia, to make a speech. "I am amazed to hear that efforts are being made to make it appear that I have been 'sacrificed' by Gov. Smith to further his own election and that my personal friends should vote against me to prevent such sacrifice. . . . Let me get this straight at once. I was not dragooned into running for governor." He hurried to leave Georgia that weekend. Awake at last, he was heading toward the fight.

A WEEK AND A half later, a young Democratic Party official made his way to a ferry dock on the west side of Manhattan. Samuel Rosenman had been reassigned to help the new gubernatorial candidate get up to speed with issues in New York State. He was to meet Franklin on the ferry to Hoboken, New Jersey; from there they'd travel north by rail to make a tour of New York cities west of the Hudson. Rosenman had heard that Franklin was weak and hapless, a "playboy and an idler." But encountering Franklin, seated happily in his car as the ferry chugged toward New Jersey, Rosenman was immediately taken in. Something about Franklin's affect—"the broad jaw and up-thrust chin, the piercing flashing eyes"—made him realize that the real Franklin was something altogether different from what he'd heard.

The days ahead would be packed with speeches and travel. Louis had suggested an easy campaign. Smith, he'd told Franklin, "wants to relieve you of all routine work as Governor and it is a grand time to start now." But Franklin, sensitive to appearances, had insisted on an exhaustive and exhausting tour of the state. In a space of two weeks, he would hold twenty-one major rallies, visiting all the state's major cities. "I want to make a hard fighting campaign," he told a reporter for the *Daily News*.

He flung himself joyfully onto the stump. He was not entirely flu-ent in the pressing issues of the Empire State, a fact that did not overly concern him. His chief task, he understood, was to show that he had the strength and energy for the job of governor. He poked at Herbert Hoover as a soulless bean counter, heir to the funereal Calvin Coolidge. The country ought not, he warned, "substitute an adding machine for an ice box."

On train rides between cities, Franklin flipped quickly through thick folders that Rosenman provided on items in the party platform. When it came time to draft speeches, Rosenman was startled to find that Franklin had a complete command of the issues and could sum-mon obscure facts from the research materials. Rosenman admired Franklin's gift for translating complex policies into emotional drama. Presented with a speech attacking Republican efforts to sell water-power rights in New York to private interests, Franklin quickly penned a new opening: "This is a history and a sermon on the subject of water power, and I preach from the Old Testament. The text is 'Thou Shalt Not Steal.'"

Between his large-venue appearances, Franklin made outings to small towns and villages by car. Arriving in a town square in an open-top car, he would lift himself to a standing position, lean against the back of the passenger seat, and deliver impromptu remarks. Then, seated again in the car, he would invite locals to come speak to him. Upon reaching the front of a long line, New Yorkers were pleased to discover this famous Roosevelt seemed intensely interested in whatever topic they had to tell him about. The next day, the papers would run pictures of him in a car, looking not like an invalid but a dashing man on the go. "Too bad about this unfortunate sick man," Franklin would shout to hoots of laughter and cheers from the people in his crowds.

Soon, his performance was attracting national attention. *Time* magazine cheekily led its national-affairs section with a telegram sent to Franklin's campaign: "I WANT TO BE THE FIRST TO PREDICT YOUR NOMINATION FOR THE PRESIDENCY IN 1932." (The clear implication being Franklin might well win the governorship even while Smith's presidential campaign went down in flames.)

Franklin never let on how grueling it all was simply to make it through the day. His smile during the outdoor addresses in his car distracted from the careful choreography of hoisting himself up and lowering back down. Many of the venues were up steep flights of stairs, and he had to ask his aides to carry him. "He never got ruffled," Rosenman observed. "Having been set down, he would adjust his coat, smile, and proceed calmly to the platform for his speech."

Anna joined her father's entourage when his tour looped back through New York City. At one scheduled stop on the Upper East Side, access to the stage required walking up a staircase and then along narrow aisles through the already assembled crowd—an approach with far too much risk of a public fall. The only option for Franklin was to be carried up a fire escape from the outside and then lowered directly onto the stage. Anna watched her father dangle onto the stage, take his son Jimmy's arm, and then summon the force to swing his heavy braces out in front of him, one after the other, as they proceeded to the speaker's stand. He retained his affable composure; only when she saw that his shirt was drenched in sweat did Anna realize how taxing it all had been.

The Democratic activist Frances Perkins, who had offered her help to the campaign and was fast becoming a Roosevelt family intimate, was watching in the wings that day too. Perkins remembered well what Franklin had been like in the days before polio—delightfully charming and talented but "with a streak of vanity and insincerity." In time, Perkins would come to believe that polio was at the heart of his greatness. "I would like to think that he would have done the things he did without his paralysis," she said, "but . . . I don't think he would have unless somebody had dealt him a blow between the eyes. . . . An old priest whom I know once said to me, 'Well, you know, humility is the first and greatest of the virtues. If we don't learn it of our own accord, the Lord will surely teach it to us by humiliation, because there's no other way to live.'"

Franklin continued to make his usual efforts to conceal his condition. Pulling up to one public engagement, he saw newsreel cameras in the press swarm. "No movies of me getting out of the machine, boys," he instructed, and, in that moment, the film photographers obliged. But with his reemergence as a candidate, he'd forfeited the control he and Louis had exerted over his public image. For the first time, the papers ran unobstructed pictures of his seated form, his hefty steel braces plainly on display.

Beyond his "unfortunate sick man" jesting, Franklin made little mention of his disability when he appeared before campaign audiences. One notable exception came at a late-night speech in Rochester that was broadcast on statewide radio. Working his way through his stump speech, he sounded familiar notes from the Democratic program on labor legislation, old-age pensions, and higher minimum standards for teachers. But then he turned to the topic of rural healthcare, observing that in New York State, "more than one hundred thousand adults and children [were] crippled from infantile paralysis and other diseases, most of them so seriously that they are unable to live normal or useful lives." Providing for these people's medical care, he argued, was not just an obligation but an opportunity for the state to reap the rewards of their restored productivity.

"I dislike to use this personal example," he went on, "but do so because it fits. Seven years ago I was completely put out of any sort of useful activity by an attack of infantile paralysis. By personal good fortune I was able to obtain the best medical care. Today I am on my feet and entirely capable, at least from the physical point of view, of running any business, private or that of the State of New York."

It was a revealing window into what his years of convalescence had taught him about politics and public policy. Need and adversity, he now understood, not only caused suffering; they also robbed people of the dignity and purpose that comes from feeling useful. An enlightened and progressive government therefore should use its resources not just to alleviate need but to help people gain confidence that they have something to contribute to the greater good.

People who'd known Franklin before polio marveled at how the disease had literally brought him down to earth. In 1920, he had approached speaking engagements as a series of physical feats: this tall and handsome man, flying into the room, uttering a series of platitudes, then flinging himself into the crowd, shaking as many hands as he quickly could before flying away once more. Now the speeches were stronger, more carefully constructed and thoughtfully delivered. Afterward, he still greeted his crowds, but they came to him. When they approached, he looked at them intently, willing to hear them out.

"He listened," Perkins later observed, "and out of it, [he] learned . . . that 'everybody wants to have a sense of belonging, of being on the inside.' . . . He became thoroughly familiar with the concept that good and evil, hope and fear, wisdom and ignorance, selfishness and sacrifice are inseparably mixed in most human beings."

Franklin himself was no exception to this mixture. Take the text of his Rochester speech: "Today I am on my feet and entirely capable," he said, a phrase that was technically accurate but intentionally misleading. It was a fitting preview of what his friends and foes in politics would come to learn. Franklin's life may well have been dedicated to noble, altruistic aims. But he was perfectly willing to use evasion, deception, and dishonesty to bring those aims to pass.

ON ELECTION DAY, HE voted in Hyde Park and then headed into Manhattan to wait for returns. After dinner, Franklin joined Smith at the 71st Regiment Armory on Park Avenue at 34th Street, where the candidate's Tammany friends had arranged a watch party. Franklin settled into a seat in the front row, just in front of Smith, who nervously flitted an unlit cigar from one side of his mouth to the other. The last time Franklin's name was on an election-night ballot, in 1920, candidates and their staff had been blissfully oblivious of radio coverage, an experimental oddity with only a smattering of listeners. Now large speakers dominated the room, living reminders of the broadcasters' unquestioned position as the voice of authority. Like everyone else, Franklin submitted, listening carefully as their first verdict came through at nine-thirty. New York State, declared the announcer from WNYC, "appears to have swung into the Hoover column." Behind Franklin's shoulder, Smith's unlit cigar stopped moving. A few minutes later, the voice of judgment resounded once more: "Indications now appear certain that Herbert Hoover has been elected."

A heavy hush overtook the room. Smith tried to keep the emotion off his face—he was surrounded by pols and reporters—but rose quickly and headed home to the Biltmore Hotel. The governor had lost New York by more than 125,000 votes. Meanwhile, his national performance was shaping up to be a historic embarrassment. Under the weight of the Republicans' anti-Catholic smear campaign, even the Democrats' Solid South had cracked: Virginia, Florida, North Carolina, and Texas would each give their electoral votes to the Republicans for the first time since Reconstruction. In his Biltmore suite, Smith sank into bitter fatalism. "Well," he would later reflect, "the time just hasn't come when a man can say his beads in the White House."

Back in his own headquarters, downstairs in the same hotel, Franklin assumed the news would be bad for him too. Traditionally, upstate Democrats could win statewide only when helped by huge margins from their downstate brethren and Tammany Hall, and Smith had somehow managed to underperform in Manhattan by a hundred thousand votes. Concluding that his gubernatorial campaign was probably finished, Franklin and Eleanor headed home.

Not every resident of the East 65th Street townhouses was ready to call it a night, however. Whatever she thought of the unseemly business of politics, Sara Roosevelt, with her unyielding Delano competitiveness, felt compelled to stay at headquarters until the true verdict was delivered. Well after midnight, scattered bits of encouraging news started to trickle in from precincts where Franklin was outperforming Smith. They continued in a steady stream until, miraculously, at four in the morning, party officials delivered word that Franklin had managed to carry the state. Frances Perkins had joined Sara in keeping vigil. The two women "had a private if exhausted jubilation," Perkins recalled, "and I saw her home as the dawn was breaking."

And so Franklin woke the next morning in a house humming with joyous news: His exile in convalescence was truly over. He would be the next governor of New York. He stayed in bed until noon, languorously receiving well wishers and chatting with reporters on the phone.

ELEANOR COULD NOT BRING herself to feign delight over Franklin's victory. "No, I am not excited about my husband's election," she told the press. "I don't care. . . . If the rest of the ticket didn't get in, what does it matter?" Taking questions from her desk at the Democratic Party headquarters two days after the election, she said that she had no intention of giving up her responsibilities at Todhunter School or at Val-Kill Industries. She was still figuring out how to balance her teaching with her responsibilities as first lady in Albany. "I suppose I shall have to pile it up, come to New York along about Tuesday night and stay until Friday night or something like that."

She was not willing to resume the role of adoring, self-sacrificing wife—at least not yet. When asked what toll his new responsibilities might take on her husband's health, Eleanor said she had only one concern: "I hardly see how he can avoid getting fat." Prolonged exercise in the waters at Warm Springs, she explained, had allowed Franklin to stay light enough to improve his movement without putting too much strain on his legs. "But now that he's going to Albany," she went on, "well, without the proper exercise, he's bound to get fat."

Franklin had said he would return to Warm Springs following the election—win, lose, or draw—and at week's end he made good on his

word. Oddly, the farther the train got from New York, the more pow-
erfully his victory seemed to have resonated. At Raleigh, North Carolina, where he stopped to visit with Josephus Daniels, he was greeted
with a large crowd and friendly newspaper editorials mentioning him
as a potential Democratic candidate for the presidency in 1932.

Switching train tracks in Atlanta, he found an official delegation
waiting for him on the platform, led by U.S. senator William Harris,
who declared him "the hope of the party in 1932." As Franklin's train
made its way from Atlanta to Warm Springs, people stood out in the
November air, waiting for him at small-town train station after small-
town train station, holding signs saying ROOSEVELT IN 1932. When he
reached Warm Springs, four hundred people came out to see his train
pull into the station. Among them were seventeen patients from the
colony, each holding a black-and-white placard with a letter so that
together they spelled the words GOVERNOR ROOSEVELT.

Before long, there was talk in the national and even international
press of Franklin, not yet governor, as the logical choice to be the
Democratic nominee for president in four years' time. In Franklin's
younger days, reporters had fastened on to the charming narrative he
presented of a second Teddy Roosevelt. Now, once more, he had a
story with an obvious romance to it—the man felled by disease, who
had fought and worked and risen again in glory. This time, however,
the romance was due to his own hard work, not his famous family
name. Franklin's comeback, wrote one Canadian newspaper, "was one
of the most admirable, unspectacular, unassuming examples of sheer
grit that a politician has ever shown. It would have made the great
fighting Theodore, first of the Roosevelts, say 'Well done.'"

Officially, Franklin dismissed the talk of a 1932 presidential run as
the last thing on his mind. "I want definitely to step on that talk with
both feet," he told the press. This was, perhaps unintentionally, a revealing statement: An object Franklin stepped on with both feet
would hardly feel it. But whatever he said publicly, a presidential run
loomed large in his mind. As one of his first pre-election acts, he
tasked Louis with canvassing five thousand Democrats in order to

understand where the *national* party ought to go next. This effort would allow Louis to reach out to the considerable list of contacts he and Franklin had developed over the years, letting influential Democrats nationwide know that, even in his moment of busy triumph, Franklin Delano Roosevelt was thinking about them.

Franklin was now convinced that 1932 was his chance. His immediate task was to prove himself a capable and compelling leader of the Empire State. For this he had limited time—New York governors were still constrained to two-year terms—but a formidable set of tools. In his eight years as governor, Smith had wrested substantial power from the legislature for the executive, including the power to write the state's annual budgets. If Franklin was successful, he would win easy reelection in 1930. Then, two years after that, if timing and strategy and, yes, luck aligned, he would reach the presidency at last.

Another sign of his seriousness was that Louis Howe was not coming to Albany with him. Franklin and Louis agreed that the best place for the aide to serve his beloved candidate was in New York. There, Louis would continue his traditional functions—tracking and shaping and policing Franklin's image in the press, peppering the national network with friendly correspondence—and would also plot Franklin's future campaign strategy. He would be able to act more covertly, and thus more effectively, with distance between him and the governor's mansion.

It pained Louis to think of being far from Franklin and Eleanor's warm light, particularly now that a new crop of aides—Sam Rosenman and the political retainer Jim Farley first among them—had entered Franklin's circle. Louis's consolation was that he would remain in residence at East 65th Street and spend most weekends with Franklin in the governor's mansion or at Hyde Park. Save for Missy, no other aide was on such intimate terms with the Roosevelts as that.

In Warm Springs, Franklin resumed his routine as patient and paterfamilias—mornings in the pool, afternoons in the sun. He told the press he had no intention of lessening his responsibilities at the colony once he assumed the governorship. Indeed, he took on more

responsibilities—in late November, he filed paperwork naming himself as the official attorney for the town of Warm Springs.

On Thanksgiving Day, he held a ceremony in the new winter
swimming pool donated by Edsel Ford. Afterward, reporters watched
as he led the patients in a series of aquatic games—he won the "crab
race"—and a spirited contest of water football. Among the spectators
was Dr. Hubbard, the colony's medical director, whom reporters
questioned about the prognosis for Franklin's further recovery. "Mr.
Roosevelt has made an enormous improvement," he told them. "He is
showing rapid gains in the use of his legs. If he could get in Albany
the same treatment he is receiving here, there would be no question
of the continuance of the improvement."

If he could. Hubbard knew well that there was no chance of his getting the same treatment in Albany as he'd received in Warm Springs.
Franklin knew it too. He would return to Warm Springs again and
again in the years to come but never in search of the same enticing
promise. His dream of walking unaided—always fanciful but fervently pursued—had reached its end.

FRANKLIN RETURNED NORTH IN the middle of December and
spent Christmas with his family at Hyde Park. On the last day of the
year, he left for Albany, where he would be inaugurated as governor
the next day. Arriving at the governor's mansion, the Roosevelts were
greeted by "Jeff" Smith, an exuberant Great Dane who flung himself
out the front door, the only member of the Smith household who was
happy to see the next governor of New York State. Smith's resent-
ments had not subsided in the weeks since his presidential loss. Convinced that his successor was not up for the job, Smith had pressured
Franklin to keep in place Smith's two closest aides, Belle Moskowitz,
the secretary to the governor, and Robert Moses, the secretary of
state. Moskowitz and Moses had been brought from the margins to
the center of power through the beneficence of Al Smith. Shrewd and
merciless inside players, they owed the old governor everything, the
new one nothing at all.

When Franklin told Smith he preferred to name his own secretary and secretary of state, Smith took it as yet another rejection. He stubbornly clung to his prerogatives as incumbent, ordering that, despite Franklin's preference for an outdoor ceremony, Franklin's inauguration would be held inside the legislative chamber. Indoors was better, a Smith lieutenant patronizingly explained to Franklin, for he could enter the "chamber from Speaker's room having only one low step."

When he at last exited the mansion, Smith's gloom seemed to take over everything else. A waiting band played "Auld Lang Syne." Eleanor, watching, began to weep. But the next morning, a snow-covered New Year's Day, Franklin was greeted by hearty cheers when he arrived at the state capitol. The papers were calling him "the man who came back." A crowd of 1,800 had gathered to see him take his oath of office and announce his agenda for the coming year. In a farewell address, Smith cloaked his resentment inside pleasantry: "Frank, I congratulate you. I hope you will be able to devote that intelligent mind of yours to the problems of the state."

Franklin made his way to a desk at the center of the room to recite his oath of office. That day, he'd received instructions from Dr. Hubbard of Warm Springs for how to preserve his health in his new position:

"Remain in bed until 9:30 doing your work in bed if you choose . . .

"Rest a full hour at lunch time . . .

"Exercise in warm water in a swimming pool as soon as that is possible . . .

"Keep away from frills, the endless round of hand shakers and official dinners . . ."

This last would not be possible. The job was a performance, and Franklin knew that. Even the simple act of reciting the oath was fraught: Raising one hand in the air, Franklin placed his other on an old family Bible. His palm pressed down hard, bearing the full force of his weight. But his voice did not waver as he recited the closing words of his vow: "*. . . to the best of my ability.*"

Chapter 25

———

The Long Fight

AUGUST 1929–DECEMBER 1931

E IGHT MONTHS LATER, ON A HOT AFTERNOON IN MID-
August 1929, Governor Franklin D. Roosevelt stood in the back of an
open-top car, watching a parade of 1,300 troops pass in front of him.
Wearing khaki uniforms and carrying wooden rifles, they marched
tightly in three battalions, accompanied by a bugle corps and band. It
was the sort of scene that had thrilled him in his Navy Department
days and the kind of display that he'd longed for in the days immediately following the Great War.

But the parade did not captivate him in the way that it once might
have. Indeed, on this day, his actions and his interests had less in common with those of the ambitious young Franklin of the Navy Department than with those of "Old Dr. Roosevelt," the man concerned
with the well-being of others, the guiding force behind Warm Springs.

The troops parading in front of him were not members of the military. They were inmates at the reformatory in Elmira, New York, a
state detention center for teenagers and young adults. Franklin had
come to the reformatory as part of a multiday tour of New York's
Southern Tier, the region of farms and factory towns that stretched
along the state's border with Pennsylvania.

After eight months in office as governor, he was taking advantage
of a break in the legislative calendar to raise his profile in far corners
of his state. Another politician might have pursued this mission with
visits to county fairs and rotary clubs and chambers of commerce. But

Franklin had chosen instead to visit the less palatable parts of the sprawling state bureaucracy he led—prisons, hospitals, and homes for the mentally ill, among other institutions.

On these inspection visits, Franklin assumed the detached thoroughness he'd used to track patients' progress at Warm Springs and employed the attention to detail he'd learned when examining his own damaged limbs. Touring the reformatory, he peppered officials with questions about the construction of the buildings, the conditions under which inmates lived, what they ate, and how they spent their days. The answers he received did not satisfy him. The building was a "fire trap," he pronounced. "I shall again recommend the rebuilding of the cells in the north extension," he said. "Mere plumbing does not make a cell habitable. Inmates in this institution should live in rooms rather than cells."

While Franklin was pleased by what he'd seen in the military parade, he cautioned the institution's leaders that if, as they claimed, they were running a military academy, they had to change their attitude toward the inmates. "This institution should be a reform school rather than a prison."

While in Elmira that day, he met with a delegation of local leaders. One person mentioned in passing that the city's Rotarians had set up a private home for children who'd had polio. Franklin, who remembered hearing about the "Elmira Home," as it was known, asked to be taken there at once. Word quickly reached the home that the governor was on his way.

When he arrived, he found the young patients waiting for him outside. Some were on crutches; others were lying in cots that had been wheeled out to see him. At first, the children hung back shyly from their esteemed visitor. But Franklin offered them a smile—not "the politician's smile," one local newspaper reporter recorded, but something more sincere. Soon they were making their way toward Franklin. "How's the arm?" he asked one child. "How's the leg coming along?" to another. "Even the youngsters who were helpless in cots asked to meet him," the next day's *Elmira Star-Gazette* reported.

When one boy was wheeled over to him, Franklin inspected his braces. Speaking softly and earnestly, he described his own illness and the braces on his own legs.

DESPITE FRANKLIN'S SUCCESS IN the 1928 election, both New York's State Senate and Assembly were controlled by Republicans. Assuming the governorship, Franklin had pledged an "era of good feeling" with the opposition, pledging to work with Republican leaders on legislation. The era was brief: In mid-spring 1929, Republicans announced that they would ignore Franklin's proposed budget in favor of their own priorities. By summer, the feud between the two branches of government had found its way to the courts, where both Franklin and the legislative leaders were claiming they had primacy over the allocation of the state's finances.

Franklin knew that with only two years in his term, he could not wait for the judicial branch to sort things out. He would need a record of accomplishments or, at least, action, if he hoped to win reelection. Since playing nice with Republican legislators hadn't made them his governing partners, he would have to try political pressure. By showing his face to New Yorkers outside the corridors of Albany, he had a chance to make his case directly to the voters.

So he'd devoted much of his first summer in office to inspections of the state government's neglected places in far corners of the state. In early summer, he'd set off on a barge tour of New York's old extensive canal system. Coming ashore at various inland stops, he'd get in a car and go off to the local asylum, hospital, or soldier's home, to see whether New York State was living up to its commitment to the forgotten, downtrodden, and dispossessed.

Eleanor accompanied him in these early expeditions around the state. Life as the governor's wife had not proved as miserable as she had expected. As she'd promised, she retained her teaching position at Todhunter in Manhattan. Her week was divided into independent city life and interdependent coexistence with Franklin. On Wednesday afternoons, she would arrive in Albany in time to host an "at home" at the governor's mansion. She would usually stay in the capital for several days, appearing with Franklin at endless rounds of private dinners and formal functions. On Sunday evenings, she would make a pre-dinner appearance with guests in the governor's mansion before swiftly saying her goodbyes and hurrying to the New York train.

The style of living in New York's executive mansion in Albany suited the Roosevelts' unusual marital bond. A hulking mash-up of nineteenth-century architectural styles, the mansion looked like a country house that had swallowed a clock tower and felt more like a hotel than a private home. Other families might have had a difficult time adjusting to life in this sprawling, not-quite-private home. But Franklin and Eleanor had long since discovered that their partnership worked best in semi-public settings.

One of their children was always coming to stay (the youngest boys, Franklin Jr. and John, were studying at Groton by the time Franklin and Eleanor moved into the governor's mansion). Eleanor's friends Marion Dickerman and Nancy Cook were occasional guests, spending time with Franklin even when Eleanor was away in the city.

Eleanor could frequently hear Missy's laughter in the hallways. Missy was a permanent resident of the mansion, with a room of her own next to Franklin's, connected by a small door. When in town, Eleanor slept in a back bedroom on another corridor. "It was not unusual to enter his sunny corner room and find Missy with him in her nightgown," the Roosevelts' son Elliott would later write of these days. "I would go in at the start of the day, and the three of us would talk with no embarrassment between us."

Meanwhile, Eleanor, like Franklin, was discovering that she could have her own court of supplicants. In the 1928 campaign, she had come to rely on her personal secretary Malvina Thompson. When the campaign ended, Eleanor had asked "Tommy" to stay at her side, where she would remain for much of the next three decades.

A more surprising addition to Eleanor's retinue of admirers was

Earl Miller, her new bodyguard from the New York State troopers. Brawny, athletic, and thirteen years Eleanor's junior, Miller was an accomplished boxer and gymnast—not the typical profile for an Eleanor Roosevelt confidant. But their personalities meshed instantly; together they would spend long days riding horses, sharing jokes, and engaging in banter that was, to anyone's eyes (and to many of Eleanor's acquaintances' amazement), deeply flirtatious.

Though scant evidence survives to indicate that Eleanor was sexually involved with her bodyguard, people who observed them together felt an erotic current. In his memoir, written after the death of both of his parents, Jimmy Roosevelt speculated that the tie with Miller "may have been [Eleanor's] one real romance outside of marriage." Perhaps not surprising given the age in which they lived, none of the Roosevelt children were inclined to give much weight to the far more voluminous evidence of their mother's same-sex romances. Indeed, the infatuation with Miller is a notable exception in a period where most of her passionate connections were with women.

The one thing that may have made life as the governor's wife most bearable for Eleanor was the simple fact that Franklin clearly needed her and valued what she had to contribute to his work. On their tours of hospitals, prisons, and asylums in the early summer, Franklin found that wardens and administrators were happy to talk up the virtues of their facilities, but his limited mobility made it impossible to do a thorough physical inspection himself.

His solution was to send Eleanor, with detailed instructions on how to tell if the institutions actually ran the way their management claimed. "I learned to look into the cooking pots on the stove . . . to find out if the contents corresponded to the menu," Eleanor would write in *This I Remember,* her 1949 memoir covering these years. "I learned to notice whether the beds were too close together, and whether they were folded up and put in closets or behind doors during the day, which would indicate that they filled the corridors at night." Before long, she adopted as her own the habits of unflinching scrutiny that Franklin had developed in his convalescent years. These powers would prove essential to her work in the years to come.

———

BY THE TIME FRANKLIN assumed the governorship in early 1929, the "big bull market" had long since become a topic of public fascination, a mystical force. Beginning in 1925, the Dow-Jones Industrial Average started growing at a pace that quickly became astonishing; by 1927, the value of the Dow was more than three times what it had been at the beginning of the climb. In the American mind, the market was no longer just a measure of the worth of American companies but a sleek modern invention where savvy stock purchasers could turn a little bit of cash into a lot.

Every so often, the papers contained worried admonitions from economists that the boom could not go on forever and that the soaring stock prices reflected public enthusiasm for the market's get-rich-quick promise more than the value of the underlying assets. And, occasionally, the market would suffer a startling period of decline, leaving the hordes of new investors momentarily terrified, before the market soared onward to even greater heights. "Will it ever end?" people asked, idly, of the boom, and the boosterish headlines answered, implicitly, "Probably not."

At its outset, the autumn of 1929 seemed like more of the same, with the market reaching a record high on September 3. Then came a series of disconcerting drops—no greater than the kind the Dow had suffered occasionally along its way up but more frequent. At first, market savants shrugged it off; as late as mid-October, financial leaders were counseling that there was no need to panic. But then on Thursday, October 24, traders liquidated stocks in such staggering quantities that the leaders of Wall Street's great investment houses banded together to take collective action.

It was not enough. After the Dow lost 13 percent of its value on October 28, full-blown panic settled over Wall Street. By the end of the next day, Black Tuesday, the demand to sell shares was so great that the New York Stock Exchange had to stay open until 7:45 P.M. In the final tally, investors had dumped an astonishing 16.4 million shares that day, erasing more than 11 percent of the Dow's worth.

In the weeks that followed, Franklin sensed a shift in the national mood. After his bruising vice-presidential loss in 1920, he'd observed that the country was entering a long period of materialism; the country would elect Republican presidents, he'd predicted, until an economic crisis brought that age to an end. Now, it seemed, that moment had arrived.

In his Thanksgiving message that November, he began to speak tentatively to the public's emerging disillusionment with heedless consumerism. "A Thanksgiving is set aside each year to give thanks to Divine Providence," he said. "It is especially befitting that in an age in which material things have so greatly . . . occupied our minds we should this year endeavor to devote a larger consideration to things spiritual."

WHEN CONSIDERING THE LONG shadow of the Great Depression, it is surprising how long it took for the economic crisis that began in late 1929 to become the dominant issue in American political life. Throughout the first two years of the crisis, many Americans—at least those who were still able to put food on the table—seemed strangely unmoved by the decimation of the global economy. Journalists and politicians struggled to explain it. It took time, of course, for big economic forces to flash their effects in people's daily lives. The job losses came first in the big industrial cities. Even there, not all workers suffered equally. A 1931 survey showed that while unemployment had reached 15 percent, those out of work were disproportionately under twenty-five or over sixty.

Others saw something deeper and perhaps more sinister in the country's apathy to its new condition, what the historian Arthur Schlesinger Jr. would later call a "numbness" in the body politic. For all the talk about the tough pioneer realism, the American character had long been prone to unwarranted optimism and its handmaiden, denial. Things *couldn't* be quite as dire as the papers made them out to be, could they? The sun still shone, the streetcars still ran, President

Hoover and his advisers still promised the worst would soon be over. People wanted to believe it.

As he plotted his campaign for reelection as governor in 1930, Franklin intuited this mood and was careful not to get in front of it. In his annual message to the legislature at the beginning of the year, he did not act like a leader focused on a single consuming crisis. Instead, he spoke at length of the need to reform the state's prisons and of his proposals to make Saratoga Springs into a spa retreat for the state's unwell. His chief concern that year was a fight over control of the significant hydroelectric power generated by the St. Lawrence River along New York's border with Canada.

When the stock market experienced a brief rebound in the first part of 1930, there were hopes that the nation's economic troubles might abate. "I am convinced we have now passed the worst," President Hoover told the country in May 1930, "and with continued unity of purpose we shall rapidly recover." But before long it was clear the president had lost touch with reality. As foreign economies began to crater, the demand for American goods dried up. Prices and wages flatlined; factories swelled with unclaimed surplus. Farmers began dumping their harvest and destroying their livestock. And no one, anywhere, was hiring. By midyear, four million Americans were out of work.

In his reelection campaign, Franklin used the country's mounting troubles to make the case that Republicans could not be trusted with governance. His opponent was Charles Tuttle, the Republican U.S. attorney for the Southern District of New York, but Franklin's campaign made Tuttle a stand-in for a Republican administration that the American people increasingly saw as inadequate to the times.

Still, Franklin didn't want to terrify voters. His program did not call for a dramatic state response to the crisis. Rather, he emphasized that, despite the turmoil, New York State's finances remained on sound footing and promised a focus on many of the same issues he'd stressed in his first two years—municipal control of water power, farm and forest policy, and prison reform.

It was the right strategy: On November 4, 1930, Franklin defeated Tuttle by nearly three-quarters of a million votes. He won all but sixteen of the state's sixty-two counties, an unprecedented showing for a Democrat of the era. For more than a decade, Franklin had been trying to sell himself to the national party as that rare Democrat who could win New York State with substantial support beyond New York City. At last, he had the proof.

Panic finally began to spread that fall, as cash-strapped Americans contemplated a long winter without the funds to feed their families. In November and December, an average of sixty banks each week suspended operation in the United States.

In the new year, 1931, as Franklin began his second term as governor, things took an even more catastrophic turn. European economies were approaching insolvency, and Hoover ordered a moratorium on the collection of foreign war debts. But by then public anxiety was impossible to contain, as the gold standard—the cornerstone of the international financial system—faltered. In September, the United Kingdom defaulted on its foreign obligations.

Global commerce, teetering for two years, was on the brink of collapse. Facing the prospect of ruin, some countries were turning toward a new and sinister extremism. With its economy decimated by the decline in exports from its home islands, imperial Japan embraced a policy of militant nationalism and ferocious expansion, the brutality of which would be demonstrated by the country's invasion of Manchuria in the fall of 1931. On the streets of beleaguered Weimar Germany, there were bloody clashes between communists and the brown-shirted storm troopers of the national socialists, whose charismatic leader, Adolf Hitler, was gaining in popularity and power. The republic's prospect was coming closer to oblivion.

Back in the United States, Democrats could see that the terrifying turn in the nation's fortunes had a political upside: They had a clear shot of winning the White House in 1932. As party leaders began to consider candidates, Franklin's virtues were obvious. His electoral record in the two governor's races showed he could deliver the must-win state of New York. He had also proved himself over the course of two years as a gifted speaker, attuned to the cadences of the radio age. Best of all, he had an inspiring story: Dealt a setback by life, he refused to give in to despair and had instead fought his way back to the corridors of power.

WHILE FRANKLIN TOILED IN the governor's mansion in Albany through the first months of 1931, claiming he was entirely focused on affairs in New York State, a sprawling, sophisticated campaign organization was operating out of an office tower in midtown Manhattan. There, dozens of workers sent a slew of mailers out into the country, touting Franklin's historic margins in upstate New York counties, his accomplishments as governor, and positive mentions of him in the press.

At the head of this enterprise stood the frail form of Louis Howe. Now sixty years old and beset by respiratory illnesses that had plagued him since his youth, he conducted much of his business recumbent on a dingy couch in the campaign's Madison Avenue headquarters. Louis, who jealously guarded his relationship with the Roosevelts, had never easily shared power at the helm of any campaign, but he formed a close partnership with James Farley, the New York State Democratic chair. Louis knew himself well enough to see that Farley was affable, easygoing, and adaptive—everything Louis wasn't. He knew too that Franklin *wanted* Farley, an Irish American who'd been the Democrats' boss in Rockland County, at the top of the Roosevelt for President campaign. In time, Farley and Louis worked out an amicable division of labor: Farley would go out into the world gathering information and report back to Louis, who would synthesize it and decide how to incorporate it into the campaign's plans.

Canvassing the country, they gleaned that Democrats were tired of losing presidential elections and were worried that the party's old regional and cultural divisions would doom it once more in 1932. So Franklin's campaign tailored a simple message for Democratic bosses: Roosevelt, and *only* Roosevelt, could unite the party and sweep the country. Their strategy was to make Franklin seem unstoppable. In their communications with local officials, they emphasized Franklin's strong 1930 margins in rural Republican upstate New York counties. They also played up his strong ties to Georgia and the South. They made it clear that while he was nominally a Wet, the prohibition issue was not one he cared to dwell on at any length. (It didn't hurt that Franklin's own wife was a Dry.) In their artful framing, Franklin Roosevelt was the one candidate who could appeal to all the party's warring factions.

By year's end, Franklin's advisers felt they'd made great strides in locking up the loyalty of party bosses across the country. Their idea was that if Franklin could build up enough pledges of support from state machines and could enter and win enough of the state-primary contests—which served in those days as a kind of trial heat for the convention-floor vote—he could come to the convention as the prohibitive favorite. More than once in the prior twelve years, Democratic conventions had been the settings for riveting drama. This time, however, if all went according to plan, the Democratic convention would be a tremendous bore.

Soon enough, though, the Roosevelt forces realized that presenting Franklin to the convention as the inevitable nominee might prove harder than they'd planned.

"NOW, DON'T PHONE ME too early," Al Smith had shouted as he boarded a train for New York City on Franklin's first day as governor in January 1929. "I have no job and I am going to take a long sleep."

Smith needn't have worried. In the weeks that followed, the calls from Albany, or at least from the governor's mansion, had been few and far between. When Franklin did call Smith, he was all praise and pleasantries. "There are many things I would like to talk to you about," he assured Smith in a letter a month after assuming office. But when they did get together, Smith found the visits disappointing. Franklin was always surrounded by people, and when Smith finally got him alone, Franklin was solicitous but vague, responding to Smith's ideas with platitudes rather than plain talk.

Smith found the whole business appalling. Deep down, he had always seen Franklin as a spoiled child of privilege. Smith believed that by arranging Franklin's gubernatorial nomination in 1928, he had bestowed that child with an exquisite gift. But Franklin couldn't even be bothered to say thanks.

The Roosevelts and their intimates would always marvel at Smith's gall. Smith expected, it seemed, to rule over New York as a kind of regent. That Smith ever believed Franklin would go along with such a scheme, Eleanor thought, showed how poorly he understood her husband. "One of Franklin's main qualities," she said, "was that he never assumed any responsibility that he did not intend to carry through. It never occurred to him that he was not going to be the governor of New York with all the responsibility and work the position carried."

Yet surrendering autonomy to an elder statesman is one thing; tending to his ego is another altogether. What Smith really wanted was to feel valued, respected, *needed,* to be a mentor and father figure to a talented but untested junior. Franklin easily could have accomplished this. Cultivating such a man while simultaneously amassing power and demonstrating independence was not beyond him. (As Josephus Daniels, James M. Cox, and half the great men of Wilson-era Washington could attest, this was one of Franklin's finest gifts.) Franklin could see how hurt Smith was by being left out and how easy it would be to let him in.

Instead, he chose to do nothing at all. He knew there would be a cost in alienating his predecessor. But he also knew that there was something to gain. He remembered well the trauma of the 1924 Democratic convention; he remembered the loathing toward Smith he had encountered in the South; he remembered, clearly, the staggering margin of Smith's loss in 1928. He knew too that his own most noticed appearances in the past eight years had been two spirited addresses making the case for Smith. Political insiders could list the myriad differences between the two New York governors. But the average voter? As he prepared his own campaign for the presidency, he had to demonstrate that *this* was an altogether different kind of

Democrat than the country had seen before. Falling out with Smith would not be pleasant, but it would get the job done.

And so it was that Al Smith, surprised by obsolescence, came to see Franklin Roosevelt as the source of his woe. Back in the city, he settled into a new life: a well-paid job, a limousine, his family, his resentment, and his contempt. These last he reserved for the man in his old seat in Albany.

In the months following the crash in the stock market, Smith began to understand that while the reversal in the nation's luck might be bad for him (Smith had invested heavily in the months leading up to the crash), bad for his new circle of wealthy friends, bad for the country, and bad for the civilized world, it might well be very good for the Democrats. It might be especially good for a Democrat like Franklin, with a ready-made message and program aimed at protecting the people from the greed of moneyed interests. Herbert Hoover, up for reelection in 1932, suddenly looked altogether beatable by the Democratic nominee. Smith saw what everyone else saw: Franklin was in an excellent position to take on Hoover and win.

Soon Smith would view that as an unbearable, unthinkable fate. He had sworn off politics, sworn he no longer wanted to be in the White House himself. On some days that was even true. At any rate, the presidency was no longer his first ambition. No: What he now wanted was to prevent Franklin Delano Roosevelt from ever becoming president of the United States. He would use all his influence to ensure it. And he would not be the only one.

Chapter 26

"You Must Let Me
Be Myself"

JANUARY–JULY 1932

FOR MUCH OF THE 1920S, WILLIAM RANDOLPH HEARST HAD turned his back on the East Coast and on politics, preferring to focus on his holdings in media. By then, his empire included newspapers in twenty-six American cities, magazines in America and Europe, and a substantial presence on the radio. He'd been engrossed in Hollywood and the stars who populated it, first and foremost his romantic companion, the actress Marion Davies. His obsession had been the castle he built for himself on California's central Pacific Coast near the village of San Simeon. Hearst had always had a knack for matching public tastes. Like so many Americans in that decade, he gave over large portions of his life to the pursuit of pleasure.

With the onset of the Depression, though, he had returned to his primary occupation: the pursuit of *power*. By 1932, his newspapers described an America that had become unrecognizable, a country of endless breadlines, eight million out of work, and city blocks overrun by people in employment lines. Of city dwellers who waited for garbage trucks to unload their cargo and then scrounged for scraps of food. Of farmers in the countryside, protesting in armed gangs.

As Hearst saw it, America's problems sprang from all the things he had been warning about for years: the evils of internationalist foreign policy, the perils of the gold standard, the mediocrity and mendacity of Herbert Hoover. The country needed a man who could get rid of Hoover and get America moving again. Nearing seventy years old, Hearst knew that he'd made too many enemies in both parties to be that man. But he still viewed himself as the people's protector and the people's voice. He was determined to use all his power to select the Democrats' Hoover-slayer himself.

He had the means to do it. He had his newspapers, of course, read by working people in American cities. And he had California, now the sixth-largest state in the union. By 1932, the lord of San Simeon had spent enough money and had won enough fights in the Golden State to believe its delegation to the Democratic convention would be his to control.

Hearst knew that Franklin was the obvious frontrunner for the Democratic nomination. Still, Hearst, who'd never cared much for any Roosevelts, couldn't quite bring himself to back Franklin. He remembered 1922, when Franklin and Eleanor's support of Al Smith had helped doom Hearst's candidacy for governor of New York. But Franklin's real problem, in Hearst's eyes, was his long record of support for the League of Nations and his ties to the moneyed East Coast establishment. Franklin, Hearst suspected, was a cursed "internationalist."

That word had become a more powerful epithet since the onset of the Depression. In the aftermath of the Great War, isolationists like Hearst had attacked the idealism of the internationalists as a front for surrendering America's interests to those of Europe. The country's economic collapse, the isolationists now argued, was the cost of this surrender, a strong and vigorous American economy dragged down by its ties to the Old World.

At the dawn of the election year, Hearst had given a half-hour speech over the radio with the title "Who Will Be the Next President?" In the speech, broadcast by eighty-two stations nationwide, he announced that his preferred Democratic presidential candidate was John Nance Garner, the taciturn Texan who was the new Speaker of the House. Garner hadn't planned a presidential run that year. A few weeks before Hearst's speech, Garner had been surprised at his Washington residence by a visit from a Hearst reporter. After a brief interview, the reporter had informed Hearst that Garner was "opposed to all foreign entanglements" and "unalterably opposed to the cancelation or modification of war debts owed to the United States by Europe." That had been enough for Hearst to launch the Garner for President campaign. No further consultation with Garner was required.

Hearst's real interest was who the next president should *not* be. Franklin Roosevelt, he warned, was an internationalist and a disciple of Woodrow Wilson, "inheriting and fatuously following his visionary policies of intermeddling in European conflicts and complications." That, Hearst believed, disqualified Franklin and other internationalist candidates for president:

> Unless we American citizens are willing to go on laboring indefinitely merely to provide loot for Europe, we should personally see to it, all of us, that a man is elected to the Presidency this year whose guiding motto is "America First."

Determined to save the nation in its time of trial, Hearst now believed his most pressing task was putting an end to Franklin Roosevelt's presidential dreams.

A FEW DAYS LATER, in January 1932, Franklin stood before the New York State legislature in Albany to deliver what he hoped would be his last annual message as governor. His eyes were already looking beyond the state he governed; he spoke that day of an entire country gripped by economic peril.

The collapse of the global economy and the attendant humanitarian catastrophe had finally become inescapable in most people's lives. In 1932, aggregate national income would be only slightly more than half what it had been in 1929. Even for those Americans lucky enough to still have money coming in, the suffering of others was now impossible to ignore. Unemployed workers, their savings exhausted, defaulted on their mortgages and abandoned their homes in the night, transforming pleasant neighborhoods into blighted wastelands. In the first months after the crash, private charities had swooped in to offer assistance that the federal government would not. But after two years, most had depleted their financial resources. The Hoover administration adamantly refused to organize a large-scale national relief effort as the charities dwindled away. Thus, the destitute, with no place to turn for help, lined up at understocked soup kitchens and slept in the streets.

In the speech, Franklin argued that the nation's troubles were rooted in policies that had alienated workers from the fruits of their labors and put them at the mercy of forces far greater than their individual efforts. "We have lost in recent years," he said, "the economic liberty of the individual—this has been swallowed up in specialization of industry, agriculture and distribution and has meant that the cog can move only if the whole machine is in perfect gear."

The problem of the Depression, Franklin now told the legislators, had been compounded by Hoover's callous and immoral refusal to act. Franklin pledged to do his part to restore the American worker's sense of security, but there was only so much a mere governor could do. "The complete solving of these economic problems, which are national in scope, is an impossibility without leadership and a plan of action by our national government."

The implication was obvious: Only if Franklin was installed in the White House could *he* do what was necessary to get the country back on track. His speech to the legislature marked a new phase of his campaign. Later that month, he would officially announce his candidacy for the presidency. Newspapers across the country covered his speech with appropriate gravity: It was a prescription for addressing the country's ills from the man who might well be the next president of the United States.

THROUGHOUT THE PREVIOUS THREE YEARS, Franklin's national press coverage had been favorable and sometimes fawning. Two days after his speech to the legislature, however, it began to take a more negative turn. The apparent cause was a column by William Randolph Hearst, featured prominently in papers nationwide under the headline WHOM DID GOVERNOR ROOSEVELT HAVE IN MIND?

In it, Hearst focused on Franklin's observation that the country's problems required *national* leadership. True enough, Hearst wrote, but Franklin was hardly the man to make that case. Franklin's loyalty was not to the national but the international, Hearst claimed, as evidenced by Franklin's long-standing support of the League of Nations, the crown jewel of the internationalist cause. He mocked a line from Franklin's speech that said Americans wanted "a leadership practical, sound, courageous and alert" by proclaiming, "And AMERICAN. You forgot AMERICAN, Governor Roosevelt, and that is the most important word of all."

Franklin and his advisers were alarmed by the prospect of a long primary campaign fielding Hearst's fire. They hastily sought to make peace. Jim Farley paid a call to top Hearst editors in New York and offered Hearst a private audience with Franklin, in which the governor could demonstrate he was really no internationalist at all. Hearst was unmoved by the offer. "Please give my compliments to Mr. Farley," he wrote to one of his editors, "but tell him I beg leave to say that if Mr. Roosevelt has any statement to make about his not now being an internationalist, he should make it to the public publicly and not to me privately." To underscore his point, Hearst published this response prominently in the pages of his own papers.

Franklin could see that he was caught. His support for the league had left him in two places he did not want to be—crossways with public opinion and crossways with William Randolph Hearst. Accordingly, in a speech before the New York Grange, he declared that he no longer favored America's entry into the League of Nations. The body, he declared, had not lived up to Woodrow Wilson's vision. "Too often," he said, "its major function has been not the broad overwhelming purpose of world peace, but rather a mere meeting place for the political discussion of strictly European political difficulties. In these the United States should have no part."

No one much believed Franklin had had a genuine change of heart on the league or on international questions generally. To supporters of the league, the idea that there was such a thing as "strictly European political difficulties" was preposterous. Within living memory, after all, America had concluded it had enough interest in "European political difficulties" to send its boys to face slaughter in the fields of France. Franklin's old Wilsonian friends, for whom an American-led league remained a great, unrealized dream, felt abandoned.

Eleanor, who had walked the killing fields of France with her husband in the winter of 1919, felt especially betrayed. International peace, and nourishing the global institutions that would support it, had been one of her great causes in the past decade. It was a depressing sign that serving Franklin's interests might come at the expense of her own ideals.

Franklin knew what he'd done had upset his wife. His efforts to make amends were typically indirect. He invited Agnes Brown Leach, a friend of Eleanor's and a peace advocate, to lunch with him at East 65th Street. Leach surprised him with her response. His speech had been "a shabby statement," she wrote to him. "I just don't feel like having lunch with you today."

Franklin, responding immediately, expressed his dismay. "One reason I wanted you here today," he wrote to Leach, "is that Eleanor is very fond of you and you can make peace between us. She hasn't spoken to me for three days." If Leach was worried that her brashness would alienate her from the Roosevelts, she was put at ease by a phone call. "Agnes," Eleanor purred into the line, "you are a sweet, darling girl. I hear you upset Franklin very much. I didn't know you had it in you."

Whispers circulated in the party, doubts about Franklin's campaign and about Franklin himself. These doubts had always been there, pressed just beneath his shimmering surface of success. His candidacy was haunted too by a persistent perception that he was a lightweight. This idea was espoused most openly by the prominent *New York Herald Tribune* political columnist Walter Lippmann. In a blistering piece for his syndicated column, Lippmann described Franklin as "a highly impressionable person, without a firm grasp of public affairs." Lippmann found the idea that Franklin might shake up the established order laughable. "He is a pleasant man who, without any important qualifications for the office, would very much like to be President.

"Nobody knows where he stands on any of the great questions which require practical, sound, courageous leadership," Lippmann wrote. "And those who think he can supply such leadership next are playing their hunches."

IN THE EARLY SPRING, as doubts about Franklin's candidacy mounted, two Columbia University professors, Raymond Moley and Rexford Tugwell, called on Franklin at the governor's mansion in Albany. They had been brought by Samuel Rosenman, who was assembling a group of advisers to add policy heft to the struggling Roosevelt campaign. This group, later known as the "Brains Trust," would serve as an incubator for what came to be the New Deal. After dinner with Eleanor and Missy, Franklin took the academics into his living room, where he asked them some broad questions about the economic situation. He then sat and listened as Tugwell launched into an hours-long lecture.

Tugwell left his meeting with the governor starstruck but concerned. Franklin was jolly, magnetic, and inviting—and seemed to lack a basic understanding of the underpinnings of economics. His questions were broad and elementary, Tugwell later wrote, his thoughts "reasonable but oversimple reactions which were obviously insufficient as guides to policy."

But Moley was less worried. A gifted writer and student of character, Moley could tell there was more to Franklin than what he showed the world. In a letter he wrote to his sister that spring, Moley shared his impressions of the qualities he was coming to know in Franklin:

He seems quite naturally warm and friendly—less because he genuinely likes many of the people to whom he is pleasant (although he does like a lot of people of all sorts and varieties) than because he just enjoys the pleasant and engaging role, as a charming woman does. And being a born politician he measures such qualities in himself by the effect they produce on others. He ... particularly enjoys sending people away who have completely forgotten (under his spell) the thing they came to say or ask.

Moley agreed with Tugwell that Franklin's grasp of economic principles was limited, but he viewed Franklin's "complete freedom from dogmas" as a blessing. "Heaven knows Hoover is full of information and dogmas but he has been imprisoned by his knowledge," he wrote. "God save us from four more years of that!"

Both Moley and Tugwell probably underestimated how much their new pupil really understood. From his illness, Franklin had long experience in dealing with experts who assumed he knew very little about their topic of specialty. He had developed techniques for gleaning information from such men. When encountering a new specialist in the treatment of infantile paralysis, Franklin did not launch into a lecture on the progress of his own symptoms or the nature of his disease, seeking to impress the specialist with what he already knew. He had learned instead to present himself as supplicant, eagerly absorbing a doctor's assumptions and prejudices, remaining, as Moley put it, "pleasant and engaging" throughout.

But all the while he would silently compare what they were saying with what other doctors had told him previously. From this absorptive approach, he was able to weigh subtle variations in doctors' treatments before committing to any one approach. Often, the path he did choose would be his own, a synthesis drawing on the differing advice of the wise men he had questioned and flattered along the way.

Sure enough, before long, his new economics tutors were startled by the quick progress Franklin made in absorbing their lessons. Tugwell noted that, after only a few months of meeting with the Brains Trust, Franklin was fluent in the complex interrelationship between the nation's industrial, agricultural, and banking spheres and their relation to international trade and the stock market. He was struck too by Franklin's calm steadiness. The candidate himself seemed unconcerned with the churn of events in the Democratic Party; he was adamant that his seminars be geared toward developing policy for the *general* election campaign, not for the convention or the state primaries. Here too he was drawing on his experience with polio, which punished impulse and overreaction and rewarded planning and patience.

But as various state primaries for the presidential nomination loomed, Franklin's once-mighty campaign appeared decidedly weak. It was not required or even expected in those days that presidential contenders would enter every state's contest (most states' delegations to the conventions were not bound by the results of their primaries and caucuses). Franklin, though, had planned to compete broadly, in the hopes of arriving at the convention with such a large lead in delegates that he would be seen as unstoppable. Still, the papers now spoke of an "open war on Roosevelt."

BY EARLY 1932, IT HAD become clear that Al Smith intended to be a candidate for the presidential nomination himself. He did not seem to harbor any illusions of actually *winning* the nomination. Smith no longer attempted to finesse the differences between the party's disparate camps, no longer tried to ingratiate himself to the South and West. The animating purpose of Smith's campaign was more base, and more achievable: keeping Franklin off the ticket. One journalist reported that Smith felt "Roosevelt fails to measure up to the demands of this critical period for a candidate of vigorous character"—a not-so-subtle reminder of Franklin's disability.

Realizing, too late, that he needed to tend to Smith's ego, Franklin invited him to lunch at East 65th Street. The get-together was a rare failure of Franklin's charm. He was agreeable and solicitous as ever but, seeking to avoid unpleasant topics, he never brought up the campaign at all. Smith left feeling even more affronted. Meeting afterward with Clark Howell, the editor of *The Atlanta Constitution*, Smith was apoplectic. "By God, he invited me to his house . . . and did not even mention to me the subject of his candidacy."

As Howell later reported to Franklin, Smith then "got on the subject of prohibition and became quite violent . . . indicating that you were 'dodging.' Why in the hell don't he speak out?" Seeking to make peace, Howell ventured to Smith that he couldn't totally forsake his old friend: "The country expects you to support him and it will not believe that you can possibly do otherwise."

Smith's reply came quickly: "The hell I can't."

IN APRIL, WITH THE Smith and Garner forces gaining momentum, Franklin and his advisers decided the time had come to define his positions more clearly. They chose to do it not in a speech to party leaders, as would have been the traditional approach, but in a direct radio address to the American people.

The Depression had done nothing to loosen radio's grip on the American mind. In 1931, the year of economic carnage, the radio industry had seen the largest profits in its history. Without money to spend for a night on the town, Americans opted to stay home, listening to Al Jolson or Jack Benny or Bing Crosby or Kate Smith.

Up to that point, Franklin's behemoth national campaign had been chiefly geared toward the party bosses, who turned out votes in primaries and who, at the conventions, selected a nominee. It had provided little opportunity for him to show off his personal connection with individual voters, but by now it was obvious that, in the years since polio, this had become one of his greatest political skills. As New York governor, he had continued his inspection tours of the state. These often brought him into startlingly intimate contact with people in need. On one visit, in the far-upstate city of Watertown, he encountered a New York State trooper who had broken his back in a motorcycle accident and was using a wheelchair. Franklin leaned in close and spoke so softly that reporters strained to hear what he was saying. They made out only the end of the conversation. "Don't quit fighting, my boy, I know what it is," Franklin told the trooper before adding, "Let me hear from you."

The radio, a medium best known for its serial dramas and soap commercials, might have seemed an imperfect medium to communicate that human touch. But Franklin's advisers, who had heard him deliver a number of radio addresses as governor, knew that he had a unique ability to draw in listeners with the simplicity and sincerity of his remarks. So it was that on Thursday, April 7, 1932, *The Lucky Strike Hour* turned over its first twelve minutes to an aspiring candidate for the Democrats' presidential nomination, the sitting governor of New York.

At the program's outset, an announcer with a thick and tinny New York accent introduced the evening's speaker. Racing through his text, slurring his words together until he reached the end of a phrase, the announcer recalled key moments from the life of *"Frank-Lin Dee Rose-VELT,"* including his "long and winning fight against illness" and "the willing self-sacrifice with which he responded to his party's call to run for the governorship of New York."

There was a pause after this introduction, as if Franklin was allowing his listeners' ears to clear. When he at last began to talk, his voice was deep and soothing where the announcer's had been clipped and raw. "Good evening, my friends!" He went on slowly, deliberately, inviting his listeners to settle in. "I do not want to feel that I am addressing an audience of Democrats, nor that I am speaking merely as a Democrat myself. For the present condition of our national affairs is too serious to be viewed through partisan eyes for partisan purposes."

Having established these friendly terms with his listeners, he proceeded with an address that was filled with fire. Franklin explained that the root cause of the Depression was a system that privileged the interests of the powerful and the wealthy over programs that "put their faith once more in the forgotten man at the bottom of the economic pyramid." The Hoover administration had failed to arrest the country's economic devastation because it had catered its policies to "the top of the social and economic structure" and "sought temporary relief from the top down rather than permanent relief from the bottom up."

The performance was a hit, the first national installment in what would become a Roosevelt genre: short radio dramas in which Franklin used vivid imagery to explain a problem and propose a solution. The text of the speech was drafted by Moley, but its core idea—that government should promote policies that empower the individual to take control of his own economic destiny—was one that Franklin had been explaining for years. In July 1929, nearly four months *before* the Wall Street crash dashed the nation's faith in the wonders of big business, he had argued that America's years of abundance had delivered too much power to the owners of capital at the expense of workers' liberty. "Are we in danger of a . . . new feudal system," he'd asked, "of the creation in these United States of such a highly centralized industrial control that we may have to bring forth a new Declaration of Independence."

The image that would live with the April 1932 speech in history— "the forgotten man"—had a special resonance for Franklin as well. Though he might have been a privileged child of the American aristocracy, Franklin's years of illness and convalescence had taught him what it felt like to be forgotten, humiliated, and overlooked as unimportant. They had taught him too what the forgotten man longs for: the simple dignity of usefulness, the feeling that opportunity and improvement are within his own control. Perhaps not coincidentally, in describing the country's challenge, Franklin called on the imagery of disease. "A real economic cure," he told his listeners, "must go to the killing of the bacteria in the system rather than to the treatment of external symptoms."

The radio address left Al Smith aghast. Who was Franklin Roosevelt, squire of Hyde Park, to lecture anyone on the concerns of the common man? In a speech at the Democrats' annual Jefferson Dinner in Washington a few days later, Smith assailed the address in terms so bitter, the assembled Democrats grew uncomfortable. "I will take off my coat and vest and fight to the end against any candidate who persists in any demagogic appeal to the masses of the working people of this country to destroy themselves by setting class against class and rich against poor."

Two weeks later, in the Massachusetts primary, Smith showed he could indeed fight hard, trouncing Franklin and gaining thirty-six delegates. "These results dispose completely of the Roosevelt propaganda that he is the idol of the masses, opposed only by the international bankers," Lippmann declared in his *Herald Tribune* column. When common folk looked at Franklin, he said, they saw "something hollow in him, something pretended and calculated."

Meanwhile, Hearst doggedly poured resources into stopping Franklin's candidacy in the California primary. In his adopted home state, where he held considerable sway, Hearst was able to persuade William Gibbs McAdoo, the thwarted Dry presidential candidate of 1924, to back Garner's candidacy. McAdoo had no particular affection for Hearst or Garner, but he knew that if the convention failed to nominate Franklin, it might well end up deadlocked and in search of a compromise candidate. Like so many men who had tried for the presidency and failed, McAdoo nourished a dream that he would still get a chance.

That spring, McAdoo also took a call from Herbert Bayard Swope, the New York journalist and man-about-town who acted as a retainer for the financier Bernard Baruch. In the interest of stopping Franklin, Swope wondered, would McAdoo be willing to join forces with Al Smith? This was quite an ask. Few living Democrats could forget the bitter enmity that had divided Smith and McAdoo, and nearly destroyed the party, in 1924. But McAdoo said he would indeed be happy to take up arms alongside Smith. He had one stipulation: Once Roosevelt had been dealt with, would Smith allow McAdoo to join the group of party elders who chose the compromise nominee? Smith, who had been sitting silent by Swope's side, answered right away. "I'll do more than that," he said. "Unless he's included, I'll refuse to be a conferee myself."

The Hearst–McAdoo alliance was strong enough to deliver California to Garner, another embarrassing disappointment for Franklin.

Going into the convention, the Golden State delegation would be combined with that of Texas, eagerly pledged to Garner their native son. Altogether it made Garner—or, more accurately, Hearst—a force to be reckoned with in the ultimate selection of the nominee.

FRANKLIN'S CANDIDACY WAS FURTHER snarled that spring by a tempest surrounding Jimmy Walker, the extravagantly crooked mayor of New York City. Walker, a proud son of Tammany who'd been groomed by Al Smith, wore immaculately tailored suits, kept a "hang-over room" in city hall for recovery after long nights on the town, and spent much of his mayoral term on vacation in Europe.

For two years, Samuel Seabury, a dogmatic and publicity-savvy anti-Tammany judge, had led investigations of corruption in the city's politics. He worked his way through the municipal courts and the offices of the New York sheriff and district attorney. By early 1932, he'd produced a sensational array of corruption charges against Mayor Walker himself, including the revelation of a secret "tin box" in which the mayor and other highly placed officials had accumulated large sums in under-the-table payments from business owners bidding for city contracts.

In late May, while deposing the mayor, Seabury had definitively proved Walker's malfeasance by pressing him to account for inexplicable transactions stretching back to the middle of the previous decade. Afterward, Seabury, who harbored his own ambitions for high office, had said that not he but Governor Roosevelt was the one who must now act. Under authority granted him by the legislature, New York's governor had it within his power to remove a New York mayor who'd acted against the public interest. An upright and just governor, Seabury implied, wouldn't hesitate to act.

This suggestion outraged Franklin. It was no coincidence, he felt, that Seabury had decided to hang Walker and Tammany around his neck a month before the convention. Walker's offenses were so egregious and had gotten so much attention beyond New York that they posed a dire threat to Franklin's chances at the convention. But that very fact, Franklin felt, tied his hands. How could he claim to be an impartial judge of Walker's fate, he reasoned, if his political interests compelled him to act in a certain way?

Even many of Franklin's closest supporters failed to follow his logic. He should remove Walker, they told him, because it was both the right thing to do *and* the politically smart thing to do. One evening, Marion Dickerman sat with him at the governor's mansion and urged him to act. "The convention will never nominate a Tammany-controlled candidate," she told him, "and that's what your enemies will call you. You *must* remove the mayor."

The look in Franklin's eyes when she'd finished speaking filled Marion with horror. He began to respond, his words electric with uncontained rage. "Never," he shot back at her, "*never* will I let it be said that I climbed to a position of power on the back of someone else!"

Dickerman was genuinely terrified. She had spent countless hours with Franklin and Eleanor over the past decade but could hardly ever recall seeing him so overcome with anger. It was that rarest of occasions: Franklin pulling back his mask of pleasantness to reveal true emotion. Decades later, in an interview with the historian Kenneth Davis, Dickerman would recall how Franklin, sensing her distress, had immediately put the mask of friendliness back on. Then he calmly explained why he was hesitant to act in the Walker case.

Experience had taught him, he said, that it was dangerous to adopt someone else's logic for how to solve a problem without fully believing it yourself. Though the advice might make good sense in the moment, it might lose its efficacy as circumstances changed. Then, he went on, "the path that you are following is not the one that you would have chosen by yourself, and because it isn't, you make mistakes.... You must let me be myself. Only when I am myself can I fit into my own pattern and find my way."

It was a rejoinder not just to the criticisms of his handling of the Walker matter but to Walter Lippmann and William Randolph Hearst and everyone else who had spent the past months attacking him for refusing to say exactly what he thought and what he planned to do. His reluctance to take clear stands on issues was not evidence of a lack of conviction. Quite the opposite. His experience in recovery had taught him the importance of sincere belief. To commit to a long and difficult program of rehabilitation, he had had to believe in the underlying logic. Equally must he believe in any program he recommended for salvaging the country from the ravages of the Depression. Otherwise, when events complicated matters, as they certainly would, he would not know which way to turn. He had to have faith in his own actions.

JUNE ARRIVED, WITH THE convention mere weeks away. Although Franklin had amassed a commanding lead in pledged delegates that spring, he was far from the two-thirds majority he would need to secure the nomination.

His strategy of making the convention a terrific bore had failed. As Democrats converged on Chicago at the end of the month, an array of exciting possibilities beckoned for the days ahead. Just before the convention opened, Bernard Baruch, a conservative Democrat and one of the party's largest donors, convened a secret conference between Al Smith and William McAdoo in his suite at the Blackstone Hotel. At Baruch's suggestion, the two former foes recommitted to a convention alliance to stop Roosevelt.

Baruch also knew that William Randolph Hearst would be an invisible but essential player on the convention floor. Leaving his contact information with Hearst's office, Baruch asked for a number in Los Angeles where Hearst could be reached during the convention week. Hearst replied promptly by telegram: TELL BARUCH PARKWAY TWO FIVE THREE FOUR FROM NOON TO EIGHT COAST TIME OTHER HOURS AND SUNDAY SANTA MONICA TWO FIVE SEVEN FOUR.

Al Smith, William McAdoo, William Randolph Hearst—these men had spent much of the past decade in bitter feuds with one another. But for the moment, at least, they were united in a common goal: cutting Franklin D. Roosevelt's throat.

The Prize

JUNE–JULY 1932

A FEW DAYS BEFORE THE CONVENTION, RAYMOND MOLEY came to the executive mansion in Albany to meet with Governor Roosevelt. For weeks, Moley and the Brains Trust had been working on Franklin's speech to accept the Democratic nomination for the presidency. The group viewed this as the culmination of their workshops with him that spring, a synthesis of the ideas they had considered as solutions to the economic crisis. At the onset of his general-election campaign, Franklin would declare himself once and for all.

Arriving for his meeting with the governor, Moley saw another visitor making his way out. It was Joseph P. Kennedy, the tycoon who had been an early and eager backer of Franklin's campaign. Kennedy, a son of Irish East Boston, had made a fortune investing in commodities on Wall Street and in the burgeoning movie business on the West Coast. Now he was looking to get involved in politics in similarly sensational fashion. He had come to Albany to lunch with Franklin before heading off to the convention at Chicago.

As they said their goodbyes, Kennedy offered Franklin an assurance: "I will keep my contact with W.R. on a day-and-night basis."

Moley knew enough to know that "W.R." stood for William Randolph.

Franklin himself would not be heading to Chicago. The 1932 gathering would be the first Democratic convention in twenty years he didn't attend. He was abiding by long-standing protocol under which

it was considered bad form for announced candidates for the presidency to politick as the delegates met. The logic of this custom was
bizarre—*unannounced* candidates were free to attend and campaign
as much as they liked, no matter how obviously they wanted the job.
Al Smith—who claimed, incredibly, that his candidacy was not intended to secure the nomination but rather to affect the selection of
the eventual nominee—had arrived in Chicago early and was parading around the city. (The House of Representatives planned to meet
in Washington during the convention, sparing Speaker John Nance
Garner, Hearst's ambivalent candidate, from having to make the trip
to the Midwest.)

So Franklin would stay in Albany, with Eleanor, Sara, and Missy
to keep him company, along with his sons Elliott and John. In his
place, he would send a large delegation of not only floor captains and
political aides but members of his inner circle, including his other
children—Anna, Jimmy, and Franklin Jr.—and family intimates
Marion Dickerman and Nancy Cook.

And, of course, he would send Louis Howe. Louis, who'd been
planning this convention for so many years, had designed a vast ap-
paratus to make it feel like Franklin *was* there. As a center of operations, he secured a suite in the Congress Hotel and envisioned
ushering delegates there to talk to Franklin by a special hotline connected straight to Albany.

For much of the past decade, Louis's ambitions for Franklin had
been in combat with Louis's frail health. Now it seemed both were
approaching a fateful climax. He left for Chicago by afternoon train
on June 23, accompanied by Marion and Nancy. They dined together
on the train that evening, and he was in good spirits. But when Louis
failed to appear for breakfast the next morning, the two women were
alarmed and sent for a conductor, who took them to Louis's quarters.
There they found him overcome by fever and asthma, barely able to
breathe. They worried he might not make it to Chicago alive.

When Jim Farley, greeting the train at the station, laid eyes on
Louis, he thought he "looked like death." Louis insisted on proceed-
ing to the Congress Hotel suite as planned. There, he spent the next

week prostrate and sweltering, barking orders even as he struggled to find air to fill his lungs. A common sight in the opening days of the convention was Farley, just back from the stadium, lying on the floor beside his colleague, whispering fresh reports in his ear.

The news was all bad. In the opening days of the convention, Franklin's support seemed shakier than ever. For months, Franklin and his advisers had considered advocating for abandoning the rule that required a candidate to secure the support of two-thirds of the delegates to become the party's nominee. Instead, a simple majority would suffice. This made good sense for the party—such a rule change would have spared the Democrats the debacle of 1924, when the prolonged fight between Smith and McAdoo had doomed the party's chances in the general election—as well as served Franklin's interest. But openly endorsing the rule change risked alienating Franklin's southern supporters, who trusted the two-thirds requirement to give them a veto over any unacceptable northern nominee. Franklin sent his lieutenants to Chicago with the clear suggestion that he hoped the party would drop the two-thirds rule but without clear instructions to make it happen.

This a-little-bit-pregnant approach had a predictably disastrous result. At a pre-convention meeting of pro-Roosevelt leaders, Huey Long, Louisiana's swashbuckling and self-serving senator, took it on himself to announce that Franklin's campaign would indeed seek to abandon the two-thirds rule. Franklin's coalition shook with rancor; several of his pledged delegations threatened to bolt. Eventually, Franklin sent word from Albany that he, in fact, believed the rule should stay in place. In the press, he hinted that the whole thing had been Farley's fault, that Franklin certainly hadn't known of the effort to alter the rules and wouldn't have supported it if he had. But the affair made Franklin look weak—he was unable to control his own supporters, let alone the whole party. Worse, it had furthered the perception that Franklin *couldn't* win the nomination under the existing rules.

There were whispers swirling around the hotels about Franklin's physical condition and his fitness for the job of president. In a remarkably nasty missive, a close Al Smith ally assailed Franklin's candidacy: "The Democratic Party has a golden opportunity, but for the party to select the weakest man cannot bring success. Governor Roosevelt has utterly failed in his last two attempts to sell himself to the people. There is a wealth of material before the convention . . . why consider the one man who is weakest in the eyes of the rank and file?"

Franklin had been especially sensitive about the spotlight on his health in the months leading up to the convention. In a letter that spring, he'd complained about "yellow journalism" focusing on his disability. "I cannot see the importance of all this nonsense when I am in perfect health and get through three times as much work in the average day as three ordinary men do."

Leaning into the emphasis on Franklin's supposed "weakness," Al Smith tried to frame himself as the opposite, popping up everywhere in Chicago to shake hands and pose for photos, making sure reporters knew he was playing golf every day.

The message was breaking through. In the bars and lobbies, reporters and pols guessed that former secretary of war Newton Baker or Maryland governor Albert Ritchie would end up as the convention's compromise choice. Some were so impressed by the apparent enthusiasm for Smith that they wondered if the Happy Warrior might be able to fight his way to the nomination once more. Few who wanted to sound smart were expressing much confidence in the Roosevelt effort.

THROUGH THE EARLY HOURS of the convention, Farley consoled himself with numbers: Franklin had a towering majority of delegates; no other candidate came close. It was simply a question of finding the states that would move into Franklin's corner and put him over the top. He and Louis brainstormed creative combinations, but again and again he came back to the two delegations pledged to Garner—Texas and California. The two delegations controlled by William Randolph Hearst.

With Garner in Washington and Hearst far away in California, Farley sought out Sam Rayburn, an affable party stalwart who'd represented Texas in the House for three decades. The best thing for the party, Farley argued, would be to settle on a nominee early. To help that along, he suggested, Texas could declare its votes for Garner in the roll call of the first ballot and then switch to Roosevelt before the final tally was announced. In exchange for this act of generosity, he suggested, Franklin might well consider Garner a top contender to be the party's vice-presidential nominee.

Rayburn wasn't interested in a deal. "We have come to Chicago to nominate Speaker Jack Garner for the presidency if we can," he said. Still, Rayburn opened the door ever so slightly, recalling the endless balloting of the calamitous 1924 convention: "But we don't intend to make it another Madison Square Garden."

On the afternoon of June 30, the convention began considering nominations for the presidential ticket. Texas senator Tom Connally nominated John Garner, and Massachusetts governor Joseph Ely nominated Al Smith, and their respective supporters flooded the stadium with shouts and songs. As midnight approached, Franklin was the last candidate to be nominated. By the time the speeches extolling his virtues began, the crowd was tired and bored. The succession of orators nominating Franklin fell flat. Louis, still in agony in his suite at the Congress, listened to the radio coverage from the stadium in sickly horror. A pipe organ was screeching through the verses of "Anchors Aweigh," Franklin's oddly lifeless campaign song. "For God's sake," Louis wheezed, "tell 'em to play something else."

As the speakers droned on, Farley approached Rayburn once more with a proposal. If Garner would commit to release Texas and California to a Roosevelt stampede on the first ballot, Franklin was prepared to guarantee him the vice presidency. Rayburn continued to play coy: "Well, we just must let the convention go for a while, even if we are interested in the vice presidency, and I'm not saying that we are."

THE JOYLESS ROOSEVELT NOMINATING speeches went on and on, until dawn was not far away. Bone-tired, Farley and the other Roosevelt leaders considered whether to call for an adjournment until the following afternoon or to proceed to balloting straightaway. All night, the events in Chicago had been broadcast over a loudspeaker in the executive mansion's ballroom. Cloistered in his study with Eleanor, Sara, Missy, Elliott, and John, Franklin sat listening to the broadcast on another set. When Farley called to consult him, Franklin agreed that they should go right to the balloting. Their position was too precarious to wait another day.

And so at 4:28 A.M., Montana senator Thomas Walsh, the convention chairman, began calling the first ballot. Getting through all the states took an agonizingly long time. Farley hovered on the convention stage, adding up figures as each delegation reported its votes. At last, after two hours, the roll call was completed. Waiting for the totals to be officially tallied, Farley felt a momentary rush of triumph: The Roosevelt campaign had amassed an overwhelming majority of delegates, 666.25, besting his nearest rival, Smith, by 464.5 votes.

In past conventions, such a staggering lead would have signaled that the party had a winner. Holdout delegations, hoping to get in good with the surefire nominee, would have rushed to change their votes before the final tally was announced. Perhaps, Farley hoped, a stampede was about to come his way.

But his relief quickly lapsed into horror. Not a single delegation budged. No one thought Franklin Roosevelt was the surefire anything.

It was now past six in the morning. In Albany, Franklin, still listening in his study, was brought breakfast on a tray. As the second roll call of the states began, he diligently kept a tally on paper. The convention again made its way slowly through the states. Between the first and second ballots, he had picked up only a measly 11.5 votes. This was an artificial sign of progress—Farley had arranged in advance to save these votes for a second ballot, to give the impression of momentum and help move recalcitrant Democrats off the fence. But no one had been spontaneously tempted to move Franklin's way.

Outside, the summer sun was blaring high in the sky. In Chicago,

Farley feared yet another inconclusive ballot. He had been telling party insiders he could hold Franklin's support together for three to five ballots. If three ballots failed to make Franklin the nominee, his candidacy would start to look mortally wounded. The drowsy delegates dutifully began their way through a third ballot. This time Franklin gained a mere five votes. This paltry showing was enough for his opponents. They allowed the convention to adjourn until that evening, confident that the Roosevelt juggernaut had been stopped.

Farley stumbled out of the arena, feeling glum as he made his way back to the Congress Hotel. There he found Louis, a wretched puddle on the floor. Farley, exhausted, stooped to whisper in his colleague's ear: "Texas is our only chance."

But a secret rescue operation for Franklin's candidacy had already been launched. Early that morning, as the second ballot was being called, as Farley had counted and worried, as Louis had suffered and writhed, and as Franklin had silently tallied votes with his pen, Joseph Kennedy, the dapper man Franklin had lunched with in Albany the week before, placed a call to William Randolph Hearst's castle in San Simeon. It was early, 5:00 A.M. Pacific Time, but Hearst had taken the call. He listened carefully as Kennedy began to talk.

IN ALBANY, A GROUP of reporters covering Franklin had spent the night in the executive mansion's garage, following the news from Chicago. After the convention adjourned, they were ushered in to see Franklin. Greeting them, he buoyantly declared that he was certain he would be the nominee. "The boys in Chicago are pleased and confident," he said, taking great liberties with the truth. The reporters noted that his linen suit was still crisp and he seemed considerably more alert than his two sons, who were drowsy at his side. He said he planned to take a nap for a few hours. "After that I expect I shall be pretty busy on the telephone."

When Franklin finished, the reporters dispersed to file their stories and get some sleep of their own. Lorena Hickok, the correspondent charged with covering the Roosevelts for the New York office of the Associated Press, was walking to her car with another reporter when she spotted Eleanor Roosevelt on the mansion's porch. Eleanor asked if they'd like to come inside and have something to eat. Dying of hunger, the two reporters gratefully said yes.

Hickok studied Eleanor curiously as she served them breakfast. Hickok had been covering New York's first lady for several years and, though she did not know Eleanor well, had long found her fascinating. That morning, Eleanor seemed "withdrawn" and closed off. "She showed little interest in the night's proceedings," Hickok would later write, and "appeared unwilling to discuss the subject. That was perhaps natural. But there was something else—something I couldn't define or understand."

After thanking Eleanor for the breakfast, Hickok said her goodbyes. "That woman is unhappy about something," she said as she and the other reporter drove away.

She was right. A few days before, Eleanor had sent a letter to Nancy Cook at the Democratic convention in Chicago. In it, she despaired at the prospect of Franklin's nomination and life as the president's wife, sacrificing her work, her friends, her happiness, for the sake of her husband's career. She did not restrain herself in the letter; she said she wanted to leave Franklin, leave her family altogether, and start a life. Nancy was so startled by this missive and its implications for Franklin's candidacy that she and Marion took it to Louis. After reading it, Louis ripped the letter to shreds and threw it in the wastebasket. "You are not to breathe a word of this to anyone, understand?" Marion would later recall him saying. "Not to anyone."

In the countless hours he'd spent alone with Eleanor over the course of the past twelve years, Louis had almost certainly heard similarly bold and impetuous declarations. He knew that Eleanor had fears about life in the White House, that there would be nothing there for her to do. He knew too that she didn't really intend to leave her husband. She believed too much in him and in their shared ideals. In her memoirs years later, recalling her ambivalence toward Franklin's candidacy, Eleanor judged herself harshly: "From the personal standpoint, I did not want my husband to be president.... It was pure selfishness on my part, and I never mentioned my feelings on the subject to him."

It is worth considering, however, why the suspenseful hours before his nomination left her particularly bereft. In the years since the crisis over Lucy Mercer, Eleanor had been guided by a watchword: independence. In that time, she had to abide her share of unpleasantness—Franklin's frequent absences, Missy's constant presence, Sara's lingering judgment. None of it rattled her for very long. Only in the moments when Franklin's needs had threatened her independent life—the first winter of his convalescence, the first months of his governorship in Albany—had she lost her composure and surrendered, however temporarily, to woe.

She had made the best of being the governor's wife, clinging to her job as a teacher at Todhunter and zealously guarding her time there each week. But that wouldn't be possible with Franklin in Washington. The terms of the arrangement she'd worked out with Franklin so many years ago would be rendered meaningless—the American people would not tolerate a wife who left her husband alone in the White House so that she could teach school in New York.

Those nervous hours of waiting for news from Chicago were almost certainly a painful reminder not just of all Eleanor had to lose but how little she had to gain. Seated in his study, listening to the radio, Franklin juggled an eager horde of supplicants offering information—Farley, Moley, Rosenman, Kennedy, Louis, and many others besides. Eleanor would have witnessed him gobbling up their intelligence, taking their counsel graciously but always carefully keeping his own thoughts, his own grand strategy, to himself. He never showed anyone exactly what he really thought. Not Farley, not Louis. Not her. Her choice was not between a life with Franklin or a life apart. It had never been that. The prospect of a life lived chiefly as Franklin's wife seemed, ultimately, the promise of a lonely life, on her own.

———

IN CHICAGO THAT MORNING, Al Smith's campaign stayed busy, telling reporters they had Franklin stopped. Smith was pleased by the way things were turning out; he might not just succeed in stopping Franklin, he might even win the nomination for himself.

As the day wore on, however, Smith began to notice an unsettling pattern. He couldn't reach anyone on the telephone. In their pre-convention meeting, he and McAdoo had agreed to work together in the event the convention was deadlocked. But despite several attempts, he could not connect with his old rival. Sensing something was up, he had his aides try to track down Garner in Washington. Garner too could not be reached. When Smith aide Belle Moskowitz finally got through to the manager of the Washington Hotel, Garner's residence, the manager assured her that Garner was in fact at home. "The reason you can't get him is that he refuses to answer the telephone."

Then came a disturbing rumor that the delegations of California and Texas planned caucuses that afternoon in their adjacent suites at the Sherman Hotel. California and Texas had two things in common: Both were pledged to John Nance Garner, and both were under the influence of William Randolph Hearst.

Everyone had been trying to get through to Hearst in California over the past twenty-four hours. The publisher had mostly refused the calls. But when Joe Kennedy's early-morning call came through, he took it. Hearst had gotten to know Kennedy in Hollywood and trusted him. Kennedy told Hearst the plain facts: It was possible he could stop Roosevelt from being nominated. But he could not have his pick of the president. Indeed, if Roosevelt was successfully stopped, the nomination was likely to go to Newton Baker—a Wilsonian, an internationalist, and a man Hearst had long loathed.

Kennedy's argument revealed an ironic new reality: If Hearst truly wanted to claim responsibility for selecting the Democrats' nominee, Franklin Roosevelt was his man. If Franklin's support fell apart on the next ballot, his delegations would most likely scatter to an assortment of other candidates. To reach a two-thirds majority, a compromise candidate would have to build a coalition from the ground up. Hearst's delegates would be useful in that process, but they would not be sufficient. Only Franklin, who was just over a hundred votes shy of the majority, needed exactly the number of delegates that Hearst could provide. What's more, Franklin was willing to trade something in return for Hearst's support—a Garner vice presidency, say, or firm pledges about the international entanglements.

Hearst had a talent for forgetting old grudges as his interest required. Listening to Kennedy, he agreed to a call with Louis and then a call with Franklin. Then came a slew of additional phone calls: Albany to Chicago, Chicago to San Simeon, San Simeon to Washington, Washington to Chicago. Farley got involved, as did Sam Rayburn and Garner.

That evening, as Franklin sat down to dinner with his family at the governor's mansion, he was summoned to take a call from Louis. He was grinning when he put down the receiver.

BACK IN CHICAGO, the delegates gathered in the stadium for another session. As the fourth ballot began, Bess Furman, an industrious reporter for the Associated Press, positioned herself near the Roosevelt family's box. She watched with interest as seventeen-year-old Franklin Roosevelt Jr. slid under a rope to join his family, hurriedly explaining that he was late because he'd been detained by a police officer. Then, as the roll call reached California, she heard one of the young Roosevelts exclaim, "This is it!"

William McAdoo had climbed up to the convention stage to speak for his state. "California," he said, "came here to nominate a president of the United States. She did not come here to deadlock this convention or to engage in another desolating contest like that of 1924."

Al Smith was stricken as he heard these words. Seated by the radio in his suite at the Congress Hotel, he knew that his campaign had come to an end. His brief alliance with McAdoo had mattered little; the memory of 1924 and the hunger for revenge was everything.

"When any man," McAdoo went on, "comes into this convention with the popular will behind to the extent of almost seven hundred votes—"

At this, the galleries, now aware as well that Smith was sunk, filled the room with wrathful jeers so that, for several minutes, it was impossible for McAdoo to go on.

Jim Farley bolted toward the stage, a wide grin on his face. He was patting McAdoo on the back by the time the other man finished his speech: "And so, my friend, California casts forty-four votes for Franklin D. Roosevelt!"

The Roosevelts had been expecting this moment, but when they heard McAdoo's words come over the radio in Franklin's study, they were overcome all the same. Even Eleanor cast aside her glumness, throwing her arms around Missy. Soon the speakers blared happy pandemonium from Chicago Stadium, where state after state flooded the aisles to join a Roosevelt parade. When at last the roll call commenced, it was clear it was all over: Texas too cast her votes for Roosevelt. By the end of the ballot, Franklin had secured a two-thirds majority and the nomination.

Before the balloting was even concluded, most of Franklin's opponents had withdrawn from consideration and announced their support of Franklin as the party's 1932 nominee. Delegates listened to a message that Garner had telegraphed to Franklin: HEARTIEST CONGRATULATIONS. YOUR NOMINATION MEANS YOUR ELECTION.

The true warmth of these congratulations was hard to discern. After a conversation with Hearst that afternoon, Garner had ordered Sam Rayburn to release the Texas delegation. He'd gone to bed at nine o'clock that night, not even bothering to listen to radio coverage from Chicago. The telegraph of congratulations had been composed on his behalf by a Hearst writer. From conception to concession, then, the Garner campaign was mainly a Hearst invention. But the Texan's involuntary passage through presidential politics had not yet reached its end: The next day, in accordance with the Hearst–Roosevelt deal, the convention would nominate him unanimously for the vice presidency.

As the convention adjourned for the night, Democrats poured into the Chicago streets, awash in good feeling. Louis's suite in the Congress Hotel swarmed with well-wishers, including some of the men who had been plotting Franklin's downfall mere hours before.

There was one notable absentee. When reporters offered Al Smith a chance to extend his own warm message to Franklin that night, he declined, saying simply that he was going to bed. The next day he left Chicago, without ever endorsing the party's newly christened nominee.

Smith had underestimated Franklin. McAdoo, Bernard Baruch, Walter Lippmann, Hearst—they had all underestimated him too. All these men had known Franklin for decades. When they thought of him, they assumed he was still the man he'd been in his thirties—charming and charismatic, impulsive and insubstantial. A politician notices what is in his interest to notice, and none of them had had cause to assess the ways that Franklin's years *out* of politics might have changed him.

For it was the things he'd gained in those years that delivered the nomination to Franklin. Ultimately he had relied, and would continue to rely, on patience and faith in himself. Even with his closest aides, he had cultivated an aura of mystery. Neither Moley nor Rosenman nor Farley nor even Louis knew exactly what Franklin's strategy was for the campaign. He alone saw all the cards he was playing, and he believed that would be enough. Belief in his own powers had brought him back from illness. Now it had nearly put the presidency in his hands.

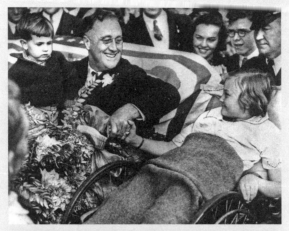

Franklin on the campaign trail and with a fellow
polio survivor in the fall of 1932. Greeting voters
seated in his car, he could both conceal the full
extent of his disability and appear closer to
the common man and woman.

PART VIII

Out of Every Crisis

———

JULY 1932–MARCH 1933

"One word more: Out of every crisis, every tribulation, every disaster, mankind rises with some share of greater knowledge, of higher decency, of purer purpose."

—FRANKLIN DELANO ROOSEVELT,
SPEECH ACCEPTING THE DEMOCRATIC
NOMINATION FOR PRESIDENT,
JULY 2, 1932

Chapter 28

"Pray for Me"

JULY–NOVEMBER 1932

I T WAS EARLY THE NEXT MORNING, JULY 2, 1932, WHEN FRANKLIN and Eleanor arrived at an airstrip near Albany. Franklin had decided to forgo the old custom in which a candidate waited several weeks to be officially notified of his nomination and then accepted it in his hometown. Instead, he had asked the convention to remain in session so that he could accept the nomination in front of the delegates. He would fly to Chicago from Albany.

It was a stunt, a signal to the country that, unlike Hoover, a President Franklin Roosevelt would act, and act fast. And it also carried an additional message, obvious to one and all. "A quick jump across the country," *The New York Times* reported, "would help to dispel the belief that the Governor was incapable, because of his physical condition, to fulfill the duties of the Presidency."

In Albany, Franklin climbed aboard the thirteen-person plane. He was joined by Eleanor, Missy, his sons Elliott and John, and several other advisers, bodyguards, and staff. On board, he sat behind a makeshift desk, where he revised the acceptance speech he was to give that evening, handing pages to Grace Tully to type. The flight—nine hours long thanks to headwinds and refueling stops—was terrifyingly bumpy. John Roosevelt got sick promptly after takeoff. As the other passengers held their stomachs and feared for their safety, Sam Rosenman looked over at Franklin: "The Governor—on his way to accept a nomination that was almost tantamount to an election to the Presidency of the United States—was sound asleep."

Franklin's three other children, along with Louis and Farley, greeted the plane at the airport in Chicago late that afternoon. Louis, temporarily revived from his physical agonies, clambered into the car that was waiting to take Franklin to the stadium. No sooner had the nomination been secured the night before than Louis had gone into a rage over the draft that Moley, Rosenman, and others submitted for Franklin's acceptance speech. The speech was bad politics, he said, populist and interventionist at a time when Franklin needed to sound measured and constrained. His real objection was probably that he hadn't written it. "I see Sam Rosenman in every paragraph of this mess," he'd complained.

From the car, Franklin waved to the large crowd that had come out to greet him on the way to Chicago Stadium. Louis hectored him throughout the drive, presenting an alternative speech he'd composed in a hurry. Franklin pointed out that it was a little late to switch speeches—the crowd at the stadium was already seated. But Louis persisted, expounding on all the flaws in the existing version. "Damn it, Louis," Franklin finally snarled, "I'm the nominee."

Most likely, the true source of Louis's agitation that day was the new reality of his and Franklin's lives. The plan that he had hatched all those years ago, the vision that he'd used to entice Franklin back into life, had at last reached its intended goal. Never again would Franklin's career and Franklin's interests be only Louis's to look after, to plan and to promote. The idea of a President Franklin Delano Roosevelt no longer belonged to just Louis and Franklin. From that night on, it would transfix the country and the world.

Inside the stadium, Franklin took James Roosevelt's arm. As they made their way across the speaker's platform, Franklin observed his crowd, smiled broadly, and raised his arm in greeting. It was, as always, a vulnerable and potentially dangerous moment. Yet on this day, when James left his father at the speaker's rostrum, Franklin straightened his back, emanating calm.

Cutting into a solemn silence, Franklin acknowledged the precedent he was shattering by appearing before the convention at all. "Let it be the task of our party to break foolish traditions. We will break these traditions and leave it to the Republican Party to break promises." At this, the crowd laughed and cheered.

He then launched into his speech, a sweeping plan of action. Over the next twenty minutes, he described a program that was not just an array of policies but a moral crusade to fundamentally realign the relationship between the federal government and the broader populace. For the first time, he offered a phrase that would go on to live in history alongside his name: "I pledge you, I pledge myself to a new deal for the American people."

But it was only at the very end of the speech that Franklin gave a hint of what would be the heart of his presidency, the deep wisdom that would distinguish him from almost every other person to occupy the White House before or since:

"One word more: Out of every crisis, every tribulation, every disaster, mankind rises with some share of greater knowledge, of higher decency, of purer purpose. . . . To return to higher standards we must abandon the false prophets and seek new leaders of our own choosing."

Out of crisis comes knowledge, higher decency, purer purpose. He meant these words. He believed these words. He had lived these words in his own life.

EARLY ON THE MORNING of July 3, a Navy plane dropped a stack of newspapers on Rapidan, President Herbert Hoover's retreat in Virginia's Blue Ridge Mountains. Hoover had followed the events in Chicago with interest. He'd listened to the second ballot over the radio while eating his breakfast in the White House and perched by his set for the drama of the fourth ballot that night. But he'd been en route to Rapidan when Franklin had made his arrival at the convention. Opening the papers, President Hoover read the text of Franklin's speech:

> . . . Republican leaders not only have failed in material
> things, they have failed in national vision, because in disaster

they have held out no hope, they have pointed out no path for the people below to climb back to places of security and of safety in our American life. . . .

Putting the papers aside, the president took a pen and paper and began scribbling lines for his own acceptance speech.

The early press coverage predicted the general election would be a civil fight between two men who'd long enjoyed an affectionate acquaintance. "In Wartime Washington, they used to be good friends and see much of each other at informal Sunday suppers," *Time* magazine told its readers. "That old relationship ought to save the campaign from getting personal and dirty." But, in fact, the well of amity between Franklin and Hoover, never especially deep, had already run dry. The president had been outraged by the tenor of Franklin's attacks, which he viewed as reckless, overly personal, and unfair.

The Roosevelts too had come to resent Hoover's actions toward them. That spring, Franklin had been invited to attend a White House reception for the nation's governors. Eleanor, knowing that a visit with a president generally involved a great deal of waiting around, had worried about all the time Franklin would have to spend standing, leaning on someone's arm for support. They'd arrived early through a separate entrance to avoid cameras catching his slow progress. Sure enough, the Hoovers kept them waiting for half an hour. When Franklin was offered a chair to rest in, he refused, afraid it would make him look weak. Eleanor suspected the Hoovers' tardiness was by design. "It seemed," she later wrote, "he was being put through an endurance test."

Hoover was pleased with the opponent the Democrats had given him. Like Franklin's Democratic rivals, he too had known the young Franklin Roosevelt of the Navy Department days and did not highly rate that man's intellect, character, or talent. Franklin was "a trimmer," he said, lacking seriousness and conviction. "He's a sick man," Hoover told an aide. "He wouldn't last a year in the White House."

Hoover's faith in his own chances was delusional. With each month that year, as food lines across the country had grown, the nation became repulsed with a president who appeared obstinate, uncaring, and out of touch. And in just a few weeks' time, events would conspire to permanently foreclose the possibility of his winning a second term.

The cataclysm came in late July, when Washington was shocked by violence in its streets. For months, some 20,000 veterans of the Great War had been camped in the capital, demanding relief from the government. In 1924, an act of Congress had authorized a bonus payment for veterans of the war: one dollar for each day of domestic service, a dollar and a quarter for each day served overseas. The bonus was to be paid to every former soldier—but not for another twenty-one years, in 1945. This long wait had been tantalizing and bizarre in good economic times, but as the Depression wore on, it came to feel like base cruelty. The group of veterans, who called themselves the Bonus Expeditionary Forces, had descended on Washington demanding immediate payment, a request Hoover had adamantly refused.

The veterans, many of whom had brought their families with them, lived primarily in a large camp in a part of the southeast quadrant of the city known as the Anacostia Flats. A smaller group lived in abandoned government-owned buildings on the east end of Pennsylvania Avenue. On July 28 the attorney general had, with Hoover's blessing, ordered the removal of the occupants of the Pennsylvania Avenue camp. When the Washington police moved to enforce the order, the veterans rioted. In response, Hoover called on the Army to restore order and "clear the affected area without delay."

A series of unthinkable scenes followed: troops marching over the Memorial Bridge and massing on the Ellipse just south of the White House; tanks rolling through the streets of the nation's capital. Leading the response was General Douglas MacArthur, the Army chief of staff who was still in the early years of a career marked by persistent belief in his own greatness and in the mediocrity of the elected officials giving him orders. Under his direction, saber-wielding cavalry had taken control of the city and terrorized not just members of the Bonus Forces but civilians in their way. Ignoring a narrow directive from Hoover, MacArthur took it on himself to cross the Anacostia

River and take out the larger camp of the Bonus Forces, using tear gas to subdue the veterans and fire to destroy the site.

The violent crackdown shocked the country and further inflamed public sentiment against Hoover. The plight of the Bonus Forces resonated with Franklin's broader critique of the Republicans' handling of the Depression—the penniless veterans assailed by MacArthur's troops were quintessential forgotten men. Felix Frankfurter, a campaign aide, was with Franklin as he read accounts of the confrontation. His response was succinct: "Well, Felix, this will elect me."

By fall, even Hoover knew that Franklin was right. From the fortress walls of his White House, signs of a coming Roosevelt landslide were not hard to spot. When, around Labor Day, the White House elevator broke down, a repair company was called to restore it to service. As the repair truck drove away, a sign could be spotted on its rear: VOTE FOR ROOSEVELT.

FRANKLIN KNEW THAT HOWEVER assured his victory might seem, he had one remaining challenge: demonstrating to the public that he was physically up to the job. By fall, Republicans were spreading word that Franklin was sicker than he let on, that, indeed, his illness was degenerative and would soon take hold of his brain. One rumor even had it that John Nance Garner had agreed to take the vice-presidential slot on the Democratic ticket only after reviewing a secret medical report that said Franklin had less than a year to live.

To demonstrate his virility, Franklin used the same tactic he'd used in 1928 while campaigning in New York, announcing that he would go on an extensive and exhausting tour. In doing so, he claimed—perhaps a bit disingenuously—that he was going against the advice of his advisers, who preferred that he stay closer to home. But, he said, given the scope of the nation's problems, he felt it was important to go on a "fact-finding" mission to see as much of the varied effects of the Depression as possible. Plus, he said, "I'm stubborn and I like to travel." In mid-September he left Albany in a $20,000 private railcar dubbed the "Roosevelt Special," on an itinerary that would take him

8,900 miles through nineteen states—as ambitious an itinerary as any presidential candidate had ever undertaken.

Eleanor stayed behind in the East for the first half of the journey. "Mrs. Roosevelt remained at home to send . . . Franklin Jr. and John to school," Franklin would tell campaign audiences. In her place, he had Anna, James, and James's wife, Betsey. At whistle stops, Franklin used this family group to put on a show from the back of his car. "Pa developed a little family act," James later wrote. "He would come out on my arm, smiling at the crowd, then take his stance at the rail . . . then Pa would present the two blonde glamour girls—Anna and Betsey." After that he'd turn toward James, who towered over him and most everyone else, with exaggerated effect. "And this is my little boy, Jimmy," he would say, waiting a beat, then saying, "I have more hair than he has!"

Just as on Franklin's 1920 vice-presidential campaign rail journey, this campaign train was a movable feast of Roosevelt family, political staffers, and press. As a reward for his service in Chicago, Joseph Kennedy was invited to join Franklin's entourage. Kennedy, who had set his sights on a position in the Roosevelt administration, was a buoyant, flattering presence on board, but in private communications he made clear to Hearst where his true allegiance lay. In October, when Hearst sent Kennedy a large check to deliver to the campaign, Kennedy wrote to thank him. "You may rest assured," he said, "that whenever your interests in this administration are not served well, my interest has ceased."

Hearst's papers, never particularly concerned with consistency, now reliably proclaimed Franklin as a savior in waiting, poised to rout the Hoover menace and restore American greatness. When Franklin's train reached Los Angeles, Hearst organized a gathering of movie stars to celebrate him, including Helen Hayes, Constance Bennett, and Joan Crawford.

Even with Hearst in his corner, Franklin knew he could not count on universally favorable treatment in the news media. Concerns about his coverage in the nation's newspapers, disproportionately owned by Republicans, had helped compel the train trip. Out on the plains,

Franklin could woo and charm the reporters covering him for conservative outlets. These correspondents would then fill their dispatches with flattering copy about Franklin. Even if editors back in the city rooms then diluted this praise, the net effect was more positive coverage than any Democrat would have otherwise expected.

One reporter, John Boettiger of the *Chicago Tribune,* got particularly close to the Roosevelt family. The *Tribune,* a titan of American media in the 1930s, was published by Colonel Robert McCormick, an archconservative who deeply mistrusted Franklin, despite an acquaintance that stretched back to Groton. "Tammany wants Mr. Roosevelt to run for Governor again this fall and Cactus Jack Garner has announced that . . . he will run again for Congress down in Texas," the *Tribune* wrote in an editorial a few days after Franklin's nomination. "Somehow it doesn't look as though the Democrats felt just absolutely certain of electing their national ticket in November."

Shortly after he arrived in Albany to cover the Roosevelt campaign in the summer of 1932, Boettiger was hospitalized with an infected throat. Learning of the *Tribune* reporter's illness, Franklin insisted that after his release he spend a few days convalescing at Hyde Park. There, despite the *Tribune's* enmity toward Franklin, Boettiger formed a friendship with the Roosevelt family, and with one Roosevelt in particular.

Anna Roosevelt's marriage to Curtis Dall had not proved a happy one. Curtis's career in finance stalled after the crash of 1929; their finances became so strained that Anna, Curtis, and their two children moved into Franklin and Eleanor's East 65th Street townhouse. By the summer of 1932, Anna and Curtis's marriage was effectively over. She formed a close attachment to Boettiger that quickly blossomed into love. One day on the campaign train, Anna's son John would later write, reporters discovered them kissing on the platform between two cars.

Slowly making his way back east, Franklin stopped in Williams, Arizona, for a day of rest at the ranch of Isabella Greenway, one of Eleanor's oldest and closest friends. Eleanor flew west to join up with the campaign entourage there. The press was told that the visit to the

Greenway ranch would be nonpolitical and private. But reporters were outraged to discover that one of their number, John Boettiger, had been invited to join the Roosevelts.

Lorena Hickok, the AP reporter, was particularly affronted. When she saw Eleanor that day, she shared her grievance. As she spoke, she noted that Eleanor seemed different, more open and accessible than she'd been before. Her impression was confirmed when Eleanor offered a modifying proposal: perhaps Hickok would like to join as well. "The story didn't amount to much," Hickok later wrote. "I saw some cowboys roping steers and trying to stay on bucking broncos. . . . But Mrs. Roosevelt came and sat with me for quite a long time in the car and told me about her girlhood friendship with Isabella Greenway."

Eleanor was starting to see Hickok as more than just a reporter. Hickok was the only woman charged with covering Franklin's campaign train. Eleanor knew how alienating the fraternity of traveling political men could be, but Hickok was impressively unflappable. Returning to the station after one whistle stop, Hickok learned that the train had left without her. Instantly, she hailed a taxi and demanded the driver catch the Roosevelt party; at her urging, he drove so fast his taxi caught fire.

Hickok's life story was a testament to her formidable will and grit. Persecuted by an unstable and abusive father, she left home at age fourteen and worked as a domestic laborer while finishing school. Starting at local newspapers in the Midwest, she had risen to become one of the most prominent women reporters in the nation. She was, in other words, a reminder to Eleanor, held temporarily captive to her husband's ambition, of a woman empowered to guide her own life's course. Eleanor decided that Hickok was the kind of woman she could admire—and the kind of woman she could trust.

Hickok quickly became enamored. As the campaign train made its way back east, her dispatches were increasingly concerned with the Democratic candidate's accomplished, indefatigable wife. The connection between them deepened that fall when the AP assigned Hickok to cover Eleanor full-time. Through long days of campaign travel, Eleanor told Hickok all about her life—her unhappy child-hood, the revelation and deliverance she had felt at Mademoiselle Souvestre's Allenswood, the unhappiness of her years in Washington, the liberation and satisfaction she'd gained from her work in politics. Before long, the other woman was not "Miss Hickok" from the Associated Press but "Hick," Eleanor's dearest and most intimate friend.

FRANKLIN CONCLUDED HIS CAMPAIGN on the night before Election Day with a speech in Poughkeepsie. The city's streets were drenched in red light to celebrate him, and people began lining up to enter the city's Columbus Hall hours before his address. At ten o'clock, with Sara and Eleanor seated silently beside him, Franklin began his speech, broadcast live over the radio. His tone was solemn, even grave. He explained to his national audience that he had concluded all his campaigns in Poughkeepsie, since his first run for the state legislature twenty-two years before. "A man comes to wisdom in many years of public life," he said. "He knows well that when the light of favor shines upon him, it comes not, of necessity, that he himself is important. Favor comes because for a brief moment in the great space of human change and progress some general human purpose finds in him a satisfactory embodiment."

When most politicians say things like this, they are protesting too much. Certainly, at many moments in the thirty-year quest that had brought Franklin to this point, he'd thought himself sufficiently important to assume leadership of his countrymen. But that night, speaking in the city of his father and grandfather, he had reason to feel humbled and perplexed by the mysteries of fate. All his adult life, he had chased after the "light of favor." Now the light was at last shining on him. But the favor it offered him was a crushing load of near-insolvable problems, the custody of a nation in danger of collapse.

In the car with Hick later that night, Eleanor spoke of what was facing her husband. She too sounded solemn. "Of course Franklin will do his best if elected," she told Hick. "He is strong and resourceful. And he really cares about people. The federal government will have to do something. But will it be enough? Can it be enough? The responsibility he may have to take is something I hate to think about."

In the morning, November 8, 1932, Franklin voted in Hyde Park. Then the entire family, Sara included, began a joyous caravan down to New York City, where they would watch the returns come in. Crowds lined the Post Road as they moved through the lower Hudson Valley, in Poughkeepsie, Ossining, and Tarrytown.

After hosting a reception for campaign staff and the press who'd covered the campaign, the Roosevelts headed to the Biltmore Hotel to wait on the results. Outside Franklin's suite, twenty "telephone girls" fielded reports of the vote totals from all over the country. Their dispatches were unfailingly good. That day nearly 23 million Americans would vote for Franklin Roosevelt. He easily returned the entire Solid South, the place he had spent so much time in the past six years, to the Democrats' column. He captured as well every state he'd journeyed through on his western voyage, including California, Hoover's home state. He did what Al Smith failed to do in 1928—draw enough votes from both the city and upstate to carry their shared home state of New York. In the end, he carried all but six states: Maine, New Hampshire, Vermont, Connecticut, Pennsylvania, and Delaware.

It was a landslide. By nine o'clock in the East, that was clear. The hallways of the Biltmore swelled with Democrats offering their congratulations to the obvious president-elect. In the study of his home in Palo Alto, California, where he'd gone to vote, Herbert Hoover received a note. Outside the house, Stanford students were literally singing his praises—"Sis-boom-bah! President and Mrs. Hoover!"— but the news was bad: Franklin had won New York State. That was it, Hoover knew; he'd lost the presidency after a single term. After a few minutes, he released a telegram of congratulations to Franklin that was studiously correct if not especially warm:

I CONGRATULATE YOU ON THE OPPORTUNITY THAT HAS COME TO YOU TO BE OF SERVICE TO THE COUNTRY AND I WISH

FOR YOU A MOST SUCCESSFUL ADMINISTRATION. IN THE COM-
MON PURPOSE OF ALL OF US I SHALL DEDICATE MYSELF TO
EVERY POSSIBLE HELPFUL EFFORT.

At the Biltmore, Louis Howe poured from an old bottle of sherry. For twenty years, he said, he'd been saving this bottle for a special occasion: the moment Franklin Roosevelt was elected president of the United States.

IT WAS NEARLY TWO in the morning when Franklin returned home to East 65th Street, but Sara greeted him at the door. Mother and son were now seventy-eight and fifty, but their old rule still reigned: Accentuate the positive all the time. "This is the greatest night of my life," Franklin said.

When he retired to his bedroom that night, his mood was more sober. James Roosevelt helped his father into bed. It was the same bedroom in which, eleven years before, James, just home from boarding school, had found him newly released from the hospital, his body and life transformed. Seeing tears in his son's eyes that day, Franklin had been warm and welcoming, trying to reassure the boy that there was no need for fear. In the years between, James, more than anyone, had been at Franklin's side in his delicate, public moments of peril—getting out of the car, making his way to a podium as the wide world looked on. For those other eyes, Franklin flashed his winning smile. James alone felt his father's nervous fingers, clutching his arm.

"You know, Jimmy, all my life I've been afraid of just one thing—fire," Franklin said. "Tonight I think I'm afraid of something else ... I'm just afraid that I may not have the strength to do this job."

Before his eyes closed that night, Franklin said, he would pray. "I am going to pray that God will help me, that He will give me the strength and the guidance to do this job and to do it right."

He looked at the son he had comforted years ago, now a man. "I hope you will pray for me too, Jimmy."

Chapter 29

Spreading Fire

NOVEMBER 1932–FEBRUARY 1933

SINCE THE EARLY REPUBLIC, NEW PRESIDENTS HAD BEEN inaugurated on March 4, the anniversary of the birth of the federal government in 1789. (In those years when March 4 fell on a Sunday, the president's swearing-in was postponed until the next day.) This four-month interval—equivalent to more than 8 percent of a president's entire term—had been a necessity in the nation's infancy, when service in the capital had required a long journey from the far-flung states, through treacherous winter conditions. But in the fast-moving world of 1932 and 1933, it was a practical disaster. With their votes at the beginning of November, the people had stingingly, unambiguously rejected Hoover's leadership in the crisis of the Depression. Yet that leadership would remain unchanged until spring was nearly at hand.

The election result had left Hoover embittered but not humbled. Like many defeated incumbents, he consoled himself that his sense of duty had cost him the election. As president, he had had an obligation to act in a responsible, if politically unpopular, fashion, while his challenger had been free to make whatever promises he liked. To Hoover, the long interregnum offered an opportunity to school Franklin Roosevelt in the reality of the world.

A few days after the election, Franklin was surprised to receive a long telegram from the man he had just defeated. In it, Hoover went on at length about the imminent predicament of European debt to the United States. In accord with the U.S. government's moratorium policy of 1931, France and Britain were due to make payments of $95.5 million and $19.9 million to the U.S. treasury in mid-December. Both had indicated they would be unable to make these payments. Hoover proposed that he and Franklin meet in the hopes they might come to an understanding on how to proceed.

Franklin was wary but agreed to stop in Washington on his way south to Warm Springs, where he planned, as usual, to spend Thanksgiving. On November 22, he and Raymond Moley called on Hoover and his Treasury secretary, Ogden Mills, at the White House. Franklin tried to reestablish chummy terms, but Hoover merely launched into an hour-long lecture on the debt problem. Though the president was intense and emphatic, he was unable even to look his successor in the eye, preferring to keep his gaze fixed on the floor.

In response to this presentation, Franklin stayed mostly quiet, asking only a set of basic questions about the debt problem. Hoover left the meeting aghast and feeling vindicated. Franklin "did not get it at all," he said.

In fact, Franklin had kept quiet because he saw a trap. In his presentation, Hoover had laid out two bad options—force payment from the European states, triggering a default, or postpone the debt payments, further undermining faith in international credit. Hoover had proposed that Franklin join with him in appointing commissioners to a conference charged with coming up with a long-term solution to the question of European debt.

As Franklin and his advisers saw it, Hoover was trying to assign Franklin political responsibility for the debt problem without actually giving Franklin any control over the policy. Throughout the campaign, Hoover had presented solving the debt question as central to ending the Depression. This view, shared by Wall Street and most doctrinaire economists, conflicted with Franklin's own campaign message—that the Depression could be solved only by addressing fundamental inequities in the domestic economic system.

If Franklin accepted the debt crisis as his own, he would create a number of short-term political problems. Hearst, for one, would be outraged to see his handpicked president, after all his campaign promises to disavow internationalism, entangle himself in European affairs before his presidency had even begun. The long-term damage was even greater. If Franklin acknowledged the primacy of the debt question, he would undermine the political urgency for his expansive, if still somewhat unformed, domestic program, which had come to be known as the New Deal. Hoover, having lost the election, was now asking Franklin to concede its central argument.

So Franklin did what came naturally to him, adopting a posture of cordial aloofness. Whenever further communications from Hoover came, he took days to respond, and when he did, he was careful not to make firm commitments. Hoover seethed: Franklin *was* the man he'd seen in the campaign—ignorant, insignificant, and dishonest.

The crisis swelled. The stock market sank, and financial institutions continued to fail—by 1933, more than 40 percent of banks that were in business at the time of the 1929 crash had closed their doors. Those that remained open scoured ruthlessly for liquidity; thousands of farmers, unable to sell their crops and thus pay their mortgages, faced imminent foreclosure. Slowly, the country inched toward restiveness, if not outright revolution. In states like Iowa, Kansas, and Nebraska, bankers and lawyers charged with carrying out foreclosures faced protest, violence, and even lynching.

Franklin's true task on assuming the presidency was becoming clear: to ensure that the federal republic would endure. Whatever his doubts about Franklin, the columnist Walter Lippmann now saw him as the nation's only hope. Visiting Franklin during the interregnum, Lippmann spared no drama: "The situation is critical, Franklin, you may have no alternative but to assume dictatorial powers."

Franklin had to do something; still, he gave few hints of *what* he intended to do. His economic advisers Moley and Rexford Tugwell were now stars in the press, reputed to be the wise men who had the president's ear. But even they weren't sure exactly what Franklin was thinking. They would believe they'd sold him on a broad program of domestic spending to restore employment and the individual's purchasing power, but then someone would pay a call on Franklin and report that he seemed preoccupied with balancing the federal budget.

In January, William Randolph Hearst, mindful of all he'd done for the president-elect, sent a top editor to inspect Franklin for signs of postelection heresy. Franklin assured the editor his cabinet would be "radical," with "no one in it who knows the way to 23 Wall Street," the legendary headquarters of J. P. Morgan. (Receiving this report, Hearst was uncharacteristically, if impermanently, smitten, pronouncing himself "in enthusiastic accord" with Franklin "about practically everything.") And yet when Bernard Baruch, who certainly knew the way to 23 Wall Street, called on Franklin, the president-elect was quick to offer assurances that his policy agenda would fall squarely in the mainstream.

Old hands from the Roosevelt organization noted the ever-expanding crop of supplicants fawning over Franklin. They also noted, and resented, the ease with which Franklin invariably fawned back. In January, an exasperated Hoover sent Henry Stimson, the workhorse Republican statesman, to Hyde Park, hoping he could convince Franklin of the wisdom of Hoover's economic course. Franklin's advisers were shocked as Franklin was charming and pleasing with this interloper; Franklin even seemed to hold Stimson's ideas in high regard. The old campaign hands were experiencing the same pain that Louis and Eleanor had to overcome in the past. Devotion to Franklin was a deceptively tricky business. His love was always on offer, and yet, somehow, there was never quite enough of it.

Franklin made no apology for his vagueness. In his own mind, he was not inconstant but *flexible*, and flexibility was precisely what the times required. "Let's concentrate upon one thing," he told a friend. "Save the people and the nation, and if we have to change our minds twice every day to accomplish that end, we should do it." What's more, he knew that any clarity he offered on what he planned to do as president would muffle the dramatic effect when it came time to actually do it. He had long since learned to resist the temptation to act simply for the sake of acting. Patience had restored him to his career in politics, had won him the Democratic nomination and the presidency. Until his hour was at hand, he would wait, contemplate, and keep his true plans to himself.

———

FRANKLIN KNEW WHAT HE really needed in the meantime: Time to rest and swim, to collect his thoughts and gather his strength. And he needed the sun. He made two trips to Warm Springs, once in November and again in January. He stayed in a newly completed cottage he had designed and built for himself, away from the colony, on Pine Mountain. A six-room colonial, it was painted white with four columns sheltering its entrance. It bore a striking resemblance, in miniature, to another white house, in Washington, that he would soon call home.

At the end of January, he returned to the St. Johns River near Jacksonville for a ten-day cruise of Florida and the Bahamas. The accommodations on this trip were a considerable improvement from what they had been in his *LaRooco* days. He would be the guest of Vincent Astor, his Hudson Valley neighbor, aboard Astor's opulent yacht.

During his voyage, a horde of Democratic office-seekers, along with the political press corps, decamped to Miami, to be at the president-elect's beck and call. But from the seas, Franklin's party sent only the occasional chirpy telegram. WE ARE ALL SPENDING THE DAY SWIMMING OFF A SWELL BEACH, read one dispatch from the Bahamian port of Eleuthera.

When the yacht arrived back in Miami on February 15, he invited the press on board. Tanned and recharged, he professed to be utterly detached from the news. "I haven't really seen a newspaper since I left, except the Nassau paper yesterday."

As evening fell, twenty thousand people gathered in Miami's Bayfront Park. Franklin's aides had made it known that, after disembarking, he would stop in the park for a brief address before boarding a train north that night. In the audience was Lillian Cross, a Miami housewife, who, along with her husband and a friend visiting from Atlanta, hoped to catch a glimpse of the president-elect. Arriving at the park, she and her friend left her husband behind and pushed to the front of the crowd, near the bandstand where Franklin was to speak.

Franklin traveled in an open-top car, accompanied by Miami mayor R. D. Gautier and Marvin McIntyre, Franklin's assistant. Riding behind him in a second car was Raymond Moley, who had traveled south to brief the president-elect on progress in filling the Cabinet posts. Along with Moley were Vincent Astor and some of the other guests from the yachting trip. As they made their way to the park, they passed through mobs of people who had come out to greet Franklin. Astor noted the anonymity offered by the encroaching darkness and the swelling crowds. An ideal setting, he observed morbidly, for an assassin to do his work.

When they reached the park, Franklin's car pulled up to the bandstand. Propped in a standing position in the back seat, Franklin spoke into a microphone. His remarks were friendly but brief. "I am not going to attempt to tell you any fish stories," he said, "and the only fly in the ointment on this trip has been that I have put on about ten pounds." When he'd finished, Lillian Cross, seated some fifteen feet away, stood up on her bench to get a better look. She saw Franklin sitting once again in the car's back seat, as the scene around him grew chaotic. Then she felt the bench buckling underneath her and, worried that she'd lose her balance, she turned. A small man with curly hair had stood up on the bench behind her. "Don't do that, please," she said. "You're going to knock me off." As her eyes fixed on the man, she shook with horror: He was holding a gun.

From his seat in the back of the car, Franklin was greeting the surge of well-wishers. He turned to see a familiar face: Anton Cermak, the mayor of Chicago. Cermak, who'd helped to organize the anti-Roosevelt forces at the convention, had come to Miami to make amends with Franklin's organization and hopefully gain Franklin's future political support. "Hello, Tony!" Franklin said warmly. The two men shook hands and spoke for a moment, before Cermak disappeared around the back of the car.

Next someone else approached, clutching a lengthy telegram. Franklin hunched his body forward, trying to hear the man explain what the telegram said. He was still leaning forward when he heard an explosion, like a firecracker, ricochet through the air. The series of identical blasts that followed and the screams that rose from the crowd said it all: Someone was trying to shoot him.

In quick succession, five bullets flew through the air. The first victim, a woman visiting from New Jersey, suffered a non-fatal wound to the head. The second bullet hit Mayor Cermak in the abdomen, and he fell in a pile on the ground. A third bullet struck a woman standing on the bandstand, sending her tumbling down the steps. Two more bullets nicked two men at the scene.

All five shots had come from a .32-caliber revolver belonging to a man named Giuseppe Zangara. Thirty-two years old, Zangara, an Italian-born naturalized American citizen, was the small, curly-haired man standing behind Lillian Cross on the bench. "He's going to kill the president!" Cross later said she'd thought when she saw him raise his gun. As he began shooting, she lunged at him, grabbing at his arm and thrusting it up into the air. She held her grip on him, even as he continued shooting. Had she not done so, one of his shots almost certainly would have struck Franklin.

Men in the crowd had set upon Zangara, tearing him down off the bench into the crowd. With the shooting over, Franklin, enveloped by a phalanx of Secret Service, hoisted himself up in the car once more. "I'm all right!" he cried, reassuring the crowd. "I'm all right!"

The Secret Service, wary of the surging crowd, commanded Franklin's driver to move out of the area, but just after they passed the bandstand, Franklin ordered the driver to halt once more. He could see Mayor Cermak, his white shirt turned a horrific shade of crimson, being carried away from the bandstand. Quickly, Franklin signaled to have the wounded Cermak brought to him. They headed to a hospital, Franklin clutching Cermak's near-lifeless frame, trying to support it as best he could. He searched for a pulse but couldn't find one. When a Miami policeman, riding in the car, offered a dire assessment—"I don't think he is going to last"—Franklin concurred: "I am afraid he isn't."

After another block, Cermak seemed to revive and return to consciousness. "Tony, keep quiet, don't move," Franklin told him. "It won't hurt you if you keep quiet." Franklin wondered why the trip to the hospital was taking so long, but he offered soothing words of encouragement to the wounded man: They would be there soon; everything would be all right. When at last they arrived, doctors found that the bullet had lodged in Cermak's spine. (Cermak would never leave the hospital, succumbing to complications from his wounds two-and-a-half weeks later.)

In New York that evening, Eleanor had just finished a speaking engagement when she learned of the shooting. She'd planned to travel on a late-night train for an engagement in Ithaca the next day, but she returned to East 65th Street to await further news. Along with Lorena Hickok, she watched a hysterical Louis scream, "Operator!" over and over as he unsuccessfully tried to get a long-distance call through to Miami. To Hickok, Eleanor seemed stricken but resigned. "This is what it's like to be in public life, Hick," she said.

Finally, Franklin called from the hospital to say that he was unhurt. He described the car ride with Cermak and said he intended to stay at the hospital until he'd been updated by the doctors attending to the mayor. Eleanor offered soothing words to the press—Franklin was "all right" and "not the least bit excited"—and then caught her train to Ithaca as planned.

Canceling his plans to travel north that night, Franklin kept vigil at the hospital past eleven o'clock. His would-be assassin spent that night in the Miami jail. When authorities learned that Giuseppe Zangara had recently come to Miami from Chicago, some suspected that Cermak, not Franklin, had been his intended target. Others wondered if he was a communist, hoping his actions would light the spark of revolution across the land. The truth was sadder and more pedestrian: A bricklayer by training, Zangara was out of work, hungry, and suffering from mental illness. Like other disturbed killers before him, he had latched on to the simple logic of anarchism. "I hate all presidents," he said in an interview with the police, "and I hate officials and anybody who is rich."

When he finally left the hospital, Franklin returned to the yacht to spend the night. Observing him there, others in the party expected a break in his composure, an acknowledgment of how close he had come to death. But, Moley later wrote, "There was nothing—not so much as the twitching of a muscle, the mopping of a brow, or even the hint of a false gaiety—to indicate that it wasn't any other evening in any other place."

Of course, this was Franklin Roosevelt: There was little reason to believe that he showed his friends what he really felt. Perhaps that night as he said his prayers, he contemplated the same mystery he'd pondered in the early days of his illness: *Why had he survived?* Once more, he had come close to death. Once more, he had been spared. *God* had spared him, that he believed. If the Almighty had a plan for Franklin, it was still to be revealed. But there was still more good for him to do.

The next day, news of the failed attempt on the life of the president-elect was everywhere. The details were ghoulish, but their combined effect provided the nation with an unexpected pick-me-up. For the first time in a long time, the nation had been spared the worst: A madman had tried to kill the man they'd selected to be the next president, but he had not succeeded. Not only that: The president-elect had handled the whole ordeal with poise, good humor, and courage; he'd even acted heroically in an attempt to save another man's life! For so long, the news had been bad; for so long, people had hoped for better and gotten worse. Perhaps, people thought, America's luck had finally begun to change.

In fact, the incident demonstrated what the country had really found: a president, and a First Lady, who had long since learned how to go on living through times of anxiety and trial. Greeted by reporters in Ithaca the morning after the shooting, Eleanor downplayed the whole affair. "That's apt to happen to any man in public life," she said. "He must always face the possibility, and so must his family. But it's best not to think about it."

She grew quiet for a moment before going on: "One cannot live in fear."

ON THE NIGHT OF the shooting, Herbert Hoover had been roused from bed with news of the events in Miami. He'd promptly sent Franklin a telegram:

TOGETHER WITH EVERY CITIZEN I REJOICE THAT YOU HAVE
NOT BEEN INJURED. I SHALL BE GRATEFUL TO YOU FOR NEWS
OF MAYOR CERMAK'S CONDITION.

These were perhaps the only congenial thoughts that Hoover had
to offer his successor in the course of their four-month interregnum.
The sitting president's exhaustion and his antagonism toward the
man who had defeated him had only grown. So had the country's
problems. The failure of the nation's banks had accelerated rapidly
since the beginning of February. Americans were withdrawing between $10 million and $15 million from the nation's banks each day,
and the trend suggested even larger drainage to come. Hoover's advisers warned that panic was spinning out of control so fast that by early
March, the banking system might be insolvent.

Hoover believed all of it was Franklin's fault. As the incumbent
president saw it, he had been well on his way to solving the problem
of the Depression in 1932. Then Franklin, with his talk of realigning
the compact between capital and labor, had spooked the markets and
seized up credit. Again and again in the days since the election,
Hoover had tried to make Franklin his governing partner, only to be
rebuffed. He noted with bitterness an impertinent and highly publicized comment Rexford Tugwell had made, predicting that the nation's financial collapse might well be at hand and that the Hoover
administration would surely carry the blame for it.

In the time he had left, Hoover was determined to force Franklin
to put the country first. On February 17, as his successor made his way
back to New York by train, Hoover sat down to write Franklin another impassioned letter.

"My dear Mr. President Elect," he wrote. "A most critical situation
has arisen in the country of which I feel it is my duty to advise you
confidentially. I am therefore taking this course of writing you myself
and sending it to you through the Secret Service for your hand direct
as obviously its misplacement would only feed the fire and increase
the dangers."

———

THE FOLLOWING EVENING, FRANKLIN attended a banquet at the
Astor House, on Fifth Avenue. The occasion was the annual "Inner
Circle" gala, at which New York's political press corps performed skits
and songs lampooning the state's highest-ranking politicians, most of
whom were present in the room. Among the attendees that night was
the state's new governor, Herbert Lehman, as well as his two most
recent predecessors, Franklin Roosevelt and Al Smith. In one scene, a
reporter playing Jim Farley encountered a reporter dressed as Smith
at Franklin's inauguration in Washington.

"Well," said the Smith character, "I just came to tell you I won't
accept any Cabinet position."

"Well," Farley replied, "I think the president will listen to that."

In the audience, the real Smith and Franklin both roared.

Raymond Moley was sitting at Franklin's table. As the acts went
on, he saw Franklin subtly signaling to him. The president-elect
slipped him, under the table, a document he had just been handed by
the Secret Service. It was Hoover's letter:

> ... there is a steadily degenerating confidence in the future
> which has reached the height of general alarm. I am convinced
> that a very early statement by you upon two or three policies of
> your administration would serve greatly to restore confi-
> dence ...

Skimming the letter, Moley was first stunned and then appalled.
The situation the president described was indeed dire. But even more
shocking were the steps Hoover proposed Franklin take: issuing a
statement in which he would offer "prompt assurance that there will
be no tampering or inflation of the currency" and "that the budget
will be unquestionably balanced, even if further taxation is necessary."
In essence, it seemed to Moley, Hoover was trying to dictate the policy of his successor's administration.

This was, in fact, an accurate interpretation. "If these declarations be made by the president-elect," Hoover gloated after writing the letter, "he will have ratified the whole major program of the Republican administration; that is, it means the abandonment of 90 percent of the so-called New Deal."

Shaken by what he was reading, Moley looked up, expecting to see some of the anxiety he felt mirrored in Franklin's face. It wasn't there. Admiring the ongoing performance before them, Franklin shone, carefree. He lingered after the performances were over, chatting and signing autographs, as if he had all the time in the world.

Late that night at the townhouse on East 65th Street, he and his advisers discussed the crisis. The response to Hoover's letter would be the same one Franklin had been using for months: evasion. He would wait ten days to respond to Hoover's message, an unthinkable lag for any communication with a president, let alone on such a grave matter as this. When he finally did write, Franklin explained the delay by saying, incredibly, that a secretary had misplaced Hoover's letter. "I am equally concerned with you in regard to the gravity of the present banking situation," the letter went on, "but my thought is that it is so very deep-seated that the fire is bound to spread in spite of anything that is done by way of mere statements."

Chapter 30

An Unfamiliar City

FEBRUARY 27–MARCH 3, 1933

FRANKLIN SPENT HIS LAST DAYS IN NEW YORK FINALIZING his Cabinet and White House staff. In late February, he appointed William Woodin as his Treasury secretary. Woodin was a Republican and an industrialist, and while he was not precisely a child of the international banking system, he would have had little trouble finding his way to 23 Wall Street in a pinch. Woodin immediately entered into painful, protracted talks with Ogden Mills, the man he would replace in the Treasury Department, about a joint approach to the banking crisis. These talks were fruitless from the outset: Franklin simply wasn't interested in doing anything jointly.

His mind was on Inauguration Day. Since the fall, Franklin had been thinking about the speech he would give at his swearing-in. The address, he believed, would come at a perilous moment in the nation's history. No president since Lincoln in 1865 had addressed the country in a moment so fraught with peril. It was, Franklin believed, his best chance to shape the country's image of his presidency, and of him. He would finally cast aside doubt about what he stood for and what he planned to do.

On the night of February 27, after dinner at Hyde Park with Moley, Missy, and a stenographer, Franklin presided in the living room, leading a revision of Moley's text. Outside, the wind raged, but a healthy fire warmed the room as Franklin conducted the drafting of the speech like a symphony. He seamlessly moved from big idea to big idea, touching on policy, ethics, faith, and presidential history. Moley scrawled notes: "talk of [Benjamin] Franklin (he was shallow) Jefferson best. Franklin read Moley's sentences aloud, editing as he spoke so the stenographer could take down new versions. After midnight, Moley rose theatrically and tossed his old draft in the fire. "This is your speech now," he said good-naturedly.

Before he went to bed that night, Franklin insisted on writing out the revised draft by hand. Louis would review it the next day, he explained, and would "have a fit" if he believed it was created by someone else. But when he insisted on writing it in his own hand, Franklin may well have had more than Louis's fragile ego in mind. After the inauguration, he would append a note on White House stationery: "This is the original manuscript of the Inaugural Address as written at Hyde Park on Monday, February 27, 1933. I started in about 9:00 P.M. and ended at 1:30 A.M. A number of minor changes were made in subsequent drafts but the final draft is substantially the same as this original." Future scholars finding this note might have pictured Franklin sitting in solitary concentration at a lamplit desk, pouring his thoughts onto the page. Franklin likely sensed that the speech would live in history, and he wanted to be sure he'd get the credit for it.

The closing lines of the speech *were* entirely his, written spontaneously that late February night: "In this dedication of a Nation we humbly ask the blessing of God. May He protect each and every one of us. May He guide me in the days to come."

In the weeks before his inauguration, Franklin spoke more than usual of the Almighty. On March 2, the Roosevelts left New York for Washington on a special train. The train was packed with family, supporters, and press, and the mood on board was festive and light. But Franklin sat in his car at the back in comparative isolation, quiet and serene. Jim Farley, who would serve in the new administration as postmaster general, joined him there. The two men had been on many train trips together, and Farley was used to seeing Franklin as a joking, gossiping, carefree traveling companion. On that day, though, Farley would later write, "He seemed fully conscious of the gravity of the moment at hand and for this reason was inclined to be serious in his mood and thoughts."

To get through its time of trouble, Farley recalled Franklin saying, "The faith of the people was far more important than any other single element." The train rolled south, like the one that delivered Lincoln to a troubled capital in 1861. "He talked for some little time in the same vein," Farley wrote, "saying that in the end the salvation of all peoples, including our own, would depend upon a proper attitude toward God."

ON FRIDAY, MARCH 3, the day before Franklin's inauguration, the Roosevelts woke in their suite on the seventh floor of Washington's Mayflower Hotel. Franklin's advisers had set up a court-in-waiting at the hotel, and he remained ensconced there for the morning. But Eleanor was up and out of the hotel suite early. It was her last full day as a private citizen, and she had a deeply personal pilgrimage planned.

Downstairs, she found Lorena Hickok waiting for her in a cab. The night before, when they'd gotten off the train from New York, Eleanor had asked Hickok to meet her in the morning at the building's side entrance, away from the eyes of the press. "There's something I'd like to show you," she told Hickok. "It's something that used to mean a very great deal to me when we were in Washington before."

This had not been a politician's wife speaking to a reporter. Eleanor and her "Hick" had become much more than that. Hick had continued to cover Eleanor for the AP after the election, writing copy that showed off the unrivaled access she had secured to the new First Lady. Readers did not know that Hick was keeping to herself the best story of all: that Mrs. Roosevelt was deeply despondent over the prospect of life as the president's wife.

The months since the election had been hard on Eleanor. The morning after Franklin's victory, she'd returned to work at the Todhunter School, her sanctuary, and found her role transformed. However much she protested, students and other faculty members refused to think of her as Mrs. Roosevelt anymore. She was the wife of the president-elect. She knew that she would have to give up her teaching job, but she had intended to keep her position editing the parenting magazine *Babies, Just Babies.* When her plans were publicized, there had been an outcry at the idea of a working First Lady. "As a matter of dignity," one editorial read, "and in keeping with the exalted position her husband is about to hold she ought to abandon some of her present occupations."

For years Eleanor had been accustomed to speaking her mind on matters domestic and global. Now, as the wife of the incoming president, even her innocuous thoughts seemed to invite censure. In one speech that winter, she touched on a familiar subject, the demands on youth in a rapidly changing world. "The average girl of today," she said, "faces the problem of learning very young how much she can drink of such things as whiskey and gin and sticking to the proper quantity." Prohibition advocates were incensed. Such statements, said a Kansas alliance of conservative women's groups, had "placed a severe strain upon the loyalty of countless American women."

Her treasured freedom to come and go as she pleased was gone. When she walked down Park Avenue in New York, she was followed, photographed, pointed at. She was instructed, despite her protests, to travel with a Secret Service detail. In January 1933, on a one-day visit to Washington to inspect the living quarters in the White House, she'd scandalized the city by refusing a chauffeured car and walking the five blocks from the Mayflower Hotel to the executive mansion. Even if Franklin might let her live an independent life, the rest of the world would not.

A touch of Eleanor's discontent found its way into the public eye, thanks to Hick's pen. In the AP's postelection stories, Eleanor was a woman of liberal outlook, used to taking care of herself. She was forthright in explaining her decision to take the job editing *Babies, Just Babies.* "I went into it because I wanted money," she said. "I have a small income of my own, but I need more money to do a lot of the things I like to do." She was uninterested in the title "First Lady": "I suppose they will call me that . . . but there isn't going to be any 'first lady of the land.' There is going to be plain, ordinary Mrs. Roosevelt, and that's all." Indeed, Eleanor's ambivalence about her new position shone through Hick's prose. "I never wanted to be a President's wife," Eleanor said in one story, "and I don't want it now."

But for all the revealing glimpses Hick provided, she concealed much more. The Roosevelts' unconventional living habits, the marital difficulties of the Roosevelt children, Franklin and Eleanor's painful marital past—these things Hick kept to herself, without instruction. Thus, in Hick, Eleanor found what she'd longed for: someone who was safe, strong, and interested in what she had to say.

In the space of just a few months, the two women's lives had become thoroughly and intimately enmeshed. Hick was Eleanor's closest confidant, then something more. For Christmas 1932, Hick presented Eleanor with a diamond-and-sapphire ring. Eleanor boldly put it on her finger, where it would stay for years. "Hick darling," she wrote in a letter that spring. "Oh! How good it was to hear your voice, it was so inadequate to try & tell you what it meant, Jimmy was near & I couldn't say *je t'aime et je t'adore*' as I longed to do but always remember I am saying it & that I go to sleep thinking of you & repeating our little saying."

The precise nature of Eleanor's attachment to her other close women friends remains a matter of mystery and conjecture. But in the case of Hick, as Eleanor's biographer Blanche Wiesen Cook has convincingly shown, there is little doubt they shared a passion that was consuming, romantic, and sexual. Hick burned many of the letters that passed between the two women, but the ones that survive tell the tale clearly enough: "I've been trying today to bring back your face," Eleanor would write to Hick later that year. "Most clearly I remember your eyes and the feeling of that soft spot just northeast of the corner of your mouth against my lips."

Thus, when Eleanor got into Hick's cab that morning outside the Mayflower, she was joining a woman to whom she had decided to give her heart. Now Eleanor would show Hick the places she had known long ago, when Eleanor's world had come apart.

The cab made its way up Connecticut Avenue. In the Roosevelts' old Washington life, the avenue had been the central thoroughfare of the capital's society, shooting out toward Chevy Chase like the bone of a tight corset. At the corner of N Street, Eleanor and Hick could nearly glimpse the home of Anna "Bamie" Roosevelt Cowles, Eleanor's aunt, where the Roosevelts had lived at the beginning of Franklin's Navy Department days, the place where Eleanor had watched as Uncle Teddy's White House gardener lovingly tended the modest grounds. But Mrs. Cowles had been dead for going on two years, and now no Roosevelts lived there at all.

Next they passed the site of the old British embassy, which, in the Navy Department years, had been the glittering heart of the city's social life. A year earlier, the British legation had moved to a larger campus and the grand old building had been torn down. A Goodyear tire and filling station now stood in its place.

After making their way through the traffic at Dupont Circle, they drove down R Street, the place where she and Franklin had spent their difficult, final Washington years. On the lawn in front of the house, a sign had been erected, reading FORMER RESIDENCE OF FRANKLIN D. ROOSEVELT. Eleanor hurried the cab along.

When they reached the Rock Creek Cemetery, Eleanor got out of the cab and led the way up a hill to a grove of evergreens. There, still standing, was *Grief,* the memorial to Clover Adams by Augustus Saint-Gaudens. Hick looked up at the large bronze statue of a seated woman, her head and body covered by robes. "Only her face was visible," Hick would later recall of the statue. "It was a face that no one would ever forget."

Eleanor gave Hick the whole story: how Clover Adams, brokenhearted from her husband's betrayal, had committed suicide by drinking potassium cyanide. How her husband, Henry Adams, sick with grief and guilt, had commissioned the statue from Saint-Gaudens and then had never spoken of Clover again.

Eleanor went on to describe the special meaning that the place held in her own life. She spoke of the days after Franklin's affair with Lucy Mercer, when she had come to the monument—"the most beautiful thing in Washington"—seeking solace and release. "In the old days," Eleanor explained, "I was much younger and not so very wise. Sometimes I'd be very unhappy and sorry for myself. When I was feeling that way, if I could manage it, I'd come out here, alone, and sit and look at that woman. And I'd always come away somehow feeling better. And stronger. I've been here many, many times."

Looking at the statue, Hick could see in the face of Clover the pain that Eleanor had seen all those years before, and perhaps also something greater. "All the sorrow humanity had ever had to endure was expressed in that face. . . . Yet in that expression there was something almost triumphant. There was a woman who had experienced every kind of pain, every kind of suffering known to mankind and come out of it serene—and compassionate."

The two women sat there in the cold, silently studying the statue. After a while, they left to hail another cab. They made their way back, down Connecticut Avenue to the Mayflower. The White House was just a few blocks away. Contemplating a life that felt like a prison sentence, Eleanor may have comforted herself that *Grief* was nearby, to offer her escape and solace once more. But though she would return to the statue in her White House years, her visits would be far less frequent than they had been in the old days. Sooner than she knew, she would discover that Washington was not the same as it had been in her younger days. More important, neither was she.

THAT AFTERNOON, THE ROOSEVELTS left the Mayflower to call on the Hoovers. Franklin and Eleanor brought James and Betsey along with them in the hopes the young couple would help keep things light. At the White House, they were greeted by the chief usher, Irwin "Ike" Hoover. The usher—no relation to the outgoing president—was a Washington institution, who had served in the executive mansion since the days of Eleanor's uncle Ted. "It's good to have another Roosevelt in the White House," he said genially. Then, with the tactful discretion of an attendant to the powerful, he informed Franklin quietly that Ogden Mills, the Treasury secretary, and Eugene Meyer, the chairman of the Federal Reserve, were expected imminently at the White House.

Franklin understood the message: President Hoover intended to surprise him with one more attempt to force Franklin's hand. Calmly, Franklin sent word to have Raymond Moley informed of Mills's and Meyer's presence and to ask if Moley could join them at the White House as well.

The Hoovers and Roosevelts proceeded with their social visit in strained discomfort. The outgoing president, who'd never excelled at small talk, looked near dead from exhaustion. Relations had so deteriorated between the two men that even Franklin's attempts at charm came out sounding like half insults. He assured Hoover that he need feel no pressure to return the Roosevelts' call. "Mr. Roosevelt," Hoover replied, "when you are in Washington as long as I have been, you will learn that the President of the United States calls on nobody."

Moley had been napping in his suite at the Mayflower when he was roused by the summons from Franklin. Racing to the White House, he imagined what Hoover was planning to spring on his successor. The nation's banking system was on the brink of death. By end of business that day, thirty-four states had closed their banks. The contagious fear of further failures was so acute it seemed likely that the next day, a Saturday, depositors would rush to withdraw their savings from banks in the remaining fourteen states that had remained open. Among those states that had not yet closed but whose banks had reached a point of dire peril was New York, the epicenter of American finance.

If the big banks on Wall Street failed, the worst would follow. It was possible that in the minutes immediately before or immediately after Franklin took his oath of office, the American financial system would cease to function. Hoover, Moley surmised, wanted Franklin to join him in taking the blame for shuttering the nation's banks. But he would leave it to Franklin to figure out how, once closed, the nation's financial system could ever get up and running again.

The ice never broke during the Roosevelts' call on the Hoovers. "We downed our tea," James Roosevelt recalled, "Mother and Mrs.

Hoover made desultory conversation, and then it was time to go." As the others prepared to depart, Hoover signaled to Franklin that he wanted to continue their conversation in private. Eavesdropping from the other side of an open door, Eleanor heard the exchange between the two men grow more heated. Hoover was unsure if a national bank holiday was necessary but was open to calling for one in conjunction with Franklin. "Will you join in a joint proclamation closing all of the banks?" Hoover asked, boxing the other man in. Franklin's reflexive pleasantness vanished: "Like hell I will!" he said. "If you haven't the guts to do it yourself, I'll wait until I'm president to do it."

When Moley arrived, he found the president and president-elect, along with Mills and Meyer, in a "tense discussion" of logistics and legalisms. In time, Franklin softened a little, moved, Moley surmised, by Hoover's palpable aura of depletion and defeat. He indicated that if Hoover wanted to close the banks in his remaining hours in office, Franklin would try to give him public cover. "I shall be waiting at my hotel, Mr. President, to learn what you decide."

Aides to the two presidents worked together through the long night, fielding reports from the New York Fed and the country at large. Finally, at 2:30 A.M., Governor Herbert Lehman of New York sent word that he was ordering a closing of the state's banks. Banks in the remaining thirteen states would close by the end of that day. The run on withdrawals from the nation's banks had been paused without an explicit push from Hoover and Roosevelt. The crisis had not abated; dramatic, unprecedented action would be required. But, with luck, it could wait until Franklin put his hand on the Bible to swear the oath of office.

Eleanor spent the evening in her room at the Mayflower with Hick, worrying over news of the deteriorating situation in the banks. "Anything could happen," Eleanor said. "How much can people take without blowing up?" Late that night, Franklin, still awake in his own room, monitoring reports, sent Eleanor a final copy of the speech he would give the next day. Eleanor paged through it, reading aloud as she went. "It's a good speech," she said. "It has hope in it. But will people accept it? Will they believe him?"

Chapter 31

Fear Itself

MARCH 4, 1933

FRANKLIN SLEPT PAST EIGHT ON THE MORNING OF HIS IN-auguration as the thirty-second president of the United States. As his children and grandchildren hurried about the hotel, he breakfasted and then dressed in striped pants and "morning" coat before leaving the Mayflower for the last time, clutching James's arm.

At a quarter past ten o'clock, the Roosevelt family arrived at St. John's Church, the historic "Church of the Presidents" on Lafayette Square. At Franklin's request, a simple service of prayer and hymns had been organized for the incoming president and his Cabinet. "A private citizen is going to church before a great undertaking," explained the church's rector, "and he is going to say his prayers."

It had been bitter and gray when they left the Mayflower, but as the Roosevelts took their seats in the pew reserved for presidents of the United States, a broad, brilliant bar of light streaked through the church's stained-glass windows. The Roosevelts joined in the singing of the hymns they'd selected: "Faith of Our Fathers," "Eternal Father, Strong to Save," and "O God, Our Help in Ages Past." Endicott Peabody, the venerable rector of Groton who'd married Franklin and Eleanor twenty-eight years earlier, spoke the final prayers:

> O Lord, our Heavenly Father . . . bless Thy servant, Franklin, chosen to be the President of the United States, and all others in authority; and so replenish them with the grace of

Thy Holy Spirit, that they may always incline to Thy will and
walk in Thy way.

The service lasted only twenty minutes, but Franklin remained in
his pew afterward, head down in silent prayer.

From St. John's, the Roosevelts made their way around Lafayette
Square to the White House. There, Franklin sat in his open-top car
at the North Portico, waiting for Hoover to join him for the ride to
the Capitol for the inauguration. This was an act of courtesy on
Hoover's part. By protocol, a new president was expected to come in
to the White House to meet the man he was replacing before they
exited the mansion together and rode on to the inauguration. But
Franklin, eternally conscious of the ungainly sight made by his exits
from automobiles, had requested to remain in his car. Hoover had
not objected.

This change in custom redounded to Franklin's benefit. Newsreels
captured the moment when Hoover departed the White House to
join Franklin waiting outside. In the sequence, the outgoing president
looked feeble and deflated, while Franklin, grinning eagerly in the
back seat, looked healthy and eager, in a hurry to get to work. The
departing president's staff got some small revenge in the press. That
evening's *Washington Star* would report that, on his final walk to the
Oval Office, Hoover inspected the ramps that had been newly installed for the convenience of his successor.

The president and president-elect sat awkwardly in the back seat
as their chauffeured car made its way slowly to the Capitol. There had
not been a presidential transition in the midst of such a dire national
crisis since Abraham Lincoln succeeded James Buchanan in March
1861. When those presidents had ridden together on Lincoln's inauguration, Buchanan, who longed to return to Wheatland, his Pennsylvania home, expressed his relief at having the nation's burdens
lifted from his back. "If you are as happy on entering the White
House as I shall feel on returning to Wheatland," he said, "then you
are a happy man indeed." Hoover emanated nothing, save for exhaus-

tion and contempt. The car inched forward, guided by soldiers on horseback, but he refused to say a word.

The sun that illuminated St. John's Church had now broken through to clear the sky. That afternoon, there would be an inaugural parade along Pennsylvania Avenue. A crowd of half a million people had already gathered. The normally broad and breezy avenues of Washington were packed so thick with people, it was nearly impossible to move. One journalist asked a policeman to help her make her way through the crowd. "Lady," replied the officer, "General MacArthur and his staff couldn't ride their horses through that crowd."

Franklin smiled and waved eagerly at the masses while Hoover stared ahead, rigid and unmoved. Sensing the other man's discomfort, Franklin eventually restrained his impulses and sat motionless too. But he found the silence impossible to bear. When they passed the Commerce Department Building, constructed during Hoover's term as Commerce secretary, Franklin at last thought of something to say: "Lovely steel!" he chirped enthusiastically. Hoover offered no reply.

THEY ARRIVED AT THE Capitol ahead of schedule, but the crowd on the plaza beneath the speaker's platform had started to gather at dawn. There were radio broadcasters everywhere—at the Capitol, along Pennsylvania Avenue, on the White House grounds. Sensing that the new American president would play a decisive role in its fate, the world at large was eager to hear what he had to say. Franklin's remarks that day would be broadcast live not just across the country but on stations in Paris, London, and Berlin.

Supported by James, Franklin moved from his car up a specially constructed ramp into the Senate side of the Capitol. There, he had two long hours to wait for his swearing-in. People came and went, many of them old acquaintances from his long career in politics. So many of his old friends and old rivals had descended on the capital that day. Josephus Daniels was there, filled with pride for his brilliant young Navy Department protégé. James M. Cox, Franklin's running mate in 1920, was there, as was William Gibbs McAdoo. Al Smith was there, ready to march in New York's delegation for the inaugural parade. The presidency would never be his, and his bitterness toward Franklin would never really subside. But for that day he was happy to have a small portion of the crowd's cheers.

William Randolph Hearst was not there. A few weeks later, he would come to Washington and have a private audience with the new president. It would not go well. "I was greatly disappointed," he would tell one of his editors afterward. "The President didn't give me a chance to make suggestions. He did all the talking."

Dozens of Roosevelt and Delano relations were gathered at the Capitol for the happy day. Anna was there with her two children, as was John Boettiger, the *Chicago Tribune* reporter she would marry following her divorce from Curtis Dall the next year. Sara Roosevelt was there, proud if unsurprised that the world had chosen to acknowledge the talent and wonder of her splendid little boy. Sara, now a great-grandmother, would live to see two more of her son's inaugurations.

Also there was Frederic Delano, Franklin's "Uncle Fred," the man who had once offered his nephew "fatherly advice":

> To my mind, Philosophy means in substance, "making the best of the situation," or in other words taking things as they are, analyzing the facts, above all not fooling yourself and by intelligent reasoning determining the right course to pursue. I never worry, I accept things as they are, I look forward and not back.

Eleven years had passed since the hours in late summer 1921 when Uncle Fred had written those words. Now Franklin faced a new crisis, one in which he could call on the world's foremost experts for advice. And yet the counsel his uncle had given him—*never worry, accept things as they are, look forward and not back*—would be at the very core of Franklin's message to the country that day.

Also in attendance, waiting in a special section that Franklin had picked for them, was a delegation of forty-two patients from Warm

Springs. The colony had grown remarkably since Franklin's first visit eight years before; some 275 people would come there for treatment in winter 1933. Under the guidance of a considerably augmented staff, these patients followed rehabilitation programs tailored to their individual needs. But all their treatment was designed to foster the key element Franklin had identified as essential to a polio patient's recovery: "belief on the patient's part that the muscles are coming back." In one newspaper the day after the inauguration, an admirer would describe the remarkable spirit of the patients from Warm Springs: "I have yet to detect a feeling among them of discouragement or despondency. They seem to be unusually optimistic in this period of Depression; more so than the average citizen one meets in travel or at home. Our new President has been an inspiration to every person in the colony."

As he waited that day, Franklin may have thought too of the people who weren't there. Several key figures who helped him in his years in the wilderness had not lived to see this triumphant day. Robert Lovett, the doctor who had diagnosed Franklin's polio on Campobello, had died. So had Tom Loyless, the man whose seductive salesmanship first brought Franklin to Warm Springs. Perhaps most tragic was the absence of Livingston Davis, Franklin's close friend from college. During Franklin's recovery, Davis had cheered him the best he knew how with funny stories and dirty jokes. "You are constantly in my thoughts," he'd written Franklin in the first months of Franklin's illness, "and I wish to gosh there was something I could do." In January 1932, just a few days before Franklin announced his campaign for the presidency, Davis had shot himself in the head in a small shed on the back of his property in Brookline, Massachusetts.

Franklin may have thought too in those moments of his father, James, gone for three decades now. James had never known the adult Franklin, never seen him run for office, never heard him give a political speech. Yet his father's teachings—*Help all who are suffering. Man is dear to man*—animated the work that Franklin was now determined to do.

As the hour of his swearing-in drew near, Franklin thought once more of the Almighty. He looked down at the final copy of the speech he was about to deliver. The opening sentence was too long and too pedestrian. His presidency should begin on a higher plane. In pen, he wrote a new sentence atop the page to begin his remarks.

Just after one o'clock, he emerged on the platform erected on the east front of the Capitol as a band played "Hail to the Chief." John Nance Garner had already been sworn in as vice president in a ceremony in the Senate chamber moments before. With James standing close at hand, Franklin leaned against the lectern as he looked toward Chief Justice Charles Evan Hughes. He placed his hand on a Bible printed in the year 1686, the oldest Bible ever used for a presidential inauguration. Written in Dutch, it had belonged to Nicholas Roosevelt, Franklin's first Roosevelt ancestor to have been born in North America. At Franklin's direction, the book was opened to I Corinthians 13:12: *For now we see through a glass, darkly; but then face to face: now I know in part; but then shall I know even as also I am known.*

Hughes recited the oath that the new president was to swear. Franklin's predecessors in the office had usually listened to the oath and simply offered an assent: "I do." But Franklin preferred to repeat the entire oath out loud, start to finish:

> I, Franklin Delano Roosevelt, do solemnly swear that I will faithfully execute the office of President of the United States and will, to the best of my ability, preserve, protect, and defend the Constitution of the United States, so help me God.

At this, the crowd below the platform erupted in cheers. When they quieted, he began his address with the words he had written a short time before:

"This is a day of national consecration."

He spoke for only twenty minutes. He did not smile as he recited his text, but his voice, swelling toward the ends of his sentences, offered a nourishing reassurance. The newspapers the next day would focus on his muscular tone, the images of war he evoked as he described the extraordinary efforts his government would make to confront the country's ills. In newsreels that week, the key line was a virile call to arms: "This nation asks for action, and action now."

But in the weeks that followed, it became apparent that the lines that had resonated most with the millions of Americans listening over the radio that day came in the declaratory sentences at the outset of Franklin's remarks:

> This is preeminently the time to speak the truth, the whole truth, frankly and boldly. Nor need we shrink from honestly facing conditions in our country today. This great Nation will endure, as it has endured, will revive and will prosper.
>
> So, first of all, let me assert my firm belief that the only thing we have to fear is fear itself—nameless, unreasoning, unjustified terror, which paralyzes needed efforts to convert retreat into advance.

Eleanor's questions on reading the speech the night before had been reasonable: *Will people accept it? Will they believe him?* From the lips of another politician, these sentences might well have fallen flat. Americans in March of 1933 had countless real causes for anxiety: fear that they would lose their homes and their livelihoods, fear that their children would starve, fear that their republic of liberty would vanish from the earth. Who was this man to speak to *them* of fear?

Yet when Franklin spoke those words—*the only thing we have to fear is fear itself*—people opened their hearts because they could tell that he believed them to be true.

The people he was now charged to lead did not know all the details of his illness or of his long, lonely struggle to return to the halls of power. They knew little of steel braces or cramped train journeys or disappointing doctors' reports. They simply knew that when Franklin Delano Roosevelt spoke of the struggle against fear, he was describing a struggle that he himself had fought and would continue to fight. He had been broken and forsaken, and yet he had chosen to believe in hope. On that day of consecration, they believed in it too.

Epilogue

The Spirit of Warm Springs

IN NOVEMBER 1933, FRANKLIN LEFT WASHINGTON FOR HIS FIRST visit to Warm Springs as president. In keeping with tradition, he planned a two-week holiday in Georgia, the highlight of which would be a large Thanksgiving dinner with the colony's patients and staff.

On arrival in Warm Springs, Franklin found that the tiny town had embraced the prominence brought on by its famous adopted son. A new paved road heading toward Atlanta was called "Franklin D. Roosevelt Highway." People now referred to Franklin's cottage on Pine Mountain as "the Little White House." Warm Springs neighbors who had once only smiled at him in passing now chased after him in town, eager to get close to a man who increasingly looked like the greatest statesman of the age.

Though only eight months old, Franklin's presidency already seemed destined to be among the most significant in American history. In his first days in office, he had successfully averted the collapse of the nation's financial system by issuing an executive order to keep banks closed nationwide for an extended period. Then, after just hours of consideration, Congress had passed his Emergency Banking Act, providing for a reopening of the banks under federal supervision. When, nine days after he assumed the presidency, the banks began to reopen, deposits outpaced withdrawals and the stock market rallied to its best performance since 1929, signaling public confidence that competent leadership had been restored to the country at last.

In his opening months in office—already, by the latter part of 1933, known as the Hundred Days—he had fulfilled his inauguration promise of "action, and action now," sending fifteen messages to Congress that resulted in fifteen pieces of major legislation. Together, they would remake American life. These included bills to bring immediate help to the neediest Americans: the Emergency Farm Mortgage Act, refinancing and securing the home credit of farmers who could not sell their crops; the Federal Emergency Relief Act, allocating funds to make direct payments to the out of work; and the National Industrial Recovery Act, providing for $3.3 billion in public works.

At Franklin's urging, Congress had established the Tennessee Valley Authority and the Civilian Conservation Corps, massive new programs that would put millions to work remaking the nation's interior. And with legislation like the Agricultural Adjustment Act and the Glass–Steagall Act, securing bank deposits and prohibiting commercial banks from engaging in investment banking, the New Deal Congress had taken major steps to make the system more just and responsive to the needs of the forgotten man.

Even those who disliked these policies were grateful for Franklin's dynamic, self-assured stewardship of a nation in crisis. He had stayed in close touch with the American public—presiding twice a week at freewheeling Oval Office press conferences and updating the country on his administration's progress with intimate radio addresses known as "fireside chats." Again and again, he'd returned to the message from his inaugural address—that deliverance from the economic crisis would depend on Americans believing in their country and in themselves. "When Andrew Jackson ... died," he said in a fireside chat in July, "someone asked, 'Will he go to Heaven?' and the answer was 'He will if he wants to.' If I am asked whether the American people will pull themselves out of this depression, I answer, 'They will if they want to.'"

Franklin spent much of his time in Warm Springs that November in the seclusion of the "Little White House," meeting with advisers imported from Washington and basking in the sun. To fill their downtime, White House correspondents who'd come along for the trip acquainted themselves with the Georgia Warm Springs Foundation, now the temporary home of some two hundred patients, many of whom were children. The reporters spent one afternoon talking to Michael Hoke, the esteemed orthopedist Franklin had recruited two years earlier to serve as the foundation's medical director.

In their conversation, Hoke explained that beyond medical treatment and physical therapy, some of the foundation's most important work was fostering what Franklin called "the spirit of Warm Springs," a chain of positive feeling that encouraged recovering polio patients to believe in the possibilities life offered to them.

He gestured toward a small child using a wheelchair, struggling to push his own way up a hill. "Notice that no nurse or aide is running over to help with that chair. . . . That child will make a victory by doing this thing himself. It will be one more step toward proving to himself his own self-confidence." Children at Warm Springs, Hoke said, "become little giants of confidence.

"No one can really explain it," Hoke told the reporters, "but when . . . a polio victim recovers, there comes not a resignation but a cheerful acceptance of the challenges of life."

The more the doctor talked, the more reporters could see the similarities between the spirit of Warm Springs and the spirit of Franklin's nascent presidency. "Are you explaining Roosevelt to us?" one reporter asked.

Hoke smiled. "I'm just talking."

IN 2021, AS I completed this book on Franklin Delano Roosevelt, a Democratic president, Joe Biden, took charge of an America unsettled by the global pandemic, pledging a federal response on par with the one Franklin had offered in the Depression. Critics saw in Biden's policies a dangerous turn toward socialism, the same allegation that critics had made about Franklin's New Deal in the 1930s. Searching for precedent, political pundits scoured the history of Franklin's policy victories and his approach to legislative strategy. As so often in the three-quarters of a century since Franklin's death, he seemed destined to cast a large shadow over the politics of the 2020s.

It seemed to me, however, that all the talk about Franklin's presidency missed an essential element of its success: the ways his experience dealing with personal crisis informed his approach to solving the crises facing the country. By then I had completed my study of the years in which his character was challenged and remade. Returning to the histories, memoirs, and press coverage of Franklin's time in the White House, I looked for evidence of how his experience with polio affected his handling of the Depression and World War II.

It was easy to see why, at the beginning of my project, it had taken me some time to see the true impact of Franklin's illness and recovery. The longer Franklin spent in the White House, the less that reporters wrote about his experience battling back from polio. They no longer needed to humanize Franklin Roosevelt for their readers. Thanks to his energetic public appearances and his reassuring radio addresses, Franklin had become, for millions of Americans, an intimate friend.

Franklin himself rarely spoke of his years recovering from polio. In late June 1933, after the conclusion of the Hundred Days, he returned to Campobello for the first time since the awful August of 1921 when he'd taken ill. It was an emotional and triumphant moment; the island's residents all gathered to greet him on arrival, many with tears in their eyes. Franklin was clearly moved by their reception, but his remarks on arrival were spare: "I remember I was brought here because I was teething forty-nine years ago, and I have been coming here for some months ever since until about twelve years ago. Since then there has been a gap." That was about as much emotional revelation as Franklin Roosevelt was ever willing to volunteer.

In his twelve years as president, Franklin would transform Americans' relationship with Washington, enacting programs like Social Security, rural electrification, and the Works Progress Administration. He would forge a coalition of working people—organized labor, farmers, and racial and ethnic minorities—that would create a dominant Democratic majority for a generation. He would be the only president to seek and win four terms in office. And he would build lasting faith that, in America, the forgotten man could get a fair shake.

He would skillfully, if cautiously, steer American foreign policy through the 1930s, as Adolf Hitler terrorized Europe and the world descended once more into war. And, after the attack on Pearl Harbor in December 1941, Franklin would take charge of the war against global fascism, a war whose successful outcome he would bring about but whose end he would not live to see.

Through it all, he would remain perpetually careful to conceal and downplay the lingering impacts of his disease. In public, he continued to deliver speeches standing, his weight supported by his podium. He still walked, slowly but determinedly, with a cane in one hand and a companion's arm in the other. He never stopped challenging his body with punishing travel—train, plane, and sea voyages across the country and, in wartime, around the world. For much of his time in office, the physical challenges were evident only in small details—the ramps in the White House, the sewn patches in his suit pants where the edges of his steel braces had broken through.

But by looking only for the visible signs of polio in Franklin's presidency, I had missed its true influence—hidden, unspoken, but ever present. Now that I knew to look for it, I saw it in nearly every important moment of his time in the White House.

It was there, movingly, in his first major challenge as president, the banking crisis that threatened the nation's financial system. His immediate response was the extended bank holiday. It was a straightforward solution: In order to stop a run on banks nationwide, Americans were forbidden to withdraw funds. At first glance, it required very little of the American people. All they had to do was sit quietly and wait for the banks to reopen once the nation's anxiety had cooled.

Franklin knew, though, that in a time of crisis, being told to do nothing could be a kind of torture. His own lowest moments had come in the days immediately following his polio diagnosis on Campobello. Instructed by Dr. Lovett to move as little as possible, he had lain in his bed, wanting to *do* something, worrying, and waiting for progress that did not come. He had learned from this experience that enforced idleness, unless accompanied by consistent explanation and reassurance, can create panic, the very thing the bank holiday was seeking to avert.

One week after assuming the presidency, with the banks still closed, he went on the radio for the first of his fireside chats. Speaking in a reassuring but resolute voice, he made his listeners feel that their inaction was a kind of courageous action and that they were full and essential partners in his approach to recovery. "You people must have faith," he said, "you must not be stampeded by rumors or guesses. Let us unite in banishing fear. We have provided the machinery to restore our financial system; it is up to you to support and make it work."

Franklin's presidency drew constantly on the lessons learned in his own recovery and that of other polio patients he had known. In the pool at Warm Springs, he had learned the gratification and motivation that comes from accurately measuring progress, watching how, over time, his strengthened muscles allowed him to stand in increasingly shallow water. He had seen similar pride in Warm Springs patients, reviewing the careful notes on how their mobility and muscle strength had improved during their time in Georgia. In a fireside chat in the second year of his presidency, he encouraged Americans to look for similar strides: "The simplest way for each of you to judge recovery lies in the plain facts of your own individual situation. Are you better off than you were last year? Are your debts less burdensome? Is your bank account more secure? Are your working conditions better? Is your faith in your own individual future more firmly grounded?"

At the heart of Franklin's relationship with the American people was his unique ability to envision their fears, hopes, and needs. Frances Perkins, Franklin's friend of four decades who served as his secretary of Labor, recalled observing him in the White House, broadcasting his fireside chats. "I realized how unconscious he was of the twenty or thirty of us in that room," she later wrote, "and how clearly his mind was focused on the people listening at the other end. As he talked, his head would nod and his hands would move in simple, natural, comfortable gestures. His face would smile and light up as though he were actually sitting on the front porch or in the parlor with them. People felt this and it bound them to him in affection." Perkins, who had known Franklin before and after polio, believed that the "horror of his illness and his crippling" had given him "the capacity to associate himself with great numbers of people."

This remarkable empathy shaped the Roosevelt administration's landmark policies. His own experience had taught him that for a person facing catastrophic setbacks, the restoration of dignity is not a long-term goal but an immediate and essential necessity. Nursing Franklin in the first months of his recovery, Eleanor and Louis hadn't been able to instantly restore his body to its old condition, but they had been able to restore elements of his old life—inviting interesting visitors to the house; providing him with books to read; supplying him political news, gossip, and insight.

So too as president, Franklin did not promise the nation's impoverished an immediate end to their suffering, but he did take steps to swiftly restore their sense of dignity and purpose. He was drawn to programs like the Civilian Conservation Corps and the Works Progress Administration, in which the government gave work directly to the unemployed. Critics on the right, who saw these programs as a path toward socialism, argued that the government should simply make cash payments to the unemployed and save the added costs associated with housing, feeding, and transporting workers in its employ. Those critics, Franklin argued in a 1935 speech, failed to grasp the indignity experienced by the unemployed. "Most Americans want to give something for what they get. That something, which in this case is honest work, is the saving barrier between them and moral disintegration."

Franklin's approach to solving the problems of the Depression could often appear chaotic and contradictory. This too was a legacy of his years recovering from polio, during which he had gotten used to seeking out the advice of world-class experts, then synthesizing it with the advice of other experts and his own beliefs. Applying this approach to the country's economic problems sometimes landed Franklin in trouble. In 1937, after years of bolstering the economy by expanding the size of the federal government, he impulsively reversed course and slashed federal expenditures by nearly 40 percent. Henry

Morgenthau Jr., the secretary of the Treasury, had chosen a striking metaphor to urge this course on Franklin, arguing it was time "to throw away the crutches and see if American enterprise could stand on its own feet." It was the same flight of fancy Franklin had occasionally talked himself into in the 1920s—that he could dispose of his crutches and braces and simply *will* himself back on his feet. The result was the same: The dramatic cutbacks sent the economy spiraling into recession. Franklin soon reversed course once again.

But his eclectic approach to policy solutions reflected the essential lesson of his illness: What is promised and what comes to pass are rarely the same thing. He was happy to listen to academic theories, but he put his faith only in what was real.

PERHAPS THE GREATEST IMPACT of Franklin's years of illness and rehabilitation was the partnership he and Eleanor brought to the White House. Two months after Franklin's inauguration, she published *It's Up to the Women,* a book on how members of her sex could help to end the Depression. "There have been other great crises in our country," she wrote, "and I think if we read our history carefully, we will find that the success of our nation in meeting them was very largely due to the women in those trying times."

Franklin and Eleanor's private time of trial—polio—had put Eleanor under enormous strain, but it had also liberated her to take on a new role, representing the Roosevelts in the wider world while Franklin recuperated at home. So too did the crisis of the Depression provide the excuse for her to reinvent the role of First Lady. With so many Americans out of work and underfed, it was only natural that a president's wife should concern herself with more than just parties and place settings.

One afternoon in the Roosevelts' first spring in the White House, Eleanor and Louis Howe visited Fort Belvoir in Virginia. There, members of the Bonus Forces—the World War I veterans who had clashed with the active U.S. Army in the streets of Washington the summer before—had set up camp. On arrival, Louis told Eleanor to inspect the camp on her own while he remained in the car. Making her way, Eleanor encountered men who might have been hostile toward the president's wife: Like Hoover before him, Franklin did not intend to give in to the veterans' demand for payment of the wartime bonus. But Eleanor quickly endeared herself to the men by sharing stories of her 1919 visit to the World War I battlefields and asking them direct questions about the conditions in which they were living. When she departed, they waved her off warmly, shouting, "Goodbye and good luck to you."

To Washington insiders, the visit looked like a brilliant Roosevelt strategy for preventing another bloody clash with the Bonus Forces on Washington's streets. "Hoover sent the Army," one veteran said approvingly. "Roosevelt sent his wife." In fact, the outing was a success because of the unique combination of qualities Eleanor had cultivated over the previous twelve years: compassion and curiosity, fellowship and fearlessness. She would use those gifts on countless fact-finding missions during Franklin's presidency, visiting mines, military bases, factories, and work camps.

In the White House, the Roosevelts kept up the arrangement they had worked out in the 1920s: keeping separate courts and leading separate lives. Franklin's presidential social life revolved around evening gatherings called "the Children's Hour," where, with Missy by his side, he mixed cocktails for a revolving cast of friends, close aides, and visitors from out of town. Eleanor rarely appeared at these rollicking gatherings, preferring to fill her evenings with the things that had long sustained her—books, friends, and work.

For a time, it seemed that Louis might continue to serve as a bridge between Franklin's and Eleanor's worlds. But not long after the Roosevelts came to the White House, it became clear that Louis's perpetually frail health was entering into permanent decline. By the middle of 1935, Louis was living in Bethesda Naval Hospital, where he tried to dictate the management of Franklin's political affairs from the inside of an oxygen tent. Louis couldn't help noticing how seldom Franklin paid a call on him in the hospital, a cruel irony considering the unending vigil Louis had kept by *Franklin's* sickbed a decade before. "Not only were the demands of the presidential office remorse-less," wrote Eleanor's friend and biographer Joseph Lash, but Franklin had a habit of "blotting out people who were unable to keep up with him. It was Eleanor, who had taken so long to appreciate Louis, who was steadfast to the end."

The end came in April 1936—a quarter century after Louis Howe had first met a talented young Albany politician named Roosevelt and seen the makings of a future president of the United States. Franklin was concluding a speech before the Gridiron Club, a frater-nity of Washington journalists, when he learned of Louis's death. Re-porters in the room were struck by a rare expression on Franklin's face: genuine sadness and distress. "It was," Eleanor later wrote, "one of the greatest losses that my husband sustained."

With Louis gone, the expanse between the Roosevelts grew. Elea-nor resented many of Franklin's White House political advisers, par-ticularly a cadre of white southern men who counseled him not to risk alienating the Solid South by embracing the cause of civil rights. As the years wore on, the fight against racial segregation became one of Eleanor's great passions, a cause she embraced publicly, whether or not she was in accord with her husband's stated policies. In 1938, she traveled to Birmingham, Alabama, for the Southern Conference for Human Welfare, a mixed-race event aimed at confronting racial in-justice. Arriving at the event, Eleanor was dismayed to discover that police had divided the room by race. She seated herself in the black section, but a white police officer approached her and told her she had to move. Rather than join the white group, she pointedly picked up her chair and moved it to a space between the white and black sec-tions. For the remainder of the conference, she carried a folding chair with her, a visual rebuke to the segregated seating system.

Easy affection never returned to the Roosevelts' marriage, but El-eanor's respect for her husband grew with the years as she saw how much of himself he was willing to give to make a more just and hu-mane world. Occasionally, she made sure Franklin knew how deep her admiration ran. "Dearest honey," she wrote in an undated letter from the White House years, "I want you to know that I feel this should be a happy day because you have done much for many people. Everyone has happier feelings & you are doing a grand job. Just go on thinking of others & not of yourself & I think an undreamed of future may lie ahead for the masses of people not only here but everywhere."

POLIO MADE FRANKLIN A great leader, but it did not make him a saint. In the White House, his lifelong allergy to unpleasant scenes combined with the talent for deception he had developed during his years of recovery. On more than one occasion, congressional leaders, urging him to pursue a policy course, would note him nodding along and saying, "Yes, yes." They would leave feeling reassured that he agreed with their view. Only later, when he flagrantly ignored their counsel, would they realize that his nodding could have been interpreted not as agreement but as a mere signal that he heard what they were saying.

By the latter years of his presidency, many in Washington had concluded that, however charming he might come off in person, however sincere he sounded in his communication with the American people, Franklin Roosevelt was not a man you could trust. Not long after Franklin selected Harry Truman to be his running mate in the 1944 election, a friend asked Truman what Franklin was really like. Truman's answer was succinct: "He lies."

Yet if Franklin's deceptions revealed a cold, ruthless streak in his character, they were also essential to his success as president. Nowhere was this more evident than in his navigation of foreign policy in the years before America's entry into World War II. After the outbreak of hostilities in September 1939, it was plain to Franklin that the United States would most likely have to join the fight against the Axis powers eventually. Still, he was also clear-eyed about the enduring appeal of isolationism, a force that had figured in his political fortunes for much of the past two decades. Rather than directly challenge the nation's hostility to foreign entanglements, he accommodated it. "Your boys are not going to be sent into any foreign wars," he promised in the last days of his 1940 campaign for a third term. Careful listeners could note the wiggle room provided by the word "foreign"—what if the war came to American interests or territories abroad? Just as in 1928, when Franklin had boasted of being back "on my feet," the precise meaning of his words was not the same as their intended effect.

To many at the time, and many since, Franklin's hesitancy to make the moral case for American intervention was both a failure of courage and of compassion. "The president," complained his Treasury secretary, Henry Morgenthau Jr., "would rather follow public opinion than lead it." Yet Franklin knew that an early, aggressive stance for American involvement would have alienated him from the war-wary electorate and would have increased the likelihood of an isolationist or even pro-Axis regime rising on American shores. By forswearing interest in joining the fight, he bought himself time to educate the public on the threat of national socialism, all the while aiding the Allied effort where he could and increasing American readiness.

His fight back from polio, after all, had taught him that if he wanted to meet a great challenge, what mattered most were planning, patience, and timing. These were, he had come to believe, the essential political skills. As the war came closer and closer, he knew his task was the same as it had been in his years of convalescence: to wait, to watch, and to prepare.

BY NOVEMBER 1941, AMERICA'S entry into World War II seemed near at hand. Much of the world had been at war for nearly two years, and nearly all of the European continent had fallen under Hitler's control. Though Britain had thwarted a Nazi invasion after months of punishing German air assault, it was unclear how long it could last without the support of the United States. A future for America as a lonely island of freedom, fighting off a Nazi-dominated world, seemed altogether possible.

Through the fall of 1941, Franklin's government had been in a tense standoff with Germany's Axis ally, Japan, over that country's aggres-

sive wartime expansion in the Pacific. Efforts between the two countries to reach a peaceful accommodation seemed doomed by late
November. Franklin's advisers warned him that a surprise Japanese
attack on American forces somewhere in the Pacific could come at
any time.

Dealing with the crisis in the Pacific derailed Franklin's plans to
host his traditional Thanksgiving Day celebration with the patients at
Warm Springs that year. Still, he was determined to journey to Georgia for a brief visit. A few days after Thanksgiving, he left Washington
for Warm Springs, where he would hold a delayed version of his annual turkey dinner with the colony's patients and staff. The day he
departed was November 29, 1941. Franklin did not know it, but as he
traveled south, a flotilla carrying Japanese air squadrons was making
its way in secret toward an audaciously selected target: the U.S. naval
base at Pearl Harbor.

Franklin reached Warm Springs on November 30. The visit began
with a sad errand. The previous summer, Missy LeHand had suffered
a massive stroke, leaving her paralyzed and unable to talk. A distraught Franklin had arranged for her to recuperate at Warm Springs.
Her absence had been devastating for him; in almost nine years in the
White House, no one had spent more time with Franklin than Missy
or provided him with more tender care. He found her in the cottage
he'd provided for her, a frail shadow of the lively, loving woman who
had enriched his life for twenty years.

The year 1941 had been one of loss. In late August, eighty-six-year-
old Sara Delano Roosevelt had taken gravely ill while visiting her
home on Campobello. She was brought home to Hyde Park, where
Franklin rushed to be by her side. She had outlived her husband,
James, by forty years and seen their only son inaugurated president
three times. To the end, she was the indomitable mistress of Springwood. In that house, in the midst of a blizzard in January 1882, Sara
had brought Franklin Delano Roosevelt into the world. Under the
same roof, fifty-nine years later, Franklin had sat by his mother's side
as she took her last breath.

Franklin stayed with Missy in her cottage for only a short time; no matter how deeply he cared for her and felt her pain, he would never be able to bear the most unpleasant things. He spent that afternoon driving around Warm Springs, trying to make the most of his brief holiday, soaking in the sun. Seeking diversion, he turned on a radio broadcast of the annual Army–Navy football game. But reminders of the world's burden intruded even here. Those young, strong boys on the football field: Into what kinds of danger would Franklin be forced to send them in the days that lay ahead?

That night, the staff and patients of Warm Springs gathered for their delayed Thanksgiving dinner. Franklin was the center of attention: He carved the turkey, he watched the patients perform a satirical skit about the colony, he punctuated their performance with his hearty belly laugh. The Warm Springs patients kept their eyes on Franklin throughout the evening: He was president in an hour of great consequence but, for them, something more too. They did not know Franklin as intimately as the patients had in the mid-1920s, when he led exercises in the pool and tracked patients' muscles in precise progress reports. Still, Franklin's story and his spirit were essential to every Warm Springs patient's recovery.

A few years earlier, a Warm Springs patient named George McLaurine had written an essay to the outside world, explaining the ethos of the colony. "We cannot possibly convey to you able-bodied people," he wrote, "the transformation made by the realization that the twist of fate which banished us forever from the carefree life of the physically perfect may have been the twist which meant a better, fuller life. Perhaps you cannot understand that the paralysis which made us weaker animals might compensate by making us stronger men."

But, as every Warm Springs patient knew, there was one person who *did* understand. In President Roosevelt, polio survivors saw magnificent proof that a life of meaning and purpose was still within their reach. After all, McLaurine wrote, "Mr. Roosevelt came up from the blow of infantile paralysis to heights he might never have reached as an able-bodied man. That is the inspiration which feeds the spirit of Warm Springs."

That night, the spirit of Warm Springs also nourished Franklin, just as it always had. Near the end of the evening, he addressed the dinner guests. Speaking without a prepared text, he said how happy he was to be back with his "family" at the colony. "I want to express the hope that the Warm Springs family will never really grow up," he said. "Because after all, Warm Springs, to be successful in the future, has got to make some progress every year . . . the same progress that we have been making the past thirteen or fourteen years."

His mind then drifted to a more serious place. Since the first days of his recovery, he had spoken more honestly and more tenderly with other polio survivors than he did with nearly anyone else. Looking around at the patients, he revealed the heavy burdens he felt in those waning days of 1941. He talked of how he'd felt that afternoon, listening to the Army–Navy football game on the radio. In those days of war, he wondered, "How many other countries in the world have things like that going on? So I think we have very great cause to be thankful. . . . We need to be thoroughly thankful that these years of peace were given to us."

Were given to us. There were reporters in the room, and now they were recording his words carefully: This was Franklin talking more plainly and personally about the prospect of imminent war than he had at any point that fall.

"At the same time," he went on, "we should think not only of our selfish purposes for this country of ours, but also think a little bit about other people, people in other countries which have been overrun, people in countries which have been attacked, and, yes, people in those countries which are doing the attacking.

"I think," he said, "we can offer up a little silent prayer. . . . We hope that these people will next year be able to hold a Thanksgiving more like the American Thanksgiving. It is something for us to dream about perhaps, especially in days like these. . . . It may be that next Thanksgiving these boys of the Military Academy and of the Naval Academy will be actually fighting for the defense of these American institutions of ours." Indeed, he told his audience, "certain dangers that have been overhanging the future of this country" might require him to return to Washington as soon as the following morning.

All the same, Franklin told the patients, he was glad for what little time in Warm Springs he had. His visit, he said, had "given me faith and hope in the United States."

Faith and hope, the things he had found in his hardest days, the things that would sustain him in the hard days ahead. Somewhere in the Pacific, the Japanese fleet was heading toward Pearl Harbor. In just over a week's time, America would be at war. But for a brief moment that night, the last night of the last month of peacetime, Warm Springs was the center of Franklin's world. Finishing his speech, he promised the patients that he would wait by the door to receive them personally as they departed. Before they made their way into the darkness that night, each one of them would encounter Franklin Roosevelt, smiling warmly and offering his hand.

ACKNOWLEDGMENTS

=====

Anyone who sets out to write about the lives of Franklin and Eleanor Roosevelt relies on the work of the many scholars who have studied their lives and careers in the seventy-seven years since Franklin's death. Absorbing numerous Roosevelt biographies from earlier eras, I was particularly helped by the work of Frank Freidel, Arthur Schlesinger Jr., Joseph Lash, and Kenneth Davis. In our own time, Geoffrey Ward's magisterial volumes on Franklin's early life and career and Blanche Wiesen Cook's authoritative works on Eleanor's life have provided essential maps of the Roosevelt landscape that will no doubt guide scholars for many generations to come. The memoirs of Eleanor Roosevelt, Elliott Roosevelt, James Roosevelt, and Lorena Hickok were especially helpful in shaping my understanding of this unique American family. I am grateful to thoughtful staff at all the various archives consulted for this project, especially the Franklin D. Roosevelt Library in Hyde Park which is a living tribute to Franklin Roosevelt's historical vision and the Roosevelt family's commitment to his legacy.

At various points researching this book, I was helped enormously by the expert assistance of Jessica Gallagher. Jessica is a gifted researcher who is unfailingly resourceful and admirably unflappable. Thanks as well to Taylor Beck and Stephanie Gorton. Carol Poticny's immersive research produced gorgeous photos for the book and I am grateful for her diligence and knowledge.

Once again it has been my great good fortune to have Kate Medina as my editor at Random House. Kate has all the gifts a writer wants in an editor—taste, vision, patience, decisiveness and sensitivity—

as well as an uncanny intuition for exactly which of these traits is required in a given moment. I am so very lucky to have her in my corner. Noa Shapiro provided valuable insights on the manuscript and was a helpful guide through the publication process, as was Louisa McCullough. I am grateful for all the talented professionals at Random House who have produced a beautiful book and done so much to launch it in the world. Thanks especially to Andy Ward, Avideh Bashirrad, Ayelet Durantt, Greg Kubie, Dennis Ambrose, Rebecca Berlant, Kevin Garcia, and Barbara Bachman.

Andrew Wylie provided excellent representation, shrewd judgment, and sound advice. He is a pleasure to work with, always. My thanks as well to everyone at the Wylie Agency, especially Jacqueline Ko, Kristi Murray, and Bonnie McKiernan.

Anna Pitoniak was an early supporter of this project at Random House; she graciously agreed to stay involved after she left to focus on her own fantastic work as a novelist and was an invaluable editor and reader. I am grateful for her wisdom and friendship. Two other accomplished writers, and dear friends, Ceridwen Dovey and Julie Bosman, were thoughtful and careful readers whose insightful contributions and encouraging support made this a better book.

Evan and Oscie Thomas were early readers and I am deeply grateful for their advice, enthusiasm, and friendship. Thanks as well to friends and family who provided assistance on the road to publication: Will Darman and Lizzie Holt, Emmet Darman, Dick and Jackie Lawler, Ken Mehlman, Jon and Keith Meacham, Jeremy Peters and Brendan Camp, Elise Jordan and Mike Hogan, Maria Comella, Linnea Goldstein, Josh Eriksen and the Osmosis team, Mark Kirby and Erin Owens, Sabrina Geer and Bryan Gunderson, Susanna Mitchell and Reed Simonds, and Alex Schemmer.

Above all, this book would not have been possible without the faith and support of my partner, James Lawler. His rare gifts as a storyteller and problem solver enrich my work each day as do his humor and affection. In the preceding pages, I have tried to tell a story about the sustaining power of hope, joy, and love. I am blessed to know about each of these things because I share my life with James.

NOTES

PROLOGUE: DESTINIES

ix   "Every time you meet a crisis," Eleanor Roosevelt, *You Learn by Living* (New York: Harper Perennial ePub Edition, 2011), 37.

xiii   **A convention, he knew, was a kind of game** An artful description of the code governing presidential selection around the time of the Democrats' 1920 convention appears in Clinton W. Gilbert's *The Mirrors of Washington* (New York: Knickerbocker Press, 1921), 18: "The presidency, the one great prize in American public life, is attained by no known rules and under conditions which have nothing in them to make a man work hard or think hard, especially one endowed with a handsome face and figure, an ingratiating personality, and a literary style."

xiv   **State after state** Damon Runyon, "Belasco Touch Opens Party Drama," *San Francisco Examiner*, June 29, 1920.

xiv   **Franklin had watched** Charles T. White, "Clash Among NY Delegates on the Floor," *New-York Tribune*, June 29, 1920.

xv   **Of course, this breezy convention hall** For San Francisco convention setting, see "The Winning Ways of the West," *The Boston Globe*, June 27, 1920.

xvi   **"could set the matinee girls hearts throbbing"** "Is a Fighter Like T.R.," *The Washington Post*, March 16, 1913.

xvi   **"the figure of an idealized college football player"** *New York Evening Post*, Aug. 10, 1920; *The Washington Post*, March 16, 1919.

xvi   **"like some amazing stag"** Geoffrey Ward, *A First-Class Temperament* (New York: Vintage Books, 2014), 109.

xvii   **Soon he was in an outright struggle** My account of the fight scene on the floor was derived chiefly from newspapers' accounts, including *San Francisco Examiner*, June 29, 1920; *New-York Tribune*, June 29, 1920; *Poughkeepsie Eagle*, June 29, 1920; *The Brooklyn Daily Eagle*, June 29, 1920; *Minneapolis Star Tribune*, June 29, 1920; *Los Angeles Times*, June 29, 1920.

xvii   **And few would forget how splendid** During his years in the White House, he displayed the standard, framed, in his office at home in Hyde Park, with a handwritten note: "This is the original Standard of N.Y. at the S.F. Convention which F.D.R. took possession of after a free for all fight! FDR."

xviii   **A portrait of Woodrow Wilson** "President is 'Whole Show' on Big Field," *Greenville News*, June 28, 1936.

xix   **As Franklin's car moved** *The New York Times*, June 27, 1936. For setting inside the convention on the night of FDR's speech, see *The Philadelphia Inquirer,* June 28, 1936.

xx **Now his challenge was the opposite** H. L. Mencken's dispatch from the convention that night shows that while FDR strove to conceal signs of his disability, the public was not in the dark about his condition. "The official stand was so low," wrote Mencken, "that few if any of the spectators on the field could see it. It had to be made so because of the president's lameness. He is unable without great difficulty to ascend stairs so a ramp was built in the alley behind the stand" (*The Baltimore Sun,* June 28, 1936).

xx **Among them was Edwin Markham** "Edwin Markham Writes Poetic Keynote Speech," *Harrisburg Evening News,* June 27, 1936.

xxi **A chaotic scene followed** For Franklin's near-fall at the 1936 convention, see Arthur Schlesinger Jr., *The Politics of Upheaval* (Boston: Houghton, Mifflin Co., 1960), 583–84. James Roosevelt gave a brief description of the fall in *Affectionately, F.D.R.: A Son's Story of a Lonely Man,* co-written with Sidney Shalett (New York: Harcourt, Brace, 1959), 157–58. Franklin later recalled his anger in the moments after he toppled forward but also remembered maintaining a calm exterior while those around him struggled to refasten his brace. "There I was, hanging in the air like a goose about to be plucked, but I kept on waving and smiling, and smiling and waving. . . ." See Ward, *A First Class Temperament,* 783–84 citing Walter Trohan, *Political Animals* (Garden City, New York: Doubleday, 1975), 82–83. However, Franklin's distress was evident to those in his near vicinity. Franklin was "badly shaken . . . white and worried," his Secret Service agent Michael Reilly later said in *Reilly of the White House: Behind the Scenes with FDR* (New York: Simon and Schuster, 1947), 99–100. Grace Tully, Franklin's secretary, recalled that later that night, after delivering his acceptance speech to a rapturous crowd, FDR was still worked up over the incident, saying, "I was the damnedest, maddest white man at that moment you ever saw." Grace Tully, *F.D.R., My Boss* (New York: Charles Scribner's Sons, 1949), 202. Franklin would later call the incident "the most frightful five minutes of my life." William D. Hassett, "The President Was My Boss," *Saturday Evening Post,* October 10, 1953, 119.

xxi **Just after ten o'clock** "F.D.R. Opens 'Survival of Democracy' War," *Greenville News,* June 28, 1936.

CHAPTER 1: ON CAMPOBELLO

5 **He'd lost the use of much of his body below the neck** The most extensive, factually accurate surviving description of Franklin's early illness in his own words is his letter to William Egleston, Oct. 11, 1924, Franklin D. Roosevelt Papers Pertaining to Family, Business and Personal Affairs, 1882–1945, Box 4, FDR Library (hereafter FDRL).

7 **When their father had appeared on the island** Elliott Roosevelt and James Brough, *An Untold Story: The Roosevelts of Hyde Park* (New York: G. P. Putnam's Sons, 1973), 137–38.

7 **The last day of the Roosevelt family's old life** For FDR's activities on August 10, see *Eleanor Roosevelt, This Is My Story* (New York: Harper & Brothers, 1937), 329–31; James Roosevelt and Sidney Shalett, *Affectionately, F.D.R.: A Son's Story of a Lonely Man* (New York: Harcourt, Brace, 1959), 141–42; Roosevelt and Brough, *Untold Story,* 138–39.

8 **Anna hurried into a closet** John R. Boettiger, *A Love in Shadow* (New York: W. W. Norton, 1978), 88; see also Anna Roosevelt Halsted, "My Life With F.D.R.: How

Polio Helped Father," *The Woman*, July 1949; Bernard Asbell, *Mother and Daughter: The Letters of Eleanor and Anna Roosevelt* (New York: Coward, McCann & Geoghegan, 1982), 30.

8 **"What do you want, dear?"** Boettiger, *A Love in Shadow*, 72.

10 **Franklin's face showed no hint** Eleanor Roosevelt interview transcript, Robert D. Graff papers, Box 4, FDRL.

CHAPTER 2: THE PATH

15 **"everybody"** "Parade Jam is City's Greatest," *The New York Sun*, March 26, 1919. The March 25 Fifth Avenue parade was the city's first opportunity to officially celebrate the end of World War I. Troops returning from the European war had been arriving in New York Harbor throughout early 1919, but the War Department had forbidden the city to put on an official parade for troops who came from other areas of the country.

15 **"New York's own flesh and blood"** "Thousands Ashore to See Ship Arrive," *New-York Tribune*, March 7, 1919.

17 **This was where Franklin knew he had to be** Among the aspects of his Navy Department position FDR valued most highly were the opportunities it afforded for pomp and circumstance, formal displays of power. See Kenneth S. Davis, *FDR: The Beckoning of Destiny: 1882–1928* (New York: G. P. Putnam's Sons, 1971), 318. Franklin had specific ideas about the role of civilian leaders in observing military parades. In March 1916, he joined Woodrow Wilson's reviewing party at the inaugural parade and was dismayed to find Wilson separated from the marching troops by a glass barrier. "Awful mistake to review troops from behind glass cage," he wrote in his diary afterward; FDR Diary, March 5, 1916, Papers as Assistant Secretary of the Navy (hereafter ASN Papers), Box 33, FDRL.

17 **For Franklin and Eleanor Roosevelt** Franklin and Eleanor Roosevelt (hereafter ER) were en route to Europe on board the USS *George Washington* when they received this telegram: EX PRESIDENT THEODORE ROOSEVELT DIED THIS MORNING COLORS ARE TO BE HALF MASTED UNTIL SUNSET THIS EVENING. Twenty 12006. U.S. Naval Radio Service to Geo Washington Radio, Telegraph, 7 P.M., Jan. 6, 1919, ASN Papers, Box 58, FDRL. "We were shocked by the news of Uncle Ted's death," Eleanor wrote to her mother-in-law two days later, "and I think much of Aunt Edith for it will leave her very much alone. Another big figure gone from our nation and I fear the last years were for him full of disappointment." Letter from ER to Sara Delano Roosevelt (hereafter SDR), Jan. 10, 1919, in *F.D.R.: His Personal Letters, Vol. II, 1905–1928*, Elliott Roosevelt, ed. (New York: Duell, Sloan and Pearce, 1948), 445.

18 **By the time he reached adulthood** "Reminiscences of Langdon Parker Marvin and Mary Vaughan Marvin," 1949, Columbia University Oral History Collection, 78.

18 **This path was** The story of Franklin as a young Wall Street lawyer envisioning his path through politics was recounted by Grenville Clark in the *Harvard Alumni Bulletin*, vol. 47, Apr. 28, 1945, 452. Clark's account appears in Davis, *Beckoning of Destiny*, 214.

18 **Along the way, he carefully molded** Attending the 1912 Democratic convention, his first sustained contact with the national leadership of the Democratic Party, Franklin frequently told influential party members that his cousin Teddy preferred Speaker of the House Champ Clark as a potential Democratic opponent over Woodrow Wilson, who he thought would be harder to beat; Josephus Daniels, *The*

Wilson Era: Years of Peace—1910–1917 (Chapel Hill: University of North Carolina Press, 1972), 125. After the convention nominated Wilson, Franklin relayed the inside dish on the Roosevelt family's preference to Wilson himself; "Messages of Good Will Pour in on Governor Wilson at Sea Girt," *The Baltimore Sun,* July 4, 1912.

19 **"the greatest blow"** "World and Nation Eulogize Former President," *New York Tribune,* Jan. 8, 1919.

CHAPTER 3: THE PARADE

20 **a "year of endless hope"** "A New Year of Endless Hope Dawns on this Day," *San Francisco Examiner,* Jan. 1, 1919.

21 **the words bellowed out** *San Francisco Examiner,* Jan. 21, 1919.

22 **"He really didn't like people very much"** Frances Perkins, *The Roosevelt I Knew* (New York: Penguin, 2011), 11.

23 **"I got the Jerry who got me"** "City's Greatest Tribute Paid to Heroes," *The New York Evening World,* March 25, 1919.

23 **"You must resign"** Kenneth Davis, *FDR: The Beckoning of Destiny: 1882–1928* (New York: G. P. Putnam's Sons, 1971), 459, citing Frank Freidel, *Franklin D. Roosevelt: The Apprenticeship* (Boston: Little, Brown and Company, 1952), 301. ER describes the visit with Theodore Roosevelt (henceforth TR), in *Eleanor Roosevelt, This Is My Story* (New York: Harper & Brothers, 1937), 249–50.

23 **"Neither you nor I"** Davis, *Beckoning,* 460. See also Josephus Daniels, *The Wilson Era: Years of Peace—1910–1917* (Chapel Hill: University of North Carolina Press, 1972), 130.

23 **"For every fifty men"** Candice Millard, *Hero of the Empire: The Boer War, A Daring Escape, and the Making of Winston Churchill* (New York: Doubleday, 2016), 105, citing Winston Churchill, *Ian Hamilton's March* (London: Longmans, Green, & Co., 1900), 123. Franklin would long remain sensitive about his wartime service. In a letter written years later, he lobbied to be included in a list of Groton alumni who had served in the war, on the grounds that a 1918 visit to the front in his Navy Department capacity had brought him close to combat danger. "I believe that my name should go in the first division of those who were 'in the service,' especially as I saw service on the other side, was missed by torpedoes and shells"; James MacGregor Burns, *Roosevelt: The Lion and the Fox* (New York: Open Road Media, 2012), e-book. In his heart of hearts, though, he knew the difference between desk warfare and service on the ground.

24 **"Along the road"** Eleanor Roosevelt, *My Story,* 281.

24 **The landscape "was ghastly in its desertion"** FDR to SDR and children, Jan. 18, 1919, excerpted in *F.D.R.: His Personal Letters, Vol. II, 1905–1928,* Elliott Roosevelt, ed. (New York: Duell, Sloan and Pearce, 1948), 461.

24 **Midday approached, and the rest** My account of the Fifth Avenue parade relies heavily on coverage in the New York newspapers. For background on and preparations for the parade, see especially the *New-York Tribune* from January through March 1919. For the scene at the 84th Street reviewing stands, see *The New York Sun,* the *Tribune,* and *The New York Times* from March 26. For descriptions of chaos and fights along the parade route, see *The New York Evening World* from March 25 and *The New York Times* from March 26. For Hearst's displacement of Roosevelt, see *The New York Times* and especially *The New York Sun* from March 26. David Nasaw notes the *Times* account of Hearst's displacement of Roosevelt in *The Chief: The Life of William Randolph Hearst* (New York: Mariner Books, 2000), 273.

CHAPTER 4: BROKEN GLASS

27 **"We are approaching the campaign"** "GOP Chiefs Lambasted by Roosevelt," *Louisville Courier-Journal,* May 30, 1919.

27 **"Franklin D. Roosevelt burst into the limelight"** *Battle Creek Enquirer,* May 30, 1919.

28 **In his hands, he held a suitcase** "Circular Left by Bomb Plotters," *New-York Tribune,* June 3, 1919; "Bomb Explosion at Attorney General's Home Starts Nation-Wide Round-up of Anarchists," *Washington Evening Star,* June 3, 1919; "Red Bombs Palmer's House; Dies Himself; Family Is Not Injured," *The Washington Post,* June 3, 1919, and "Palmer's Family in House, But All Escape Injury," *New-York Tribune,* June 3, 1919. See also *Chicago Tribune, The Boston Daily Globe,* and *San Francisco Chronicle* from June 3, 1919.

29 **Lying beside his son's bed** "Find Anarchist's Spine in House," *The Washington Times,* June 3, 1919.

29 **Bursting into the house** James Roosevelt with Bill Libby, *My Parents: A Differing View* (Chicago: Playboy Press, 1976), 44. James's recollection of the night of the blast differed from that of his mother. Writing to Sara Roosevelt the morning after the explosion, Eleanor downplayed the incident's impact on her son, saying he was not awakened by the sound of the blast, only by the screams that followed it. In his first memoir, James disputed this claim and also noted his mother's bizarrely uncaring first words to her son on arriving home that night: "What are you doing out of bed at this hour, James? . . . Get yourself straight to bed." Roosevelt, James and Sidney Shalett, *Affectionately FDR: A Son's Story of a Lonely Man* (New York: Harcourt Brace & Company, 1959), 60.

29 **We will kill because it is necessary** "Bomb Explosion," *Washington Evening Star,* June 3, 1919; "Circular," *New-York Tribune,* June 3, 1919.

CHAPTER 5: THE PRECIOUS CHILD

31 **"I tried continually to study him"** Sherwood, Robert E. *Roosevelt and Hopkins, An Intimate History* (New York: Harper, 1948), 9.

33 **Checking in on the Roosevelts** Kenneth S. Davis, *FDR: The Beckoning of Destiny: 1882–1928* (New York: G. P. Putnam's Sons), 1972, 52.

33 **But inside, all was calm** Clara and Hardy Steeholm, *The House at Hyde Park* (New York: Viking, 1950), 79–81.

34 **"They tell me he has faults"** Sara Delano Roosevelt, as told to Isabel Leighton and Gabrielle Forbush, in *My Boy Franklin* (New York: Ray Long & Richard R. Smith, Inc., 1933), 18.

34 **"I do not believe I have ever seen"** Ibid., 13–14.

34 **"In fact," she wrote** Ibid., 33.

35 **But only once does the book recall** Ibid., 19. My understanding of the importance placed on pleasantness in Franklin's childhood owes a debt to Geoffrey Ward's volume on Franklin's early years, *Before the Trumpet* (New York: Vintage, 1985, 2014).

35 **"I will show you"** FDR to SDR, 1888–89, as printed in *F.D.R.: His Personal Letters, Vol. I, Early Years,* Elliott Roosevelt, ed. (New York: Duell, Sloan and Pearce, 1947), 13.

36 **James and Rebecca purchased a substantial farm** Over the course of his lifetime, James would buy several properties adjoining his and Rebecca's initial purchase, creating an estate of more than 600 acres.

37 **Inside was a large entrance hall** James and Rebecca purchased Springwood after Mount Hope, the original Roosevelt family home in the Hudson Valley, was de-

stroyed by a fire. In recollections on Roosevelt history in Hyde Park written just before his death in 1945, Franklin recalled family lore about the provenance of the fire in Mount Hope. "The tradition was that they had rented it during the summer to a New York family and this family's butler was thoroughly bored with the country and wished to go back to New York. He is supposed to have set the house on fire in order to return to the city." Eleanor Roosevelt, *Franklin D. Roosevelt and Hyde Park: Personal Recollections of Eleanor Roosevelt* (U.S. Dept. of the Interior/National Park Service, 1949), 3.

37   **"He never took his eyes off her!"** Rita Halle Kleeman, *Gracious Lady: The Life of Sara Delano Roosevelt* (New York, London: D. Appleton-Century Company, 1935), 101.

38   **After the ceremony** Steeholm, *The House at Hyde Park,* 68.

39   **"nearly nude and hideously dirty"** James's address to the guild is in the Roosevelt Family Papers at FDRL. Quoted in Ward, *Before the Trumpet,* 155–56. Christine Wicker offers astute analysis of James's speech in *The Simple Faith of Franklin Delano Roosevelt* (Washington: Smithsonian Books, 2017).

40   **"Franklin and his mother"** Ward, *Before the Trumpet,* 145.

41   **Franklin didn't hesitate** Sara Delano Roosevelt, *My Boy Franklin,* 23–26.

41   **Soon after his arrival** Ward, *Before the Trumpet,* 182.

41   **"I am getting on finely"** FDR to SDR and James Roosevelt, Sept. 18, 1896, in *Letters, Vol. I,* Elliott Roosevelt, ed., 35.

41   **"a quiet, satisfactory boy"** Frank Ashburn, *Peabody of Groton* (Cambridge, Mass.: Riverside Press, 1967), 346.

42   **At the *Crimson*** Philip M. Boffy, "Franklin Delano Roosevelt at Harvard," *Harvard Crimson,* Dec. 13, 1957.

42   **Society girls thought him a "feather duster"** The originator of the epithet may have been Alice Roosevelt, Franklin's cousin and Teddy Roosevelt's eldest daughter, known to history by her married name, Alice Roosevelt Longworth. "We used to call him Feather Duster (for Franklin Delano) because he pranced around and fluttered," she told the writer Michael Teague, recounted in *Mrs. L: Conversations with Alice Roosevelt Longworth* (Garden City, N.Y.: Doubleday, 1981), 156.

42   **"I am so glad"** FDR to SDR and James Roosevelt, Nov. 23, 1900, in *Letters, Vol. I,* Elliott Roosevelt, ed., 434.

42   **"At 2:20 he merely slept away"** Kleeman, *Gracious Lady,* 209.

CHAPTER 6: LOVE MATCHES

43   **Franklin, beginning his second year** FDR to SDR and James Roosevelt, Nov. 13, 1898, in *F.D.R.: His Personal Letters, Vol. I Early Years,* Elliott Roosevelt, ed. (New York: Duell, Sloan and Pearce, 1947), 230.

44   **When, in his junior year** "Cousin Frank," flyer, FDRL. "A cousin of President Roosevelt has just been elected secretary of the Crimson," a Boston newspaper wrote in the fall of 1902. "Franklin D. Roosevelt, like the president, is thoroughly democratic"; Rita Halle Kleeman, *Gracious Lady: The Life of Sara Delano Roosevelt* (New York, London: D. Appleton-Century Company, 1935), 224.

44   **It was his distant cousin** Blanche Wiesen Cook, *Eleanor Roosevelt, Vol. 1: 1884–1933* (New York: Penguin, 1993), 132.

45   **"She remembered my standing in the door"** Eleanor Roosevelt, *This Is My Story* (New York: Harper & Brothers, 1937), 104.

45   **"more claim to good looks"** *Town Topics,* March 19, 1905, quoted in Hazel Rowley, *Franklin and Eleanor* (New York: Farrar, Straus and Giroux, 2010), 37.

46 He "simply could not believe" Cook, *Eleanor Roosevelt, Vol. 1,* 138.

46 "I am so happy" ER to FDR, Nov. 24, 1903, FDRL, quoted in ibid., 139.

46 "Now, dear Franklin" Geoffrey Ward, *A First-Class Temperament* (New York: Vintage Books, 2014), 13.

46 "I am as fond of Eleanor" TR to FDR, Nov. 29, 1904, Box 20, FDRL.

47 "I cannot remember" Eleanor Roosevelt, *My Story,* 126.

CHAPTER 7: THE ORPHAN GIRL

48 A pair of vignettes tell the tale The story of young Franklin's difficult passage home from England appears in Rita Halle Kleeman, *Gracious Lady: The Life of Sara Delano Roosevelt* (New York, London: D. Appleton-Century Company, 1935), 152–53. It was indeed a near miss: The force of the wave knocked the ship's captain unconscious and stripped the vessel of its lifeboats. See also Geoffrey Ward, *Before the Trumpet* (New York: Vintage, 1985, 2014), 115–16. For the story of Eleanor's family's calamitous aborted journey to Europe, see Blanche Wiesen Cook, *Eleanor Roosevelt, Vol. 1: 1884–1933* (New York: Penguin, 1993), 48–49, and Joseph P. Lash, *Eleanor and Franklin: The Story of Their Relationship, Based on Eleanor Roosevelt's Private Papers* (New York: W. W. Norton & Company, Inc., 1971), 29–30.

50 Anyone who ever met Eleanor's mother Anna's beauty was a central fact of Eleanor's life: Nearly half a century after her mother's death, Eleanor would begin her own memoir with the following words: "My mother was one of the most beautiful women I have ever seen." *Eleanor Roosevelt, This Is My Story* (New York: Harper & Brothers, 1937), 1.

50 "She seems to me" Cook, *Eleanor Roosevelt, Vol. 1,* 43.

50 Life was a struggle For comparisons between Theodore and Elliott Roosevelt, see David McCullough, *Mornings on Horseback* (New York: Simon & Schuster, 2003), 128. Even in early adulthood, as his life became troubled, Elliott still merited favorable comparison alongside his brother. "Elliott as a young man," said one family acquaintance, "was a much more fascinating person than Theodore Roosevelt." Edmund Morris, *The Rise of Theodore Roosevelt* (New York: Random House, 1979), 95.

51 "Believe me" Joseph P. Lash, *Eleanor and Franklin: The Story of Their Relationship, Based on Eleanor Roosevelt's Private Papers* (New York: W. W. Norton & Company, Inc., 1971), 19.

51 "I shall never feel you are really your dear old self" Cook, *Eleanor Roosevelt, Vol. 1.,* 54.

51 "You have no looks" Ibid., 62, and Eleanor Roosevelt, *My Story,* 11.

52 Stroking Anna's hair Eleanor Roosevelt, *My Story,* 13.

52 "Someday I would make a home for him again" Ibid., 20.

53 "cried like a little child for a long time" Corinne Roosevelt Robinson to Anna Roosevelt Cowles, Aug. 15, 1894, Theodore Roosevelt Collection, Harvard College Library, quoted in Morris, *Rise of Theodore Roosevelt,* 488.

53 "Tell her her father is so very sorry" Corinne Roosevelt Robinson to Anna Roosevelt Cowles, Aug. 15, 1894, quoted in Cook, *Eleanor Roosevelt, Vol. 1,* 88.

54 "the warmest heart" Lash, *Eleanor and Franklin,* 82.

54 Allenswood turned Eleanor's attention For influence of Mademoiselle Souvestre, see ibid. and Eleanor Roosevelt, *My Story,* 53–61. At Allenswood, Eleanor would later write, she learned "that the underdog was always the one to be championed!" a tidy summation of both Eleanor's Christian faith and her politics.

54 "I feel lost without you somewhere near" Eleanor's letters to Franklin during his absence with Sara, Box 14, FDRL, quoted in Cook, *Eleanor Roosevelt, Vol. 1,* 158.

55 **"Bonheur!"** Lash, *Eleanor and Franklin,* 140.

55 **"It is deliciously cool"** FDR to SDR, June 16, 1905, in *F.D.R.: His Personal Letters, Vol. II, 1905–1928,* Elliott Roosevelt, ed. (New York: Duell, Sloan and Pearce, 1948), 21.

55 **The whole episode** Eleanor describes her feelings during the unhappy visit to Cortina—"jealous beyond description"—in *My Story,* 130, and identifies Franklin's female hiking companion as a "Miss Kitty Gandy." In 1937, she wrote, "Perhaps I should add that Miss Gandy has since become one of my very good friends!"

CHAPTER 8: MR. AND MRS. ROOSEVELT

57 **Franklin, the only child of Sara and James** Franklin's desire to have a large family helped to scuttle his most serious pre-Eleanor romance, with Alice Sohier, a girl from Boston's North Shore. Sohier later told her granddaughter this was because "I did not wish to be a cow"—her life given over to the production of offspring. See Geoffrey Ward, *Before the Trumpet* (New York: Vintage, 1985, 2014), 253–4. See also Rowley, Hazel *Franklin and Eleanor* (New York: Farrar, Straus and Giroux, 2010), 28–29.

57 **"So many years later"** Eleanor Roosevelt, *This Is My Story* (New York: Harper & Brothers, 1937), 165.

57 **A profile in *The New York Times*** "Senator FD Roosevelt, Chief Insurgent at Albany," *The New York Times,* Jan. 22, 1911.

58 **Performing a satirical song** *Glens Falls Post Star,* Apr. 28, 1911.

58 **"I took an interest in politics"** Eleanor Roosevelt, *This Is My Story* (New York: Harper & Brothers, 1937), 173.

59 **"How would I like it"** Josephus Daniels, *The Wilson Era: Years of Peace—1910–1917* (Chapel Hill: University of North Carolina Press, 1972), 124. In making the case for Franklin's nomination, Daniels assured President Wilson that Franklin was "one of our kind of liberal"; ibid., 126.

CHAPTER 9: GOLDEN BOY

60 **"There's another Roosevelt on the job today"** Jean Edward Smith, *FDR* (New York: Random House, 2007), 103, citing *The New York Sun,* March 13, 1913. Stories about the second coming of an assistant Navy secretary Roosevelt began appearing in the first weeks of Franklin's time in Washington—see *The Washington Post,* March 11, 1913, and *St. Louis Post-Dispatch,* Apr. 11, 1913—and continued throughout Franklin's tenure. Over time, some reporters began to note the differences in the two men's temperaments and presentation as well. See, for example, "Another Roosevelt," *The New York Times,* July, 2, 1918. During the Wilson years, the difference in Franklin and Theodore Roosevelt's parties became a more substantial barrier to their personal relations, due to Teddy's loathing for the Democratic president. Franklin wrote lengthy, solicitous letters about his Navy responsibilities, boldly addressed to "*Uncle Ted.*" But Teddy showed little interest in sharing confidences; his own letters were brief and perfunctory, usually asking Franklin's assistance in securing a commission, lightened only by a "with dearest love to Eleanor" at the end. Still, the family affection remained. When Franklin came down with debilitating pneumonia after a visit to the war front in 1918, Teddy wrote to express his concern: "We are deeply concerned about your sickness and trust you will be well. We are very proud of you"; TR to FDR, Sept. 23, 1918, ASN Papers, Box 58, FDRL.

61 **Wilson, with his bizarre hybrid** Jonathan Daniels describes Washington society's

apprehension toward the Wilsonian invaders in *Washington Quadrille: The Dance Beside the Documents* (Garden City, N.Y.: Doubleday, 1968).

62 **"Whenever a Roosevelt rides"** Josephus Daniels, *The Wilson Era: Years of Peace— 1910–1917* (Chapel Hill: University of North Carolina Press, 1972), 124–27.

62 **"I wish you would throw that cigarette away"** "Boy with Cigarette Was Franklin Roosevelt," *The Tennessean,* Jan. 23, 1918.

62 **In the years before the Great War** David Brinkley, *Washington Goes to War* (New York: Alfred A. Knopf, 1988), 32.

63 **"Franklin, why are you grinning"** Daniels, *Wilson Era,* 129.

63 **"Somehow I don't believe I shall be long in Washington"** FDR to ER, August 20, 1918 in in *F.D.R.: His Personal Letters, Vol. II, 1905–1928,* Elliott Roosevelt, ed. (New York: Duell, Sloan and Pearce, 1948), 440.

64 **When he got back, he put out word to the papers** See "Roosevelt May Quit," *The New York Times,* Oct. 31, 1918.

CHAPTER 10: BREATHLESS AND HUNTED

67 **"Nothing ever happens to us"** Eleanor Roosevelt, *You Learn by Living* (New York: Harper Perennial ePub Edition, 2011), 82.

70 **"daughter of Mrs. Carroll Mercer"** "Another Washingtonian Goes into Business," *The Washington Times,* Nov. 12, 1916.

70 **think of Lily Bart** A further Wharton resonance: In 1920, after the conclusion of her affair with Franklin, Lucy Mercer married Winthrop Rutherfurd, a wealthy and handsome New York socialite who had been a "childhood crush" of Edith Wharton herself; Hermione Lee, *Edith Wharton* (New York: Knopf, 2007), 728.

70 **Lucy "had the same brand of charm as Father"** Elliott Roosevelt and James Brough, *An Untold Story: The Roosevelts of Hyde Park* (New York: G. P. Putnam's Sons, 1973), 82.

71 **After the birth of John in 1916** Ibid., 81.

71 **Their romance became consuming passion** Details from the "hot summer of 1917": FDR to ER, July 16, 1917, in *F.D.R.: His Personal Letters, Vol. II, 1905–1928,* Elliott Roosevelt, ed. (New York: Duell, Sloan and Pearce, 1948), 347; FDR to ER, July 25, 1917; in ibid., p. 352. No account of Franklin and Lucy's romance survives from Franklin or Lucy themselves. Ironically, then, any chronology of their relationship depends most heavily on two sources: Franklin's letters to Eleanor during wartime summer separations and Eleanor's version of the story as told to her friend and biographer Joseph Lash. The most extensive alternative versions come from Joseph Alsop in *FDR: A Centenary Remembrance* (New York: Viking, 1982), 67–73, and Alice Roosevelt Longworth in Michael Teague, *Mrs. L: Conversations with Alice Roosevelt Longworth* (Garden City, N.Y.: Doubleday, 1981), 157–59. Both of these accounts draw on the recollections of Eleanor's aunt Corinne Roosevelt Robinson (Alsop's grandmother and Longworth's aunt) and are decidedly less sympathetic to Eleanor's point of view than is Lash's account. See also Jonathan Daniels, *Washington Quadrille: The Dance Beside the Documents* (Garden City, N.Y.: Doubleday, 1968), 143–48.

71 **"I saw you out driving"** Teague, *Mrs. L,* 158.

71 **"Isn't it horrid"** Joseph P. Lash, *Eleanor and Franklin: The Story of Their Relationship, Based on Eleanor Roosevelt's Private Papers* (New York: W. W. Norton & Company, Inc., 1971), 222.

72 **Sara's opposition to his leaving Eleanor** For Sara's threat, see Alsop, *Centenary Remembrance,* 70. Alsop's version, via Sara's friend Corinne Roosevelt Robinson, has

Sara declaring "that she 'would not give him another dollar' if he left 'a wife and five children for another woman.'" Given the dynamics of the relationship between ~~mother and son, Sara's displeasure~~ as much as any financial implications, would have been meaningful to Franklin.

72 **Yet her letters from the summer of 1919** Blanche Wiesen Cook adroitly evokes the juxtaposition between the smallness of Eleanor's worldview in the summer of 1919 with the momentous events going on around her in Ch. 10 of *Eleanor Roosevelt, Vol. 1: 1884–1933* (New York: Penguin, 1993). For Eleanor's letters to Franklin, see *Letters: Vol. II*, Elliott Roosevelt, ed., 479–81. For a detailed and disturbing account of the persecutory white mobs in Washington in the summer of 1919, see "The Deadly Race Riot Aided and Abetted by the Washington Post" *The Washington Post*, July 15, 2019.

73 **"This past year"** ER to Isabella Greenway, July 11, 1919, Papers of Anna Eleanor Roosevelt, Family and Personal Correspondence, FDRL.

74 **"passionately longing"** "Women Will Choose the Next President, Says Mrs. Carrie Chapman Catt," *Buffalo Times*, July 27, 1919.

74 **As was the case with nearly every event** *The Washington Times*, Aug. 3, 1919.

75 **"had she insisted"** *Eleanor Roosevelt, This Is My Story* (New York: Harper & Brothers, 1937), 300.

76 **"I didn't want to spoil the fun"** See Alsop, *Centenary Remembrance*, 260, and Teague, *Mrs. L*, 160. Alsop implies the scene occurred in wartime, but Blanche Wiesen Cook credibly places it in the latter part of 1919. It is not clear whether Eleanor's distress at the dinner dance sprang from Franklin's dancing with Lucy Mercer; Washington newspapers from December 1919 show Eleanor and Lucy overlapping at society events. See "Society," *The Washington Herald*, Dec. 18, 1919. Alsop's account indicates the story of Eleanor on the doorstep was well known in Washington society at the time. It was circulating in Washington during the latter years of Franklin's presidency; see "Reminiscences of Marquis W. Childs," 1958, individual interviews Oral History Collection, Columbia University Center for Oral History. Eleanor wrote about the incident, without the broader context of the Lucy Mercer affair, in *You Learn by Living: Eleven Keys for a More Fulfilling Life* (New York: Olive Editions, 2016).

CHAPTER II: PERSECUTORS

77 **"I just can't stand"** Joseph P. Lash, *Eleanor and Franklin: The Story of Their Relationship, Based on Eleanor Roosevelt's Private Papers* (New York: W. W. Norton & Company, Inc., 1971), 243.

77 **The strain on Franklin and Eleanor's nerves** Multiple sources contribute to a picture of the early months of 1920 as an emotional low point in Franklin's adult, pre-polio life. Encountering Franklin out for an early-morning walk, his neighbor Bertie Hamlin found him looking unwell, in a disagreeable mood, and "not himself"; Kenneth Davis, *FDR: The Beckoning of Destiny: 1882–1928* (New York: G. P. Putnam's Sons, 1971), 593–95. Several weeks later, when a visitor proposed he consider a run for the presidency on a ticket with Herbert Hoover, Franklin seemed distracted and unmoved; Louis B. Wehle, *Hidden Threads of History: Wilson Through Roosevelt* (New York: Macmillan, 1953), 81–82.

77 **found it hard to make ends meet** See FDR to SDR, Feb. 11, 1920, in *F.D.R.: His Personal Letters, Vol. II, 1905–1928*, Elliott Roosevelt, ed. (New York: Duell, Sloan and Pearce, 1948), 486.

78 **After a few weeks, he was loudly** Lawrence R. Murphy, *Perverts by Official Order* (New York: Harrington Park Press, 1988) 10–11.

78 **In early 1919, Ervin Arnold** Box 4-6, Louis Howe Papers, FDRL, and Sherry Zane, "I Did It for the Uplift of Humanity and the Navy: Same-Sex Acts and the Origins of the National Security State, 1919–1921," *New England Quarterly*, Vol. XCI, No. 2, June 2018, 279.

78 **"This department"** FDR to A. Mitchell Palmer, March 22, 1919, in *The Providence Journal*, March 19, 1920.

79 **Arnold's innovative method** Murphy, *Perverts*, 22–25.

80 **"It is requested"** FDR to chief of Naval Intelligence, May 5, 1919, quoted in Murphy, *Perverts*, 72; Geoffrey Ward, *A First-Class Temperament* (New York: Vintage Books, 2014), 441–42.

81 **"I heard something recently"** Ward, *First-Class Temperament*, 466–67.

82 **Daniels made a point of telling reporters** "John R. Rathom Charges 'Vile Practices' in Prosecuting Seamen," *The New York Times*, Jan. 20, 1920.

CHAPTER 12: LONELY ISLAND

83 **Yet while political insiders** Though the passage of the nineteenth amendment was a testament to women's prowess as political organizers, newspapers in 1920 consistently questioned the seriousness of female voters. A jokey poem published in newspapers nationwide read: "If you want to win the female vote, Here is your one best bet / Just write and send to her a note, enclosed in a hair net." *Wilkes-Barre Times Leader*, Sept. 9, 1920.

84 **plans for a new law firm** Emmet, Marvin & Roosevelt announcement, March 17, 1920, ASN, Box 47, FDRL.

85 **Only Campobello felt like hers** For background on the Roosevelts' Campobello, see Rita Halle Kleeman, *Gracious Lady: The Life of Sara Delano Roosevelt* (New York, London: D. Appleton-Century Company, 1935), 137, 148–49. For Sara's gift of the house to Eleanor and Franklin, see *Eleanor Roosevelt, This Is My Story* (New York: Harper & Brothers, 1937), 178–77.

85 **"I was always part"** Eleanor Roosevelt, *My Story*, 311.

86 **On Sundays** James Roosevelt and Sidney Shalett, *Affectionately, F.D.R.: A Son's Story of a Lonely Man* (New York: Harcourt, Brace, 1959), 66.

86 **She struggled too as a parent** For the differences in Eleanor and Franklin's parenting styles and the dynamic with Sara Roosevelt, see Ch. 3 and 4 of James Roosevelt with Bill Libby, *My Parents: A Differing View* (Chicago: Playboy Press, 1976), 35–36: Eleanor "tried to do what was right for us," James wrote, "but had no confidence in her ability to do so. Sara had confidence in her own ability to do anything." See also Anna Roosevelt Halsted Oral History interview, FDRL; FDR's 1918–25 correspondence with Anna Roosevelt gives a sense of his easy, comfortable connection to his children—and his frequent absences from their daily lives. ("I can't wait to see you," Anna wrote to her father in September 1918, "please come soon or I will burst.") In Ch. 3 of *A Love in Shadow* (New York: W. W. Norton, 1978), Anna's son, John R. Boettiger, contrasts Eleanor's "pattern of impersonal constraint and inadequate warmth" with Franklin's "more physically and emotionally relaxed" way with his children. See also Bernard Asbell, *Mother and Daughter: The Letters of Eleanor and Anna Roosevelt* (New York: Coward, McCann & Geoghegan, 1982), 14–15.

86 **"I am more your mother than your mother"** James Roosevelt, *My Parents*, 25.

87 **"You were a goosy girl"** FDR to ER, July 16, 1917, in *Letters: Vol. II*, Elliott Roosevelt, ed., 347.

87 **The rest of the city seemed to be in on** There is good reason to believe that Franklin and Lucy's affair was well known in the capital's society circles at the time. By the latter years of Franklin's presidency, it was well trafficked in Washington political and journalistic circles as well—thanks, perhaps, to Franklin and Eleanor's vengeful loose-lipped cousin, Alice Roosevelt Longworth. It was on the radar of FDR's early biographers: Writing in the 1950s, while Eleanor was still alive, James MacGregor Burns gingerly suggested the possibility of an affair. The first lengthy account of the affair appeared after ER's death, in Jonathan Daniels's *The Time Between the Wars* (New York: Doubleday, 1966). At the time of publication, Franklin and Eleanor's son Franklin Jr. publicly disputed Daniels's account. "My mother and my father had a beautiful and ideal life together," Franklin Jr., said; "Kin Deny Account of F.D.R. Romance: Describe Mrs. Rutherfurd and President as Friends," *The New York Times*, Aug. 13, 1966. But Franklin Jr.'s three elder siblings—Anna, James, and Elliott—all subsequently confirmed knowledge of Franklin and Lucy's affair and, in James's and Elliott's case, wrote about it in family memoirs.

87 **"She inquired if you had told me"** ER to FDR, undated, FDRL. A good exploration of the scene between Alice and Eleanor in the Capitol and their relationship c. 1918 appears in Mark Peyser and Timothy Dwyer's wonderful *Hissing Cousins* (New York: Nan A. Talese, 2015), 105–06.

89 **IT WOULD HAVE DONE YOUR HEART GOOD** Eleanor Roosevelt, *My Story*, 310.

89 **"I am very much pleased"** "Plan to Welcome Roosevelt," *The Boston Post*, July 12, 1920, in ASN Papers, Box 38, FDRL.

90 **"I still hope to leave Saturday p.m."** FDR to ER, July 17, 1920, in *Letters: Vol. II*, Elliott Roosevelt, ed., 494.

CHAPTER 13: IN A HURRY

91 **"A Young Men's Candidate"** Box 38, ASN, FDRL.

91 **It was a bittersweet, passing-of-the-torch moment** For Cox–Roosevelt visit, see James M. Cox, *Journey Through My Years* (Macon, Ga.: Mercer, 2004), 241–45, and Frank Freidel, *Franklin Roosevelt: The Ordeal* (Boston: Little, Brown & Co., 1954), 73–74. For the scene outside the White House, see *The New York Times*, *The Washington Post*, and *New-York Tribune* from July 19, 1920. The emotional scene at the White House appears to have overwhelmed Franklin's preference to dwell on the positive. "I don't quite like to write of the meeting with the President," he wrote to Eleanor, "so I will wait till I can see you on Sunday"; FDR to ER, July 20, 1920, quoted in *F.D.R.: His Personal Letters, Vol. II, 1905–1928*, Elliott Roosevelt, ed. (New York: Duell, Sloan and Pearce, 1948), 495.

92 **"like an enthusiastic schoolboy"** *The Kansas City Post*, Oct. 10, 1920, 1920 VP Papers, Box 13, FDRL.

92 **"as much like Theodore as a clam"** "The One Half of One Percent Roosevelt," *Chicago Tribune*, Aug. 13, 1920.

92 **In their efforts to de-Roosevelt Franklin** "He does not have the brand of our family," Theodore Roosevelt Jr. said at a campaign stop in Wyoming. For Eleanor, the Oyster Bay Roosevelts' menacing of Franklin during the 1920 campaign would be a lasting source of bitterness. See Blanche Wiesen Cook, *Eleanor Roosevelt, Vol. 1: 1884–1933* (New York: Penguin, 1993), 278.

93 **"I have something to do with the running"** Franklin's visit to Butte looked promising on the day of his fateful speech. Previewing his performance, a local paper observed that Franklin "appears to have at least one of the qualities that are associated with his family name and that is strenuosity"; *Butte Montana Miner,* quoted in the *Poughkeepsie Star,* Aug. 25, 1920, in 1920 VP Papers, Box 16, FDRL.

93 **"We would very much like to know"** For the Hearst editorial, see *New York American,* Aug. 27, 1920, 1920 VP Papers, Box 15, FDRL.

94 **to save himself** "Roosevelt Misquoted," *The New York Times,* Sept. 3, 1920. The press was skeptical of Franklin's defense: "There you are again. It is always the stenographer, reporter or linotyper who is to blame when a speaker says something he afterward discovers he ought not to have said"; *Utica Herald,* Sept. 8, 1920, 1920 VP Papers, Box 16, FDRL.

94 **"You who have been bludgeoned"** "Sudden Sensitiveness," *The New York Times,* August 19, 1920, ASN Papers, Box 38, FDRL.

94 *Drop clippings and suggestions* "FD Roosevelt Says Missouri and Ohio Will Vote for Cox," *St. Louis Times,* Oct. 4, 1920, 1920 VP Papers, Box 16, FDRL.

95 **"clean shaven and fairly spark[ling] with virility"** "Nation's Next Vice-President Makes Big Hit," *Wheeling Register,* Sept. 30, 1920, 1920 VP Papers, Box 13, FDRL.

95 **In Washington, he had frequently** Elliott Roosevelt and James Brough, *An Untold Story: The Roosevelts of Hyde Park* (New York: G. P. Putnam's Sons, 1973), 20.

95 **"jealousy . . . of a one-man dog"** Oral History Interview with Samuel Irving Rosenman, 1959, Columbia Center for Oral History, Columbia University.

96 **Soon they were inseparable** Eleanor Roosevelt, *This Is My Story* (New York: Harper & Brothers, 1937), 316–19; Lela Stiles, *The Man Behind Roosevelt: The Story of Louis McHenry Howe* (Cleveland, Ohio: World Publishing Company, 1954), 72–73.

96 **"silent vote"** "FD Roosevelt Bases Hope on Silent Vote," *New-York Tribune,* Oct. 26, 1920.

96 **"Please take the enclosed"** Unknown to "Pryor," Oct. 19, 1920, 1920 VP Papers, Box 9, FDRL.

97 **"Who is that fellow?"** *New-York Tribune,* Nov. 3, 1920.

97 **But soon the radio** KDKA, owned by Westinghouse, received updates on balloting by telephone from the *Pittsburgh Post.* "The first program," a Westinghouse vice president later recalled, "which ran from about 8 P.M. to some time after midnight, consisted only of the election returns repeated into our microphone by [an announcer] from what he heard by phone from the Post downtown, interspersed with recorded music." *American Heritage,* Vol. 6, Issue 5, Aug. 1955.

97 **"Every war brings after it"** FDR to Matthew Hale, Nov. 6, 1920.

98 **"We move to N.Y."** FDR to Early, Dec. 12, 1921, in *Letters: Vol. II,* Elliott Roosevelt, ed., 514.

CHAPTER 14: HURTLING

99 **Then, a few weeks after her return** Eleanor Roosevelt, *This Is My Story* (New York: Harper & Brothers, 1937), 324–26.

100 **Catt's "clear cold reason"** ER to FDR, Apr. 11, 1921, quoted in Blanche Wiesen Cook, *Eleanor Roosevelt, Vol. 1: 1884–1933* (New York: Penguin, 1993), 291.

100 **"an indefatigable worker"** *New York Daily News,* May 10, 1921.

100 **good food and refined conversation** Eleanor Roosevelt, *My Story,* 324–25.

100 **In Read and Lape's home** Cook, *Eleanor Roosevelt, Vol. 1,* 296–97.

101 **Cast away from high purpose** Ibid., 304–305, and Joseph P. Lash, *Eleanor and Franklin: The Story of Their Relationship, Based on Eleanor Roosevelt's Private Papers* (New York: W. W. Norton & Company, Inc., 1971), 265.

101 **COMMITTEE READY** Josephus Daniels to FDR, July 12, 1921, Papers Pertaining to Family, Personal and Business Affairs, FDRL, quoted in Geoffrey Ward, *A First-Class Temperament* (New York: Vintage Books, 2014), 570.

102 **"That Franklin D. Roosevelt"** Alleged Immoral Conditions at Newport Naval Training Station. Report of the Committee on Naval Affairs (Washington D.C.: Government Printing Office, 1921).

102 **The headlines the next morning** "Lay Navy Scandal," *The New York Times*, July 20, 1921; "Used Enlisted Men Improperly to Catch Moral Perverts," *The Great Falls Tribune*, July 20, 1921.

103 **On board, he mixed congenially** For visit to the Boy Scout camp, see *The New York Evening World* and *The New York Herald*, July 28, 1921.

103 **"so cold it seemed paralyzing"** Elliott Roosevelt and James Brough, *An Untold Story: The Roosevelts of Hyde Park* (New York: G. P. Putnam's Sons, 1973), 138. "I'd never felt anything as cold as that water," FDR would tell Earle Looker; Looker, *This Man Roosevelt* (New York: Brewer, Warren & Putnam, 1932), 111.

103 **what felt like a summer cold** Missy LeHand to ER, Aug. 23, 1921, FDR Family, Business, and Personal Affairs Papers, Box 4, FDRL.

104 **When he tried to stand** First night of illness see Roosevelt and Brough, *Untold Story*, 139; Eleanor Roosevelt, *My Story*, 330–31; FDR to William Egleston, Oct. 11, 1924, Family, Business, and Personal Affairs Papers, Box 4, FDRL; Looker, *This Man*, 111–12. (FDR's account, as published by Looker in 1932, condenses the timeline on Campobello but, excepting the Egleston letter, is nonetheless the most extensive record of FDR's own recollection leading up to paralysis.)

CHAPTER 15: STRANDED

109 **"I don't know what's the matter"** Lela Stiles, *The Man Behind Roosevelt: The Story of Louis McHenry Howe* (Cleveland, Ohio: World Publishing Company, 1954), 76.

110 **In the first years of the twentieth century** Naomi Rogers, *Dirt and Disease: Polio Before FDR* (New Brunswick, N.J.: Rutgers University Press, 1992), 10–11.

111 **In 1916, New York City** See ibid., 11–33; *The New York Times*, July 9, 1916; *The Philadelphia Inquirer*, July 9, 1916; *The New York Sun*, July 29, 1916.

111 **"The infantile paralysis in N.Y. and vicinity"** FDR to ER, July 7, 1916, quoted in *F.D.R.: His Personal Letters, Vol. II, 1905–1928*, Elliott Roosevelt, ed. (New York: Duell, Sloan and Pearce, 1948), 304. The Roosevelts' concerns about the risks of infantile paralysis led Eleanor and the children to prolong their annual summer holiday, remaining out of Washington well into the fall.

112 **It was also widely** Rogers, *Dirt and Disease*, 19–21.

112 **He was, in fact, *more* likely** Naomi Rogers writes of the 1916 New York epidemic: "Polio victims in rural counties in New York State were older than urban children and more likely to die. These figures reflect not only the widespread immunity among adults in urban and congested areas but also the endemic mild cases of polio missed by most physicians"; *Dirt and Disease*, 13.

112 **The stresses and strains of the past year** James Tobin explores the impact on Franklin's immune system of his emotionally trying summer in *The Man He Became* (New York: Simon & Schuster, 2013), 37–40.

113 **In the winter of 1911** Stiles, *The Man Behind Roosevelt*, 30–34.

114 **Louis called himself Franklin's "toe weights"** Ibid., 40.

114 **"His whole object in life"** Josephus Daniels interview transcript with Frank Freidel, Box 8, FDRL.

114 **"unless you want him to jump"** Stiles, *The Man Behind Roosevelt,* 53.

114 **The boy was "the only person in the world"** Louis Howe to Grace Howe, Oct. 9, 1919, Louis Howe Personal Papers, FDRL.

115 **Louis met Keen that evening** For background on Keen, see *St. Louis Post-Dispatch,* Nov. 3, 1918; *St. Petersburg Times,* July 20, 1985; and *American Heritage,* Vol. 8, Issue 6, Oct. 1957, which is cited in Geoffrey Ward, *A First-Class Temperament* (New York: Vintage Books, 2014), 585.

116 **The misdiagnosis came at a high cost** Tobin, *Man He Became,* 58–62. By closely examining medical evidence, Tobin's account adds valuable perspective to the story of Franklin's illness and infection. Tobin speculates that had the Roosevelts sought out the opinion of Franklin's personal physician, George Draper, during the early days of illness on Campobello, Draper would have "dropped everything to locate the closest anti-poliomyelitis serum" and possibly arrested Franklin's progress toward paralysis.

116 **"Louis and I are rubbing him"** ER to James R. Roosevelt in *Letters, Vol. II,* Elliott Roosevelt, ed., 524.

117 **"I dread the time"** Ibid., Aug. 18, 1921, 525.

118 **After reviewing the symptoms** Frederic A. Delano to ER, Aug. 20, 1921, Family, Business, and Personal Affairs Papers, Box 23, FDRL . For more on Delano's meeting with Samuel Levine, see Tobin, *Man He Became,* 327, drawing on Levine's unpublished notes.

118 **"A telegram to his office will get him"** Frederic A. Delano to ER, Aug. 20, 1921, Family, Business, and Personal Affairs Papers, Box 23, FDRL.

118 **"On Uncle Fred's urgent advice"** ER to James R. Roosevelt, Aug. 23, 1921, *Letters: Vol. II,* Elliott Roosevelt, ed., 526.

119 **"read . . . that story again"** Julie M. Fenster, *FDR's Shadow: Louis Howe, the Force That Shaped Franklin and Eleanor Roosevelt* (New York: Palgrave Macmillan, 2009), 135.

119 **"no one could tell where they stood"** Robert Lovett to George Draper, Sept. 12, 1921, Robert W. Lovett Papers, Francis Countway Library, Harvard University.

119–20 **"the prospect is so bright"** Quoted in Elliott Roosevelt and James Brough, *An Untold Story: The Roosevelts of Hyde Park* (New York: G. P. Putnam's Sons, 1973), 144.

CHAPTER 16: PLANS

121 **Louis Howe watched** My description of Franklin's escape from Campobello draws on Lela Stiles, *The Man Behind Roosevelt: The Story of Louis McHenry Howe* (Cleveland, Ohio: World Publishing Company, 1954), 79–80; Elliott Roosevelt and James Brough, *An Untold Story: The Roosevelts of Hyde Park* (New York: G. P. Putnam's Sons, 1973), 148–49; and Geoffrey Ward, *A First-Class Temperament* (New York: Vintage Books, 2014), 598–99. (Ward interviewed the daughter of the Roosevelt cottage caretaker and the two youngest Roosevelt sons.) See also Eleanor Roosevelt, *This Is My Story* (New York: Harper & Brothers, 1937), 333–34, and James Roosevelt and Sidney Shalett, *Affectionately, F.D.R.: A Son's Story of a Lonely Man* (New York: Harcourt, Brace, 1959), 144.

121 **"Few people possess the courage"** Stiles, *The Man Behind Roosevelt,* 81.

122 **"dominated circumstances"** Julie M. Fenster, *FDR's Shadow: Louis Howe, the Force That Shaped Franklin and Eleanor Roosevelt* (New York: Palgrave Macmillan, 2009), 116.

122   **"You have been a rare wife"** Roosevelt and Brough, *Untold Story*, 144.

123   **"What a pity he is not still in the Navy"** James R. Roosevelt to ER, Aug. 20, 1921, FDRL.

123   **"Don't worry, chicks"** Ward, *First-Class Temperament*, 599; Roosevelt and Shalett, *Affectionately*, 144.

124   **"Your Aunt Annie"** Frederic Delano to Eleanor Roosevelt, Aug. 28, 1921, Family, Business, and Personal Affairs Papers, Box 23, FDRL.

124   **Franklin was not even able to hold a pen** Roosevelt and Brough, *Untold Story*, 147.

124   **"I have made an attempt"** Missy LeHand to Eleanor Roosevelt, Aug. 23, 1921, Family, Business, and Personal Affairs Papers, Box 4, FDRL.

125   **"Franklin D. Roosevelt, former Assistant Secretary of the Navy"** *The New York Times* and *New-York Tribune*, Aug. 29, 1921.

125   **"Dearest Mama"** ER to SDR, Aug. 27, 1921, cited in Hazel Rowley, *Franklin and Eleanor* (New York: Farrar, Straus and Giroux, 2010), 107.

125   **"brave . . . & beautiful"** SDR to Frederic Delano, Sept. 2, 1921, Family, Business, and Personal Affairs Papers, Box 23, FDRL.

126   **"My thoughts are with you"** SDR to ER, Sept. 4, 1921, Roosevelt Family Papers Donated by the Children, Box 8, FDRL.

126   **So he'd encouraged** Frank Freidel, *Franklin Roosevelt: The Ordeal* (Boston: Little, Brown & Co., 1954), 101–02.

126   **When they reached land** Eleanor Roosevelt, *My Story*, 333.

127   **F. D. ROOSEVELT IS BETTER** *The New York Times*, Sept. 15, 1921.

127   **"was unable to walk or to sit up"** *Rochester Democrat and Chronicle, Ogden Standard-Examiner, Oakland Tribune*, Sept. 15, 1921.

128   **"looked like his old self"** *Poughkeepsie Eagle*, Sept. 16, 1921.

128   **The reality of the scene** Ernest K. Lindley, *Franklin D. Roosevelt: A Career in Progressive Democracy* (Indianapolis, Ind., Bobbs-Merrill Co., 1931); Stiles, *The Man Behind Roosevelt*, 80; and Kenneth Davis, *FDR: The Beckoning of Destiny: 1882–1928* (New York: G. P. Putnam's Sons, 1971), 662.

128   **"F.D. ROOSEVELT HAS PARALYSIS IN MILD FORM"** *New York Tribune*, September 16, 1921.

128   **"He definitely will not be crippled"** *The New York Times*, Sept. 16, 1921; Ward interprets Draper's actions in *First-Class Temperament*, 603. "I feel immensely relieved"; FDR to Adolph Ochs, Sept. 16, 1921, FDRL.

CHAPTER 17: THE WILL AND DETERMINATION OF THE PATIENT

130   **"I am very much concerned"** George Draper to Robert Lovett, Sept. 24, 1921, Lovett Papers, Francis Countway Library, Harvard University.

131   **The mind of a patient** Jerome Groopman's classic, *The Anatomy of Hope: How People Prevail in the Face of Illness* (New York: Random House, 2004), was invaluable in my understanding of the role of hope in recovery from serious illness. Of hope's power to physically ease pain, Groopman writes: "Belief and expectation, cardinal components of hope, can block pain by releasing the brain's endorphins and enkephalins, thereby mimicking the effects of morphine"; 170. See also Kathryn T. Hall, Joseph Loscalzo, and Ted J. Kaptchuk, "Genetics and the Placebo Effect: The Placebome," *Trends Mol Med.*, 21(5), May 2015, 285–94.

133   **"You thought you were coming to see an invalid"** Kenneth Davis, *FDR: The Beckoning of Destiny: 1882–1928* (New York: G. P. Putnam's Sons, 1971), 664.

134 **"I came to the conclusion"** Frederic Delano to FDR, Sept. 4, 1921, Family, Business, and Personal Affairs Papers, Box 23, FDRL.

135 **ROOSEVELT IS IMPROVING** *The New York Herald,* Oct. 2, 1921;

135 **"Mr. Pell"** FDR to Herbert Pell October 8, 1921, Box 3 General Political Correspondence 1920–28, FDRL.

135 **"Nothing but an accident"** Lela Stiles, *The Man Behind Roosevelt: The Story of Louis McHenry Howe* (Cleveland, Ohio: World Publishing Company, 1954), 31.

136 **Sara Roosevelt was ready to resume control** Davis, *Beckoning,* 667–69.

136 **"You have good common sense"** Stiles, *The Man Behind Roosevelt,* 82.

137 **"You are a man of destiny"** Ibid., 82–84.

CHAPTER 18: NOTHING TO DO BUT THINK

138 **painfully out of place** Bernard Asbell, *Mother and Daughter: The Letters of Eleanor and Anna Roosevelt* (New York: Coward, McCann & Geoghegan, 1982), 30.

138 **"the birds and the bees"** Asbell, *Mother and Daughter,* 19; Elliott Roosevelt and James Brough, *An Untold Story: The Roosevelts of Hyde Park* (New York: G. P. Putnam's Sons, 1973), 167.

139 **a choice Eleanor would later regret** Eleanor Roosevelt, *My Story,* 338.

139 **"It was great to hear how well father was getting on"** James Roosevelt to ER and FDR, Fall 1921, Roosevelt Family Papers Donated by the Children, Box 20, FDRL.

139 **he'd remembered his father taking him** James Roosevelt and Sidney Shalett, *Affectionately, F.D.R.: A Son's Story of a Lonely Man* (New York: Harcourt, Brace, 1959), 144–45

139 **Nervously climbing the stairs** James Roosevelt with Bill Libby, *My Parents: A Differing View* (Chicago: Playboy Press, 1976), 73–74.

140 **"Mother had changed completely"** Reminiscences of Anna Roosevelt Halsted, 1973, individual interviews, Oral History Collection, Columbia University Center for Oral History.

142 **"Anna, I will hear no more from you"** Elliott Roosevelt and James Brough, *An Untold Story: The Roosevelts of Hyde Park* (New York: G. P. Putnam's Sons, 1973), 167.

142 **Dr. Lovett paid a call on him** Geoffrey Ward, *A First-Class Temperament* (New York: Vintage Books, 2014), 609–10.

143 **a place designed** ER interview, Freidel Papers, FDRL.

143 **"A year or two in bed"** Lela Stiles, *The Man Behind Roosevelt: The Story of Louis McHenry Howe* (Cleveland, Ohio: World Publishing Company, 1954), 83.

143 **"will give you a time for reflection"** Frederic Delano to FDR, Sept. 4, 1921, Family, Business, and Personal Affairs Papers, Box 23, FDRL.

144 **"began to see the other fellow's point of view"** Stiles, *Man Behind Roosevelt,* 83.

144 **"found that the muscles behind the knees"** FDR to William Egleston, Oct. 11, 1924, Family, Business, and Personal Affairs papers, Box 4, FDRL. See also Davis, *Beckoning,* 668.

144 **The brutality startled the family** Geoffrey Ward, *A First-Class Temperament* (New York: Vintage Books, 2014), 623.

145 **"The doctors are most encouraging"** FDR to Josephus Daniels, Oct. 3, 1921, Family, Business, and Personal Affairs Papers, Box 2, FDRL.

145 **"By next Autumn"** FDR to Richard E. Byrd, November 21, 1921, Box 1 Family, Business and Personal Affairs Papers FDRL

146 **"You have been in my thoughts"** James Cox to FDR, Nov. 29, 1922, Family, Business, and Personal Affairs Papers, Box 1, FDRL.

146 **"Except for my legs"** FDR to James Cox, Dec. 8, 1922, Family, Business, and Personal Affairs Papers, Box 1, FDRL.

146 **"You are constantly in my thoughts"** Livingston Davis to FDR, Oct. 21, 1921, Family, Business, and Personal Affairs Papers, Box 2, FDRL.

147 **"I read in our English press"** G. S. Barrows to FDR, Sept. 20, 1921, Family, Business, and Personal Affairs Papers, Box 23, FDRL.

147 **"I hope you will pardon me for not answering"** FDR to G. S. Barrows, Oct. 31, 1921, Family, Business, and Personal Affairs Papers, Box 23, FDRL.

147 **"I am delighted to be able"** G. S. Barrows to FDR, Nov. 26, 1921, Family, Business, and Personal Affairs Papers, Box 23, FDRL.

148 **"I too am getting along well"** FDR to G. S. Barrows, Dec. 8, 1921, Family, Business, and Personal Affairs Papers, Box 23, FDRL.

148 **"I really think I would be walking today"** Lawrence Erving Brown to FDR, Sept. 20, 1921, Family, Business, and Personal Affairs Papers, Box 23, FDRL.

148 **"That was a most generous offer"** FDR to Lawrence Erving Brown, Sept. 27, 1921, Family, Business, and Personal Affairs Papers, Box 23, FDRL.

149 **"By golly"** James Roosevelt, *My Parents,* 74.

CHAPTER 19: MEANS OF GRACE

150 **She felt tears running down her face** For the scene of ER dissolving into tears, see *Eleanor Roosevelt, This Is My Story* (New York: Harper & Brothers, 1937), 339–40, and Elliott Roosevelt and James Brough, *An Untold Story: The Roosevelts of Hyde Park* (New York: G. P. Putnam's Sons, 1973), 170. "That is the one and only time in my entire life I remember having gone to pieces in this particular manner," ER wrote.

150 **"the most trying winter of my entire life"** Eleanor Roosevelt, *My Story,* 336.

151 **"Mrs. R is pretty much at the end of her tether"** George Draper to Robert Lovett, March 25, 1922, Lovett Papers, Francis Countway Library, Harvard University.

153 **And so, on a mild afternoon** Kenneth Davis, *Invincible Summer* (New York: Atheneum, 1974), 13; Joseph P. Lash, *Eleanor and Franklin: The Story of Their Relationship, Based on Eleanor Roosevelt's Private Papers* (New York: W. W. Norton & Company, Inc., 1971), 277–78.

153 **"Franklin Roosevelt for Governor"** *The New York Times,* March 25, 1922.

153 **"to be kept strictly confidential"** FDR to Livingston Davis, May 27, 1922, Family, Business, and Personal Affairs Papers, Box 2, FDRL.

153 **"Below the knee"** Draper to Lovett, March 25, 1922, Lovett Papers, Francis Countway Library, cited in James Tobin, *The Man He Became* (New York: Simon & Schuster, 2013), 144.

154 **"I am glad you and Franklin"** SDR to ER, Aug. 9, 1922, Papers Donated by the Children, Box 9, FDRL.

154 **"I shall have to make sure"** Anna Roosevelt Halsted, "My Life with FDR," *The Woman,* July 1949.

155 **At the sight of their car** For Cook and Dickerman's first visits to Hyde Park, see Reminiscences of Marion Dickerman, 1971, individual interviews, Columbia University Oral History Collection.

155 **"immense joie de vivre"** Davis, *Invincible Summer,* 17.

157 **"The water put me where I am"** James Roosevelt and Sidney Shalett, *Affectionately, F.D.R.: A Son's Story of a Lonely Man* (New York: Harcourt, Brace, 1959), 162.

157 **To mark the eighth anniversary** "Anti-War Parade Fails to Convince," *The New York Times*, July 30, 1922.

157 **"there is a growing assumption"** "Lloyd George Sees Seeds of New War" in ibid., July 29, 1922.

159 **"Dear Al"** "Will Al Smith Run? Roosevelt Queries,"*The New York Herald*, Aug. 15, 1922.

159 **"the nomination of such candidates"** "Hearst Candidacy Given Fresh Volt by Women Voters," *New York Evening World*, June 23, 1922.

159 **"the attitude of the women"** Vote for Hearst Soap is Put Out to Skid Him In ... Followers Worry Over Defiance of Women," *New York Tribune*, June 22, 1922.

160 **"to see the women"** Frances Perkins, *The Roosevelt I Knew* (New York: Penguin, 2011), 22.

160 **"What do you think, Mrs. M.?"** Robert A. Slayton, *Empire Statesman: The Rise and Redemption of Al Smith* (New York: Free Press, 2001), 130.

160 **"Have something you want to say"** Eleanor Roosevelt, *My Story*, 352; Marion Dickerman, Columbia University Oral History Collection.

161 **Now it was Eleanor** "Upstate Democratic Women for Smith Without Compromise," *New-York Tribune*, Sept. 29, 1922.

161 **"The combination of warm weather"** FDR to Cox, December 8, 1922, Box 1, Family Business and Personal Affairs, FDRL.

161 **One October morning** My account of Franklin's fall in the lobby of 120 Broadway relies on the opening pages of Turnley Walker's *Roosevelt and the Warm Springs Story* (New York: A. A. Wyn, Inc., 1953), 6–9.

CHAPTER 20: TIME IN THE SUN

165 **"Human relationships"** Eleanor Roosevelt, *You Learn by Living* (New York: Harper Perennial ePub Edition, 2011), 86.

169 **Rather than bothering with it all** For FDR's time on the *Weona II*, see Geoffrey Ward, *A First-Class Temperament* (New York: Vintage Books, 2014), 660 63.

169 **"The result has been"** FDR to Robert Lovett, Apr. 12, 1924, Family, Business, and Personal Affairs Papers, Box 23, FDRL.

169 **"What I am looking for"** Elliott Roosevelt and James Brough, *An Untold Story: The Roosevelts of Hyde Park* (New York: G. P. Putnam's Sons, 1973), 154.

170 **"I will send you $100"** FDR to George E. Bilyon, Jan. 4, 1920, Family, Business, and Personal Affairs Papers, Box 23, FDRL.

170 **His son James would later recall** James Roosevelt and Sidney Shalett, *Affectionately, F.D.R.: A Son's Story of a Lonely Man* (New York: Harcourt, Brace, 1959), 169–70.

170 **"I want to be as little of a burden"** Frank Freidel interview with ER, July 13, 1954, in Freidel Papers, FDRL.

171 **"When we anchored at night"** Eleanor Roosevelt, *This Is My Story* (New York: Harper & Brothers, 1937), 345.

171 **"I'm up to my eyes"** ER to FDR, Feb. 6, 1924, quoted in *It Seems to Me: Selected Letters of Eleanor Roosevelt*, Leonard C. Schlup and Donald W. Whisenhunt, eds. (Lexington, Ky.: University Press of Kentucky, 2001), 20–21.

171 **"the older generation has made"** "Present Generation Praised at Y.M.C.A," *Brooklyn Standard Union*, May 12, 1924.

172 **DEMOCRATIC WOMEN WIN** *The New York Times*, Apr. 16, 1924. See also: *New York Daily News*, Apr. 16, 1924.

172 **"Like you I have fought"** FDR to Josephus Daniels, May 26, 1924, Family, Business, and Personal Affairs Papers, Box 2, FDRL.

172 **"You need not be proud of me"** ER to FDR, Feb. 6, 1924. Quoted in Eleanor Roosevelt, *It Seems to Me.*

173 **"shared a familiar life in all its aspects"** Roosevelt and Brough, *Untold Story*, 197, 258; James Roosevelt with Bill Libby, *My Parents: A Differing View* (Chicago: Playboy Press, 1976), 104–05.

174 **"I took lunch with some of the Albany boys"** Louis Howe to FDR, Feb. 25, 1924, Louis Howe Personal Papers, Box 40, FDRL.

174 **"I much hope that"** FDR to Reginald Bulkley, July 17, 1924, Family, Business, and Personal Affairs Papers, Box 23, FDRL.

175 **jolting dormant nerve centers** In his quest for healing, Franklin was drawn to faddish mid-twenties' theories on the ability of powerful light to regenerate nerves. "I am about to try out a new artificial light for use this winter," he wrote to one fellow polio sufferer in the fall of 1923. "My theory is that by exercise we can only develop the muscles up to a certain point. That is necessary to build up the nerve centers of the lower spine in order to make more exercise possible." FDR to Paul Hasbrouck, Oct. 17, 1923, Family, Business, Personal Affairs Papers, Box 23, FDRL.

175 **"I know that it is doing the legs good"** FDR to SDR, Feb. 22, 1924, in *F.D.R.: His Personal Letters, Vol. II, 1905–1928,* Elliott Roosevelt, ed. (New York: Duell, Sloan and Pearce, 1948), 543–44.

176 **"There may not be enough Kluxers"** *The Baltimore Evening Sun,* June 26, 1924, quoted in *Politico,* March 7, 2016. The definitive source on the Madison Square Garden convention in 1924 is Robert K. Murray, *The 103rd Ballot: Democrats and the Disaster in Madison Square Garden* (New York: Harper, 2016).

177 **Smith's cronies could do all the wheeling and dealing** Even as they accepted the supremacy of the Smith aides, Franklin and Louis ran an independent Smith campaign effort from 65th Street, reinventing Smith as a unifying figure who had plenty to offer the world beyond New York. They did what they could to dilute the New York City influence on Smith's convention plans. "Unfortunately, the Committee has grown so large that it has become unwieldy," Franklin wrote to one New Yorker who wanted to add his name to the campaign effort. However, he advised, "if you have any friends in other states, we will be pleased to receive a list of their names and addresses." FDR to J. Lewis Amster, May 26, 1924, 1924 Campaign Papers, Box 2, FDRL.

178 **with the help of his son James** Roosevelt and Shalett, *Affectionately,* 204. Of Franklin's preparation for the walk to the podium, Marion Dickerman would later say, "Nobody knows how that man worked"; Dickerman Oral History Interview, FDRL.

178 **special upholstered chair** A photo in the *New York Daily News* from June 30, 1924, of Franklin's special convention chair surrounded by heaps of litter, the detritus of a single day at the convention, shows how treacherous Franklin's path to and from his place on the convention floor would have been.

178 **"The work of restoring his limbs"** "Roosevelt Boom Grows Despite his Reticence," *New York Herald,* June 28, 1924.

179 **"Franklin Roosevelt sits in his wheelchair"** *Chicago Tribune,* June 27, 1924.

179 **"gray faced and tired"** *The Boston Globe,* June 26, 1924.

179 **"a vigorous young man"** *San Francisco Examiner,* June 27, 1924.

179 **"It was Roosevelt but . . ."** *Nashville Tennessean,* June 27, 1924.

179 **Waiting beside his father on the platform** Roosevelt and Shalett, *Affectionately,* 205–06.

181 **"I saw around him all those fat slob politicians"** Frances Perkins Oral History, Columbia University Oral History Project.

181 **"This fellow Roosevelt"** *San Francisco Examiner,* June 27, 1924.

182 **"Marion," he said, "I *did* it!"** Marion Dickerman, 1971, individual interviews, Columbia University Oral History Collection.

CHAPTER 21: THE WAY IT FEELS

183 **at a place called Warm Springs** FDR to Byron Stookey, Sept. 4, 1924, quoted in Frank Freidel, *Franklin Roosevelt: The Ordeal* (Boston: Little, Brown & Co., 1954), 193.

184 **"I am very much disheartened"** George Draper to Robert Lovett, Feb. 11, 1924, Lovett Papers, Francis Countway Library, Harvard University.

185 **"I have a hunch"** FDR to Van Lear Black, Sept. 24, 1924, Family, Business, and Personal Affairs Papers, Box 1, FDRL.

186 **"How grand to be able to do that"** My description of Franklin's first swim in the Warm Springs waters depends on Turnley Walker, *Roosevelt and the Warm Springs Story* (New York: A. A. Wyn, Inc., 1953), 27–29.

187 **"If they were not satisfied"** *The Baltimore Sun,* June 28, 1924.

188 **"The legs are really improving"** FDR to ER, Oct. 1924, Roosevelt Family Papers Donated by the Children, Box 12, FDRL.

188 **After hauling himself out of the pool** Cleburne Gregory, "FDR Will Swim to Health," *Atlanta Journal,* October 26, 1924; "Former Vice Presidential Nominee Becomes Man-Fish to Cure Infantile Paralysis," *St. Louis Post-Dispatch,* October 26, 1924.

189 **"his home in New York became"** Ibid.

189 **Franklin would later suggest** See Franklin's column in *The Macon Telegraph,* Apr. 16, 1925, Family, Business, and Personal Affairs Papers, Box 41, FDRL. See also *F.D.R., Columnist,* Donald Scott Carmichael, ed. (Chicago, Cuneo Press, 1947), 27–29. "There I was," Franklin wrote, "large as life, living proof that Warm Springs, Georgia, had cured me of 57 different varieties of ailments. Most of the diseases from which I had suffered were apparently fatal, but Warm Springs evidently had got each just in time, giving me a chance to go out and catch another incurable malady and dash back here to get rid of it."

190 **"I knew when the first"** *St. Louis Post-Dispatch,* Oct. 26, 1924.

190 **"Have you ever heard of Warm Springs"** Fred Botts, "Where Infantile Paralysis Gets Its Walking Papers," Family, Business, and Personal Affairs Papers, Box 61, FDRL.

190 **"eight long years"** Ibid.

190 **Swim your way back to health** Ibid.

191 **"How are you getting on?"** FDR to Paul Hasbrouck, Jan. 4, 1925, Family, Business, and Personal Affairs Papers, Box 23, FDRL.

191 **"Consultation with the University physician"** Paul Hasbrouck to FDR, Jan. 11, 1925, Family, Business, and Personal Affairs Papers, Box 23, FDRL.

191 **"I really believe"** FDR to Hasbrouck, Jan. 12, 1925, Family, Business, and Personal Affairs Papers, Box 23, FDRL.

192 **"Georgia is somewhat distant"** ER to FDR, June 29, 1926, quoted in Blanche Wiesen Cook, *Eleanor Roosevelt, Vol. 1: 1884–1933* (New York: Penguin, 1993), 336.

193 **"Catch hold"** Botts, "Where Infantile Paralysis Gets Its Walking Papers."

193 **"The following treatment"** FDR to William Egleston, Oct. 11, 1924, Family, Business, and Personal Affairs Papers, Box 4, FDRL.

195 **Mr. Botts from Pennsylvania** Geoffrey Ward, *A First-Class Temperament* (New York: Vintage Books, 2014), 728.

195 **"It looks as if I had bought Warm Springs"** FDR to SDR, March 7, 1926, in *F.D.R.: His Personal Letters, Vol. II, 1905–1928,* Elliott Roosevelt, ed. (New York: Duell, Sloan and Pearce, 1948), 600.

195 **"You needn't worry"** FDR to SDR, October 13, 1926 in ibid.; Elliott Roosevelt and James Brough, *An Untold Story: The Roosevelts of Hyde Park* (New York: G. P. Putnam's Sons, 1973), 232. For Franklin's abortive plans to relaunch Warm Springs as a resort for the wealthy, see *The Atlanta Constitution,* May 1, 1927. Within a month of this boosterish piece, Franklin's second thoughts about the idea were evident: "Do send me some nice souls this coming winter," he wrote, "but not the kind who insist on full dress for dinner every evening"; FDR to Anna Roosevelt Cowles, June 29, 1927, in *Letters: Vol. II,* Elliott Roosevelt, ed., 624.

196 **"We have so many cases"** FDR to SDR, Nov. 19, 1927, in ibid., 632.

CHAPTER 22: THE SOUL THAT HAD BELIEVED

199 **"What about the schools for Negro children?"** Turnley Walker, *Roosevelt and the Warm Springs Story* (New York: A. A. Wyn, Inc., 1953), 32.

200 **"I think you ought to ask her down"** Elliott Roosevelt and James Brough, *An Untold Story: The Roosevelts of Hyde Park* (New York: G. P. Putnam's Sons, 1973), 232.

200 **"Eleanor left again at 7:30"** SDR to FDR, June 7, 1922, Papers Donated by the Children, Box 9, FDRL. Sara's letters to Franklin during this period reveal her mastery of criticism disguised as support. "Tomorrow I join Eleanor in her 'Women's Trades Union tea,'" she wrote Franklin in 1924. "So many people decline that I think it will be a small affair"; SDR to FDR, March 15, 1924, in ibid.

200 **"I wish you could read"** James Roosevelt and Sidney Shalett, *Affectionately, F.D.R.: A Son's Story of a Lonely Man* (New York: Harcourt, Brace, 1959), 151.

201 **"But aren't you girls silly"** Kenneth Davis, *Invincible Summer* (New York: Atheneum, 1974), 35.

201 **"I have been awfully busy"** FDR to Anna Roosevelt, July 20, 1925, Papers Donated by the Children, Box 12, FDRL.

202 **"Much love to Nan & to you"** ER to Marion Dickerman, Feb. 5, 1926, Dickerman Papers, Box 3, FDRL.

202 **"I hate to think you have been unhappy"** Ibid., May 18, 1926.

202 **"Marion dearest"** Ibid., Aug. 27, 1925.

202 **Prominent women in their circles** At the 1924 convention, the formidable Democratic activist Elisabeth Marbury took a seat near the front of the New York delegation. She intended to stay there, she told any reporter who listened, until she found a husband. This was a joke whose double meaning Marbury's friends would have especially appreciated—she shared a life, and several homes, with the famed designer Elsie de Wolfe. See *New York Daily News,* June 25, 1924.

203 **"Eleanor is so happy over there"** SDR to FDR, March 2, 1926, Papers Donated by the Children, Box 9, FDRL.

203 **"held the most powerful positions"** Blanche Wiesen Cook, *Eleanor Roosevelt, Vol. 1: 1884–1933* (New York: Penguin, 1993), 366.

204 **"Here was the answer"** "Tells 'Ambitious' Women What is Wrong with Them," *The Des Moines Register,* Nov. 30, 1930.

204 **"Seated at a small desk"** "A Woman Speaks Her Political Mind," *The New York Times,* Apr. 8, 1928.

204 **"I've written two editorials"** ER to FDR, Oct. 17, 1926, quoted in Joseph P. Lash, *Eleanor and Franklin: The Story of Their Relationship, Based on Eleanor Roosevelt's Private Papers* (New York: W. W. Norton & Company, Inc., 1971), 305.

204 **"It takes me exactly five minutes"** *The Des Moines Register*, Nov. 30, 1930.

205 **One society reporter who visited** "Prominent New York Women at Home," *Moline Dispatch*, Nov. 9, 1926 (originally published in *The New York Evening World*).

205 **"a buyer in a department store"** "Women Political Leaders Prepare for Vote Battles," *Reading Times*, Aug. 16, 1928.

205 **She caused a national stir in a 1928** "Women Must Learn to Play the Game as Men Do," *Redbook*, No. 50, Apr. 1928, in Eleanor Roosevelt Papers Project, Department of History, Columbian College of Arts & Science, GW University, accessed https://erpapers.columbian.gwu.edu/women-must-learn-play-game-men-do.

207 **"Braces are of course laid aside"** FDR to SDR, Aug. 26, 1925, in *F.D.R.: His Personal Letters, Vol. II, 1905–1928,* Elliott Roosevelt, ed. (New York: Duell, Sloan and Pearce, 1948), 588.

207 **Plastridge came to stay** Geoffrey Ward interviewed Alice Plastridge for *A First-Class Temperament* (New York: Vintage Books, 2014); the story of Plastridge's visit to Hyde Park appears on pp. 734–37. See also Jay Schleichkorn, "Physical Therapist, 98, Recalls Rehabilitating Franklin Roosevelt," *P.T. Bulletin*, March 16, 1988, and Alice Plastridge Oral History, Tugwell Collection, FDRL.

208 **the heart of Plastridge's teaching** "Corrective Walking," *The Polio Chronicle*, Oct. 1932, in Family, Business, and Personal Affairs Papers, FDRL.

208 **He would not, she believed** Theo Lippman, *The Squire of Warm Springs: FDR in Georgia, 1924–1945* (Chicago: Playboy Press, 1977), 56–57.

209 **"Our rate is $42 a week"** FDR to Paul Hasbrouck, March 25, 1927, Paul Hasbrouck Papers, Box 1, FDRL.

209 **"I'll be back in ten days"** Letters from Warm Springs, 1927, Hasbrouck Papers, Box 1, FDRL.

210 **"The complete gallantry of all the patients"** Eleanor Roosevelt, *The Autobiography of Eleanor Roosevelt,* 143.

210 **"turned quite pink"** *Shreveport Times*, Oct. 28, 1928.

211 **"We don't always agree"** "Those Democratic Roosevelts," *Muncie Star Press,* Nov. 16, 1928.

211 **"I can only give you two minutes"** "Wives of Great Men," *Hanover Evening Sun,* Jan. 9, 1925.

212 **"pull a curtain down and go to sleep"** Frank Freidel interview with ER, Sept. 3, 1952, Freidel Papers, FDRL.

213 **"A great deal of love to you both"** Cook, *Eleanor Roosevelt, Vol. 1,* 326–27.

213 **"much closer into a very real partnership"** Anna Roosevelt Halsted, 1973, individual interviews Oral History Collection, Columbia University Center for Oral History.

213 **"a blessing in disguise"** Eleanor Roosevelt, *The Autobiography of Eleanor Roosevelt* (New York: Harper Perennial, 2014), 142.

213 **On her clipping** Lash, *Eleanor and Franklin,* 245.

214 **"You are entitled to one life"** Lash describes Eleanor's interest in Patri, ibid., 302.

214 **"The night that John came here"** Franklin D. Roosevelt Jr. to ER and FDR, 1922, Papers Donated by the Children, Box 19, FDRL.

214 **"time available to think"** Roosevelt Halsted, Oral History Collection, Columbia University.

215 **"were driven by their destinies"** James Roosevelt with Bill Libby, *My Parents: A Differing View* (Chicago: Playboy Press, 1976), 69.

215 **"didn't help me a bit"** Bernard Asbell, *Mother and Daughter: The Letters of Eleanor and Anna Roosevelt* (New York: Coward, McCann & Geoghegan, 1982), 32–33.

215 **"I was *mad*"** Ibid., 40.

216 **150 days** Lippman, *Squire of Warm Springs,* 60.

216 **"Democratic success"** "Franklin Roosevelt, Supporter of Al Smith, Addresses Leaders in Gerogia," *Brooklyn Times-Union,* Feb. 27, 1927.

216 **"the New York–Georgia-farmer-politician"** *The Atlanta Constitution,* Oct. 2 and 3, 1928.

216 **"Jefferson Davis's splendid home"** *The Macon Telegraph,* Apr. 30, 1925, Family, Business, and Personal Affairs Papers, Box 41, FDRL.

216 **"There, stretching out for many miles"** Ibid. Apr. 18, 1925, in *F.D.R., Columnist,* Donald Scott Carmichael, ed. (Chicago, Cuneo Press, 1947), 31. Given the course of future events, perhaps the most disturbing column FDR wrote for *The Macon Telegraph* was on relations between Japan and the United States. "Anyone who has traveled in the Far East," he wrote, "knows that the mingling of Asiatic blood with European or American blood produces, in nine cases out of ten, the most unfortunate results. In this question, then, of Japanese exclusion from the United States, it is necessary only to advance the true reason—the undesirability of mixing the blood of the two people." Ibid., "The Average American and the Average Japanese" Apr. 30, 1925, 58–60.

217 **"She loved the pool"** Walker, *Warm Springs,* 24.

217 **"How Hot Sun"** *Tampa Tribune,* Apr. 4, 1926.

218 **"Helping humanity more satisfying"** *Brooklyn Daily Times,* Aug. 26, 1927.

218 **"assure them that you are still"** Alfred B. Rollins Jr., *Roosevelt and Howe* (New York: Knopf, 1962), 224.

CHAPTER 23: THE CALL

220 **"Women, women, women"** *Reading Times,* Aug. 16, 1928.

221 **"Victory is his habit"** Placing Alfred E. Smith in Nomination, June 27, 1928, Franklin D. Roosevelt, Master Speech File, Box 18, FDRL.

221 **"I do not know yet"** FDR to Van Lear Black, July 25, 1928, Family, Business, and Personal Affairs Papers, Box 1, FDRL.

222 **"The weather is heavenly"** FDR to SDR, Sept. 21, 1928, in *F.D.R.: His Personal Letters, Vol. II, 1905–1928,* Elliott Roosevelt, ed. (New York: Duell, Sloan and Pearce, 1948), 643.

223 **THE REAL PRESSURE** Elliott Roosevelt and James Brough, *An Untold Story: The Roosevelts of Hyde Park* (New York: G. P. Putnam's Sons, 1973), 249.

224 **"Everyone makes me so uncomfortable"** ER to FDR, Sept. 30, 1928, FDRL.

224 **GROWTH OF ROOSEVELT'S BOOM** *Rochester Democrat and Chronicle,* Oct. 1, 1928.

224 **PLEASE LET ME KNOW** Louis Howe to FDR, Sept. 26, 1928, Louis M. Howe Papers, Box 19, FDRL.

225 **GO AHEAD AND TAKE IT** Anna Roosevelt Halsted, 1973, individual interviews, Oral History Collection, Columbia University Center for Oral History. "I remember thinking it would be very exciting if he got into politics, and sending him a wire," Anna explained.

225 **"Confirming my telephone message"** *The Baltimore Sun,* Oct. 2, 1928.

225 **would "make a good candidate"** Emily Smith Warner with Hawthorne Daniel, *The Happy Warrior: The Story of My Father, Alfred E. Smith* (Garden City, N.Y.: Doubleday, 1956), 239.

226 **They found an operator** Kenneth Davis, *FDR: The New York Years: 1928–1933* (New York: Random House, 1985), 20.

226 **"I never presume to speak for my husband"** "F.D. Roosevelt Picked to Run in Al's Chair," *Chicago Tribune*, Oct. 2, 1928.

227 **At the school in Manchester** Davis, *Beckoning*, 848, and Freidel, *The Ordeal*, 253.

228 **"The gentleman who heads the Republican ticket"** *New York Times*, October 3, 1928; "They Say That Women . . ." *The Atlanta Constitution*, Sept. 27, 1928.

228 **"Hello, Frank"** Eleanor Roosevelt, *The Autobiography of Eleanor Roosevelt* (New York: Harper Perennial, 2014), 150.

228 **"Don't you dare"** Roosevelt and Brough, *Untold Story*, 253. See also Geoffrey Ward, *A First-Class Temperament* (New York: Vintage Books, 2014), 793–94.

228 **To certain sympathetic listeners** Grace Tully, *F.D.R., My Boss* (New York: Charles Scribner's Sons, 1949), 36.

229 **it was beyond his capacity** On the question of whether Franklin would ever regain the ability to walk unaided, Alice Plastridge was definitive: "He had below 50 percent use of muscles in his lower extremities. After five years you can't expect to get improvement." Theo Lippman, *The Squire of Warm Springs: FDR in Georgia, 1924–1945* (Chicago: Playboy Press, 1977), 56.

229 **"She was firmly convinced"** Tully, *My Boss*, 36.

230 **BULLETIN. Rochester, N.Y.** *New York Daily News*, Oct. 2, 1928.

CHAPTER 24: ON MY FEET

236 **"I'll be back in Warm Springs"** "Roosevelt Held Out to the Last Minute," *The New York Times*, Oct. 3, 1928.

236 **"By way of congratulations"** Geoffrey Ward, *A First-Class Temperament* (New York: Vintage Books, 2014), 798.

236 **"They nominated today"** "Al's Choices Endorsed by Convention," *New York Daily News*, Oct. 3, 1928.

236 **"Who can defend"** "An Unfair Sacrifice," *New York Herald Tribune*, October 3, 1928.

236 **"Of course," Smith protested** *Brooklyn Standard Union*, Oct. 3, 1928.

237 **"fine qualities of mind and heart"** "Franklin D Roosevelt and the Governorship," *Binghamton Press & Sun-Bulletin*, Oct. 3, 1928.

237 **"I am amazed to hear"** "Roosevelt No 'Sacrifice,'" *New York Daily News*, Oct. 5, 1928.

237 **"playboy and an idler"** Samuel Rosenman, *Working with Roosevelt* (New York: Harper & Brothers, 1952), 15–16.

238 **"wants to relieve you"** Alfred B. Rollins Jr., *Roosevelt and Howe* (New York: Knopf, 1962), 238.

238 **"an adding machine for an ice box"** "Ice Box Cal," *New York Daily News*, Oct. 21, 1928.

238 **When it came time to draft** Rosenman, *Working with Roosevelt*, 18–19, 22–23.

239 **"unfortunate sick man"** *The Brooklyn Daily Eagle*, Oct. 27, 1928.

239 **I WANT TO BE THE FIRST** "Political Notes: Robbed," *Time*, Oct. 15, 1928.

239 **"He never got ruffled"** Rosenman, *Working with Roosevelt*, 22.

239 **At one scheduled stop** Anna Roosevelt Halsted, 1973, individual interviews Oral History Collection, Columbia University Center for Oral History; James Roosevelt and Sidney Shalett, *Affectionately, F.D.R.: A Son's Story of a Lonely Man* (New York: Harcourt, Brace, 1959), 208.

240 **"with a streak of vanity"** Frances Perkins Oral History, Columbia University Oral History Project.

240 **"No movies of me getting out of the machine"** Hugh Gregory Gallagher, *FDR's Splendid Deception* (New York: Dodd, Mead & Co, 1988), 93-34.

240 **"more than one hundred thousand"** *Rochester Democrat and Chronicle*, Oct. 23, 1928.

241 **"He listened," Perkins later observed** Frances Perkins, *The Roosevelt I Knew* (New York: Penguin, 2011), 43-44.

242 **"appears to have swung"** *The New York Times*, Nov. 7, 1928; "Indications Now Appear Certain," *New York Daily News*, Nov. 7, 1928.

242 **"the time just hasn't come"** Perkins, *The Roosevelt I Knew*, 46.

243 **"had a private"** Ibid., 49.

243 **"No, I am not excited"** Joseph P. Lash, *Eleanor and Franklin: The Story of Their Relationship, Based on Eleanor Roosevelt's Private Papers* (New York: W. W. Norton & Company, Inc., 1971), 320.

243 **"I suppose I shall have to"** "Mrs. Roosevelt to Keep on Filling Many Jobs Besides Being the First Lady at Albany,"*The New York Times*, Nov. 10, 1928.

243 **"I hardly see how"** "Mrs. Roosevelt's Only Fear for New Governor is– Fat," *New York Daily News*, Nov. 8, 1928.

244 **"was one of the most admirable"** "Franklin Roosevelt has Fought his Way Back from Paralysis to Health and Success," *Edmonton Journal*, Dec. 1, 1928.

244 **"I want definitely"** "No 1932 for Roosevelt," *New York Daily News*, Nov. 12, 1928.

246 **"Mr. Roosevelt has made"** "Roosevelt Proves Physical Fitness," *The New York Times*, Nov. 30, 1928.

247 **"chamber from Speaker's room having only one low step"** Robert A. Slayton, *Empire Statesman: The Rise and Redemption of Al Smith* (New York: Free Press, 2001), 358.

247 **"Remain in bed"** "Rules for Health are Prescribed for Governor Roosevelt," *Elmira Star-Gazette*, Jan. 2, 1929.

CHAPTER 25: THE LONG FIGHT

249 **The building was a "fire trap"** "Governor Roosevelts Advocates Abolotion of Reformatory Cells,"*Elmira Star-Gazette*, Aug. 14, 1929. For more on FDR's inspection tour of the Elmira reformatory, see *The New York Times*, Aug. 14, 1929.

249 **"How's the arm?"** *Elmira Star-Gazette*, Aug. 14, 1929.

251 **"It was not unusual"** Elliott Roosevelt and James Brough, *An Untold Story: The Roosevelts of Hyde Park* (New York: G. P. Putnam's Sons, 1973), 258. Here again, Elliott and James Roosevelt's understanding of their father's relationship with Missy LeHand differed. James saw nothing romantic in Missy's bedroom attire: "Was she supposed to dress to the teeth every time she was summoned at midnight?" James asked in *My Parents: A Differing View* (Chicago: Playboy Press, 1976), 105.

252 **may have been [Eleanor's] one real romance** James Roosevelt, *My Parents*, 110. Eleanor had powerful and intimate, if presumably nonsexual, connections to other men, most especially Louis Howe and later Harry Hopkins.

252 **"I learned to look"** Eleanor Roosevelt, *The Autobiography of Eleanor Roosevelt* (New York: Harper Perennial, 2014), 154-55.

254 **"A Thanksgiving is set aside"** "Roosevelt Issues Thanks Day Edict," *Brooklyn Times-Union*, Nov. 17, 1929.

254 **A 1931 survey** David E. Kyvig, *Daily Life in the United States, 1920–1939: Decades of Promise and Pain* (Westport, Conn.: Greenwood Press, 2002), 221.

254 **"numbness"** Schlesinger, *Crisis of the Old Order*, 252-56.

255 **"I am convinced we have now"** *Chicago Tribune*, May 2, 1930.

255 **By midyear** David M. Kennedy, *Freedom from Fear: The American People in Depression and War* (New York: Oxford University Press), 59.

256 **In November and December** Ibid., 65.

257–58 **In their communications with local officials** For the FDR campaign's early attempts at national outreach, see James A. Farley, *Behind the Ballots: The Personal History of a Politician* (New York: Harcourt, Brace & Co., 1938), 69–75.

258 **"Now, don't phone me too early"** John F. Geis, "Smith Retires as Roosevelt Takes Up Reins," *The Brooklyn Daily Times*, Jan. 2, 1929.

258 **"There are many things I would like"** FDR to Al Smith, Feb. 8, 1929, quoted in Robert A. Slayton, *Empire Statesman: The Rise and Redemption of Al Smith* (New York: Free Press, 2001), 358.

259 **"One of Franklin's main qualities"** Eleanor Roosevelt, *Autobiography*, 152.

CHAPTER 26: "YOU MUST LET ME BE MYSELF"

262 **"Who Will Be the Next President?"** David Nasaw, *The Chief: The Life of William Randolph Hearst* (New York: Mariner Books, 2000), 452. **"opposed to all foreign entanglements"** *William Randolph Hearst: A Portrait in His Own Words*, Edmond D. Coblentz, ed. (New York: Simon & Schuster, 1952), 127–28.

263 **inheriting and fatuously following** "Who Will Be the Next President," *San Francisco Examiner*, Jan. 3, 1932.

264 **"We have lost in recent years"** "Gov Roosevelt Urges Boost in Taxes," *Brooklyn Times-Union*, Jan. 6, 1932.

265 **WHOM DID GOVERNOR ROOSEVELT HAVE IN MIND?** *San Francisco Examiner*, Jan. 8, 1932.

265 **"Please give my compliments"** William Randolph Hearst to Edmond Coblentz, Jan. 21, 1932, Carton 20, William Randolph Hearst Papers, Bancroft Library, University of California, Berkeley.

265 **To underscore his point** J. Willicombe to managing editors, Hearst Sunday Papers, Jan. 28, 1932, Carton 14, Hearst Papers.

265 **"Too often"** *The New York Times*, Feb. 3, 1932.

266 **felt especially betrayed** Joseph P. Lash, *Eleanor and Franklin: The Story of Their Relationship, Based on Eleanor Roosevelt's Private Papers* (New York: W. W. Norton & Company, Inc., 1971), 347.

266 **"a shabby statement"** Ibid., 347.

266 **"a highly impressionable person"** *The Des Moines Register*, Jan. 12, 1932.

267 **"reasonable but oversimple"** Rexford Tugwell, *The Democratic Roosevelt* (Garden City, N.Y.: Doubleday, 1957), 215.

267 **He seems quite naturally warm and friendly** Raymond Moley, *After Seven Years* (New York: Harper & Brothers, 1939), 10–11.

268 **Tugwell noted that** Tugwell, *Democratic Roosevelt*, 215.

269 **"vigorous character"** "Report Smith Ready to Toss Derby in Ring," *Camden Morning Post*, Feb. 5, 1932.

270 **"By God, he invited me"** Clark Howell to FDR, Dec. 2, 1931, in *F.D.R.: His Personal Letters, Vol. III, 1928–1945*, Elliott Roosevelt, ed. (New York: Duell, Sloan and Pearce, 1948).

270–71 **"Don't quit fighting"** "Meet the New President!" *Lansing State Journal*, Nov. 16, 1932.

271 **At the program's outset** Franklin D. Roosevelt radio address, from Albany, N.Y.,

Apr. 7, 1932, "The 'Forgotten Man' Speech," Gerhard Peters and John T. Woolley, The American Presidency Project: https://www.presidency.ucsb.edu/node/288092. "Forgotten Man" Speech, radio appearance for the Democratic Party on *Lucky Strike Hour*, New York City, Apr. 7, 1932, "Recorded Speeches and Utterances of FDR, 1920–1945 (completely digitized)," FDRL, https://www.fdrlibrary.org/utterancesfdr.

272 **"Are we in danger"** "Mergers Seen by Roosevelt as U.S. Menace," *Brooklyn Standard Union*, July 5, 1929.

272 **"I will take off my coat"** "Smith Launches 'Stop Roosevelt' Move at Dinner," *Washington Evening Star*, Apr. 14, 1932.

273 **"These results dispose completely"** *Charleston Daily Mail*, Apr. 30, 1932.

273 **"I'll do more than that"** Emily Smith Warner with Hawthorne Daniel, *The Happy Warrior: The Story of My Father, Alfred E. Smith* (Garden City, N.Y.: Doubleday, 1956), 252–53.

275 **"The convention will never"** In recounting Franklin's heated exchange with Marion Dickerman, I have drawn on Kenneth Davis, *Invincible Summer* (New York: Atheneum, 1974), 100–01, and Marion Dickerman, 1971, individual interviews, Columbia University Oral History Collection.

276 **TELL BARUCH PARKWAY** Edmond Coblentz to Bernard Baruch, June 23, 1932, Outgoing Box 1, Coblentz Papers, Bancroft Library, University of California, Berkeley.

CHAPTER 27: THE PRIZE

277 **"I will keep my contact"** Raymond Moley, *The First New Deal* (New York: Harcourt, Brace and World, 1966), 379.

278 **They dined together** Marion Dickerman, 1971, individual interviews, Columbia University Oral History Collection; Kenneth Davis, *Invincible Summer* (New York: Atheneum, 1974), 103.

278 **"looked like death"** Davis, *Invincible Summer*, 104.

280 **"The Democratic Party has a golden opportunity"** "Spontaneous Confusion," *Time*, July 4, 1932.

280 **"I cannot see the importance"** FDR to Russell Hungerford, March 7, 1932, quoted in Conrad Black, *Franklin Delano Roosevelt: Champion of Freedom* (New York: Public Affairs, 2003), 211.

281 **"We have come to Chicago"** James A. Farley, *Behind the Ballots: The Personal History of a Politician* (New York: Harcourt, Brace & Co., 1938), 134–35.

281 **"For God's sake"** Alfred B. Rollins Jr., *Roosevelt and Howe* (New York: Knopf, 1962), 342.

281 **"Well, we just must"** Farley, *Behind the Ballots*, 138.

282 **Waiting for the totals** Ibid., 142–43.

283 **"Texas is our only chance"** Jim Farley, *Jim Farley's Story* (New York: Whittlesy House, 1948), 23. James Roosevelt and Marion Dickerman both recalled Farley saying "Texas is our only hope." See Davis, Invincible Summer, 105 and James Roosevelt, *My Parents: A Differing View* (Chicago: Playboy Press, 1976), 134.

283 **Early that morning** David Nasaw, *The Patriarch: The Remarkable Life and Turbulent Times of Joseph P. Kennedy* (New York: Penguin Press, 2012), 177.

283 **"The boys in Chicago"** *New York Daily News*, July 2, 1932.

284 **"She showed little interest"** Lorena A. Hickok, *Eleanor Roosevelt: Reluctant First Lady* (New York: Dodd, Mead, 1962), 32–33.

284 **"You are not to breathe a word"** Davis, *Invincible Summer*, 108; Marion Dickerman, Oral History, Columbia University.

285 **"From the personal standpoint"** Eleanor Roosevelt, *The Autobiography of Eleanor Roosevelt* (New York: Harper Perennial, 2014), 160.

286 **"The reason you can't get him"** Robert A. Slayton, *Empire Statesman: The Rise and Redemption of Al Smith* (New York: Free Press, 2001), 372.

287 **He was grinning** Elliott Roosevelt and James Brough, *An Untold Story: The Roosevelts of Hyde Park* (New York: G. P. Putnam's Sons, 1973), 290.

287 **"This is it!"** Bess Furman, *Washington By-Line: The Personal History of a Newspaper Woman* (New York: Knopf, 1949), 119.

287 **William McAdoo had climbed up to the convention stage** "Gathering Is Tense as M'Adoo Speaks," *The New York Times*, July 2, 1932.

288 **The Roosevelts had been expecting** James Roosevelt, *My Parents*, 135; "Chicago Convention: Atmospherics," *Time*, July 11, 1932.

288 **HEARTIEST CONGRATULATIONS** *Austin American-Statesman*, July 2, 1932.

288 **He'd gone to bed at nine o'clock** *William Randolph Hearst: A Portrait in His Own Words*, Edmond D. Coblentz, ed. (New York: Simon & Schuster, 1952), 138–39.

CHAPTER 28: "PRAY FOR ME"

293 **"A quick jump across the country"** *The New York Times*, July 3, 1932.

293 **"The Governor—on his way to accept"** Samuel Rosenman, *Working with Roosevelt* (New York: Harper & Brothers, 1952), 76.

294 **"I see Sam Rosenman in every paragraph"** Raymond Moley, *After Seven Years* (New York: Harper & Brothers, 1939), 29.

294 **"Damn it, Louis"** James Roosevelt and Sidney Shalett, *Affectionately, F.D.R.: A Son's Story of a Lonely Man* (New York: Harcourt, Brace, 1959), 226.

294 **"Let it be the task of our party"** Address accepting the Democratic nomination at Chicago, July 2, 1932, accessed https://www.presidency.ucsb.edu/documents/address -accepting-the-presidential-nomination-the-democratic-national-convention-chi cago-1

296 **"In Wartime Washington"** "The Hoover Week," *Time*, July 11, 1933.

296 **"put through an endurance test"** Eleanor Roosevelt, *The Autobiography of Eleanor Roosevelt* (New York: Harper Perennial, 2014), 156.

296 **"a trimmer"** Charles Rappleye, *Herbert Hoover in the White House: The Ordeal of the Presidency* (New York: Simon & Schuster, 2016), 332–33.

298 **"Well, Felix, this will elect me"** H. W. Brands, *Traitor to His Class: The Privileged Life and Radical Presidency of Franklin Delano Roosevelt* (New York: Anchor, 2009), 259.

298 **VOTE FOR ROOSEVELT** "The Hoover Week," *Time*, Sept. 12, 1932.

298 **"I'm stubborn"** "Roosevelt Leaves on Trip to Coast, "*The New York Times*, Sept. 13, 1932.

299 **"Mrs. Roosevelt remained at home"** Ibid., Sept. 14, 1932.

299 **"Pa developed a little family act"** Roosevelt and Shalett, *Affectionately*, 229–230.

299 **"You may rest assured"** Joseph P. Kennedy to William Randolph Hearst, Oct. 19, 1932, Box 7, Hearst Papers, Bancroft Library.

299 **When Franklin's train reached Los Angeles** "Roosevelt Will See Spectacular Screen Pageant," *San Francisco Examiner*, Sept. 22, 1932.

300 **"Tammany wants Mr. Roosevelt to run for Governor again"** *Chicago Tribune*, July 7, 1932.

300 **One day on the campaign train** John R. Boettiger, *A Love in Shadow* (New York: W. W. Norton, 1978), 171. For John Boettiger's difficult task in 1932 triangulating between the orbits of Franklin Roosevelt and Robert McCormick, see Richard

Norton Smith, *The Colonel: The Life and Legend of Robert R. McCormick* (New York: Houghton, Mifflin, 1997), 313–14.

301 "The story didn't amount to much" Lorena A. Hickok, *Eleanor Roosevelt: Reluctant First Lady* (New York: Dodd, Mead, 1962), 38.

302 "A man comes to wisdom *The New York Times*, Nov. 8, 1932.

302 "Of course Franklin will do his best . . ." Hickok, *Reluctant First Lady* 53–55.

303 In the study of his home Rappleye, *Hoover in the White House*, 406.

303 "Sis-boom-bah!" Gene Smith, *The Shattered Dream: Herbert Hoover and the Great Depression* (New York: William Morrow, 1970), 212–13.

303 I CONGRATULATE YOU *The New York Times*, Nov. 9, 1932.

304 Louis Howe poured Lela Stiles, *The Man Behind Roosevelt: The Story of Louis McHenry Howe* (Cleveland, Ohio: Wblishing Company, 1954), 216–17.

304 "This is the greatest night of my life" "Roosevelt, Buoyant, Gets Returns Here," *The New York Times*, Nov. 9, 1932.

304 "You know, Jimmy" Roosevelt and Shalett, *Affectionately*, 232.

CHAPTER 29: SPREADING FIRE

306 Though the president was intense Raymond Moley, *After Seven Years* (New York: Harper & Brothers, 1939), 73.

306 "did not get it at all" Arthur M. Schlesinger Jr., *The Crisis of the Old Order* (Boston: Houghton, Mifflin, 1957), 444.

307 "The situation is critical" Ronald Steel, *Walter Lippmann and the American Century* (New Brunswick, N.J.: Transaction Publishers, 2008), 300, quoted in Jonathan Alter, *The Defining Moment: FDR's Hundred Days And the Triumph of Hope* (New York: Simon & Schuster, 2006), 5.

308 "the way to 23 Wall Street" *William Randolph Hearst: A Portrait in His Own Words*, Edmond D. Coblentz, ed. (New York: Simon & Schuster, 1952), 147, 151.

308 "Let's concentrate upon one thing" Schlesinger, *Crisis of the Old Order*, 455.

309 WE ARE ALL SPENDING THE DAY *The New York Times*, Feb. 14, 1933.

309 "I haven't really seen" Ibid., Feb. 16, 1933.

310 Astor noted the anonymity Moley, *After Seven Years*, 138–39.

310 "I am not going to attempt to tell you" "National Affairs: Escape," *Time*, Feb. 27, 1933. For Lillian Cross's perspective on the events of February 15th, I have relied on press accounts, especially "Woman Tells How She Seized Assassin," *New York Daily News*, February 17, 1933 and "Woman Diverted Aim of Assassin," *New York Times*, February 16, 1933.

311 "I'm all right!" Ibid.

311 "I don't think he is going to last" On the day after the assassination attempt, Franklin released a narrative statement with his precise recollections of the events before and after the shooting. That statement—which included Franklin's dialogue in the car while riding to the hospital—appeared in *The New York Times* on Feb. 17, 1933.

312 "This is what it's like to be in public life" Lorena A. Hickok, *Eleanor Roosevelt: Reluctant First Lady* (New York: Dodd, Mead, 1962), 80–81.

312 "not the least bit excited" *The New York Times*, Feb. 16, 1933.

312 "I hate all presidents" Kenneth Davis, *FDR: The New York Years: 1928–1933* (New York: Random House, 1985), 431–34.

312–13 "There was nothing—not so much" Moley, *After Seven Years*, 139.

313 "One cannot live in fear" Hickok, *Reluctant First Lady*, 80–83.

314 TOGETHER WITH EVERY CITIZEN *Richmond Times-Dispatch*, Feb. 16, 1933.

314 **He noted with bitterness** Richard Norton Smith, *An Uncommon Man: The Triumph of Herbert Hoover* (Worland, Wyo.: High Plains Publishing Company, 1984) 157–58.

315 **"I just came to tell you"** *The New York Times*, Feb. 19, 1933; *Brooklyn Times-Union*, Feb. 19, 1933.

315 **Skimming the letter** Moley, *After Seven Years*, 139–41.

316 **"If these declarations be made"** Herbert Hoover to David A. Reed, Feb. 20, 1933, quoted in Davis, *New York Years*, 438.

316 **"I am equally concerned"** FDR to Hoover, March 1, 1933, quoted in Schlesinger, *Crisis of the Old Order*, 477.

CHAPTER 30: AN UNFAMILIAR CITY

318 **"talk of [Benjamin] Franklin"** Raymond Moley, *The First New Deal* (New York: Harcourt, Brace and World, 1966), 113–14.

318 **"This is the original manuscript"** When, several years after Franklin's death, his memorandum claiming authorship became public, Raymond Moley took issue with Franklin's description as "to say the least misleading" and subsequently published his own notes from the drafting session. Moley had begun thinking about a draft of the speech as early as September of 1932. But the historian Jonathan Alter, who closely reviewed additional unpublished notes from Moley's personal papers, has convincingly demonstrated that Moley's attempts to set the record straight have left an equally deceptive impression that Franklin had little to do with the writing of the speech. "The draft language in Moley's personal papers," Alter writes in *The Defining Moment: FDR's Hundred Days and the Triumph of Hope* (New York: Simon & Schuster, 2006), "bears little resemblance to the final reading copy of the inaugural"; 207–11. Nearly a century later, it remains unclear exactly how many of the phrases in Franklin's address were born in Franklin's mind. Recovered notes and drafts tell only so much; inevitably they miss Franklin's essential tools in crafting oratory—his unique ability to articulate an idea clearly as it came to him and his habit of using genial pleasantries to subtly edit, clarify, and instruct.

318 **"He seemed fully conscious"** James A. Farley, *Behind the Ballots: The Personal History of a Politician* (New York: Harcourt, Brace & Co., 1938), 208.

319 **But Eleanor was up and out** "Mrs. Roosevelt Visits Grief Rock Creek Cemetery Statue," *Washington Evening Star*, March 3, 1933.

319 **"There's something I'd like to show you"** Lorena A. Hickok, *Eleanor Roosevelt: Reluctant First Lady* (New York: Dodd, Mead, 1962), 90.

320 **"As a matter of dignity"** Alida Black, *Casting Her Own Shadow: Eleanor Roosevelt and the Shaping of Postwar Liberalism* (New York: Columbia University Press, 1996), 21.

320 **"The average girl of today"** *Brooklyn Times-Union*, Dec. 10, 1932.

320 **"placed a severe strain"** *Chattanooga News*, Dec. 14, 1932.

320 **"I went into it because I wanted money"** *"Plain Ordinary Mrs. Roosevelt in the White House, The Boston Globe*, Nov. 10, 1932.

321 **"Hick darling"** ER to Lorena Hickok, March 6, 1933, in *Empty Without You: The Intimate Letters of Eleanor Roosevelt and Lorena Hickok*, Rodger Streitmatter, ed. (New York: Da Capo Press, 1998), 17.

321 **"I've been trying today to bring back your face"** ER to Lorena Hickok, Dec. 1933, quoted in Blanche Wiesen Cook, *Eleanor Roosevelt: Vol. II, 1933–1938* (New York: Viking, 1999), 195.

322 **"Only her face was visible"** Hickok, *Reluctant First Lady*, 91.

323 **"another Roosevelt in the White House"** Grace Tully, *F.D.R., My Boss* (New York: Charles Scribner's Sons, 1949), 63–64.

324 *Mr. Roosevelt," Hoover replied Ibid., 6 ｜*

324 **"We downed our tea"** James Roosevelt and Sidney Shalett, *Affectionately, F.D.R.: A Son's Story of a Lonely Man* (New York: Harcourt, Brace, 1959), 252.

325 **"Will you join in"** Alter, *Defining Moment*, 422, citing Dorothy Roe Lewis, "What F.D.R. Told Hoover March '33," *The New York Times*, March 13, 1981. In her piece, Lewis reported that, on returning to her hotel from the White House, Eleanor told female reporters about Franklin's harsh words with Hoover in the hopes they would run the story. Concerned that such would further destabilize the financial system, the reporters, remarkably, convinced Eleanor it was best for them to keep it to themselves.

325 **"I shall be waiting at my hotel"** Raymond Moley, *After Seven Years* (New York: Harper & Brothers, 1939), 146.

325 **"Anything could happen"** Hickok, *Reluctant First Lady*, 95.

CHAPTER 31: FEAR ITSELF

326 **"A private citizen is going to church"** *Binghamton Press & Sun-Bulletin*, March 4, 1933.

326 **O Lord, our Heavenly Father** *The New York Times*, March 5, 1933.

327 **That evening's *Washington Star* would report** *Washington Evening Star*, March 4, 1933.

328 **"Lovely steel!"** Eleanor Roosevelt, *The Autobiography of Eleanor Roosevelt* (New York: Harper Perennial, 2014), 164.

329 **"I was greatly disappointed"** *William Randolph Hearst: A Portrait in His Own Words*, Edmond D. Coblentz, ed. (New York: Simon & Schuster, 1952), 154.

330 **"I have yet to detect"** *Bloomington Illinois Pantagraph*, March 5, 1933.

EPILOGUE: THE SPIRIT OF WARM SPRINGS

334 **"When Andrew Jackson . . . died"** Third Fireside Chat (Recovery Program), July 24, 1933.

335 **"Notice that no nurse"** The scene of reporters talking with Michael Hoke appears in Charles Hurd, *When the New Deal Was Young and Gay: FDR and His Circle* (New York: Hawthorn Books, 1965), 66–67.

336 **I remember I was brought** *The New York Times*, June 30, 1933.

338 **"You people must have faith"** First Fireside Chat (Banking Crisis), March 12, 1933. Franklin D. Roosevelt, Master Speech File, Box 14, FDRL.

338 **"The simplest way for each of you"** Fifth Fireside Chat (Review of the Achievements of the 73rd Congress), June 28, 1934, Franklin D. Roosevelt, Master Speech File, Box 18, FDRL.

338 **"I realized how unconscious he was"** Frances Perkins, *The Roosevelt I Knew* (New York: Penguin, 2011), 71.

339 **"Most Americans want"** Address at Atlanta, Georgia, Nov. 29, 1935, Franklin D. Roosevelt Master Speech File, Box 23, FDRL.

340 **"throw away the crutches"** "The Morgenthau Diaries," *Collier's 82*, Sept. 27, 1947, quoted in Jean Edward Smith, *FDR* (New York: Random House, 2007), 397.

340 **"There have been other great crises"** Eleanor Roosevelt, *It's Up to the Women* (New York: Bold Type Books, 2017), 1.

341　**When she departed, they waved** Eleanor Roosevelt, *The Autobiography of Eleanor Roosevelt* (New York: Harper Perennial, 2014), 176.

341　**"Hoover sent the Army"** Arthur Schlesinger Jr., *The Coming of the New Deal* (Boston: Houghton, Mifflin, 1959), 15.

342　**"Not only were the demands"** Joseph P. Lash, *Eleanor and Franklin: The Story of Their Relationship, Based on Eleanor Roosevelt's Private Papers* (New York: W. W. Norton & Company, Inc., 1971), 434–36.

342　**"one of the greatest losses"** Eleanor Roosevelt, *Autobiography,* 186.

342　**In 1938, she traveled** For Eleanor's visit to the Southern Conference for Human Welfare, see Blanche Wiesen Cook, *Eleanor Roosevelt: Vol. II, 1933–1938* (New York: Viking, 1999).

342　**"Dearest honey"** Lash, *Eleanor and Franklin,* 511.

343　**"He lies"** David McCullough, *Truman* (New York: Simon & Schuster, 1992), 409.

343　**"Your boys are not"** Address at Boston, Massachusetts, Oct. 30, 1940, made available at the American Presidency Project, https://www.presidency.ucsb.edu/documents/campaign-address-boston-massachusetts.

344　**"would rather follow public opinion"** Smith, *FDR,* 492.

346　**"We cannot possibly convey"** *Washington Evening Star,* Jan. 28, 1934, "The Spirit of Warm Springs," Polio Chronicle, Dec. 1933, accessed https://www.disabilitymuseum.org/dhm/lib/detail.html?id=1161

347　**"I want to express the hope"** Informal remarks of the president, Georgia Hall, Georgia Warm Springs Foundation, Nov. 29, 1941, Franklin D. Roosevelt, Master Speech File, Box 62, FDRL.

SELECTED BIBLIOGRAPHY

BOOKS

Allen, Frederick Lewis. *Only Yesterday: An Informal History of the 1920's.* New York: Harper Perennial Classics, 2000.

Alter, Jonathan. *Defining Moment: FDR's Hundred Days and the Triumph of Hope.* New York: Simon & Schuster, 2006.

Alsop, Joseph. *FDR, 1882–1945: A Centenary Remembrance.* New York: Viking Press, 1982.

Alsop, Joseph, and Robert Kintner. *American White Paper: The Story of American Diplomacy and the Second World War.* New York: Simon & Schuster, 1940.

Anonymous. *Boudoir Mirrors of Washington.* Philadelphia: The John C. Winston Company, 1923

Asbell, Bernard, ed. *Mother and Daughter, The Letters of Eleanor and Anna Roosevelt.* New York: Coward, McCann & Geoghegan, 1982.

————. *The F.D.R. Memoirs.* Garden City, N.Y.: Doubleday, 1973.

Ashburn, Frank. *Peabody of Groton.* Cambridge, Mass.: Riverside Press, 1967.

Baruch, Bernard. *Baruch: the Public Years.* New York: Holt, Rinehart and Winston, 1960

Bernays, Edward. *Crystallizing Public Opinion.* New York: Boni and Liveright, 1923.

Black, Allida. *Casting Her Own Shadow: Eleanor Roosevelt and the Shaping of Postwar Liberalism.* New York: Columbia University Press, 1996.

Black, Conrad. *Franklin Delano Roosevelt: Champion of Freedom.* New York: Public Affairs, 2003.

Boettiger, John R. *A Love in Shadow.* New York: Norton, 1978.

Bowers, Claude G. *My Life: the Memoirs of Claude Bowers.* New York: Simon & Schuster, 1962.

Brands, H. W. *Traitor to His Class: The Privileged Life and Radical Presidency of Franklin Delano Roosevelt.* New York: Anchor, 2009.

Brinkley, David. *Washington Goes to War.* New York: Ballantine, 1988.

Burke, David M. Jr., and Odie A. Burke. *Images of America: Warm Springs.* Charleston, S.C.: Arcadia Publishing, 2005.

Burner, David. *The Politics of Provincialism: The Democratic Party in Transition, 1918–1932.* New York: Knopf, 1968.

Burns, James MacGregor. *Roosevelt: The Lion and the Fox.* New York: Harcourt, Brace and Company, 1956.

Carmichael, Donald Scott, ed. *F.D.R., Columnist.* Chicago, Cuneo Press, 1947.

Childs, Marquis W. *I Write from Washington.* New York: Harper & Brothers, 1942.

Coblentz, Edmond D., ed. *William Randolph Hearst: A Portrait in His Own Words.* New York: Simon & Schuster, 1952.

Cook, Blanche Wiesen. *Eleanor Roosevelt, Vol. 1: 1884–1933.* New York: Penguin, 1993.

————. *Eleanor Roosevelt, Vol. 2: 1933–1938.* New York: Viking, 1999.

Cox, James M. *Journey Through My Years.* Macon, Ga.: Mercer, 2004.

Daniels, Jonathan. *The End of Innocence.* Philadelphia: J. B. Lippincott Company, 1954.

————. *The Time Between the Wars.* New York: Doubleday, 1966.

————. *Washington Quadrille: The Dance Beside the Documents.* Garden City, New York: Doubleday, 1968.

Daniels, Josephus. *The Wilson Era: Years of Peace—1910–1917.* Chapel Hill: University of North Carolina Press, 1972.

Davis, Kenneth S. *FDR: The Beckoning of Destiny: 1882–1928.* New York: G.P. Putnam's Sons, 1971.

————. *FDR: The New Deal Years: 1933–1937.* New York: Random House, 1986.

————. *FDR: The New York Years: 1928–1933.* New York: Random House, 1985.

————. *Invincible Summer: An Intimate Portrait of the Roosevelts, Based on the Recollections of Marion Dickerman.* New York: Atheneum, 1974.

Farley, James A. *Behind the Ballots: The Personal History of a Politician.* New York: Harcourt, Brace and Company, 1938.

————. *Jim Farley's Story: The Roosevelt Years.* New York: Whittlesey House, 1948.

Fenster, Julie M. *FDR's Shadow: Louis Howe, The Force That Shaped Franklin and Eleanor Roosevelt.* New York: Palgrave Macmillan, 2009.

Freidel, Frank. *Franklin D. Roosevelt: The Apprenticeship.* Boston: Little, Brown Company, 1952.

————. *Franklin D. Roosevelt: The Ordeal.* Boston: Little, Brown, 1954.

————. *Franklin D. Roosevelt: The Triumph.* Boston: Little, Brown, 1956.

————. *Franklin D. Roosevelt: Launching the New Deal.* Boston: Little, Brown, 1973.

Furman, Bess. *Washington By-Line: The Personal History of a Newspaper Woman.* New York: Knopf, 1949.

Gallagher, Hugh Gregory. *FDR's Splendid Deception.* New York: Dodd, Mead & Co, 1988.

Gilbert, Clinton W. *The Mirrors of Washington.* New York: Knickerbocker Press, 1921.

Goodwin, Doris Kearns. *No Ordinary Time: Franklin and Eleanor Roosevelt: The Home Front in World War II.* New York: Simon & Schuster, 1994.

Groopman, Jerome. *The Anatomy of Hope: How People Prevail in the Face of Illness.* New York: Random House, 2004.

Hickok, Lorena A. *Eleanor Roosevelt: Reluctant First Lady.* New York: Dodd, Mead, 1962.

Hurd, Charles. *When the New Deal Was Young and Gay: FDR and His Circle.* New York: Hawthorn Books, 1965.

Kennedy, David M. *Freedom from Fear: The American People in the Depression and War.* New York: Oxford University Press, 1999.

Kleeman, Rita Halle. *Gracious Lady: The Life of Sara Delano Roosevelt.* New York: D. Appleton-Century Company, 1935.

Kyvig, David E. *Daily Life in the United States, 1920–1939: Decades of Promise and Pain.* Westport, Conn.: Greenwood Press, 2002.

Lash, Joseph P. *Eleanor and Franklin: The Story of Their Relationship, Based on Eleanor Roosevelt's Private Papers.* New York: W. W. Norton & Company, Inc., 1971.

Lee, Hermione. *Edith Wharton.* New York: Knopf, 2007.

Lindley, Ernest K. *Franklin D. Roosevelt: A Career in Progressive Democracy.* Indianapolis, Ind.: Bobbs-Merrill Company, 1931.

Lippman, Theo. *The Squire of Warm Springs: FDR in Georgia, 1924–1945.* Chicago: Playboy Press, 1977.

Looker, Earle. *This Man Roosevelt.* New York: Brewer, Warren & Putnam, 1932.

McCullough, David. *Mornings on Horseback.* New York: Simon & Schuster, 2003.

————. *Truman.* New York: Simon & Schuster, 1992.

Millard, Candace. *Hero of the Empire: The Boer War, A Daring Escape, and the Making of Winston Churchill.* New York: Doubleday, 2016.

Moley, Raymond. *After Seven Years.* New York: Harper & Brothers, 1939.

Moley, Raymond, with the assistance of Elliot A. Rosen. *The First New Deal.* New York: Harcourt, Brace & World, 1966.

Morris, Edmund. *The Rise of Theodore Roosevelt.* New York: Random House, 1979.

Murphy, Laurence R. *Perverts by Official Order: The Campaign Against Homosexuals by the United States Navy.* New York: Harrington Park Press, 1988.

Murphy, Robert F. *The Body Silent.* New York: H. Holt, 1987.

Murray, Robert K. *The 103rd Ballot: Democrats and the Disaster in Madison Square Garden.* New York: Harper, 2016.

Nasaw, David. *The Chief: The Life of William Randolph Hearst.* New York: Mariner Books, 2000.

————. *The Patriarch: The Remarkable Life and Turbulent Times of Joseph P. Kennedy.* New York: Penguin Press, 2012.

Perkins, Frances. *The Roosevelt I Knew.* New York: Penguin, 2011.

Persico, Joseph E. *Franklin & Lucy.* New York: Random House, 2008.

Peyser, Marc, and Timothy Dwyer. *Hissing Cousins.* New York: Nan Talese, 2015.

Pietrusza, David. *1920: The Year of the Six Presidents.* New York: Carroll & Graf Publishers, 2007.

Rappleye, Charles. *Herbert Hoover in the White House: The Ordeal of the Presidency.* New York: Simon & Schuster, 2016.

Reilly, Michael. *Reilly of the White House: Behind the Scenes with FDR* (New York: Simon & Schuster, 1947).

Rogers, Naomi. *Dirt and Disease: Polio Before FDR.* New Brunswick, N.J.: Rutgers University Press, 1992.

Rollins, Alfred B. Jr. *Roosevelt and Howe.* New York: Knopf, 1962.

Roosevelt, Eleanor. *This Is My Story.* New York: Harper & Brothers, 1937.

————. *The Autobiography of Eleanor Roosevelt.* New York: Harper Perennial, 2014.

————. *Franklin D. Roosevelt and Hyde Park: Personal Recollections of Eleanor Roosevelt.* Washington, D.C.: U.S. Dept. of the Interior/National Park Service, 1949.

————. *It's Up to the Women.* New York: Bold Type Books, 2017.

————. *You Learn by Living: Eleven Keys for a More Fulfilling Life.* New York: Harper Parennial ePub Editions, 2011.

Roosevelt, Elliott, ed. *F.D.R.: His Personal Letters, Vol. I: Early Years.* New York: Duell, Sloan and Pearce, 1947

————. *F.D.R.: His Personal Letters, Vol. II: 1905–1928.* New York: Duell, Sloan and Pearce, 1948.

————. *F.D.R.: His Personal Letters, Vol. III: 1928–1945.* New York: Duell, Sloan and Pearce, 1948.

Roosevelt, Elliott, and James Brough. *An Untold Story: The Roosevelts of Hyde Park.* New York: G. P. Putnam's Sons, 1973.

Roosevelt, James, with Bill Libby. *My Parents: A Differing View.* Chicago: Playboy Press, 1976.

Roosevelt, James, and Sidney Shalett. *Affectionately, F.D.R.* New York: Harcourt, Brace & Company, 1959.

Roosevelt, Sara Delano. *My Boy Franklin: As Told by Mrs. James Roosevelt to Isabel Leighton and Gabrielle Forbush.* New York: Ray Long & Richard R. Smith, Inc., 1933.

Rose, Lisle A. *Explorer: The Life of Richard E. Byrd.* Columbia: University of Missouri Press, 2008.

Rosenman, Samuel. *Working with Roosevelt.* New York: Harper & Brothers, 1952.

Rowley, Hazel. *Franklin and Eleanor: An Extraordinary Marriage.* New York: Farrar, Straus and Giroux, 2010.

Schlesinger, Arthur M. Jr. *The Age of Roosevelt: The Politics of Upheaval: 1935–1936.* Boston: Houghton, Mifflin & Co., 1960.

————. *The Coming of the New Deal: 1933–1935.* Boston: Houghton, Mifflin, 1959.

————. *The Crisis of the Old Order: 1919–1933.* Boston: Houghton, Mifflin, 1957.

Schlup, Leonard C., and Donald W. Whisenhunt, eds. *It Seems to Me: Selected Letters of Eleanor Roosevelt.* Lexington: University Press of Kentucky, 2001.

Shell, Marc. *Polio and Its Aftermath: The Paralysis of Culture.* Cambridge, Mass.: Harvard University Press, 2005.

Sherwood, Robert E. *Roosevelt and Hopkins, An Intimate History.* New York: Harper, 1948.

Slayton, Robert A. *Empire Statesman: The Rise and Redemption of Al Smith.* New York: Free Press, 2001.

Smith, Gene. *The Shattered Dream: Herbert Hoover and the Great Depression.* New York: William Morrow, 1970.

Smith, Jean Edward. *FDR.* New York: Random House, 2007.

Smith, Richard Norton. *The Colonel: The Life and Legend of Robert R. McCormick.* New York: Houghton, Mifflin, 1997.

————. *An Uncommon Man: The Triumph of Herbert Hoover.* Worland, Wyo.: High Plains Publishing Company, 1984.

Steeholm, Clara and Hardy. *The House at Hyde Park.* New York: Viking Press, 1950.

Steel, Ronald. *Walter Lippmann and the American Century.* New Brunswick, N.J.: Transaction Publishers, 2008.

Stiles, Lela. *The Man Behind Roosevelt: The Story of Louis McHenry Howe.* Cleveland, Ohio: World Publishing Company, 1954.

Streitmatter, Rodger, ed. *Empty Without You: The Intimate Letters of Eleanor Roosevelt and Lorena Hickok.* New York: Da Capo Press, 1998.

Teague, Michael. *Mrs. L: Conversations with Alice Roosevelt Longworth.* Garden City, N.Y.: Doubleday, 1981.

Tobin, James. *The Man He Became: How FDR Defied Polio to Win the Presidency.* New York: Simon & Schuster, 2013.

Tugwell, Rexford. *The Democratic Roosevelt.* Garden City, N.Y.: Doubleday, 1957.

Tully, Grace. *F.D.R., My Boss.* New York: C. Scribner's Sons, 1949.

Walker, Turnley. *Roosevelt and the Warm Springs Story.* New York: A.A. Wyn, Inc., 1953.

Ward, Geoffrey C. *A First-Class Temperament.* New York: Vintage Books, 2014.

————. *Before the Trumpet.* New York: Vintage, 1985, 2014.

Warner, Emily Smith, with Hawthorne Daniel. *The Happy Warrior: The Story of My Father, Alfred E. Smith.* Garden City, N.Y.: Doubleday, 1956.

Wehle, Louis B. *Hidden Threads of History: Wilson Through Roosevelt.* New York: Macmillan, 1953.

Wicker, Christine. *The Simple Faith of Franklin Roosevelt.* Washington, D.C.: Smithsonian Books, 2017.

Wilson, Daniel J. *Living with Polio: The Epidemic and Its Survivors.* Chicago: University of Chicago Press, 2005.

Winkler, John. *William Randolph Hearst: A New Appraisal.* New York: Hastings House, 1955.

SELECTED ARTICLES

For a comprehensive list of articles cited in the text, please see the source notes for each chapter.

"Franklin Delano Roosevelt at Harvard," *Harvard Crimson,* Dec. 13, 1957.

Hall, Kathryn T., Loscalzo, Joseph, and Kaptchuk, Ted K. "Genetics and the Placebo Effect: The Placebome," *Trends Mol Med.,* 21(5), May 2015, 285–94.

Halsted, Anna Roosevelt. "My Life with FDR," *The Woman,* July 1949.

Schleichkorn, Jay. "Physical Therapist, 98, Recalls Rehabilitating Franklin Roosevelt," *P.T. Bulletin,* March 16, 1988.

Zane, Sherry. "I Did It for the Uplift of Humanity and the Navy: Same-Sex Acts and the Origins of the National Security State, 1919–1921," *New England Quarterly,* Vol. XCI, No. 2, June 2018.

ORAL HISTORY, COLUMBIA CENTER FOR ORAL HISTORY

Childs, Marquis W.
Dickerman, Marion
Marvin, Langdon Parker and Mary Vaughan
Perkins, Frances
Roosevelt, Anna Halsted
Rosenman, Samuel Irving

ARCHIVAL COLLECTIONS

Franklin D. Roosevelt Library, Hyde Park, N.Y.

Franklin D. Roosevelt, Papers as Assistant Secretary of the Navy, 1913–1920
Franklin D. Roosevelt, Papers as Vice-Presidential Candidate (1920 VP)
Franklin D. Roosevelt, Papers Pertaining to the Campaign of 1924
Franklin D. Roosevelt, Papers Pertaining to the Campaign of 1928
Franklin D. Roosevelt, Master Speech File, 1898–1945
FBP/ Correspondence: Papers Pertaining to Family, Business, and Personal Affairs—General Correspondence File, 1904–1928, Papers of Franklin D. Roosevelt
FBP/ Subject: Papers Pertaining to Family, Business, and Personal Affairs—Subject File, 1904–1928, Papers of Franklin D. Roosevelt
Papers Donated by the Children: Papers Donated by the Children of FDR & Eleanor, Papers of the Roosevelt Family
Anna Eleanor Roosevelt Papers, Part 1, 2 and 3, 1884–1964
Esther Lape Papers, 1925–1978
Louis McHenry Howe Papers, 1912–1936
Louis McHenry Howe Personal Papers
Marion Dickerman Papers, 1918–1975
Paul DeWitt Hasbrouck Papers, 1922–1969
Robert D. Graff Papers

Francis A. Countway Library of Medicine, Harvard University

Robert W. Lovett Papers

Houghton Library, Harvard University

Theodore Roosevelt Collection

New York State Library

A.E. Smith Papers

Library of Congress

Papers of James A. Farley
Theodore Roosevelt Papers

Bancroft Library at University of California, Berkeley

William Randolph Hearst Papers
Edmond Coblentz Papers

PHOTOGRAPH CREDITS

Eleanor Roosevelt as a young girl with her horse. BETTMANN/GETTY IMAGES

Marie Souvestre. THE WOMEN'S LIBRARY AT THE LONDON SCHOOL OF ECONOMICS

3   Sara Roosevelt, mother of Franklin, speaks with young Eleanor Roosevelt. BETTMANN/GETTY IMAGES

Franklin and Eleanor Roosevelt at Campobello, New Brunswick, Canada, 1910. CORBIS HISTORICAL/GETTY IMAGES

Franklin Roosevelt wading in the water with daughter, Anna, at Campobello, New Brunswick, Canada, 1910. FRANKLIN D. ROOSEVELT PRESIDENTIAL LIBRARY AND MUSEUM, HYDE PARK, NEW YORK

4   Assistant Secretary of the Navy Roosevelt climbing the rigging of a naval vessel, 1913. CORBIS HISTORICAL/GETTY IMAGES

Franklin Roosevelt with former President Theodore Roosevelt and W. H. Van Benschoten, 1915. FRANKLIN D. ROOSEVELT PRESIDENTIAL LIBRARY AND MUSEUM, HYDE PARK, NEW YORK

5   Portrait of Lucy Mercer Rutherfurd, by Elizabeth Shoumatoff. HERBERT ORTH/THE LIFE PICTURE COLLECTION/SHUTTERSTOCK

Portrait of Franklin and Eleanor Roosevelt with their children and his mother, Sara, circa 1919. HULTON ARCHIVE / GETTY IMAGES

6   Vice presidential candidate Roosevelt and presidential candidate James M. Cox lead the Ohio Democratic Notification Parade in Dayton, Ohio, 1920. BETTMANN/GETTY IMAGES

Franklin Roosevelt visiting the Boy Scout camp in Palisades Interstate Park, Bear Mountain, New York, 1921. FRANKLIN D. ROOSEVELT PRESIDENTIAL LIBRARY AND MUSEUM, HYDE PARK, NEW YORK

7   Roosevelt cottage on Campobello, New Brunswick, Canada, circa 1920. ROOSEVELT CAMPOBELLO INTERNATIONAL PARK COLLECTION

Franklin Roosevelt with sons Franklin Jr. and John at his Springwood estate, Hyde Park, New York, 1922. FRANKLIN D. ROOSEVELT PRESIDENTIAL LIBRARY AND MUSEUM, HYDE PARK, NEW YORK

Leg braces used by Franklin Roosevelt made of steel, leather, and elastic. FRANKLIN D. ROOSEVELT PRESIDENTIAL LIBRARY AND MUSEUM, HYDE PARK, NEW YORK

8   Franklin Roosevelt with his personal secretary, Louis Howe, 1924. BETTMANN/GETTY IMAGES

Franklin Roosevelt nominates Al Smith for president at the 1924 Democratic National Convention at Madison Square Garden, New York City. GEORGIA STATE PARKS AND HISTORIC SITES/ROOSEVELT'S LITTLE WHITE HOUSE

9   Franklin Roosevelt poolside at Warm Springs, Georgia, 1924. CORBIS HISTORICAL/GETTY IMAGES

St. Louis Post-Dispatch headline, FORMER VICE PRESIDENTIAL NOMINEE BECOMES MAN-FISH TO CURE INFANTILE PARALYSIS, October 26, 1924. ST. LOUIS POST-DISPATCH

Letter from Franklin Roosevelt to Paul D. Hasbrouck, fellow polio victim, January 5, 1925. FRANKLIN D. ROOSEVELT PRESIDENTIAL LIBRARY AND MUSEUM, HYDE PARK, NEW YORK

10   Eleanor Roosevelt using the voting machine at the Women's Art and Industries Exhibit at the Hotel Commodore, New York City, October, 1925. BETTMANN/ GETTY IMAGES

Stone Cottage at Val-Kill, circa 1931. NATIONAL PARK SERVICE COLLECTION

Nancy Cook, Marion Dickerman, and Eleanor Roosevelt picnicking, circa 1924. NATIONAL PARK SERVICE COLLECTION

11   Franklin Roosevelt in Florida with friends, including Missy LeHand, 1924. EVERETT COLLECTION/ALAMY STOCK PHOTO

Warm Springs treatment pool, circa 1930. ROOSEVELT WARM SPRINGS VOCATIONAL REHABILITATION CAMPUS, WARM SPRINGS, GEORGIA

Franklin Roosevelt at the wedding of his daughter, Anna, to Curtis Dall, Hyde Park, New York, June 5, 1926. BETTMANN/GETTY IMAGES

12   Governor Roosevelt talks with former New York governor Al Smith. BETTMANN/ GETTY IMAGES

Frances Perkins, first woman Cabinet member, appointed by President-Elect Roosevelt to be secretary of labor in 1933. SMITH ARCHIVE/ALAMY STOCK PHOTO

13   William Randolph Hearst inside the S.S. *Rex* in New York on his way to Europe, 1936. ASSOCIATED PRESS

Hearst in War, Hearst in Peace, Hearst in the Hearts of his Countrymen. William Randolph Hearst as candidate for governor of New York, 1906. EVERETT COLLECTION

Joseph Kennedy, Sr. (fifth from right in front row) campaigning for Franklin Roosevelt (center of train platform), September 23, 1932. FRANKLIN D. ROOSEVELT PRESIDENTIAL LIBRARY AND MUSEUM, HYDE PARK, NEW YORK

14   Governor Franklin Roosevelt delivers his acceptance speech at the 1932 Democratic National Convention in Chicago. ASSOCIATED PRESS

Eleanor Roosevelt dining with Lorena Hickok, San Francisco, 1934. BETTMANN/ GETTY IMAGES

Governor Franklin Roosevelt exiting a car during a presidential campaign trip to Hollywood, California, September 1932. FRANKLIN D. ROOSEVELT PRESIDENTIAL LIBRARY AND MUSEUM, HYDE PARK, NEW YORK

15   President Herbert Hoover and President-Elect Franklin Roosevelt on their way to the U.S. Capitol for Roosevelt's inauguration, Washington, D.C., March 4, 1933. GLASSHOUSE IMAGES/ALAMY STOCK PHOTO

President Franklin Roosevelt arriving at the White House with his wife, Eleanor, and son James, March 4, 1933. BRIDGEMAN IMAGES

President Roosevelt making his inaugural address at the Capitol, Washington, D.C., March 4, 1933. NEW YORK DAILY NEWS ARCHIVE/GETTY IMAGES

Inaugural address of President Franklin Roosevelt, March 4, 1933. FRANKLIN D. ROOSEVELT PRESIDENTIAL LIBRARY AND MUSEUM, HYDE PARK, NEW YORK

16   First Lady Eleanor Roosevelt visits the indigent remnant of the Bonus Army, Fort Hunt, Virginia, May 1933. CSU ARCHIVES / EVERETT COLLECTION/ALAMY STOCK PHOTO

President Roosevelt in his car outside the Little White House in Warm Springs, Georgia, November 1935. BETTMANN/GETTY IMAGES

INDEX

═══

ER=Eleanor Roosevelt
FDR=Franklin Delano Roosevelt
TR=Theodore Roosevelt

Adams, Clover, 88, 322–323
Adams, Henry, 88, 322
Agricultural Adjustment Act, 334
Allenswood School, Wimbledon,
    England, 45, 53–54, 58, 59, 100,
    204, 302
American Orthopedic Association,
    209
Anacostia Flats, 297–298
Arnold, Ervin, 78–82
Asbell, Bernard, 215
Associated Press, 220, 284, 287, 301,
    302
Astor, Vincent, 157, 309, 310
Atlanta, Georgia, 227, 244
Atlanta Constitution, The, 216, 269
Atlanta Journal, The, 188

Babies, Just Babies magazine, 320
Bahamas, 309
Baker, Newton, 280
banking crisis, 256, 307, 314, 316, 317,
    324–325, 333
Bar Harbor, Maine, 115

Barrows, G.S., 147–148
Baruch, Bernard, 273, 276, 289, 308
Bay of Fundy, 103
Bear Mountain, 103
Bennet, E.H., 109, 115
Bennett, Constance, 299
Benny, Jack, 270
Bethesda Naval Hospital, 341
Biden, Joe, 335
Biltmore Hotel, New York, 303
Birmingham, Alabama, 312
Black, Van Lear, 98, 101, 103, 165, 170,
    185, 207
Black Tuesday, 253
Blue Ridge Mountains, 295
Boer War, 23
Boettiger, John, 300–301, 329
Bonus Expeditionary Forces, 297–298,
    340–341
Boston Globe, The, 127
Boston Post, The, 89–90, 99
Botts, Fred, 190, 193–195
Boy Scouts, 103, 111
Brains Trust, 267, 268, 277
Brown, Lawrence Erving, 107, 148
Buchanan, James, 327
Buckley School, New York City, 139
Bulkley, Reginald, 174
Bull Moose Progressive Party, 59
Bullochville, Georgia, 183, 184

Buzzards Bay, 207
Byrd, Richard E., 145

Camp, Walter, 117
Campobello Island, xviii, 5–10, 38, 69,
    85, 87, 89, 103–104, 109–111,
    114–123, 132, 150, 202, 336, 345
Catt, Carrie Chapman, 74, 99, 100
Cermak, Anton, 310–312, 314
Chevy Chase Club, Washington,
    D.C., 62–63, 75, 84, 96
Chicago Tribune, 92, 153, 300, 329
Chief (dog), 205, 214
Children's Hour, 341
Churchill, Marigold, 9
Churchill, Winston, 9, 23
City Housing Corporation, 203
civil rights, 217, 342
Civil War, xiv, 115
Civilian Conservation Corps, 334,
    339
Cleveland, Grover, 115
climate crises, xxiii
Columbia Law School, 18, 56
Columbia University, 191
Columbia Yacht Club, 102
Columbus, Georgia, 237
communism, 20–21
Connally, Tom, 281
Constitution of the United States
    Eighteenth Amendment to the, 167
    Nineteenth Amendment to the, 73,
        74, 83, 99
    Seventeenth Amendment to the, 57
Cook, Blanche Wiesen, 203, 321
Cook, Nancy, 152–153, 155, 201–204,
    212–213, 251, 278, 284
Coolidge, Calvin, 218, 238
    presidential election (1920), 84,
        92, 96
    presidential election (1924), 184, 187
    succeeds to presidency, 167

Cornell University, 215
Cowles, Anna "Bamie" Roosevelt, 60,
    92, 322
Cox, James M., xviii, 6, 91, 96, 145–146,
    161, 259, 328
Crawford, Joan, 299
Crimson (student newspaper), 42, 44
Crosby, Bing, 270
Cross, Lillian, 309–311
Cuba, 93

Dall, Curtis, 215, 300, 329
Daniels, Josephus, 16, 23, 59, 61–62, 78,
    82, 89, 93, 97, 101, 102, 114, 133, 145,
    172, 259, 328
Davies, Marion, 261
Davis, Jefferson, 216
Davis, John W., 184, 187
Davis, Kenneth, 155, 275
Davis, Livingston, 146, 153, 154, 330
Delano, Catherine Lyman, 38
Delano, Frederic Adrian, 117–118, 123,
    124, 125, 134, 143, 149, 206, 329
Delano, Warren II, 37–38
Delano family, 34
Democratic National Committee,
    Bureau of Women's Activities,
    203
Democratic National Convention
    1920, xiii–xviii, 5, 83–84, 177
    1924, 167–168, 171–172, 174–182,
        183–184, 216, 220, 259, 273, 279, 281,
        287
    1932, 262, 276, 277–283, 286–289,
        293–295, 310
    1936, xvii–xxii
Democratic State Committee,
    Women's Division of, 152
Dickerman, Marion, 155, 182, 201–204,
    212–213, 251, 275, 278
Doheny, Edward, 167
Dow-Jones Industrial Average, 9, 253

Draper, George, 128–133, 135, 151, 153, 184
Dreier, Mary, 160
Duffy (dog), 127

Early, Steve, 98
Eastport, Maine, 122, 123, 126
Economic Consequences of the Peace, The (Keynes), 84
Eighteenth Amendment to the Constitution, 167
Eleuthera, Bahamas, 309
Elmira, New York, 248, 249
Elmira Star-Gazette, 249
Ely, Joseph, 281
Emergency Banking Act, 333
Emergency Farm Mortgage Act, 334
Emmet, Grenville, 98
Emmet, Marvin & Roosevelt, 98, 170
European debt issue, 305–307

Fairhaven, Massachusetts, 69
Farley, James A., 278, 285, 294, 315
  as adviser to FDR, xxi, 245, 257, 279–283, 287–289, 318–319
  Louis Howe and, 257
farmers, 307, 334, 336
fascism, 337
Federal Emergency Relief Act, 334
Federal Reserve Board, 117
Fidelity and Deposit Company of Maryland, 6, 98, 101, 152, 161, 162, 170, 175, 190, 207
fireside chats, 107, 334, 338
Ford, Edsel, 218–219, 246
foreclosures, 307
Foreign Policy Association, 203
"Forgotten Man, The" (FDR radio address), 233
Fort Belvoir, Virginia, 340
Frankfurter, Felix, 298

Franklin, Benjamin, 318
"Franklin D. Roosevelt: Man of Destiny" (Markham), xx
Furman, Bess, 287

Galleani, Luigi, 29
Garner, John Vance, 262–263, 270, 273–274, 278, 280, 281, 286–288, 298, 300, 331
Gautier, R.B., 310
Georgia Warm Springs Foundation, 196, 334–335
Germany, 8, 73, 84, 157, 256, 344
Glass-Steagall Act, 334
global pandemic, xxiii, 335
gold standard, 256, 261
Great Depression, xix, xxii, 198, 254–256, 261, 262, 270, 271, 276, 297, 298, 305, 314, 330, 335, 336, 339, 340
Greenway, Isabella, 67, 300–301
Gregory, Cleburne, 188–189
Gridiron Club, Washington, D.C., 342
Grief (Saint-Gaudens), 88, 322–323
Groton School, Massachusetts, 17, 28, 41, 43, 54, 94, 138, 139, 251, 300
gubernatorial election
  1898, 43
  1920, 158, 187

Haiti, 93, 94
Hall, Mary Livingston Hall, 53, 54, 74–75, 88
Harding, Warren G.
  death of, 167
  presidential election (1920), 84, 92, 96
Harris, William, 244
Harvard College, 17, 18, 41–43, 46
Hasbrouck, Paul, 191, 209

Hayes, Helen, 299
Hearst, William Randolph, 25, 275, 277, 278, 280, 283, 288
    FDR and, xxvi, 262, 263, 265, 273, 276, 286–287, 289, 299, 306–308, 329
    gubernatorial candidacy of, 158, 159, 161, 262, 275, 277, 278, 280, 283, 288
    as news publisher, 21, 93, 261
Hickok, Lorena, 220, 283–284, 301–302, 312, 319–323, 325
Hitler, Adolf, 9, 256, 337, 344
Hoke, Michael, 335
Hoover, Herbert, 222, 261, 268, 295–296
    banking crisis and, 324, 325
    Bonus Forces and, 297–298, 341
    European debt issue and, 305–306
    FDR and, xxvi, 238, 296, 305–308, 313–316, 323–325
    FDR's inauguration and, 327–328
    Great Depression and, 244, 256, 271, 297, 298, 314
    presidential election (1932), xix, 220, 242, 260, 296, 298, 303–304, 305
Hoover, Irwin "Ike," 323
Hoover, Lou Henry, 324–325
House of Mirth, The (Wharton), 70
Howe, Grace, 103, 114, 119, 140
Howe, Hartley, 103, 114
Howe, Louis, 9, 103, 118, 169, 212, 312, 340
    Anna Roosevelt and, 140–142, 154
    death of, 342
    Democratic National Convention (1932), 278–281, 283, 287
    ER and, 95–96, 103, 122, 140–141, 150, 152, 159, 206, 284, 342
    FDR and, xix, 6, 95–96, 109, 112–116, 119, 121–122, 124, 126–127, 129, 135–137, 142, 144, 146, 154–155, 177,
        178, 181, 189, 218, 222, 224–225, 236, 240, 244–245, 257, 285, 289, 294, 304, 308, 318, 339, 341–342
    health of, 257, 278–279, 281, 341
    James Farley and, 257
    presidential election (1932), 257–258
Howell, Clark, 269
Hubbard, Leroy, 197, 229, 246, 247
Hudson, Erastus, 79–82
Hughes, Charles Evans, 331
Hundred Days, xxiv, 333–334, 336
Hyde Park, New York, 17, 33, 36, 37, 40, 57, 96, 97, 99, 100, 136, 154, 169, 201, 207, 300, 303, 308
Hylan, John, 16, 17, 21, 24–25

immigration, xxv, 112
Inner Circle gala, 315
internationalism, 262, 263, 265, 307
isolationism, 21, 93, 262, 343, 344
It's Up to the Women (E. Roosevelt), 340

Jackson, Andrew, 334
Jacksonville, Florida, 170, 309
Japan, 256, 344–345
Jeff (dog), 246
Jefferson, Thomas, 318
Jefferson Dinner, Washington, D.C., 272
Jim Crow, 217
Jolson, Al, 270
Joseph, Louis, 183, 185–186, 190, 207

Keen, William Williams, 115–120, 122
Kennedy, Joseph P., 277, 283, 285, 287, 299
Kent, Samuel, 81
Keynes, John Maynard, 84
Ku Klux Klan, 168, 176, 221

Lake, Kathleen, 151
Lape, Esther, 100, 202
LaRooco (barge), 169–171, 172, 174, 175, 200, 309
Lash, Joseph, 206, 342
Lawrence, John, 169
Leach, Agnes Brown, 266
League of Nations, 9, 20, 73–75, 93, 100, 144, 262, 265–266
League of Women Voters, 99–100
LeHand, Marguerite "Missy," 111–112, 124, 133, 151, 184, 227, 267, 278, 282, 285, 288, 293, 317
    ER and, 172–173, 175, 199–200
    FDR and, 172–173, 175, 199–200, 226, 228–229, 245, 251, 341, 345–346
    stroke of, 345
Lehman, Herbert, 224, 315, 325
Levine, Samuel, 118
Lincoln, Abraham, xix, 84, 317, 319, 327
Lippmann, Walter, 266–267, 273, 275, 289, 307
Lloyd George, David, 157–158
Lodge, Henry Cabot, 73, 75
Long, Huey, 279
Longworth, Alice Roosevelt, 61, 71, 87
Longworth, Nicholas, 61
Lovett, Robert Williamson, 9–10, 117–119, 121–124, 128, 130, 132, 135, 144, 151, 153–154, 156, 169, 171, 184, 330, 337
Loyless, Tom, 183–185, 188, 191–192, 199, 330
Lubec, Maine, 109, 115
Lucky Strike Hour, The (radio show), 271
Lynch, Tom, 128

MacArthur, Douglas, 297–298
Macon Telegraph, The, 216

Madison Square Garden, New York City, 175, 221
Mahoney, Helena, 218, 229
Manchester, Georgia, 227
Manchuria, 256
Marion, Massachusetts, 206–207
Markham, Edwin, xx, xxi
Marvin, Langdon, 98
May Day plot (1919), 26, 29
Mayflower Hotel, Washington, D.C., 319, 320, 323
McAdoo, William Gibbs, 276, 328
    Democratic Convention (1924), 174, 176, 184, 273, 279
    Democratic Convention (1932), 286–288
McCormick, Robert, 300
McDonald, William, 207
McDuffie, Irvin, 184, 186
McIntyre, Marvin, 310
McKinley, William, 43
McLaurine, George, 346
Mencken, H.L., 176
Mercer, Carroll, 70
Mercer, Lucy, 85, 200, 212, 215, 285, 322
    FDR and, 69–73, 86–88, 173
Mercer, Minna, 70
Metropolitan Club, Washington, D.C., 62
Metropolitan Museum of Art, New York City, 15, 16
Meyer, Eugene, 324, 325
Miami, Florida, 309
Miller, Earl, 252
Mills, Ogden, 306, 317, 324, 325
Miss Chapin's School, New York City, 138, 215
Moley, Raymond, 312–313
    as adviser and speech writer to FDR, 267–268, 272, 285, 289, 294, 306, 307, 310, 315–318, 324, 325
Moore, Virginia, 213
Morgan, J.P., 308

Morgenthau, Henry, Jr., 339–340, 344
Moore, Robert, 225, 246
Moskowitz, Belle, 160, 177, 246, 286
Murphy, Charles, xiv, 176–177

National Industrial Recovery Act, 334
National Women's Committee of the
    Democratic Party, 220
Navy Department, xiii, xvi, xxv, 6, 7, 15,
    16, 18, 19, 22, 23, 59–64, 69, 77–83,
    95, 102, 112–114, 144, 322
New Deal, xix, 267, 307, 316, 333–336,
    339
New England Oil, 114, 135
New York Daily News, 100, 229, 236,
    238
New York Grange, 265
New York Herald, 125, 135
New York Herald Tribune, 178, 236, 266,
    273
New York Journal, 21
New York Stock Exchange, 253
New York Times, 57, 82, 125, 127, 128, 129,
    293
New-York Tribune, 97, 128
New York World, xvi, 127
Newport vice allegations, 78–79,
    101–102, 112, 144
Nicaragua, 93
Nineteenth Amendment to the
    Constitution, 73, 74, 83, 99
Non-Partisan Legislative Committee,
    203
Normandy, Allied invasion of, xxii
Not Poppy (Moore), 213
Noye, Philippe de la, 37

Oak Terrace, New York, 50
Ochs, Adolph, 129
O'Connor, Basil, 162, 190
October Revolution of 1917, 21

O'Gorman, James Aloysius, 58
organized labor, 336
O'Ryan, John, 16, 25
Ossining, New York, 303
Ottinger, Albert, 235

Palisades Interstate Park, 103
Palmer, A. Mitchell, 26–28
pandemic of 1918, xxiv
Paris Peace Conference, 9, 20, 157
Parish, Susie, 46
Patri, Angelo, 214
Peabody, Endicott, 41, 326
Peabody, George Foster, 183, 185, 186,
    192
Pearl Harbor, xxii, 337, 345
Pell, Herbert, 135
Perkins, Frances, 22, 160, 243
    FDR and, 181, 239–241, 338–339
Peter Bent Brigham Hospital, Boston,
    118
Phillips House, Boston, 153–154
Pine Mountain, Georgia, 216–217, 309,
    333
Pittsburgh, Pennsylvania, 97
Plastridge, Alice Lou, 207–208
Poincaré, Raymond, 157
polio, xviii, xx–xxiii, 5–10, 103, 109–112,
    115–128, 130–134, 130–137, 142, 146,
    190, 194, 206, 240–241, 336–338,
    346
Poughkeepsie, New York, 302, 303
Poughkeepsie Eagle, 128
Presbyterian Hospital, New York
    City, 128, 138, 139
presidential campaigns and elections
    1912, 59
    1920, xvi, xviii, 5–6, 74, 77, 91–98, 144,
        158, 235, 242, 254, 299, 328
    1924, 174, 176–178, 181, 184, 187, 273
    1928, 218, 221–222, 227–229, 235–236,
        241–242, 250, 259, 303, 344

1932, xix, 220, 242, 244–245, 256–258,
  264, 267, 269, 270, 273–274, 290,
  296, 298–304
1940, 344
1944, 343
prohibition, 167–168, 217, 221, 258, 320
Proskauer, Joseph, 177
Providence Journal, The, 81, 82
Pulitzer family, 189

race riots, 73
radio, 97, 107, 180, 235, 237, 242, 257, 270,
  271, 328, 334, 336, 338
Raleigh, North Carolina, 244
Rapidan, Virginia, 295
Raskob, John Jakob, 221
Rathom, John, 81, 82
Rayburn, Sam, 280–281, 287, 288
Read, Elizabeth, 99–100, 202
Reconstruction, 242
Red Scare, 27
Redbook magazine, 205
reparations, 73, 84, 157
Republican National Convention
  (1920), 84
Ritchie, Albert, 280
Rivington Street Settlement House,
  New York City, 46
Rochester, New York, 223, 224, 240,
  241
Rochester *Democrat and Chronicle*, 224
Rock Creek Cemetery, Washington,
  D.C., 88, 322–323
Rockey, Anna, 140, 150, 151
Roosevelt, Anna (daughter), 6, 187,
  201, 278, 294, 299
  birth of, 57, 69
  childhood of, 7–8, 28, 119, 139, 214
  education of, 138, 215
  father, relationship with, 142, 201,
    213, 225, 239
  first marriage of, 215–216, 300

Louis Howe and, 140–141, 154
mother, relationship with, 138, 140,
  141, 154, 213, 215
second marriage of, 300, 329
Roosevelt, Anna Livingston Ludlow
  Hall, 45, 49–52, 57, 73, 203
Roosevelt, Betsey, 299, 323
Roosevelt, Corinne, 53
Roosevelt, Edith, 92
Roosevelt, Eleanor, xix, xxiii, 5, 169,
  182, 184, 197, 259, 267, 278, 282, 288,
  293, 296, 299, 300, 308, 325–326
  Al Smith and, 159–161, 172, 205, 223
  as Albany political wife, 58–59
  Albany residence of, 57, 85
  alcohol, views on, 94, 258, 320
  Alice Longworth Roosevelt and, 87
  anarchist bomb in D.C. and, 28, 29
  assassination attempt against FDR
    and, 312, 313
  Babies, Just Babies magazine and,
    320
  birth of, 51
  birth of children of, 57, 69, 71
  bodyguard of, 252
  campaigning by, 94–95, 205, 301–302
  on Campobello, 85, 103, 104,
    109–110, 116, 118–119, 150, 202
  childhood of, 45, 49–53, 51
  civil rights and, 342
  daughter Anna, relationship with,
    141, 154, 215
  death of baby son, 57
  death of father, 53
  death of grandmother, 74–75, 88
  death of mother, 52
  Democratic National Convention
    (1924), 171, 187
  in Democratic party politics,
    159–161, 203, 220, 222–224,
    226–228
  driving and, 156–157
  Earl Miller and, 252

Roosevelt, Eleanor (*cont'd*):
  education of, 45, 53–54
  FDR's illness and, 7, 9, 109, 116,
    118–119, 122, 150–151, 213, 339
  FDR's inaugural address and, 325,
    332
  fear of heights and of water, 49, 55
  fear of life in White House,
    284–285
  female friends of, 100, 151, 155,
    201–204, 212–213, 252, 301–302,
    319–323, 325
  financial affairs of, 77, 98
  as first lady, 319–321, 340–341
  as governor's wife, 243, 250–252, 285
  honeymoon of, 55
  It's Up to the Women by, 340
  League of Nations and, 266
  League of Women Voters and,
    99–100
  Lorena Hickok and, 301–302,
    319–323, 325
  Louis Howe and, 95–96, 103, 122,
    140–141, 150, 152, 159, 206, 284,
    342
  Lucy Mercer and, 72, 73, 86–88, 200,
    212, 215, 285, 322
  married life of, xxvi, 56–57, 71–73,
    75–76, 88, 212–214, 321, 342–343
  Missy LeHand and, 172–173, 175,
    199–200
  mother-in-law and, 56, 59, 85, 86,
    99, 125, 141, 200–201, 203, 215
  Nancy Cook and, 152–153, 155
  New York City residence of, 56, 85,
    136
  as parent, 86, 214
  parents of, 50–53
  photographs of, 66, 206
  physical appearance of, 45, 152, 220
  press and, 204–206, 211–212, 313,
    319–321
  prohibition and, 211, 258, 320

  psychological depression of, 59,
    72–73
  public profile of, 204–205
  religion and, 54
  social secretary of, 69–70, 86
  as teacher, 46, 204, 222, 243, 250, 285,
    319–320
  This I Remember by, 252
  TR and, 17, 46–47
  travel to Europe (1919), 24, 341
  Val-Kill cottage and, 201–203
  Val-Kill Industries and, 203–204,
    243
  Warm Springs and, 192, 199, 210
  Washington residences of, 60, 85,
    322
  wedding of, 17, 46–47, 54–55, 326
  women's suffrage and, 90, 99, 205
  You Learn By Living by, 67, 165
Roosevelt, Elliott (ER's father), 6, 7,
  49–54, 73, 203
Roosevelt, Elliott (son), 6, 138, 173, 221,
  251, 278, 282, 283, 293
  birth of, 57
  childhood of, 7, 28, 139, 150, 214
  education of, 251
Roosevelt, Elliott, Jr. "Ellie" (ER's
  brother), 52
Roosevelt, Franklin, Jr., 6, 278, 287, 294
  childhood of, 7, 28, 123, 138, 144, 150,
    214
  education of, 251, 299
Roosevelt, Franklin, Jr. (d. 1909), 57
Roosevelt, Franklin Delano
  Al Smith and, xxvi, 153, 158–159, 223,
    225, 226, 229, 236–237, 246–247,
    258–260, 269–270, 272–273, 280,
    289, 329
  Albany residence of, 57, 113
  ambition of, xiii, xix, 18, 80, 82, 114
  anarchist bomb in D.C. and,
    28–29, 64
  ancestry of, 36

assassination attempt against and, 310–313

as assistant secretary of Navy, xiii, xvi, xxv, 6, 7, 15, 16, 18, 19, 22, 23, 59–64, 69, 77–83, 95, 102, 112–114, 144, 248, 322

banking crisis and, 324–325, 333, 337–338

birth of, 33, 38, 345

black Americans and, 217

Bonus Forces and, 341

braces and, 145, 154, 156, 173, 175, 207, 239, 240, 250, 332, 337

Cabinet of, 317

on Campobello, 5–10, 103–104, 109–110, 114–121, 132, 336

cane, use of, 221, 222

character and temperament of, xiv, xvi, xxiv, xxv, xxvi, 22, 34–36, 40–41, 58, 61, 123–128, 134, 212, 267–268, 275, 312–313

childhood of, 34–36, 40, 45, 48–49, 56

children of, 6, 57, 138, 139, 141, 149, 155

convalescence and rehabilitation of, xix, 129, 138, 142–145, 151–155, 169–175, 183–198, 207–209, 217, 218, 228–229, 246, 276

cruise of Florida and Bahamas, 309

crutches and, 142, 145, 154, 155, 161, 162, 169, 175, 189, 208, 218, 221

death of father, 42–45

Democratic banquet speech (1919), 26–27

Democratic National Convention (1920), xiii–xvii, 5, 83–84, 89, 177

Democratic National Convention (1924), 168, 175–182, 184, 216, 220, 259

Democratic National Convention (1928), 220–221

Democratic National Convention (1932), 277–283, 286–289

Democratic National Convention (1936), xvii–xxii

destiny and, xxii

drinking and, 101, 144, 341

economic knowledge of, 267–269

education of, 17, 18, 35, 41–44, 56

empathy of, xxvi, 249, 270–271, 338–339, 346, 348

ER's female friends and, 212–213

European debt issue and, 305–307

European tours by, 40

falls by, xx–xxi, 162, 169, 190

father, relationship with, 38–39, 42, 330

financial affairs of, 77, 151, 169–170, 192, 195, 196

fireside chats of, 107, 334, 338

Florida boat trip by (1924), 170–172, 174–175

"forgotten man" radio speech by, 271–272

Frances Perkins and, 181, 239–241, 338–339

as governor of New York State, 18, 19, 22, 246–252, 256–259, 263–264, 270

gubernatorial candidacy of, xix, 143, 223–230, 235–240, 242–243

health issues and, 72, 77, 87, 101, 103, 104, 112, 280

Herbert Hoover and, xxvi, 238, 296, 305–308, 313–316, 323–325

honeymoon of, 55

Hundred Days of, xxiv, 333–334, 336

inaugural address of, 317–318, 325, 331–332, 334

inauguration as thirty-second president, 326–332

intuition of, xxvi, 35, 131, 133, 184

James Farley and, xxi, 245, 257, 279–283, 287–289, 318–319

League of Nations and, 262, 265–266

leaves Campobello for New York, 126–128

Roosevelt, Franklin Delano (*cont'd*):
  Livingston Davis and, 146, 330
  Louis Howe and, xix, 6, 95–96, 109,
    112–116, 119, 121–122, 124, 126–127,
    129, 135–137, 142, 144, 146, 154–155,
    177, 178, 181, 189, 218, 222, 224–225,
    236, 240, 244–245, 257, 285, 289,
    294, 304, 308, 318, 339, 341–342
  Lucy Mercer and, 69–73, 86–88, 173
  married life of, xxvi, 56–57, 71–73, 88,
    212–214, 321, 342–343
  Missy LeHand and, 172–173, 175,
    199–200, 226, 228–229, 245, 251,
    341, 345–346
  mother, relationship with, 31, 33–35,
    38, 40, 46, 48–49, 56, 72, 85,
    125–126, 136, 154, 195, 200, 304,
    329
  New Deal and, xix, 267, 307, 316,
    333–336, 339
  New York City residence of, 56, 98,
    136
  New York parade (1919), 15–17, 19,
    25, 64
  as New York State senator, xiii, xv,
    18, 113
  Newport vice allegations and,
    78–83, 101–102, 144
  nomination acceptance speech
    (1932), 277, 291, 293–295
  Oglethorpe University address by
    (1932), 165
  onboard *LaRooco*, 169–171, 200
  pets of, 35, 127
  photographs of, 2, 12, 30, 106, 164,
    230, 232, 240, 290
  physical appearance of, xiii, xiv, xvi,
    xvii, xviii, xxv, 42, 62, 113, 145, 179,
    221, 238
  plaster casts for, 144
  polio's effects on, xviii, xix, xx, xxi,
    xxii, xxiii, 5–10, 103, 109–112,
    115–128, 130–134, 130–137, 136, 142,

    146, 190, 194, 206, 240–241,
    336–338, 346
  presidency of, 333–344
  as president-elect, 305–316, 323–325,
    327
  presidential election (1920), xvi,
    xviii, 5–6, 91–98, 144, 158, 235, 242,
    254, 299, 328
  presidential election (1928), 218,
    221–222, 227, 228, 235–236,
    241–242, 344
  presidential election (1932), xix,
    244–245, 256–258, 264, 267, 269,
    270, 273–274, 290, 296, 298–304
  presidential election (1940), 344
  presidential election (1944), 343
  press coverage of, 124–128, 217, 239,
    264–267, 273, 283, 299–301, 307,
    331–332, 335, 336, 342, 347
  private railcar of, 298, 299
  in private sector, 6, 18, 84, 98, 101, 190
  prohibition and, 258
  radio and, 271–272, 328, 334, 336
  Raymond Moley and, 267–268, 272,
    285, 289, 294, 306, 307, 310,
    315–318, 324, 325
  re-election as governor of New
    York State, 232, 245, 255–256, 258
  reactions to disability of, 147–149,
    189–190
  religion and, 39, 54, 156, 313, 319,
    326–327, 353
  Samuel Rosenman and, 237–239,
    245, 267, 285, 289, 294
  senatorial candidacy of, 57, 143, 235,
    236
  son Jimmy and, xx–xxi, 178, 179, 180,
    181, 239, 294, 299, 304
  as speaker, xxv, 181, 257
  sports and, 41, 42, 63, 212
  stamp collection of, 155, 211
  swimming and, 156–157, 161, 164, 165,
    169, 174, 175, 185, 186, 194, 197

Tammany Hall and, xiv, 22
tonsillectomy and, 112
TR and, xv, 17–19, 46
travels to Europe by, 24, 48, 63, 72
visit to Boy Scouts camp by, 103, 111
voice of, 181, 271, 331, 338
Walker case and, 274–275
Walter Lippmann and, 266–267,
    273, 289, 307
at Warm Springs, Georgia,
    183–200, 206, 209–210, 216–219,
    222, 225–228, 235–236, 243–246,
    248, 249, 306, 309, 330, 333–335,
    338, 345–348
Washington residences of, 28, 60,
    322
wedding of, 17, 46–47, 54–55, 326
William Randolph Hearst and,
    xxvi, 262, 263, 265, 273, 276,
    286–287, 289, 299, 306–308, 329
World War I and, xvi, 23, 63–64
World War II and, xxii, 336, 337,
    343–345, 347, 348
Roosevelt, Gracie Hall "Hall," 52
Roosevelt, James (FDR's father), 33,
    36–46, 48, 85, 156, 209–210, 330, 345
Roosevelt, James "Jimmy" (son), 6, 7,
    86, 170, 173, 252, 278, 321, 323, 324,
    328, 331
    birth of, 57
    childhood of, 7, 28–29, 149, 154, 214,
        215, 304
    education of, 57, 94
    parents, relationship with, 138, 139
    as support for FDR, xx–xxi, 178,
        179, 180, 181, 239, 294, 299, 304
Roosevelt, James Roosevelt "Rosy,"
    35–37, 116–118, 123, 212
Roosevelt, John (son), 6, 278, 282, 293,
    300
    birth of, 69, 71
    childhood of, 7, 28, 123, 138, 150, 214
    education of, 251, 299

Roosevelt, Martha Bulloch, 37
Roosevelt, Nicholas, 36, 331
Roosevelt, Rebecca Howland, 36–37
Roosevelt, Sara Delano (mother), 8,
    28, 44, 54, 117, 150, 169, 170, 175,
    196, 200–201, 207, 222, 242–243,
    278, 285, 302, 303
    ancestry of, 37–38
    birth of, 38
    birth of FDR, 33
    death of, 345
    death of husband, 42
    FDR, relationship with, 31, 33–35,
        38, 40, 46, 48–49, 56, 72, 85,
        125–126, 136, 154, 195, 200, 304, 329
    FDR's illness and, 41, 125–126, 136,
        138–139
    marriage of, 37, 38
    as mother-in-law to ER, 56, 59, 85,
        86, 99, 125, 141, 200–201, 203, 215
Roosevelt, Theodore, xvi, 12, 13, 37, 52,
    58, 69, 92, 94, 98, 152, 206, 244,
    322, 323
    assumes presidency, 43
    campaigning by, 92
    childhood of, 50
    death of, 17, 19
    death of brother of, 53
    education of, 50
    ER and, 17, 46–47
    gubernatorial election (1898), 43
    idolized by FDR, xv, 17–19, 46
    political rise of, 18
    politics of, 27
    presidential election (1912), 59
    reputation of, 18
    in Spanish-American War, xv,
        23, 60
    World War I and, 63
Roosevelt, Theodore, Jr., 92, 187
Roosevelt and the Warm Springs Story
    (Walker), 186
Root, Elihu, 61–62

Rosenman, Samuel, 293
    as advisor to FDR, 237–239, 245, 267,
        285, 289, 294
Rosenvelt, Claes van, 36
Rough Riders, xv
rural electrification, 336

Sabin, Pauline, 220
St. James Episcopal Church, Hyde
    Park, 156, 170, 209–210, 216
St. John's Church, Washington, D.C.,
    326–328
St. Johns River, Florida, 309
St. Lawrence River, 255
St. Louis Post-Dispatch, 189
Saint-Gaudens, Augustus, 88, 322
San Francisco Examiner, 21, 179
San Simeon castle, California, 261, 283
Saratoga Springs, New York, 255
Schlesinger, Arthur, Jr., 254
Scudder, Townsend, 224
Seabury, Samuel, 274
Secret Service, xxi, 311, 314, 315, 320
segregation, 199, 217, 342
Seventeenth Amendment to the
    Constitution, 57
Sheehan, William, 57, 58
Sherwood, Robert E., 31
Sims, Anne, 81–82
Sims, William, 81
Sinclair, Harry, 167
Smith, Al, xxvi, 16, 17, 21, 25, 97, 160,
        210, 216, 315, 328
    Democratic Convention (1924), 174,
        176–178, 181, 184, 259, 279
    Democratic Convention (1932), 278,
        280–282, 286–289
    ER and, 159–161, 172, 205, 223
    FDR and, xxvi, 153, 158–159, 223, 225,
        226, 229, 236–237, 246–247,
        258–260, 269–270, 272–273, 280,
        289, 329

    as governor of New York State, 22,
        187, 245
    presidential election (1924), 273
    presidential election (1928), 218,
        220–229, 235, 236, 242, 259, 303
    presidential election (1932), 269,
        270, 273, 276
Smith, Catherine, 210
Smith, Kate, 270
Social Security, 336
socialism, 20, 335, 339
Somme, Battle of the, 24
Southern Conference for Human
    Welfare, 342
Souvestre, Marie, 53–55, 100, 204,
        302
Spanish-American War, xv, 23, 60
Springwood, Hyde Park, 17, 33, 34, 37,
        38, 40, 41, 45, 154, 155, 159, 201,
        207–208, 345
Stiles, Lela, 137, 144
Stimson, Henry, 308
stock market, 253, 255, 307, 333
Swope, Herbert Bayard, 273
Sylph (yacht), 71

Taft, William Howard, 59
Tammany Hall, xiv–xvi, 22, 57–59, 89,
        153, 158–159, 171–172, 176–177, 221,
        242, 274, 300
Tarrytown, New York, 303
Teapot Dome scandal, 167, 174, 187
Tennessee Valley Authority, 334
This I Remember (E. Roosevelt), 252
Thompson, Malvina "Tommy," 251
Time magazine, 239, 296
Tivoli, New York State, 44, 74
Tobin, James, 116
Todhunter School, New York City,
        204, 222, 243, 250, 285, 319–320
Treasury, U.S. Department of the,
        317

Triangle Shirtwaist Factory Fire of
    1911, 160
Truman, Harry, 343
Tugwell, Rexford, 267, 268, 307, 314
Tully, Grace, 229, 293
Tuttle, Charles, 255–256
27th Infantry Division, 15, 23–24
two-thirds rule, 279

unemployment, 254, 255, 261, 263, 339
USS *Boxer*, 79
USS *New York*, 83

Val-Kill cottage, Hyde Park, 201–203,
    213
Val-Kill Industries, 203–204, 243
Van Wyck, Augustus, 43
Vanderlip, Narcissa, 9
Versailles, Treaty of, 73, 84
veterans, 297–298, 340–341
Vireo (sailboat), 103
Volstead Act of 1919, 168
voting rights, 74, 83, 90

Walker, Jimmy, 274–275
Walker, Turnley, 186, 217
Walsh, Thomas, 282
Ward, Geoffrey, 40, 129
Warm Springs, Georgia, 164, 165,
    183–200, 206, 209–210, 216–219,
    222, 225–228, 235–236, 243–246,
    248, 249, 306, 309, 330–331,
    333–335, 338, 345–348
Washington Post, xvi
Washington Star, 327
Watertown, New York, 270
Weona II (houseboat), 169, 171

Westinghouse Electric and
    Manufacturing Company, 97
Wharton, Edith, 70
Wheatland, Pennsylvania, 327
white supremacy, xxv, 217
"Who Will Be the Next President?"
    (Hearst radio speech), 262
Williams, Arizona, 300
Wilson, Edith, 73, 75
Wilson, Woodrow, xiii, xviii, 21, 27, 84,
    102, 174, 263
    health of, xiv, 75, 91
    League of Nations and, 73–75, 93,
        265
    presidency of, 61
    presidential election (1912), 59
    World War I and, 20, 63
WNYC Radio Station, 242
Women's City Club of New York,
    203
Woodin, William, 317
Woolf, S.J., 204
workers' rights, 160
Works Progress Administration, 336,
    339
World War I, xvi, xxiv, xxv, 8, 15, 16, 20,
    21, 23, 24, 63–64, 71–73, 157, 235,
    297
World War II, xxii, 336, 337, 343–345,
    347, 348
Wright, Wilhelmine, 154

You Learn By Living (E. Roosevelt),
    67, 165
Young Men's Christian Association
    (YMCA), 171

Zangara, Giuseppe, 310–312

About the Type

This book was set in Caslon, a typeface first designed in 1722 by William Caslon (1692–1766). Its widespread use by most English printers in the early eighteenth century soon supplanted the Dutch typefaces that had formerly prevailed. The roman is considered a "workhorse" typeface due to its pleasant, open appearance, while the italic is exceedingly decorative.